Mastering Spring 5
Second Edition

An effective guide to build enterprise applications using Java Spring and Spring Boot framework

Ranga Rao Karanam

BIRMINGHAM - MUMBAI

Mastering Spring 5
Second Edition

Commissioning Editor: Richa Tripathi
Acquisition Editor: Denim Pinto
Content Development Editor: Tiksha Sarang
Senior Editor: Afshaan Khan
Technical Editor: Royce John
Copy Editor: Safis Editing
Project Coordinator: Prajakta Naik
Proofreader: Safis Editing
Indexer: Rekha Nair
Production Designer: Arvindkumar Gupta

First published: June 2017
Second edition: July 2019

Production reference: 1100719

Published by Packt Publishing Ltd.
Livery Place
35 Livery Street
Birmingham
B3 2PB, UK.

ISBN 978-1-78961-569-2

www.packtpub.com

Packt.com

Subscribe to our online digital library for full access to over 7,000 books and videos, as well as industry leading tools to help you plan your personal development and advance your career. For more information, please visit our website.

Why subscribe?

- Spend less time learning and more time coding with practical eBooks and Videos from over 4,000 industry professionals

- Improve your learning with Skill Plans built especially for you

- Get a free eBook or video every month

- Fully searchable for easy access to vital information

- Copy and paste, print, and bookmark content

Did you know that Packt offers eBook versions of every book published, with PDF and ePub files available? You can upgrade to the eBook version at www.packt.com and as a print book customer, you are entitled to a discount on the eBook copy. Get in touch with us at customercare@packtpub.com for more details.

At www.packt.com, you can also read a collection of free technical articles, sign up for a range of free newsletters, and receive exclusive discounts and offers on Packt books and eBooks.

Contributors

About the author

Ranga Rao Karanam is the founder of in28Minutes, a company that trains 300,000 developers across the globe in relation to the cloud, microservices, Spring, Spring Boot, and Containers. He loves programming, and loves consulting for start-ups on developing scalable cloud applications and following modern development practices, such as BDD, continuous delivery, and DevOps.

In his spare time, he loves hiking, cricket, and tennis. His ambition is to spend a year hiking the Himalayas.

About the reviewers

Sherwin John Calleja Tragura is currently a Java-JakartaEE-C# corporate trainer who is also a subject matter expert on Python 3, Angular 7, Ionic 3, Alfresco, CMS, DMS, and Webscripts. He is currently involved in business analysis and the technical design of a web and mobile project with a number of ongoing projects in the area of reactive programming and web frameworks. He graduated from the University of the Philippines Los Baños, where he started his career as a university lecturer. He has authored *Spring 5 Cookbook*, *Spring MVC Blueprints*, and *Jakarta EE 8 Recipes*, all published by Packt Publishing. He is continuing to explore and share new techniques in the areas of microservices, Java, C# .NET, and JavaScript frameworks, all of which will prove useful to future projects and training.

Samer Abdelkafi has over 14 years' experience as a software architect and engineer, with a primary focus on open source technologies. He has contributed to numerous projects in different sectors, including banking, insurance, education, public services, and utility billing. At the end of 2016, he created DEVACT, a company specializing in information technology consultancy.

In addition to his day job, he has reviewed many books related to Spring projects, including *Mastering Spring Cloud*, *Mastering Spring Boot 2.0*, and *Spring MVC Blueprints*.

Mohamed Sanaulla is a full-stack developer with more than 8 years' experience in developing enterprise applications and Java-based backend solutions for e-commerce applications. His interests include enterprise software development, refactoring and redesigning applications, designing and implementing RESTful web services, troubleshooting Java applications for performance issues, and TDD.

He has significant expertise in Java-based application development, ADF (a JSF-based Java EE web framework), SQL, PL/SQL, JUnit, designing RESTful services, Spring, Spring Boot, Struts, Elasticsearch, and MongoDB. He is also a Sun Certified Java Programmer for the Java 6 platform. He is a moderator for JavaRanch, and likes to share his findings on his blog.

Packt is searching for authors like you

If you're interested in becoming an author for Packt, please visit authors.packtpub.com and apply today. We have worked with thousands of developers and tech professionals, just like you, to help them share their insight with the global tech community. You can make a general application, apply for a specific hot topic that we are recruiting an author for, or submit your own idea.

Table of Contents

Preface

Spring Framework revolutionized enterprise application development in the Java world. It has been the framework of choice for almost 15 years. This book will help you understand this evolution—from solving the problems of building testable loosely coupled applications to building web applications and REST APIs. Today, various Spring Projects are available to help you build cloud-native microservices and API backends for full stack applications. We will look at some of the important Spring Projects in depth—Spring Framework, Spring Boot, Spring Cloud, Spring Data, Spring Reactive, Spring Security, and Spring Test. We will build a web application, a Todo REST API, several cloud-native microservices, and a basic full stack application to understand the various Spring Projects. Advanced features of Spring Boot will also be covered and demonstrated through powerful examples.

By the end of this book, you will be equipped with the knowledge and best practices to develop applications with Spring, Spring Boot, and Spring Cloud.

Who this book is for

This book is for experienced Java developers with a basic knowledge of Spring Framework. In this book, we dig deeper into various Spring Projects—Spring Framework, Spring Boot, Spring Cloud, Spring Data, Spring Reactive, Spring Security, and Spring Test. This book will help you develop and unit test an awesome REST API, microservices, full stack applications, and cloud-native applications with Spring Framework.

What this book covers

Chapter 1, *Spring Landscape – Framework, Modules, and Projects*, takes you through the evolution of Spring Framework, ranging from its initial versions to Spring 5.1. Initially, Spring was used to develop testable applications using dependency injection and core modules. Recent Spring Projects, such as Spring Boot, Spring Cloud, and Spring Cloud Data Flow deal with application infrastructure and moving applications to the cloud. You'll get an overview of different Spring modules and Projects.

Chapter 2, *Dependency Injection and Unit Testing*, dives deep into dependency injection, looking at the different kinds of dependency injection methods available in Spring, and how auto-wiring makes life easier. This chapter also takes a quick look at unit testing.

Chapter 3, *Building Web Applications with Spring MVC*, gives an overview of building web applications with the most popular Java web framework—Spring MVC. The beauty of Spring MVC lies in its clean, loosely coupled architecture. With a clean definition of roles for controllers, handler mappings, view resolvers, and **Plain Old Java Object (POJO)** command beans, Spring MVC makes use of all the core Spring features, such as dependency injection and auto-wiring, to make it simple to create servlet-based web applications.

Chapter 4, *Getting Started with Spring Boot*, introduces Spring Boot and discusses how it makes it easy to develop production-grade Spring-based applications. You will learn the basics of Spring Boot—Spring Initializr, auto-configuration, and starter Projects. You will use Spring Boot Actuator to monitor your applications and use Spring Boot DevTools to become a productive developer.

Chapter 5, *Digging Deeper into Spring Framework*, digs deeper into Spring Framework. You will learn about implementing cross-cutting concerns with Spring **AOP** (short for **Aspect Oriented Programming**). You will also learn how to schedule tasks and write dynamic scripts using Groovy and JavaScript with the JSR 223 API.

Chapter 6, *Building REST APIs with Spring Boot*, focuses on building great REST APIs with Spring Boot. You will start by implementing a basic REST API and then move on to adding caching, exception handling, HATEOAS, and internationalization, while making use of different features from Spring and Spring Boot frameworks.

Chapter 7, *Unit Testing REST APIs with Spring Boot*, focuses on writing great unit and integration tests for REST APIs developed with Spring Boot. You'll learn how to use Spring MockMVC and Spring Boot Test to write unit tests with mocks and integration tests launching entire Spring contexts.

Chapter 8, *Securing REST APIs with Spring Security*, looks at the most important REST API features—authentication and authorization. Spring Security is the framework of choice for securing REST APIs in the Java world—especially for applications built with Spring and Spring Boot. You'll gain an understanding of how to integrate Spring Security into a Spring Boot REST API project. You will then learn about the key building blocks behind Spring Security—filters, authentication managers, providers, and access decision managers. This chapter covers basic authentication, OAuth, and using JWT with Spring Security OAuth.

Chapter 9, *Full Stack App with React and Spring Boot*, shifts our attention to full stack applications. You will create a simple frontend application with one of the popular frontend frameworks—React—and integrate it with a Spring Boot backend. The chapter covers various challenges that you may face when doing full stack development—including security.

Chapter 10, *Managing Data with Spring Data*, focuses on the Spring Data module. Spring Data aims to introduce a common approach to talking to a wide variety of data stores—relational or otherwise. You will develop simple applications to integrate Spring with JPA and big data technologies.

Chapter 11, *Getting Started with Microservices*, explains the evolution of application architectures in the last decade. You will gain an understanding of why microservices and cloud-native applications are needed and get a quick overview of the different Spring Projects that can help you build cloud-native applications.

Chapter 12, *Building Microservices with Spring Boot and Spring Cloud*, looks at implementing microservices using projects under the Spring Cloud umbrella. We will look at configuration management, service discovery, circuit breakers, and intelligent routing. You will use Spring Cloud Config, Spring Cloud Bus, Ribbon, Eureka, Zuul, Spring Cloud Sleuth, Zipkin, and Hystrix to implement a microservice.

Chapter 13, *Reactive Programming*, explores programming with asynchronous data streams. In this chapter, you will gain an understanding of reactive programming. The chapter also takes a quick look at the features provided by Spring Framework.

Chapter 14, *Spring Best Practices*, introduces best practices for developing enterprise applications with Spring, related to unit testing, integration testing, maintaining a Spring configuration, and more.

Chapter 15, *Working with Kotlin in Spring*, introduces you to a JVM language that is quickly gaining popularity—Kotlin. This chapter offers guidance on how to set up a Kotlin project in Eclipse. You will create a new Spring Boot project using Kotlin and implement a couple of basic services with unit and integration testing.

To get the most out of this book

To get the most out of this book, you need to be an experienced Java programmer.

To be able to run through the examples in this book, you will need the following tools:

- Java 8/9/10/11/12
- Eclipse IDE
- Postman

We will use Maven embedded into Eclipse IDE to download all the dependencies that are needed.

Download the example code files

You can download the example code files for this book from your account at www.packt.com. If you purchased this book elsewhere, you can visit www.packt.com/support and register to have the files emailed directly to you.

You can download the code files by following these steps:

1. Log in or register at www.packt.com.
2. Select the **SUPPORT** tab.
3. Click on **Code Downloads & Errata**.
4. Enter the name of the book in the **Search** box and follow the onscreen instructions.

Once the file is downloaded, please make sure that you unzip or extract the folder using the latest version of:

- WinRAR/7-Zip for Windows
- Zipeg/iZip/UnRarX for Mac
- 7-Zip/PeaZip for Linux

The code bundle for the book is also hosted on GitHub at https://github.com/PacktPublishing/Mastering-Spring-5.1. In case there's an update to the code, it will be updated on the existing GitHub repository.

We also have other code bundles from our rich catalog of books and videos available at https://github.com/PacktPublishing/. Check them out!

Download the color images

We also provide a PDF file that has color images of the screenshots/diagrams used in this book. You can download it here: https://static.packt-cdn.com/downloads/9781789615692_ColorImages.pdf.

Conventions used

There are a number of text conventions used throughout this book.

CodeInText: Indicates code words in text, database table names, folder names, filenames, file extensions, pathnames, dummy URLs, user input, and Twitter handles. Here is an example: "We are defining a component scan for the com.mastering.spring.springmvc package so that all the beans and controllers in this package are created and autowired."

A block of code is set as follows:

```
<beans > <!-Schema Definition removed -->

    <context:component-scan  base-
package="com.mastering.spring.springmvc"  />

    <mvc:annotation-driven />

</beans>
```

When we wish to draw your attention to a particular part of a code block, the relevant lines or items are set in bold:

```
public class User {
    private String guid;
    private String name;
    private String userId;
    private String password;
    private String password2;
    //Constructor
    //Getters and Setters
    //toString
}
```

Any command-line input or output is written as follows:

```
mvn cf:push
```

Bold: Indicates a new term, an important word, or words that you see onscreen. For example, words in menus or dialog boxes appear in the text like this. Here is an example: "Click on the **Install** button shown in the following screenshot."

Warnings or important notes appear like this.

 Tips and tricks appear like this.

Get in touch

Feedback from our readers is always welcome.

General feedback: If you have questions about any aspect of this book, mention the book title in the subject of your message and email us at customercare@packtpub.com.

Errata: Although we have taken every care to ensure the accuracy of our content, mistakes do happen. If you have found a mistake in this book, we would be grateful if you would report this to us. Please visit www.packt.com/submit-errata, selecting your book, clicking on the Errata Submission Form link, and entering the details.

Piracy: If you come across any illegal copies of our works in any form on the Internet, we would be grateful if you would provide us with the location address or website name. Please contact us at copyright@packt.com with a link to the material.

If you are interested in becoming an author: If there is a topic that you have expertise in and you are interested in either writing or contributing to a book, please visit authors.packtpub.com.

Reviews

Please leave a review. Once you have read and used this book, why not leave a review on the site that you purchased it from? Potential readers can then see and use your unbiased opinion to make purchase decisions, we at Packt can understand what you think about our products, and our authors can see your feedback on their book. Thank you!

For more information about Packt, please visit packt.com.

Section 1: Getting Started with Spring and Spring Boot

The Spring framework revolutionized enterprise application development in the Java world. It has continued to be the framework of choice for almost 15 years.

This section will help you get started with the two most important Spring Projects: Spring Framework and Spring Boot. We will understand the modularity of the Spring Framework and discuss several Spring Modules.

The following chapters are covered under this section:

- Chapter 1, *Spring Landscape – Framework, Modules, and Projects*
- Chapter 2, *Dependency Injection and Unit Testing*
- Chapter 3, *Building Web Applications with Spring MVC*
- Chapter 4, *Getting Started with Spring Boot*
- Chapter 5, *Digging Deeper into the Spring Framework*

1
Spring Landscape - Framework, Modules, and Projects

The first version of Spring Framework 1.0 was released in March 2004. In the last decade and a half, the Spring Framework remains the number one framework of choice to develop enterprise applications in the Java world.

In this chapter, we will take a 10,000 feet look at the journey of the Spring Framework.

The Spring Framework is highly modular with more than 20 different modules. Spring Modules provide the core features of the Spring Framework—**Dependency Injection (DI)**, the Web MVC Framework, AOP, and more. Spring Modules help you to pick and choose the modules you want to use.

Architectures have continuously evolved during the last decade. Almost all enterprises are on the journey from monolith architectures to microservices architectures. The Spring Framework evolved continuously to keep up with the needs of enterprise applications.

Spring Projects explore solutions to the evolving challenges in enterprises. Some of the important Spring Projects are Spring Boot, Spring Cloud, Spring Data, Spring Batch, and Spring Security.

In this chapter, we will get a big picture of the entire Spring landscape—including the evolution of important Spring Modules and Spring Projects. We will end the chapter by looking at the new features in Spring Framework 5.0 and 5.1.

The following topics will be covered in this chapter:

- Why the Spring Framework is popular
- How the Spring Framework has adapted to the evolution of application architectures
- What the important modules in the Spring Framework are
- Where the Spring Framework fits in the umbrella of Spring Projects
- What the new features in Spring Framework 5.0 and 5.1 are

Exploring Spring and its evolution

Spring has been the number one framework of choice to develop enterprise applications in the Java world for more than a decade. In the relatively young and dynamic world of Java frameworks, a decade is a long time.

Enterprise applications evolve quickly. The main challenges in 2004, when the first version of the Spring Framework was initially released, were the difficulties in writing testable code and developing loosely coupled web applications. As time progressed, the challenges shifted to developing great web services—initially with **Simple Object Access Protocol (SOAP)** and, eventually, REST. And, in the last few years, enterprise application architectures evolved toward microservices.

The Spring Framework (including Spring Projects and Spring Modules) continues to provide solutions to meet the needs of the day with a number of Spring Projects and Spring Modules, including Spring Core, Spring MVC, Spring Web Services, Spring Boot, and Spring Cloud.

How did Spring remain so popular in a dynamic world where frameworks struggle to be relevant for more than a few years?

In this section, let's take a quick look at how the Spring Framework has kept up with the changing needs of enterprise applications.

Beginning with the first version of the Spring Framework

Java EE applications in the early 2000s were cumbersome to write and test. It was difficult to develop loosely coupled applications. Unit testing was near impossible for enterprise applications with external connections such as a database. Testing even simple features involved deploying the entire application in a container.

The Spring Framework was introduced, in 2004, as a lightweight framework aimed at making developing Java EE applications simpler.

The Spring website (`https://projects.spring.io/spring-framework/`) defines the Spring Framework as follows:

> *The Spring Framework provides a comprehensive programming and configuration model for modern Java-based enterprise applications.*

Spring Framework is used to wire enterprise Java applications. The main aim of Spring Framework is to take care of all the technical plumbing that is needed in order to connect the different parts of an application. This allows programmers to focus on the crux of their jobs—writing business logic.

The crux of the Framework is a concept called DI or **Inversion of Control (IoC)**.

Any Java class we write depends on other classes. The other classes a class depends on are its dependencies. If a class directly creates instances of dependencies, a tight coupling is established between them. With Spring, the responsibility of creating and wiring objects is taken over by a new component called the IoC Container. Classes define dependencies and the Spring IoC Container creates objects and wires the dependencies together. This revolutionary concept, where the control of creating and wiring dependencies is taken over by the container, is famously called IoC or DI. We will discuss dependency injection in complete detail in `Chapter 2`, *Dependency Injection and Unit Testing*.

The initial version of Spring also provided a very good framework to develop web applications—Spring MVC.

Let's quickly look at the reasons behind the initial popularity of the Spring Framework:

- Loose coupling and testability
- Architectural flexibility
- Reduction in plumbing code

Let's discuss each of these in detail.

Loose coupling and testability

Through DI, Spring brings loose coupling between classes. While loose coupling is beneficial for application maintainability in the long run, the first benefits are realized with the testability that it brings in.

Earlier versions of Java EE applications were very difficult to unit test. In fact, it was difficult to test code outside of the container. The only way to test code was to deploy them in a container.

DI enables unit testing by making it easy to replace the dependencies with their mocks. We do not need to deploy the entire application to unit test it.

Simplifying unit testing has multiple benefits:

- Programmers are more productive
- Defects are found earlier so they are less costly to fix
- Applications have automated unit tests, which can run in **Continuous Integration (CI)** builds, preventing future defects

 CI involves running all of the automated tests and deployments as soon as the code is committed to version control. This would ensure that any broken test or feature is found and reported immediately.

Architectural flexibility

The Spring Framework is highly modular, having more than 20 different modules—all with clearly defined boundaries. This allows applications to pick and choose the features (or the module) of the framework they would want to use. These modules are called Spring Modules. We will look at Spring Modules in detail a little later in this chapter.

In addition, the Spring Framework does not aim to be the jack-of-all-trades. While focusing on its core job of reducing coupling between different parts of the application and making them testable, Spring provides great integration with frameworks of your choice. This means you have flexibility in your architecture—if you do not want to use a specific framework, you can easily replace it with another.

Let's consider a few examples:

- If you would want to build an awesome web application, Spring offers a framework of its own—Spring MVC. However, Spring has great support for Struts, Vaadin, JSF, or any web framework of your choice.
- Spring Beans can provide lightweight implementation for your business logic. However, Spring can be integrated with **Enterprise JavaBeans (EJBs)** as well.
- To talk to a database, Spring provides its own module—the Spring JDBC module. However, Spring has great support for any of your preferred data layer frameworks—**Java Persistence API (JPA)**, Hibernate (with or without JPA), or iBatis.
- Spring provides a basic **Aspect Oriented Framework (AOP)** called Spring AOP to implement your cross-cutting concerns (logging, transaction management, security, and more). It also provides the option to integrate with a full-fledged AOP implementation such as AspectJ.

Reduction in plumbing code

Before the Spring Framework, typical J2EE (or Jakarta EE, as it is called now) applications contained a lot of plumbing code, for example, getting a database connection, exception handling code, transaction management code, and logging code.

Let's take a look at a simple example of executing a query using the prepared statement:

```
PreparedStatement st = null;
try {
st = conn.prepareStatement(INSERT_TODO_QUERY);
// business logic goes here..
} catch (SQLException e) {
    logger.error("Failed : " + INSERT_TODO_QUERY, e);
} finally {
    if (st != null) {
        try {
            st.close();
        } catch (SQLException e) {
            // Ignore - nothing to do..
        }
    }
}
```

In the preceding example, there are four lines of business logic and more than 10 lines of plumbing code.

With the Spring Framework, the same logic can be applied in a couple of lines:

```
jdbcTemplate.update(INSERT_TODO_QUERY,
bean.getDescription(), bean.isDone());
```

How does the Spring Framework do this magic?
Spring (and Spring Modules) converts most checked exceptions into unchecked exceptions. Unchecked exceptions do not need to be handled! Think about this—what can you really do if there is an exception in running a query? Not much—you would typically show an error page to the end user. If that's the case, why do you need to implement exception handling in every method in the data layer? Spring provides a way to centralize the exception handling logic and handle it in a single place. In addition, all of the plumbing code involved in getting a connection, creating a prepared statement, and so on is implemented in a wrapper class (namely, `JdbcTemplate`, in one of the Spring Modules called **Spring JDBC**) so that we do not need to repeat the logic every time you execute a query. Developers of the 2000s, like me, loved this more than anything else!

Avoiding all of the plumbing code also has another great benefit—reduced duplication in the code. Since all the code for transaction management, exception handling, and so on (typically, all of your cross-cutting concerns) is implemented in one place, it is easier to maintain.

Learning about the early years of the Spring Framework – Spring Projects

In the previous section, we discussed how the first version of Spring brought a breath of fresh air to the Java EE world. In this section, let's look at how Spring evolved with the next versions of the Spring Framework.

An important thing Spring brings in is the umbrella of Spring Projects. While the Spring Framework provides the base for core features of enterprise applications (DI, web, and data), other Spring Projects explore integration and solutions to other problems in the enterprise space. Spring Projects helped Spring to stay ahead of the game by allowing innovation outside the core Spring Framework. We will discuss the important Spring Projects in a separate section in this chapter.

As we move toward the last few years of the 2000 decade, enterprise applications started moving toward web services—initially SOAP Web Services and, by the end of the decade, toward RESTful web services.

Spring continued to evolve as follows:

- Introduced a Spring Project called Spring Web Services—to help the development of contract-first SOAP web services
- Enhanced the Spring MVC Module with excellent support for REST web services

Staying ahead of Java EE

In addition to providing excellent support for web services, Spring stayed ahead of Java EE by providing new features:

- Annotations were introduced in Java 5. The Spring Framework (version 2.5—November 2007) was ahead of Java EE in introducing an annotation-based controller model for Spring MVC. Developers using Java EE had to wait until Java EE 6 (December 2009—2 years) before having comparable functionality.
- The Spring Framework introduced a number of abstractions ahead of Java EE to keep the application decoupled from specific implementation. The caching API provides a case in point. Spring provided a transparent caching support in Spring 3.1. Java EE came up with JSR-107 for JCache (in 2014), support for which was provided in Spring 4.1.
- One of the Spring Projects called Spring Batch defines a new approach to building Java Batch applications. We had to wait until Java EE 7 (June 2013) to have a comparable batch application specification in Java EE.

Evolution toward microservices – Spring Boot and Spring Cloud

In the previous sections, we looked at how Spring evolved to meet the enterprise application needs of the late 2000s—RESTful and SOAP web services and staying ahead of Java EE.

We've evolved further in the last few years and the enterprise needs today are very different from a decade ago. Over a period of time, applications grew into monoliths, which became difficult to manage. The challenges with monolith applications lead to organizations searching for the silver bullet.

In the last few years, a common pattern emerged among all of the organizations that were successful at doing this. From this emerged an architectural style that was called **microservices architecture**. We will discuss microservices in Chapter 11, *Getting Started with Microservices*.

Microservices architecture involves building a number of small, independently deployable microservices. These bring in a couple of new challenges:

- How can we quickly build microservices?
- How can we connect the microservice to the cloud?

Let's discuss the solution Spring provides to these problems.

Building microservices quickly with Spring Boot

In the era of monoliths, we had the luxury of taking time to set the frameworks up for an application. However, in the era of microservices, we would want to create individual components faster. Spring Boot project aims to solve this problem.

Let's consider an example—I want to build a RESTful API microservice using Spring MVC and JPA (Hibernate). What are the things I would need to do? Let's take a quick look:

1. You would need to decide the compatible versions of Spring MVC, JPA, and Hibernate to use
2. You would need to start setting up Spring Context with all of the different layers integrated—the web layer, business layer, and data layer
3. You would need to decide how to do configuration management, unit testing, transaction management, logging, and security

This would take a few weeks at least. And, in the microservices world, we do not have weeks. And that's the problem Spring Boot aims to solve.

As the official website highlights:

> *Spring Boot makes it easy to create stand-alone, production-grade Spring based Applications that you can just run. We take an opinionated view of the Spring platform and third-party libraries so you can get started with minimum fuss.*

Spring Boot aims to take an opinionated view—basically making a lot of decisions for us—on developing Spring-based projects. We will talk about Spring Boot in depth in Chapter 5, *Digging Deeper into the Spring Framework*.

Connecting microservices with the cloud using Spring Cloud

The cloud comes with its own set of challenges. Spring Cloud aims to provide solutions to some commonly encountered patterns when building systems on the cloud:

- **Configuration management**: All applications have configuration that varies from one environment to another environment. Configuration is typically littered at multiple locations—application code, property files, databases, environment variables, **Java Naming and Directory Interface (JNDI)**, and system variables are a few examples. With microservices architectures, the problem of configuration management becomes multi fold. Spring Cloud provides a centralized configuration management solution for microservices called Spring Cloud Config.
- **Service discovery**: Service discovery promotes loose coupling between services. Spring Cloud provides integration with popular service discovery options such as Eureka, ZooKeeper, and Consul.
- **Circuit breakers**: Microservices must be fault tolerant. They should be able to handle the failure of backing services gracefully. Circuit breakers play a key role in providing a default minimal service in the case of failures. Spring Cloud provides integration with the Netflix Hystrix fault tolerance library.
- **API gateways**: An API gateway provides centralized aggregation, routing, and caching services. Spring Cloud provides integration with the API gateway library, Netflix Zuul.

We will explore Spring Cloud in depth in `Chapter 11`, *Getting Started with Microservices*.

Quickly revising what we learned

In this section, we looked at how Spring evolved to meet enterprise application needs during the last 15 years. What started off as a simple framework to enable testability with loosely coupled code evolved into a complete landscape of Projects and Modules, enabling the enterprise to develop web services, such as RESTful and SOAP—and microservices.

In the subsequent sections, let's take a deeper look at the important Spring Modules and Spring Projects.

Learning about Spring Modules

The modularity of the Spring Framework is one of the most important reasons for its widespread use. The Spring Framework is highly modular with more than 20 different modules having clearly defined boundaries.

The following diagram shows different Spring Modules, organized by the layer of application they are typically used in:

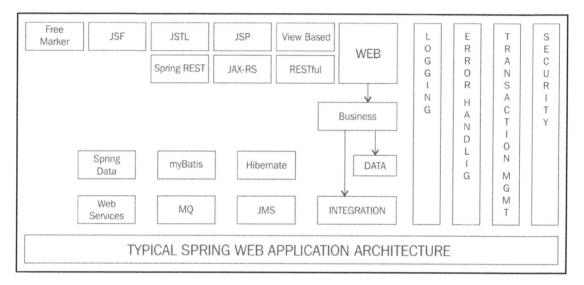

We will start by discussing the Spring Core Container before moving on to other modules grouped by the application layer they are typically used in.

Spring Core Container

Spring Core Container provides the core features of the Spring Framework—DI, the IoC Container, and the application context. We will learn more about DI and the IoC container in `Chapter 2`, *Dependency Injection and Unit Testing*.

Important core Spring Modules are listed as follows:

- `spring-core`: This is for utilities used by other Spring Modules.
- `spring-beans`: This provides support for Spring Beans. In combination with `spring-core`, it provides DI, the core feature of the Spring Framework. It includes the implementation of BeanFactory.

- `spring-context`: This implements `ApplicationContext` (which extends BeanFactory) and provides support for loading resources and internationalization, among others.
- `spring-expression`: This extends EL (Expression Language from JSP) and provides a language for bean property (including arrays and collections) access and manipulations.

Cross-cutting concerns

Cross-cutting concerns are applicable to all application layers—including logging and security, among others. AOP is typically used to implement cross-cutting concerns.

Unit tests and integration tests fit this category since they are applicable to all layers.

Important Spring Modules related to cross-cutting concerns are listed as follows:

- `spring-aop`: Provides basic support for **Aspect Oriented Programming (AOP)**—with method interceptors and Pointcuts
- `spring-aspects`: Provides integration with AspectJ—the most popular and fully featured AOP framework
- `spring-instrument`: Provides basic instrumentation support
- `spring-test`: Provides basic support for unit testing and integration testing

Web – Spring MVC

Spring provides its own MVC framework, Spring MVC, apart from providing great integration with popular web frameworks such as Struts.

Important artifacts/modules are listed as follows:

- `spring-web`: This provides basic web features, such as multi part file upload. It also provides support for integration with other web frameworks, such as Struts.
- `spring-webmvc`: This provides a fully featured Web MVC Framework—Spring MVC, which includes features to implement RESTful services as well.
- `spring-webflux`: Introduced in Spring Framework 5, this brings reactive capabilities to web applications.

We will cover Spring MVC and develop web applications and REST services with it in Chapter 3, *Building Web Applications with Spring MVC*, and Chapter 6, *Building REST APIs with Spring Boot*.

We will discuss building reactive applications with Spring Web Flux in Chapter 13, *Reactive Programming*.

The business layer

The business layer is focused on executing the business logic of the applications. With Spring, business logic is typically implemented in **Plain Old Java Object** (**POJO**).

Spring transactions (spring-tx) provide declarative transaction management for POJO and other classes.

The data layer

The data layer in applications typically talks to the database and/or the external interfaces. Some of the important Spring Modules related to the data layer are listed as follows:

- spring-jdbc: Provides abstraction around JDBC to avoid boilerplate code
- spring-orm: Provides integration with **Object-relational mapping** (**ORM**) frameworks and specifications—including JPA and Hibernate, among others
- spring-oxm: Provides an object to XML mapping integration and supports frameworks such as JAXB and Castor
- spring-jms: Provides abstraction around JMS to avoid boilerplate code

Beginning with Spring Projects

While the Spring Framework provides the base for core features of enterprise applications (DI, web, and data), other Spring Projects explore integration and solutions to other problems in the enterprise space—including deployment, cloud, big data, batch, and security, among others.

Some of the important Spring Projects are listed as follows:

- Spring Boot
- Spring Cloud
- Spring Data
- Spring Batch
- Spring Security
- Spring **HATEOAS (Hypermedia As The Engine of Application State)**

Spring Boot

Some of the challenges while developing microservices and web applications are as follows:

- Making framework choices and deciding compatible framework versions
- Providing mechanisms for externalizing configuration—properties that can change from one environment to another
- Health checks and monitoring—providing alerts if a specific part of the application is down
- Deciding on the deployment environment and configuring the application for it

Spring Boot solves all of these problems out of the box. We will look at Spring Boot in depth in two chapters—Chapter 5, *Digging Deeper into the Spring Framework,* and Chapter 7, *Unit Testing REST API with Spring Boot.*

Spring Cloud

It is not an exaggeration to say the world is moving to the cloud.

Cloud-native microservices and applications are the order of the day. We will discuss this in detail in Chapter 11, *Getting Started with Microservices.*

Spring is taking rapid strides toward making application development for the cloud simpler with Spring Cloud.

Spring Cloud provides solutions for common patterns in distributed systems. Spring Cloud enables developers to quickly create applications that implement common patterns. Some of the common patterns implemented in Spring Cloud are listed as follows:

- Configuration management
- Service discovery
- Circuit breakers
- Intelligent routing

We will discuss Spring Cloud and its varied range of features in more detail in `Chapter 11`, *Getting Started with Microservices*.

Spring Data

There are multiple sources of data in today's world—SQL (relational) and a variety of NoSQL databases. Spring Data tries to provide a consistent data-access approach to all of these different kinds of databases.

Spring Data provides integration with a varied range of specifications and/or data stores:

- JPA
- MongoDB
- Redis
- Solr
- Gemfire
- Apache Cassandra
- Neo4J for Graph Search

Some of the important features are listed as follows:

- Provides abstractions around repository and object mappings—by determining queries from method names
- Simple Spring integration
- Integration with Spring MVC controllers
- Advanced automatic auditing features, created by, created date, last changed by, and last changed date

We will discuss Spring Data in more detail in `Chapter 8`, *Securing REST API with Spring Security*.

Beginning with Spring Batch

Enterprise applications today process large volumes of data using batch programs. The needs of these applications are very similar. Spring Batch provides solutions for high-volume batch programs with high performance requirements.

Important features in Spring Batch are as follows:

- The ability to start, stop, and restart jobs—including the ability to restart failed jobs from the point where they failed
- The ability to process data in chunks
- The ability to retry steps or to skip steps on failure
- A web-based administration interface

Spring Security

Authentication and authorization are critical parts of enterprise applications, both web applications and web services. Authentication is the process of identifying the user. Authorization is the process of ensuring that a user has access to perform the identified action on the resource.

Spring Security provides declarative authentication and authorization for Java-based applications.

Important features in Spring Security are as follows:

- Simplified authentication and authorization
- Great integration with Spring MVC and Servlet APIs
- Support to prevent common security attacks—**Cross-Site Forgery Request (CSRF)**, **CORS** (**Cross-Origin Resource Sharing**), and Session Fixation
- Modules available for integration with SAML and LDAP

We will discuss how to secure web applications and RESTful APIs with Spring Security in `Chapter 9`, *Full Stack App with React and Spring Boot*.

Spring HATEOAS

HATEOAS (short for **Hypermedia As The Engine of Application State**). Though it sounds complex, it is quite a simple concept. Its main aim is to decouple the server (the provider of the service) from the client (the consumer of the service).

The service provider provides the service consumer with information about what other actions can be performed on the resource.

Spring HATEOAS provides a HATEOAS implementation, especially for the RESTful services implemented with Spring MVC.

Important features in Spring HATEOAS are as follows:

- Simplified definition of links pointing to service methods, making the links less fragile
- Support for JAXB (XML-based) and JSON integration
- Support for service consumer (client side)

We will discuss how to use HATEOAS in `Chapter 7`, *Unit Testing REST API with Spring Boot*.

New features in Spring Framework 5.0 and 5.1

Spring Framework 5.0 is the first major upgrade in the Spring Framework, almost four years after Spring Framework 4.0. In this time frame, one of the major developments has been the evolution of the Spring Boot project.

One of the biggest features of Spring Framework 5.0 is reactive programming. Core reactive programming features and support for reactive endpoints are available out of the box from Spring Framework 5.0. The list of important changes includes the following:

- Baseline upgrades
- Java 11 and 12 support
- Usage of JDK 8 features in the Spring Framework code
- Reactive programming support
- A functional web framework
- Java modularity with Jigsaw
- Kotlin support
- Dropped features

Baseline upgrades

Spring Framework 5.0 has JDK 8 and Java EE 7 as its baseline. Basically, it means that previous JDK and Java EE versions are not supported anymore.

Some of the important baseline Java EE 7 specifications are listed as follows:

- Servlet 3.1
- JMS 2.0
- JPA 2.1
- JAX-RS 2.0
- Bean Validation 1.1

There are many changes to the minimum supported versions of several Java frameworks. The following list contains some of the minimum supported versions of prominent frameworks:

- Hibernate 5
- Jackson 2.6
- EhCache 2.10
- JUnit 5
- Tiles 3

The following list shows the supported server versions:

- Tomcat 8.5+
- Jetty 9.4+
- WildFly 10+
- Netty 4.1+ (for web reactive programming with Spring Web Flux)
- Undertow 1.4+ (for web reactive programming with Spring Web Flux)

Applications using earlier versions of any of the preceding specifications/frameworks need to be upgraded at least to the previously listed versions before they can use Spring Framework 5.0.

Java 11 Support

Spring Framework 5.1 supports JDK 12 and JDK 11 and is compatible with Java 8.

Usage of JDK 8 features in the Spring Framework code

The Spring Framework 4.x baseline version is Java SE 6. This means that it supports Java 6, 7, and 8. Having to support Java SE 6 and 7 puts constraints on the Spring Framework code. The framework code cannot use any of the new features in Java 8. So, while the rest of the world upgraded to Java 8, the code in the Spring Framework (at least the major parts) was restricted to using earlier versions of Java.

With Spring Framework 5.0, the baseline version is Java 8. The Spring Framework code is now upgraded to use the new features in Java 8. This will result in more readable and performant framework code. Some of the Java 8 features used are as follows:

- Java 8 default methods in core Spring interfaces
- Internal code improvements based on Java 8 reflection enhancements
- Use of functional programming in the framework code—such as lambdas and streams

Reactive programming support

Reactive programming is one of the most important features of Spring Framework 5.0.

Microservices architectures are typically built around event-based communication. Applications are built to react to events (or messages).

Reactive programming provides an alternate style of programming focused on building applications that react to events.

While Java 8 does not have built-in support for reactive programming, there are a number of frameworks that provide support for reactive programming:

- **Reactive Streams**: A language-neutral attempt to define reactive APIs
- **Reactor**: Java implementation of Reactive Streams provided by the Spring Pivotal team
- **Spring WebFlux**: Enables the development of web applications based on reactive programming, and provides a programming model similar to Spring MVC

We will discuss reactive programming and how you can implement it with Spring Web Flux in `Chapter 13`, *Reactive Programming*.

Functional web framework

Building on top of the reactive features, Spring 5 also provides a functional web framework.

A functional web framework provides features to define endpoints using functional programming style. A simple hello world example is shown here:

```
RouterFunction < String > route = route(
    GET("/hello-world"),
    request - > Response.ok().body(fromObject("Hello World"))
);
```

A functional web framework can also be used to define more complex routes, as shown in the following example:

```
RouterFunction << ? > route =
    route(GET("/todos/{id}"),
        request - > {
            Mono < Todo > todo =
Mono.justOrEmpty(request.pathVariable("id"))
            .map(Integer::valueOf)
            .then(repository::getTodo);
            return Response.ok().body(
                fromPublisher(todo, Todo.class));
        })
    .and(route(GET("/todos"),
        request - > {
            Flux < Todo > people = repository.allTodos();
            return Response.ok().body(
                fromPublisher(people, Todo.class));
        }))
    .and(route(POST("/todos"),
        request - > {
            Mono < Todo > todo = request.body(toMono(Todo.class));
            return Response.ok().build(repository.saveTodo(todo));
        }));
```

A couple of important things to note are as follows:

- RouterFunction evaluates the matching condition to route requests to the appropriate handler function.
- We are defining three endpoints, two GET statements, and one POST statement and mapping them to different handler functions.

We will discuss Mono and Flux in more detail in Chapter 11, *Getting Started with Microservices.*

Java modularity with Jigsaw

Until Java 8, the Java platform was not modular. A couple of important problems resulted out of this:

- **Platform bloat**: Java modularity has not been a cause of concern in the last couple of decades. However, with the **Internet of Things (IOT)** and new lightweight platforms such as Node.js, there is an urgent need to address the bloat of the Java platform. (Initial versions of JDK were less than 10 MB in size. Recent versions of JDK need more than 200 MB.)
- **JAR hell**: Another important concern is the problem of JAR hell. When Java `ClassLoader` finds a class, it will not see whether there are other definitions for the class available. It immediately loads the first class that is found. If two different parts of the application need the same class from different JARs, there is no way for them to specify the JAR from which the class has to be loaded.

Open System Gateway Initiative (OSGi) is one of the initiatives, started way back in 1999, to bring modularity into Java applications.

Each module (referred to as bundle) defines the following:

- **Imports**: Other bundles that the module uses
- **Exports**: Packages that this bundle exports

Each module can have its own life cycle. It can be installed, started, and stopped on its own.

Jigsaw is an initiative under **Java Community Process (JCP)**, started with Java 7, to bring modularity into Java. It has two main aims:

- Defining and implementing a modular structure for JDK
- Defining a module system for applications built on the Java platform

Spring Framework 5.0 contains support for Jigsaw modules.

Kotlin support

Kotlin is a statically typed JVM language that enables code that is expressive, short, and readable. Spring Framework 5.0 has good support for Kotlin.

Consider a simple Kotlin program illustrating a data class, as shown here:

```
import java.util.*
data class Todo(var description: String, var name: String, var targetDate :
Date)
fun main(args: Array<String>) {
    var todo = Todo("Learn Spring Boot", "Jack", Date())
    println(todo)
        //Todo(description=Learn Spring Boot, name=Jack,
        //targetDate=Mon May 22 04:26:22 UTC 2017)
    var todo2 = todo.copy(name = "Jill") println(todo2)
        //Todo(description=Learn Spring Boot, name=Jill,
        //targetDate=Mon May 22 04:26:22 UTC 2017)
    var todo3 = todo.copy() println(todo3.equals(todo)) //true
 }
```

In fewer than 10 lines of code, we created and tested a data bean with three properties and the following functions—`equals()`, `hashCode()`, `toString()` and `copy()`.

Kotlin is strongly typed. But there is no need to specify the type of each variable explicitly:

```
val arrayList = arrayListOf("Item1", "Item2", "Item3") // Type is ArrayList
```

Named arguments allow you to specify the names of arguments when calling methods, resulting in more readable code:

```
var todo = Todo(description = "Learn Spring Boot", name = "Jack",
targetDate = Date())
```

Kotlin makes functional programming simpler by providing default variables (`it`) and methods such as `take` and `drop`:

```
var first3TodosOfJack = students.filter { it.name == "Jack" }.take(3)
```

You can also specify default values for arguments in Kotlin:

```
import java.util.*
 data class Todo(var description: String,
     var name: String,
     var targetDate : Date = Date())
fun main(args: Array<String>) {
    var todo = Todo(description = "Learn Spring Boot",
                    name = "Jack")
 }
```

We will discuss more about Kotlin in `Chapter 13`, *Reactive Programming.*

Dropped features

Spring Framework 5 is a major Spring release with a substantial increase in the baselines. Along with the increase in baseline versions for Java, Java EE, and a few other frameworks, Spring Framework 5 removed support for a few frameworks:

- Portlet
- Velocity
- JasperReports
- XMLBeans
- JDO
- Guava

If you are using any of the preceding frameworks, it is recommended that you plan a migration and stay with Spring Framework 4.3, which has support until 2019.

Learning about new features in Spring Boot 2.0 and 2.1

The first version of Spring Boot was released in 2014. The following are some of the important updates in Spring Boot 2.1:

- The baseline JDK version is Java 8
- The baseline Spring version is Spring Framework 5.1
- There's support for reactive web programming with WebFlux
- There's Lombok, Oath2, and Jersey 2 support and the Thymeleaf security extension
- There's WebMvcTest/WebFluxTest support in Spring Test 5.1

The minimum supported versions of some important frameworks are listed as follows:

- Jetty 9.4
- Tomcat 8.5
- Hibernate 5.2
- Gradle 3.4

We will discuss Spring Boot extensively in Chapter 5, *Digging Deeper into the Spring Framework,* and Chapter 7, *Unit Testing REST API with Spring Boot.*

Summary

Over the course of the last decade and a half, the Spring Framework has dramatically improved the experience of developing Java Enterprise applications. With Spring Framework 5.1, it brings in a lot of features while significantly increasing the baselines.

In the subsequent chapters, we will cover dependency injection and understand how we can develop web applications with Spring MVC. After that, we will move into the world of microservices. In `Chapter 11`, *Getting Started with Microservices*, we will cover how Spring Boot makes the creation of microservices simpler. We will then shift our attention to building applications in the cloud with Spring Cloud and Spring Cloud Data Flow.

Further reading

- Spring official website: `https://spring.io/`
- Spring Boot official website: `https://spring.io/projects/spring-boot`
- Spring Cloud official website: `https://spring.io/projects/spring-cloud`
- Spring Getting Started guides: `https://spring.io/guides`

Dependency Injection and Unit Testing

2

In this chapter, we will start with understanding what dependency is. We will explore the need for DI. We will understand the flexibility **Dependency Injection (DI)** brings in. After that, we will explore how DI is implemented in the Spring Framework.

DI is the most important feature of the Spring Framework. It makes it easy to develop loosely coupled applications. Loosely coupled applications are easier to unit test and, therefore, a lot easier to maintain.

In the Spring Framework, DI is implemented in the Spring **Inversion of Control (IoC)** container.

After the Spring Framework and DI became popular, Jakarta EE (earlier Java EE) introduced a standard specification for DI called the Java **Contexts and Dependency Injection (CDI)**. We will look at the support for CDI in the Spring Framework.

The Spring Framework makes unit testing easy and so we will end this chapter with an understanding of how you can write great unit tests with this framework.

This chapter will answer the following questions:

- What is a dependency?
- What is DI?
- How does proper use of DI make applications testable?
- How does Spring implement DI with BeanFactory and `ApplicationContext`?
- What is a component scan?
- What is the difference between Java and XML application contexts?
- How do you create unit tests for Spring contexts?

- How does mocking make unit testing simpler?
- What are the different bean scopes?
- What is CDI and how does Spring support CDI?

Technical requirements

The following software is required for this chapter:

- Your favorite IDE, Eclipse
- Java 8+
- Maven 3.x
- Internet connectivity

The code on GitHub is available at `https://github.com/PacktPublishing/Mastering-Spring-5.1/tree/master/Chapter02`

Understanding a dependency

At its core, Spring is a DI framework. Before we get started with understanding Spring, we need to understand the concepts of dependency and DI.

Object-oriented applications are built around objects and their interaction with other objects. Typical applications involve thousands of objects interacting with each other.

Let's consider an example class, `BusinessServiceImpl`, as follows:

```
public class BusinessServiceImpl {
  public long calculateSum(User user) {
    DataServiceImpl dataService = new DataServiceImpl();
    long sum = 0;
    for (Data data : dataService.retrieveData(user)) {
      sum += data.getValue();
    }
    return sum;
  }
}
```

`BusinessServiceImpl` creates an instance of `DataServiceImpl` and uses it to get the data from the database. `DataServiceImpl` is a dependency of `BusinessServiceImpl`.

Dependencies of a class are the other classes it depends on to fulfill its responsibilities.

Why do we have dependencies?

Enterprise applications have a wide range of functionality and features. Some parts of the application need to talk to the database; some parts of the application are used to show information to the user (user interface); and some parts of the application have business logic, while other parts of the application might be talking to other applications via web services.

One of the important design objectives is the **Single Responsibility Principle (SRP)**. We would want each class and component in our application to have a well-defined specific responsibility. We would not want the same class to be responsible for multiple features.

Let's consider an example—if you have Class A, which talks to a database and does some UI logic, it's not well designed. Class A has multiple responsibilities and it would not satisfy the SRP.

SRP is also applicable to application layers. To promote clear separation, all well-designed applications have multiple layers. Every layer has a well-defined responsibility:

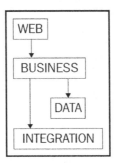

Here are some of the specific responsibilities of individual layers:

- **UI layer**: This is responsible for the View logic—how to show the data to the end user
- **Business layer**: This is responsible for Business logic
- **Data layer**: This is responsible for interacting with the database
- **Integration layer**: This is responsible for talking to other applications using web services or another connection mechanism

Consider the classes in the **Business** layer. They would need to get data from the database. How do they do that?

They would talk to classes in the **Data** layer. So, classes in the **Business** layer are dependent on classes in the **Data** layer. Classes in the **Data** layer are dependencies of classes in the **Business** layer.

In the preceding example, the `DataServiceImpl` class gets data related to the user from the database. The `BusinessServiceImpl` class is a typical business service, talking to the data service, `DataServiceImpl`, for data and adding business logic on top of it (in this example, the business logic is very simple—calculate the sum of data returned by the data service).

Enterprise applications are complex. To make applications easy to maintain, we adhere to SRP. When you implement SRP well, you would have a number of small classes with a number of dependencies.

What is DI?

Now that we understood what a dependency is and why dependencies are needed, let's shift our attention toward understanding DI.

We will start by discussing the importance of loose coupling. After that, we will understand how proper use of DI helps in developing loosely coupled applications.

Loose and tight coupling

An important design objective is *loose coupling*. You would want each of your components and classes to be loosely coupled. You would want to be able to make changes to your classes and components without affecting other classes and components.

Let's consider our earlier example of `BusinessServiceImpl`. Focus on how `BusinessServiceImpl` creates an instance of `DataServiceImpl`:

```
DataServiceImpl dataService = new DataServiceImpl();
```

`BusinessServiceImpl` is directly creating an instance of `DataServiceImpl`. This creates a tight coupling between these two classes.

If you want to change `BusinessServiceImpl` to use a different implementation of `DataService`, for example, `DataServiceImpl2`, you need to change the code in `BusinessServiceImpl`:

```
DataServiceImpl dataService = new DataServiceImpl2();
```

In the preceding example, `BusinessServiceImpl` is tightly coupled to `DataServiceImpl`. Tightly coupled code is difficult to maintain and difficult to unit test.

In the next section, let's discuss how we can make the preceding example loosely coupled.

Eliminating tight coupling and making code loosely coupled

Here's a question to think about—how do we reduce tight coupling between `BusinessServiceImpl` and `DataServiceImpl`?

Creating an interface for DataServiceImpl

The first thing we can do is to create an interface for `DataServiceImpl`. Instead of using the direct class, we can use the newly created interface of `DataServiceImpl` in `BusinessServiceImpl`.

The following code shows you how to create an interface:

```
public interface DataService {
  List<Data> retrieveData(User user);
}
```

Let's update the code in `BusinessServiceImpl` to use the interface:

```
DataService dataService = new DataServiceImpl();
```

We are now using the `DataService` interface, but `BusinessServiceImpl` is still tightly coupled as it is creating an instance of `DataServiceImpl`:

```
DataService dataService = new DataServiceImpl();
```

How do we solve that? How about moving the logic to create `DataServiceImpl` elsewhere and making it available to `BusinessServiceImpl`? Let's look at that next.

Moving creation of a dependency outside BusinessServiceImpl

Taking responsibility for creating a dependency would create a tight coupling between the class and its dependencies. We saw that, even after the creation of an interface, DataService, BusinessServiceImpl is still tightly coupled to DataServiceImpl because BusinessServiceImpl is responsible for creating its dependency—DataServiceImpl:

```
DataService dataService = new DataServiceImpl();
```

To solve this, will to create the dependency, DataServiceImpl, somewhere else and make it available to BusinessServiceImpl.

Let's add a new constructor to BusinessServiceImpl accepting DataService as an argument. The calculateSum method is also updated to use this reference. The updated code is as follows:

```
public class BusinessServiceImpl {
  private DataService dataService;
  public BusinessServiceImpl(DataService dataService) {
      this.dataService = dataService;
  }
  public long calculateSum(User user) {
    long sum = 0;
    for (Data data : dataService.retrieveData(user)) {
      sum += data.getValue();
     }
    return sum;
   }
}
```

You can see that BusinessServiceImpl is no longer tightly coupled with DataServiceImpl. You can create any implementation of DataService and pass it as a constructor argument to create BusinessServiceImpl:

```
DataService dataService = new DataServiceImpl();
BusinessServiceImpl businessService
                    = new BusinessServiceImpl(dataService);
```

Creating an interface for BusinessServiceImpl

To make the code even more loosely coupled (as we start writing the tests), let's create an interface for `BusinessService` and have `BusinessServiceImpl` updated to implement the interface:

```
public interface BusinessService {
   long calculateSum(User user);
}
public class BusinessServiceImpl implements BusinessService {
   //.... Rest of code..
}
```

Using interfaces helps to create loosely coupled code. The exact interface implementation of `DataService` to use can be changed without changing the code of `BusinessServiceImpl`.

Understanding terminology – beans, wiring, and DI

We have reduced coupling. But one question remains still—who will create the instance of the `DataServiceImpl` class and use it to create an instance of the `BusinessServiceImpl` class? If you have thousands of classes with a number of dependencies, you don't want to write the following code manually:

```
DataService dataService = new DataServiceImpl(); //Create

BusinessService businessService
  = new BusinessServiceImpl(dataService);//Create and Wire
```

That's exactly where the Spring Framework comes into the picture. The core feature of the Spring Framework is to do exactly what the preceding code does.

Before diving into the Spring Framework, let's look at some terminology:

- **Beans**: In the preceding example, we created two objects—`dataService` and `businessService`. These two instances are called beans.
- **Wiring**: `dataService` does not have any dependencies. `businessService` has one dependency—`dataService`. We created `dataService` and provided it as an argument to the `BusinessServiceImpl` constructor. This is called wiring.

- **DI**: The process of identifying beans, creating them, and wiring dependencies is called DI. This is exactly what the preceding code does.
- **IoC**: When we started this example, `BusinessServiceImpl` was responsible for creating an instance of `DataServiceImpl`. By the end, we made the code loosely coupled and `BusinessServiceImpl` was no longer responsible for creating `DataServiceImpl`. This is also called **IoC**. We are shifting the responsibility of creating dependencies to a framework.

What does the Spring Framework do?

In the previous example, we removed the tight coupling between `BusinessServiceImpl` and `DataServiceImpl` by creating appropriate interfaces and using them. However, we need to write code manually to create instances and wire them together. And that's the problem the Spring Framework solves.

The core of the Spring Framework, called the Spring IoC container, is responsible for identifying the dependencies and instantiating and wiring them together.

Before the Spring IoC container can do its magic, a couple of questions need to be answered:

1. How does the Spring IoC container know which beans to create? Specifically, how does the Spring IoC container know to create beans for the `BusinessServiceImpl` and `DataServiceImpl` classes?
2. How does the Spring IoC container know how to wire beans together? Specifically, how does the Spring IoC container know to inject the instance of the `DataServiceImpl` class into an instance of the `BusinessServiceImpl` class?

Question 1 – how does Spring IoC container know which beans to create?

We need to tell the Spring IoC container which beans to create. This is done using the `@Component` annotation. A couple of examples are shown as follows:

```
@Component
public class DataServiceImpl implements DataService

@Component
public class BusinessServiceImpl implements BusinessService
```

When the Spring IoC container sees this annotation in a class, it will create instances of the class. As we discussed earlier, these instances are called beans.

The @Component annotation is the most generic way of defining a Spring bean.

There are other annotations with more specific context associated with them. The @Service annotation is used in business service components. The @Repository annotation is used in the **Data Access Object (DAO)** components.

We use the @Repository annotation in DataServiceImpl because it is related to getting data from the database. We use the @Service annotation in the BusinessServiceImpl class as follows, since it is a business service:

```
@Repository
public class DataServiceImpl implements DataService

@Service
public class BusinessServiceImpl implements BusinessService
```

 It is recommended to use specific annotations—@Service and @Repository over the generic @Component annotation because they provide additional features. For example, @Repository provides automatic transaction management in the data layer.

Question 2 – how does the Spring IoC container know the dependencies of the bean?

The bean of the DataServiceImpl class needs to be injected into that of the BusinessServiceImpl class.

We can do that by specifying an @Autowired annotation in the instance variable of the DataService interface in the BusinessServiceImpl class:

```
@Service
public class BusinessServiceImpl {

    @Autowired
    private DataService dataService;
```

Now that we have defined the beans and their wiring, to test this, we need an implementation of `DataService`. We will create a simple, hardcoded implementation. `DataServiceImpl` returns a couple of pieces of data:

```
@Repository
public class DataServiceImpl implements DataService {

  public List<Data> retrieveData(User user) {
    return Arrays.asList(new Data(10), new Data(20));
  }
}
```

Now that we have our beans and dependencies defined, let's focus on how to create and run a Spring IoC container.

Launching a Spring IoC container

There are two ways to launch a Spring IoC container:

- BeanFactory
- `ApplicationContext`

 BeanFactory is the basis for all Spring IoC functionality—the bean life cycle and wiring. The application context is basically a superset of BeanFactory with the additional functionality typically needed in an enterprise context. Spring recommends that you use the application context in all scenarios, except when the additional few KBs of memory that the application context consumes is critical.

Let's use an application context to create a Spring IoC container.

We will use Maven to build our projects. Here are the core Spring JAR files:

```
<dependency>
 <groupId>org.springframework</groupId>
 <artifactId>spring-core</artifactId>
</dependency>

<dependency>
 <groupId>org.springframework</groupId>
 <artifactId>spring-context</artifactId>
</dependency>

<dependency>
```

```
    <groupId>org.springframework</groupId>
    <artifactId>spring-beans</artifactId>
</dependency>
```

We will use Spring BOM to manage the dependency versions. We will discuss Spring BOM further in `Chapter 14`, *Spring Best Practices*. The snippet for adding it in `pom.xml` is as follows:

```
<properties>
    <spring.version>5.1.3.RELEASE</spring.version>
</properties>

<dependencyManagement>
    <dependencies>
        <dependency>
            <groupId>org.springframework</groupId>
            <artifactId>spring-framework-bom</artifactId>
            <version>${spring.version}</version>
            <type>pom</type>
            <scope>import</scope>
        </dependency>
    </dependencies>
</dependencyManagement>
```

Importing `spring-framework-bom` in `dependencyManagement` will ensure that you would not need to specify any version of the Spring versions managed by it.

Creating a Java configuration for the application context

In the early days of the Spring Framework, all configuration for the application context was specified in XML files. However, with the evolution of annotations from Java 5, present-day applications use Java configurations based on annotations. In this book, we will use a Java annotation-based configuration for most examples.

We will start with an example of a Java annotation-based configuration. In a later section, we will see an example of an XML-based configuration.

The following example shows you how to create a simple Java context configuration:

```
@Configuration
class SpringContext {

}
```

The key is the @Configuration annotation. This is what defines this as a Spring configuration.

Launching a Java configuration

We would need to create a Java class with the main method to launch an application context. The following program shows how to launch a Java context; we use the main method to launch the application context using AnnotationConfigApplicationContext:

```
public class LaunchJavaContext {

    private static final User DUMMY_USER = new User("dummy");

    public static Logger logger =
Logger.getLogger(LaunchJavaContext.class);

    public static void main(String[] args) {

        ApplicationContext context = new
AnnotationConfigApplicationContext(SpringContext.class);

        BusinessService service = context.getBean(BusinessService.class);

        logger.debug(service.calculateSum(DUMMY_USER));

    }
}
```

The following lines of code create the application context. We want to create an application context based on the Java configuration. So, we use AnnotationConfigApplicationContext:

```
ApplicationContext context = new
AnnotationConfigApplicationContext(SpringContext.class);
```

Once the context is launched, we will need to get the business service bean. We use the getBean method that passes the type of the bean (BusinessService.class) as an argument:

```
BusinessService service = context.getBean(BusinessService.class );
```

Defining a component scan

One question remains: how does the Spring IoC container know where to search for beans?

We need to tell the Spring IoC container the packages to search for by defining a component scan. Let's add a component scan to our earlier Java configuration definition:

```
@Configuration
@ComponentScan(basePackages = { "com.mastering.spring" })
class SpringContext {
}
```

We have defined a component scan for the `com.mastering.spring` package. It shows how all of the classes we discussed so far are organized. All of the classes we have defined until now are present in this package, as follows:

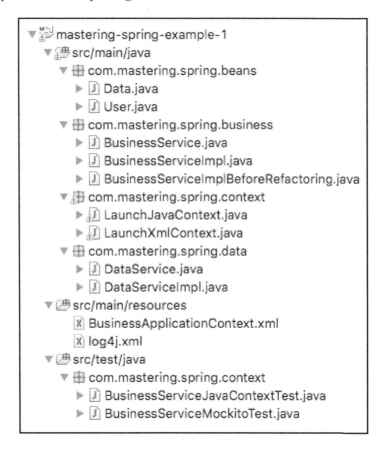

Let's take a moment and review all of the things we have done until now to get this example working:

- We defined a Spring configuration class, `SpringContext`, with the `@Configuration` annotation with a component scan for the `com.mastering.spring` package.
- We have a couple of files (in the preceding package):
  - `BusinessServiceImpl` with the `@Service` annotation
  - `DataServiceImpl` with the `@Repository` annotation
- `BusinessServiceImpl` has the `@Autowired` annotation on the instance of `DataService`.

When we launch up a Spring context, the following things will happen:

- It will scan the `com.mastering.spring` package and find the `BusinessServiceImpl` and `DataServiceImpl` beans.
- `DataServiceImpl` does not have any dependency. So, the bean for `DataServiceImpl` is created.
- `BusinessServiceImpl` has a dependency on `DataService`. `DataServiceImpl` is an implementation of the `DataService` interface. So, it matches the autowiring criteria. So, a bean for `BusinessServiceImpl` is created and the bean created for `DataServiceImpl` is autowired to it through the setter.

Running the application context

We are all set to launch the application context. All you would need to do is run the `LaunchJavaContext` program.

When you run the program, you should see the following statements printed to the console:

```
[2019-01-03 19:06:05,770] DEBUG
com.mastering.spring.context.LaunchJavaContext 30
```

Congratulations! You have successfully run a Spring application.

What's happening in the background?

Understanding what happens in the background will help us to debug problems faster when they arise. We were able to successfully launch a Spring application in the previous section. In this section, let's focus on understanding what's happening in the background. Let's look at some of the debug logs to get a better understanding.

The following are some of the important statements from the log once the context is launched using `LaunchJavaContext`.

The first few lines show the component scan in action:

```
Looking for matching resources in directory tree
[/target/classes/com/mastering/spring]

Identified candidate component class: file
[/in28Minutes/Workspaces/SpringTutorial/mastering-spring-
example-1/target/classes/com/mastering/spring/business/BusinessServiceImpl.
class]

Identified candidate component class: file
[/in28Minutes/Workspaces/SpringTutorial/mastering-spring-
example-1/target/classes/com/mastering/spring/data/DataServiceImpl.class]

defining beans [******OTHERS*****,businessServiceImpl,dataServiceImpl];
```

Spring now starts to create the beans. It starts with `businessServiceImpl`, but it has an autowired dependency:

```
Creating instance of bean 'businessServiceImpl'Registered injected element
on class [com.mastering.spring.business.BusinessServiceImpl]:
AutowiredFieldElement for private com.mastering.spring.data.DataService
com.mastering.spring.business.BusinessServiceImpl.dataService

Processing injected element of bean 'businessServiceImpl':
AutowiredFieldElement for private com.mastering.spring.data.DataService
com.mastering.spring.business.BusinessServiceImpl.dataService
```

Spring moves on to `dataServiceImpl` and creates an instance for it:

```
Creating instance of bean 'dataServiceImpl'
Finished creating instance of bean 'dataServiceImpl'
```

Spring autowires `dataServiceImpl` into `businessServiceImpl`:

```
Autowiring by type from bean name 'businessServiceImpl' to bean named
'dataServiceImpl'
Finished creating instance of bean 'businessServiceImpl'
```

In summary, the following steps are performed at the launch of a Spring application:

- A component scan is performed to identify the beans and dependencies.
- Beans are created and dependencies are wired in as needed.

 We recommend you create an example of your own using DI. Think of a class that is dependent on another class, for example, business logic needing a sorting algorithm.

Understanding the Spring Framework in depth

Until now, we created a simple application to understand what the Spring Framework does. We were focused on giving a 10,000 feet overview. In this section, let's look at some of the core features in depth.

Container Managed Beans

Instead of a class creating its own dependencies, in the earlier example, we looked at how the Spring IoC container can take over the responsibility of managing beans and their dependencies. The beans that are managed by the container are called **Container Managed Beans.**

Delegating the creation and management of beans to the container has many advantages. Some of them are listed as follows:

- Since classes are not responsible for creating dependencies, they are loosely coupled and testable. This leads to good design and fewer defects.
- Since the container manages the beans, a few hooks around the beans can be introduced in a more generic way. Cross-cutting concerns, such as logging, caching, transaction management, and exception handling can be woven around these beans using **Aspect-Oriented Programming (AOP)**. This leads to more maintainable code.

Java versus XML configuration

With the advent of annotations in Java 5, there is widespread use of Java configuration for Spring-based applications. What is the right choice to make if you have to choose between a Java-based configuration as opposed to an XML-based configuration?

Spring provides equally good support for Java and XML-based configurations. Here are some things you might need to consider when making a choice:

- Annotations lead to shorter and simpler bean definitions.
- Annotations are closer to the code they are applicable on than the XML-based configuration.
- Classes using annotations are no longer simple POJOs because they are using framework-specific annotations.
- Autowiring problems when using annotations might be difficult to solve because the wiring is no longer centralized and is not explicitly declared.
- There might be advantages of more flexible wiring using Spring context XML if it is packaged outside the application packaging—WAR or EAR. This will enable us to have a different setup for integration tests, for example.

We recommend using a Java-based configuration for all Spring applications. Whichever choice is made, it is important to have consistency across teams and projects.

Using XML configuration for the application context

In the previous example, we used a Java configuration to launch an application context. Spring also supports XML configuration.

The following example shows you how to launch an application context with an XML configuration. This will have two steps:

- Defining the XML Spring configuration
- Launching the application context with the XML configuration

Defining the XML Spring configuration

The following example shows a typical XML Spring configuration. This configuration file is created in the `src/main/resources` directory with the name `BusinessApplicationContext.xml`:

```
<?xml version="1.0" encoding="UTF-8" standalone="no"?>
<beans>   <!-Namespace definitions removed-->
```

```
        <context:component-scan base-package ="com.mastering.spring"/>
    </beans>
```

The component scan is defined using `context:component-scan`.

Launching an application context with the XML configuration

The following program shows you how to launch an application context using the XML configuration. We use the main method to launch the application context using `ClassPathXmlApplicationContext`:

```
public class LaunchXmlContext {
  private static final User DUMMY_USER = new User("dummy");
  public static Logger logger =
  Logger.getLogger(LaunchJavaContext.class);
  public static void main(String[] args) {
     ApplicationContext context = new
     ClassPathXmlApplicationContext(
     "BusinessApplicationContext.xml");
     BusinessService service =
     context.getBean(BusinessService.class);
     logger.debug(service.calculateSum(DUMMY_USER));
    }
}
```

The following lines of code create the application context. We want to create an application context based on the XML configuration. So, we use `ClassPathXmlApplicationContext` to create an application context, `AnnotationConfigApplicationContext`:

```
ApplicationContext context = new
ClassPathXmlApplicationContext (SpringContext.class);
```

Once the context is launched, we will need to get a reference to the business service bean. This is very similar to what we did with the Java configuration. We use the `getBean` method, passing the type of the bean (`BusinessService.class`) as an argument.

We can go ahead and run the `LaunchXmlContext` class. You will notice that we get output very similar to that we get when run the context with the Java configuration.

The @Autowired annotation in depth

When `@Autowired` is used on a dependency, the application context searches for a matching dependency. By default, all dependencies that are autowired are required.

The possible results are as follows:

- **One match is found**: This is the dependency you are looking for.
- **More than one match is found**: Autowiring fails.
- **No match is found**: Autowiring fails.

Cases where more than one candidate is found can be resolved in two ways:

- Use the @Primary annotation to mark one of the candidates as the one to be used.
- Use @Qualifier to further qualify autowiring.

The @Primary annotation

When the @Primary annotation is used on a bean, it becomes the primary one to be used when there is more than one candidate available to autowire a specific dependency.

Consider the following example:

```
interface SortingAlgorithm {
}
@Component
class MergeSort implements SortingAlgorithm {
  // Class code here
}
@Component
@Primary
class QuickSort implements SortingAlgorithm {
  // Class code here
}
```

In the case of the following example, there are two sorting algorithms available—QuickSort and MergeSort. If the component scan finds both of them, QuickSort is used to wire any dependencies on SortingAlgorithm because of the @Primary annotation.

The @Qualifier annotation

The @Qualifier annotation can be used to give a reference to a Spring bean. The reference can be used to qualify the dependency that needs to be autowired.

Consider the following example:

```
@Component
@Qualifier("mergesort")
class MergeSort implements SortingAlgorithm {
  // Class code here
}
@Component
class QuickSort implements SortingAlgorithm {
 // Class code here
}
@Component
class SomeService {
  @Autowired
  @Qualifier("mergesort")
 SortingAlgorithm algorithm;
}
```

In the case of the preceding example, there are two sorting algorithms available: `QuickSort` and `MergeSort`. But since `@Qualifier("mergesort")` is used in the `SomeService` class, `MergeSort`, which also has a `mergesort` qualifier defined on it, becomes the candidate dependency selected for autowiring.

Understanding DI options

In the previous example, we used a setter method to wire in the dependency. There are two types of DI that are used frequently:

- The setter injection
- The constructor injection

The setter injection

The setter injection is used to inject the dependencies through setter methods. In the following example, the instance of `DataService` uses the setter injection:

```
public class BusinessServiceImpl {
  private DataService dataService;
  @Autowired
  public void setDataService(DataService dataService) {
    this.dataService = dataService;
  }
}
```

Actually, in order to use the setter injection, you do not even need to declare a setter method. If you specify `@Autowired` on the variable, Spring automatically uses the setter injection. So, the following code is all that you need for the setter injection for `DataService`:

```
public class BusinessServiceImpl {
  @Autowired
  private DataService dataService;
}
```

The constructor injection

The constructor injection, on the other hand, uses a constructor to inject dependencies. The following code shows you how to use a constructor for injecting in `DataService`:

```
public class BusinessServiceImpl {
  private DataService dataService;
  @Autowired
  public BusinessServiceImpl(DataService dataService) {
    super();
    this.dataService = dataService;
  }
}
```

When you run the code with the preceding implementation of `BusinessServiceImpl`, you will see this statement in the log, asserting that autowiring took place using the constructor:

```
Autowiring by type from bean name 'businessServiceImpl' via
constructor to bean named 'dataServiceImpl'
```

Constructor versus setter injection

Originally, in XML-based application contexts, we used the constructor injection with mandatory dependencies and the setter injection with nonmandatory dependencies.

However, an important thing to note is that when we use `@Autowired` on a field or a method, the dependency is required by default. If no candidates are available for an `@Autowired` field, autowiring fails and throws an exception. So, the choice is not so clear anymore with Java-based application contexts.

Using the setter injection results in the state of the object changing during the creation. For fans of immutable objects, the constructor injection might be the way to go. Using the setter injection might sometimes hide the fact that a class has a lot of dependencies. Using the constructor injection makes it obvious since the size of the constructor increases.

Customizing Spring beans – scope

Spring beans can be created with multiple scopes. The default scope is a singleton.

 A Singleton, in general, is a Java class with only one instance per JVM. In the context of the Spring Framework, a singleton is a class that has one instance per Spring application context.

Since there is only one instance of a singleton bean, it cannot contain any data that is specific to a request.

The scope can be provided with the @Scope annotation on any Spring bean:

```
@Service
@Scope("singleton")
public class BusinessServiceImpl implements BusinessService
```

The following table shows the different types of scopes available for beans:

Scope	Use
Singleton	By default, all beans are of the Singleton scope. Only one instance of such beans is used per instance of the Spring IoC container. Even if there are multiple references to a bean, it is created only once per container. The single instance is cached and used for all subsequent requests using this bean. It is important to specify that the Spring Singleton scope is one object per one Spring container. If you have multiple spring containers in a single JVM, then there can be multiple instances of the same bean. So, the Spring Singleton scope is a little different from the typical definition of a singleton.
Prototype	A new instance is created every time a bean is requested from the Spring container. If a bean contains a state, it is recommended that you use the prototype scope for it.

request	This is available only in Spring web contexts. A new instance of the bean is created for every HTTP request. The bean is discarded as soon as the request processing is done. It's ideal for beans that hold data specific to a single request.
session	This is available only in Spring web contexts. A new instance of the bean is created for every HTTP session. It's ideal for data specific to a single user, such as user permissions in a web application.
application	It's available only in Spring web contexts. One instance of a bean per web application. It's ideal for things such as application configuration for a specific environment.

Other important Spring annotations

Spring provides a great deal of flexibility in defining beans and managing the life cycle of a bean. There are a few other important Spring annotations that we will discuss in the table that follows:

Annotations	Use
@ScopedProxy	Sometimes, we will need to inject a request or a session-scoped bean into a singleton-scoped bean. In such situations, the @ScopedProxy annotation provides a smart proxy to be injected into singleton-scoped beans.
@Component, @Service, @Controller, and @Repository	@Component is the most generic way of defining a Spring bean. Other annotations have more specific contexts associated with them: • @Service is used in the business service layer. • @Repository is used in the **Data Access Object (DAO)**. • @Controller is used in presentation components.
@PostConstruct	On any Spring bean, a post construct method can be provided using the @PostConstruct annotation. This method is called once the bean is fully initialized with dependencies. This will be invoked only once during a bean life cycle.
@PreDestroy	On any Spring bean, a predestroy method can be provided using the @PreDestroy annotation. This method is called just before a bean is removed from the container. This can be used to release any resources that are held by the bean. This helps you to avoid leakage of resources.

Exploring CDI

Contexts and Dependency Injection (CDI) is Java EE's attempt at bringing DI into Java EE. While not as full fledged as Spring, CDI aims to standardize the basics of how DI is done. Spring supports the standard annotations defined in *JSR-330*. For the most part, these annotations are treated the same way as Spring annotations.

 The JSR 330 titled *Dependency Injection for Java* defines standard annotations for DI for Java.

Before we can use CDI, we will need to ensure that we have dependencies for CDI JAR files included. Here's the code snippet:

```
<dependency>
  <groupId>javax.inject</groupId>
  <artifactId>javax.inject</artifactId>
  <version>1</version>
</dependency>
```

In this table, let's compare the CDI annotations with the annotations provided by the Spring Framework. It should be noted that the `@Value`, `@Required`, and `@Lazy` Spring annotations have no equivalent CDI annotations:

CDI annotation	Comparison with Spring annotations
`@Inject`	This is similar to `@Autowired`. One insignificant difference is the absence of the required attribute in `@Inject`.
`@Named`	`@Named` is similar to `@Component`. It identifies named components. In addition, `@Named` can be used to qualify the bean with a name similar to the `@Qualifier` Spring annotation. This is useful in situations when multiple candidates are available for the autowiring of one dependency.
`@Singleton`	This is similar to the Spring annotation `@Scope` ("singleton").
`@Qualifier`	This is similar to a similarly named annotation in Spring—`@Qualifier`

An example of CDI

When we use CDI, this is what the annotations on the different classes would look like. There is no change in how we create and launch the Spring application context.

CDI marks no differentiation between `@Repository`, `@Controller`, `@Service`, and `@Component`. We use `@Named` instead of all of the preceding annotations.

In the example, we use `@Named` for `DataServiceImpl` and `BusinessServiceImpl`. We use `@Inject` to inject `dataService` into `BusinessServiceImpl` (instead of `@Autowired`):

```
@Named //Instead of @Repository
public class DataServiceImpl implements DataService

@Named //Instead of @Service
public class BusinessServiceImpl {

    @Inject //Instead of @Autowired
    private DataService dataService;
```

Unit testing the Spring application context

Why do we introduce unit testing so early in this book?
Actually, we believe we are already late. Ideally, we would have loved to use **Test-Driven Development (TDD)** and write tests before code. In my experience, doing TDD leads to simple, maintainable, and testable code.

Before we write a unit test, let's understand what unit testing is.

What is unit testing?

Typically, applications are huge and have thousands of classes and methods. Unit testing involves writing independent automated tests for individual classes and methods. Instead of testing the entire application once it is deployed, unit testing focuses on writing automated tests for the responsibilities of each class and each method.

I'm a great believer that great developers write great unit tests. With unit tests, you can continuously test your code for a number of scenarios.

Unit testing has a number of advantages:

- It's a safety net against future defects
- Defects are caught early
- Following TDD leads to a better design
- Well-written tests act as the documentation of code and functionality—especially those written using the BDD Given-When-Then style

The Spring Framework provides excellent support for writing great unit tests. Before the Spring Framework, writing loosely coupled code in Java was not easy. However, the Spring Framework makes it easy to write loosely coupled code. Loosely coupled code can be easily unit tested. We can either use stubs or mock dependencies and depend on the Spring Framework for wiring them in.

In this section, let's look at writing a simple unit test for the `BusinessServiceImpl` example discussed earlier in this chapter.

Writing JUnit using the Spring context

In the previous sections, we looked at how to launch a Spring context from the main method. Now, let's shift our attention to launching a Spring context from a unit test. We will use the JUnit framework as our unit testing framework.

When we write a unit test with the Spring Framework, we need to launch an application context. The application context initializes all of the beans and dependencies. We can get the beans from the application context and check whether they return expected values.

To launch an application context in a unit test, we can use `SpringJUnit4ClassRunner.class` as a runner:

```
@RunWith(SpringJUnit4ClassRunner.class)
```

Let's launch the application context with XML configuration. Here's how you can declare this:

```
@ContextConfiguration(
    locations = {  "/BusinessApplicationContext.xml" }
)
```

Once the application context is launched, we want to get the beans from the application context and use them in the unit test. The Spring test framework provides simple annotations to use beans from the application context in the test. All that you would need to do is to define a member variable in the test with the `@Autowired` annotation. The following snippet shows how we can get an implementation of `BusinessService` autowired into the unit test:

```
@Autowired
private BusinessService service;
```

Earlier in this chapter, we created a dummy implementation of `DataServiceImpl`. The `retrieveData` method returns a list, as follows:

```
Arrays.asList(new Data(10), new Data(20))
```

The `calculateSum` method in `BusinessServiceImpl` calculates the sum 10+20 and returns 30.

We will assert for 30 in the test method using `assertEquals`:

```
long sum = service.calculateSum(DUMMY_USER);
assertEquals(30, sum);
```

The complete code of the test is as follows; it has one `test` method:

```
@RunWith(SpringJUnit4ClassRunner.class)
@ContextConfiguration(locations = {"/BusinessApplicationContext.xml" })
public class BusinessServiceJavaContextTest {
    private static final User DUMMY_USER = new User("dummy");
    @Autowired
    private BusinessService service;

    @Test
    public void testCalculateSum() {
      long sum = service.calculateSum(DUMMY_USER);
      assertEquals(30, sum);
    }
}
```

One of the important things to remember is the preceding test is not really a unit test. The test for `BusinessServiceImpl` is using the actual implementation of `DataServiceImpl`. If `DataServiceImpl` was retrieving data from the database, then the test would depend on the data present in the database.

The question now is this: how do we unit test `BusinessServiceImpl` without using a real implementation of `DataService`?

There are two options:

- Create a stub implementation of the data service, in the `src\test\java` folder, providing some dummy data. Use a separate test context configuration to autowire the stub implementation instead of the real `DataServiceImpl` class.
- Create a mock of `DataService` and autowire the mock into `BusinessServiceImpl`.

Creating a stub implementation would mean the creation of an additional class and an additional context. Stubs become more difficult to maintain, as we need more variations in data for the unit test.

In the next section, we will explore the second option of using a mock for unit testing. With the evolution of mocking frameworks (especially **Mockito**) in the last few years, you will see that we would not even need to launch a Spring context to execute the unit test.

Unit testing with mocks

Let's start with understanding what mocking is. Mocking is creating objects that simulate the behavior of real objects. In the previous example, in the unit test, we would want to simulate the behavior of `DataService`.

Unlike stubs, mocks can be dynamically created at runtime. We will use the most popular mocking framework, Mockito. To understand more about Mockito, we recommend the Mockito FAQ at `https://github.com/mockito/mockito/wiki/FAQ`.

We will want to create a mock for `DataService`. There are multiple approaches to creating mocks with Mockito. Let's use the simplest among them—annotations. We use the `@Mock` annotation to create a mock for `DataService`:

```
@Mock
private DataService dataServiceMock;
```

Next, we want `BusinessServiceImpl` to make use of the mock. We can do that using the `@InjectMocks` annotation. `@InjectMocks` will ensure that all of the dependencies of the service are autowired:

```
@InjectMocks
private BusinessService service = new BusinessServiceImpl();
```

`BusinessServiceImpl` will call the `retrieveData` method on `dataService`. We will need to make the mock return test data when this method is called. We will use the BDD style methods provided by Mockito to mock the `retrieveData` method:

```
BDDMockito.given(
        dataServiceMock.retrieveData(Matchers.any(User.class)))
    .willReturn(
        Arrays.asList(new Data(10),  new Data(15), new Data(25)));
```

When the `retrieveData` method is called on the `dataService` mock with any object of type `User`, it returns a list of three items with values specified.

When we use Mockito annotations, we will need to use a specific JUnit runner, that is, `MockitoJunitRunner`. `MockitoJunitRunner` helps to keep the test code clean and provides clear debugging information in case of test failures. `MockitoJunitRunner` initializes the beans annotated with the `@Mock` annotation and validates the usage of the framework after the execution of each test method:

```
@RunWith(MockitoJUnitRunner.class)
```

The complete list of the test is as follows. It has one test method:

```
@RunWith(MockitoJUnitRunner.class)
public class BusinessServiceMockitoTest {

    private static final User DUMMY_USER = new User("dummy");

    @Mock
    private DataService dataServiceMock;
    @InjectMocks
    private BusinessService service =  new BusinessServiceImpl();

    @Test
    public void testCalculateSum() {
        BDDMockito
            .given(
                dataServiceMock.retrieveData(Matchers.any(User.class)))
            .willReturn(
                Arrays.asList(new Data(10),  new Data(15), new
```

```
Data(25)));

        long sum = service.calculateSum(DUMMY_USER);

        assertEquals(10 + 15 + 25, sum);

    }

}
```

Writing unit tests with mocks is made simple by the @Mock and @InjectMocks annotations.

Summary

DI or IoC is the key feature of Spring. It makes code loosely coupled and testable. Understanding DI is the key to making the best use of the Spring Framework.

In this chapter, we looked at a few examples to understand what a dependency is. We understood the need for DI and explored implementing DI with the Spring Framework. We understood the basics of ApplicationContext, the BeanFactory, component scans, and bean scopes. We discussed creating application contexts with Java and XML configuration.

We wrote a few great unit tests to see the loose coupling the Spring Framework provides.

We explored the Spring Framework support for Java **Contexts and Dependency Injection (CDI)**.

In the next chapter, let's start building a web application with the Spring Framework. We will use the Spring MVC Module, which makes developing great web applications easy.

Further reading

- Spring official website, available at: https://spring.io/
- *Spring Getting Started Guides*, available at: https://spring.io/guides

Building Web Applications with Spring MVC

3

Spring MVC is the most popular web framework used to develop Java servlet-based web applications. The beauty of Spring MVC lies in its clean, loosely coupled architecture. With a clean definition of roles for controllers, handler mappings, view resolvers, and **Plain Old Java Object (POJO)** command beans, Spring MVC makes use of all of the core Spring features, such as dependency injection and autowiring, to make it simple to create servlet-based web applications. With its support for multiple view technologies, it is extensible too.

While Spring MVC can be used to create REST services, we will discuss this in Chapter 6, *Building REST APIs with Spring Boot*. We will focus on reviewing the basics of Spring MVC with simple examples.

In this chapter, we will cover the following topics:

- The Spring MVC architecture
- The roles played by DispatcherServlet, view resolvers, handler mappings, and controllers
- Model attributes and session attributes
- Form binding and validation
- Integration with Bootstrap
- The basics of Spring Security
- Writing simple unit tests for controllers

Technical requirements

The following are the requirements for this chapter:

- Your favorite IDE, Eclipse
- Java 8+
- Maven 3.x
- Internet connectivity

The GitHub link for this chapter can be found at: `https://github.com/PacktPublishing/` `Mastering-Spring-5.1/tree/master/Chapter03`.

Understanding the architectures of Java servlet web applications

The way we develop web applications has evolved continuously during the last couple of decades.

The popular approach today is to combine a REST API with a frontend framework, such as AngularJS, React, or Vue.js. We will look at architectures using a frontend framework and REST API in `Chapter 9`, *Full Stack App with React and Spring Boot*.

In this chapter, we will focus on pure Java servlet-based architectures. We will discuss the different architectural approaches to developing Java web applications and see where Spring MVC fits in:

- Model 1 architecture
- Model 2 or MVC architecture
- Model 2 with FrontController

Model 1 architecture

Model 1 architecture is one of the initial architecture styles used to develop Java-based web applications. A few important details are as follows:

- **Java Server Pages (JSP)** pages handle directly the requests from the browser.
- JSP pages make use of the model containing simple Java beans.
- In some applications of this architecture style, JSPs even perform queries to the database.
- JSPs also handle the flow logic—which page to show next.

The following diagram represents a typical Model 1 architecture:

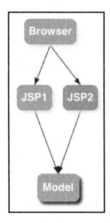

There are a lot of disadvantages associated with this approach, leading to quick shelving and the evolution of other architectures. A few important disadvantages are listed as follows:

- **Hardly any separation of concerns**: JSPs are responsible for retrieving data, displaying data, deciding which pages to show next (flow), and sometimes, even business logic as well.
- **Complex JSPs**: Because JSPs handle a lot of logic, they are huge and difficult to maintain.

Model 2 architecture

Model 2 architecture was introduced to solve the complexity involved with complex JSPs having multiple responsibilities. This forms the base for the MVC architecture style. The following diagram represents the typical Model 2 architecture:

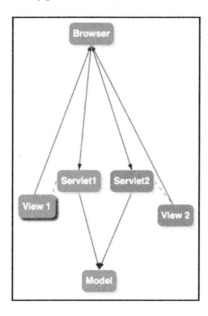

Model 2 architecture has a clear separation of roles between Model, View, and Controller. This leads to more maintainable applications. A few important details are as follows:

- **Model**: This represents the data to be used to generate a View.
- **View**: This uses the Model to render the screen.
- **Controller**: This controls the flow. It gets the request from the browser, populates the Model, and redirects to the View. Examples in the preceding diagram are **Servlet1** and **Servlet2**.

Model 2 FrontController architecture

In the basic version of Model 2 architecture, the requests from the browser are handled directly by different servlets (or controllers). In a number of business scenarios, you would want to do a few common things in servlets before we handle the request. An example would be to ensure that the logged-in user has the correct authorization to execute the request. This is common functionality that you would not want to be implemented in every servlet.

In Model 2 **FrontController** architecture, all requests flow into a single controller, called the **FrontController**.

The following diagram represents a typical Model 2 **FrontController** architecture:

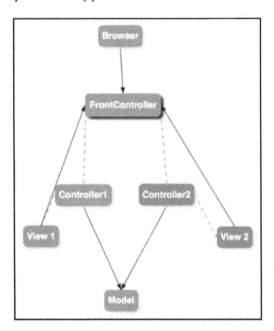

The following are some of the responsibilities of a typical **FrontController**:

- It decides which controller executes the request.
- It decides which View to render.
- It provides provisions to add more common functionality.
- Spring MVC uses an MVC pattern with **FrontController**. The **FrontController** is called `DispatcherServlet`. We will discuss `DispatcherServlet` a little later.

As you can see, **FrontController** does a lot of things. Take care to ensure that you do not put anything more than needed in your **FrontController**. Consider using filters where appropriate.

Learning Spring MVC with six basic flow examples

Spring MVC uses a modified version of the Model 2 FrontController architecture.

Before we go into detail about how Spring MVC works, we will focus on creating a few simple web flows using Spring MVC.

In this section, we will create six typical web application flows using Spring MVC. The flows are listed as follows:

- **Flow 1**: Controller without a View; serving content on its own
- **Flow 2**: Controller with a View (a JSP)
- **Flow 3**: Controller with a View and using `ModelMap`
- **Flow 4**: Controller with a View and using `ModelAndView`
- **Flow 5**: Controller for a simple form
- **Flow 6**: Controller for a simple form with validation

We will discuss how to unit test these flows in a separate section at the end of this chapter.

Setting up a Spring MVC application

Before we start with the first flow, we need to get the application set up to use Spring MVC.

We use Maven to manage our dependencies. The following steps are involved in setting up a simple web application:

1. Add a dependency for Spring MVC.
2. Add `DispatcherServlet` to `web.xml`.
3. Create a Spring application context.

Adding dependency for Spring MVC

Let's start by adding the Spring MVC dependency to our `pom.xml` file. The following code shows the dependency to be incorporated. Since we are using Spring BOM, we do not need to specify the artifact version:

```
<dependency>
    <groupId>org.springframework</groupId>
    <artifactId>spring-webmvc</artifactId>
</dependency>
```

`DispatcherServlet` is an implementation of the FrontController pattern. Any request to Spring MVC will be handled by FrontController, that is, `DispatcherServlet`.

Adding DispatcherServlet to web.xml

To enable this, we need to add `DispatcherServlet` to `web.xml`. Let's look at how to do that:

```
<servlet>

  <servlet-name>spring-mvc-dispatcher-servlet</servlet-name>

  <servlet-class>
    org.springframework.web.servlet.DispatcherServlet
  </servlet-class>

  <init-param>
    <param-name>contextConfigLocation</param-name>
    <param-value>/WEB-INF/user-web-context.xml</param-value>
  </init-param>

  <load-on-startup>1</load-on-startup>

</servlet>

<servlet-mapping>
  <servlet-name>spring-mvc-dispatcher-servlet</servlet-name>
  <url-pattern>/</url-pattern>
</servlet-mapping>
```

The first part is to define a servlet. We are also defining a context configuration location, `/WEB-INF/user-web-context.xml`. We will define a Spring context in the next step. In the second part, we are defining a servlet mapping. We are mapping a / URL to `DispatcherServlet`. So, all requests will be handled by `DispatcherServlet`.

Creating a Spring context

Now that we have `DispatcherServlet` defined in `web.xml`, we can go ahead and create our Spring context. Initially, we will create a very simple context without really defining anything specific:

```
<beans > <!-Schema Definition removed -->

    <context:component-scan  base-package="com.mastering.spring.springmvc"/>

    <mvc:annotation-driven />

</beans>
```

We are defining a component scan for the `com.mastering.spring.springmvc` package so that all of the beans and controllers in this package are created and autowired.

Using `<mvc:annotation-driven/>` initializes support for a number of features that Spring MVC supports, such as the following:

- Request mapping
- Exception handling
- Data binding and validation
- Automatic conversion (for example, JSON) when the `@RequestBody` annotation is used

That's all of the setup we require in order to be able to set up a Spring MVC application. Now, we are ready to get started with the first flow.

Flow 1 – simple controller flow without View

Let's start with a simple flow by showing some simple text that is output from a Spring MVC controller onscreen.

Creating a Spring MVC controller

Let's create a simple Spring MVC controller, as follows:

```
@Controller
public class BasicController {
    @RequestMapping(value = "/welcome")
    @ResponseBody
    public String welcome() {
        return "Welcome to Spring MVC";
    }
}
```

The following definitions explain the code in detail:

- @Controller: This defines a Spring MVC controller that can contain request mappings—mapping URLs to controller methods.
- @RequestMapping(value = "/welcome"): This defines a mapping of the /welcome URL to the welcome method. When the browser sends a request to /welcome, Spring MVC does the magic and executes the welcome method.
- @ResponseBody: In this specific context, the text returned by the welcome method is sent out to the browser as the response content. @ResponseBody does a lot of magic—especially in the context of REST services. We will discuss this further in Chapter 6, *Building REST APIs with Spring*.

Running the web application

We are using Maven and Tomcat 7 to run this web application. The Tomcat 7 server launches on port 8080 by default.

We can run the server by invoking the mvn tomcat7:run command.

Here is a screenshot of how this would appear onscreen when the http://localhost:8080/welcome URL is hit on the browser:

Flow 2 – creating a simple controller flow with a View – JSP

In the previous flow, the text to show on the browser was hardcoded in the Controller. That is not a good practice. The content to be shown on the browser is typically generated from a View. The most frequently used option is JSP.

In this flow, let's redirect from the Controller to a View.

Creating a Spring MVC controller

Similar to the previous example, let's create a simple @Controller object. Consider the example of a controller here:

```
@Controller
public class BasicViewController {

  @RequestMapping(value = "/welcome-view")
  public String welcome() {
    return "welcome";
  }

}
```

A few important things to note are as follows:

- @RequestMapping(value = "/welcome-view"): We are mapping a /welcome-view URL.
- public String welcome(): There is no @RequestBody annotation on this method. So, Spring MVC tries to match the string that is returned, welcome, to a View.

Creating a View – a JSP

Let's create welcome.jsp in the src/main/webapp/WEB-INF/views/welcome.jsp folder with the following content:

```
<html>
  <head>
    <title>Welcome</title>
  </head>
  <body>
```

```
    <p>Welcome! This is coming from a view - a JSP</p>
  </body>
</html>
```

This is a simple HTML with a head, body, and some text in the body.

Spring MVC has to map the string returned from the `welcome` method to the real JSP at `/WEB-INF/views/welcome.jsp`. How does this magic happen?

Configuring a View resolver

A View resolver resolves a View name to the actual JSP page. The View name in this example is `welcome`, and we would want it to resolve to `/WEB-INF/views/welcome.jsp`.

A View resolver can be configured in the Spring context, `/WEB-INF/user-web-context.xml`. Here's the code snippet for that:

```
<bean
class="org.springframework.web.servlet.view.InternalResourceViewResolver">

  <property name="prefix">
    <value>/WEB-INF/views/</value>
  </property>

  <property name="suffix">
    <value>.jsp</value>
  </property>

</bean>
```

The following definitions explain the code in detail:

- `org.springframework.web.servlet.view.InternalResourceViewResolver`: This is a View resolver supporting JSPs. `JstlView` is typically used. It also supports tiles with `TilesView`.
- `<property name="prefix"> <value>/WEB-INF/views/</value> </property><property name="suffix"> <value>.jsp</value> </property>`: This maps the prefix and suffix to be used by a View resolver. A View resolver takes the string from the controller method and resolves to the View—prefix + viewname + suffix. So, the View name, `welcome`, is resolved to `/WEB-INF/views/welcome.jsp`.

Here is a screenshot of how this would appear on screen when the URL is hit:

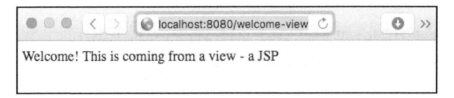

Welcome! This is coming from a view - a JSP

Flow 3 – controller redirecting to a View with a model

Typically, in order to generate the View, we need to pass some data to it. In Spring MVC, data can be passed to the View using a model. In this flow, we would set up a model with a simple attribute and use the attribute in the View.

Spring MVC controller

Let's create a simple @Controller. Consider the following example controller:

```
@Controller
public class BasicModelMapController {

    @RequestMapping(value = "/welcome-model-map")
    public String welcome(ModelMap model) {
        model.put("name", "XYZ");
        return "welcome-model-map";
    }

}
```

The following definitions explain the code in detail:

- @RequestMapping(value = "/welcome-model-map"): The URI mapped is /welcome-model-map.
- public String welcome(ModelMap model): The new parameter added is ModelMap model. Spring MVC will instantiate a model and make it available for this method. The attributes incorporated into the model will be available for use in the View.
- model.put("name", "XYZ"): This adds an attribute with the name name and the XYZ value to the model.

Creating a View

Let's create a View using the model attribute, `name`, which was set in the model in the controller. Let's create a simple JSP in the `WEB-INF/views/welcome-model-map.jsp` path:

```
Welcome ${name}! This is coming from a model-map - a JSP
```

`${name}` uses the **Expression Language** (**EL**) syntax to access the attribute from the model.

Here is a screenshot of how this would appear onscreen when the URL is hit:

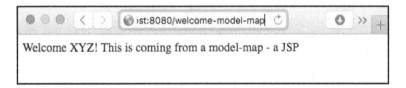

Flow 4 – controller redirecting to a View with ModelAndView

In the previous flow, we returned a View name and populated the model with attributes to be used in the View. Spring MVC provides an alternative approach, returning a single object with both the model and the View details. In this flow, we will explore this alternative approach.

Spring MVC controller

In this example, let's look at a Spring MVC Controller method, returning both the model and View details in a single object using `ModelAndView`. The `welcome` method returns a `ModelAndView` object with the View name and appropriate attributes in the Model.

Take a look at the following controller:

```
@Controller
public class BasicModelViewController {
  @RequestMapping(value = "/welcome-model-view")
   public ModelAndView welcome(ModelMap model) {
     model.put("name", "XYZ");
     return new ModelAndView("welcome-model-view", model);
   }
}
```

The following definitions explain the code in detail:

- `@RequestMapping(value = "/welcome-model-view")`: The URI mapped is `/welcome-model-view`.
- `public ModelAndView welcome(ModelMap model)`: Note that the return value is no longer a string. It is a `ModelAndView` object.
- `return new ModelAndView("welcome-model-view", model)`: This creates a `ModelAndView` object with the appropriate View name and model.

Creating a View

Let's create a View using the model attribute, `name`, which was set in the model in the controller. Create a simple JSP in the `/WEB-INF/views/welcome-model-view.jsp` path:

```
Welcome ${name}! This is coming from a model-view - a JSP
```

Here is a screenshot of how this would appear onscreen when the URL is hit:

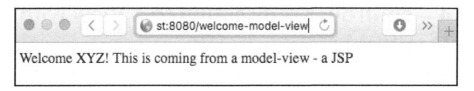

Flow 5 – controller redirecting to a View with a form

Now, let's shift our attention to creating a simple form to capture input from the user.

The following steps must be observed:

1. Create a simple POJO. We want to create a user. We will create a POJO user.
2. Create a couple of Controller methods—one to display the form and the other to capture the details entered in the form.
3. Create a simple View with the form.

Creating a command or form-backing object

POJO is short for **Plain Old Java Object**. It is generally used to represent a bean following the typical JavaBean conventions. Typically, it contains private member variables with getters and setters and a no-argument constructor.

 A form-backing Object is used to represent the values entered/shown by/to the user in a form. Model is used to populate data used to render a View—select boxes, option buttons, and so on.

We will create a simple POJO to act as a command object. Important parts of the class are listed as follows:

```java
    public class User {
private String guid;
private String name;
private String userId;
private String password;
private String password2;
//Constructor
//Getters and Setters
//toString
}
```

We are going to capture `name`, `user ID`, and `password` in the form. In the preceding class, we have fields corresponding to each of them, along with a password confirmation field, `password2`, and a unique identifier field, `guid`.

 The `Constructor`, `getters`, `setters`, and `toString` methods are not shown for brevity. This class does not have any annotations or Spring-related mappings. Any bean can act as a form-backing object.

The controller method to show the form

Let's start by creating a simple controller with `logger`:

```java
@Controller
public class UserController {
  private Log logger = LogFactory.getLog
  (UserController.class);
  }
```

Now, let's add the following method to the controller:

```
@RequestMapping(value = "/create-user",
method = RequestMethod.GET)
public String showCreateUserPage(ModelMap model) {
  model.addAttribute("user", new User());
  return "user";
}
```

The following explains the working of the preceding code block:

- `@RequestMapping(value = "/create-user", method = RequestMethod.GET)`: We are mapping a `/create-user` URI. For the first time, we are specifying a `Request` method using the method attribute. This method will be invoked only for HTTP `Get` requests. HTTP `Get` requests are typically used to show the form. This will not be invoked for other types of HTTP requests, such as `Post`.
- `public String showCreateUserPage(ModelMap model)`: This is a typical control method.
- `model.addAttribute("user", new User())`: This is used to set up the model with an empty form-backing object.

Creating the View with a form

Java Server Pages is one of the View technologies supported by Spring Framework. Spring Framework makes it easy to create views with JSPs by providing a tag library. This includes tags for various form elements, binding, validation, setting themes, and internationalizing messages. We will use the tags from the Spring MVC tag library, as well as standard `jstl` tag libraries, to create our View in this example.

Let's start by creating the `/WEB-INF/views/user.jsp` file.

Then, add the reference to the tag libraries to be used:

```
<%@ taglib uri="http://java.sun.com/jsp/jstl/core" prefix="c"%>
<%@ taglib uri="http://java.sun.com/jsp/jstl/fmt" prefix="fmt"%>
<%@ taglib uri="http://www.springframework.org/tags/form"
  prefix="form"%>
<%@ taglib uri="http://www.springframework.org/tags"
  prefix="spring"%>
```

The first two entries are for the JSTL core and formatting tag libraries. We will use the Spring form tags extensively. We provide a prefix to act as a shortcut to refer to tags.

Now, let's create a form with one field first:

```
<form:form method="post" modelAttribute="user">
 <fieldset>
   <form:label path="name">Name</form:label>
   <form:input path="name"
   type="text" required="required" />
 </fieldset>
</form:form>
```

The following definitions explain the workings of the preceding code block:

- `<form:form method="post" modelAttribute="user">`: This is the `form` tag from the Spring form tag library. Two attributes are specified. Data in the form is sent using the post method. The second attribute, `modelAttribute`, specifies the attribute from the model that acts as the form-backing object. In the model, we added an attribute with the name `user`. We use that attribute as `modelAttribute`.
- `<fieldset>`: This is the HTML element to group a set of related controls—labels, form fields, and validation messages.
- `<form:label path="name">Name</form:label>`: This is the Spring form tag to show a label. The path attribute specifies the field name (from the bean) this label is applied to.
- `<form:input path="name" type="text" required="required" />`: This is the Spring form tag to create a text input field. The `path` attribute specifies the field name in the bean that this input field has to be mapped to. The required attribute indicates that this is a `required` field.

When we use the Spring form tags, the values from the form-backing object (`modelAttribute="user"`) are bound automatically to the form, and, on submitting the form, the values from the form are automatically bound to the form-backing object.

A more complete list of the form tags, including the name and user ID fields, is as follows:

```
<form:form method="post" modelAttribute="user">
<form:hidden path="guid" />
<fieldset>
  <form:label path="name">Name</form:label>
  <form:input path="name"
   type="text" required="required" />
</fieldset>
<fieldset>
  <form:label path="userId">User Id</form:label>
  <form:input path="userId"
```

```
          type="text" required="required" />
    </fieldset>
    <!-password and password2 fields not shown for brewity-->
    <input class="btn btn-success" type="submit" value="Submit" />
    </form:form>
```

Controller get method to handle form submit

When the user submits the form, the browser sends an HTTP POST request. Now, let's create a method to handle this. To keep things simple, we will log the content of the form object. The complete listing of the method is as follows:

```
@RequestMapping(value = "/create-user", method = RequestMethod.POST)
public String addTodo(User user) {
    logger.info("user details " + user);
    return "redirect:list-users";
}
```

A few important details include the following:

- @RequestMapping(value = "/create-user", method = RequestMethod.POST): Since we want to handle the form submit, we use the RequestMethod.POST method.
- public String addTodo(User user): We are using the form-backing object as the parameter. Spring MVC will automatically bind the values from the form to the form-backing object.
- logger.info("user details " + user): This logs the details of the user.
- return redirect:list-users: Typically, on submitting a form, we save the details of a database and redirect the user to a different page. Here, we are redirecting the user to /list-users. When we use redirect, Spring MVC sends an HTTP response with the status 302, that is, REDIRECT, to the new URL. The browser, upon processing the 302 response, will redirect the user to the new URL. While the POST/REDIRECT/GET pattern is not a perfect fix for the duplicate form submission problem, it does reduce the occurrences, especially those that occur after the View is rendered.

The code for list users is straightforward and is listed as follows:

```
@RequestMapping(value = "/list-users",  method = RequestMethod.GET)
public String showAllUsers() {
    return "list-users";
}
```

Flow 6 – adding validation to the previous flow

In the previous flow, we added a form. However, we did not validate the values in the form. While we can write JavaScript to validate the form content, it is always secure to execute validation on the server. In this flow, let's add validation to the form that we created earlier on the server side using Spring MVC.

Spring MVC provides excellent integration with the Bean Validation API. JSR 303 and JSR 349 define specifications for the Bean Validation API (versions 1.0 and 1.1, respectively), and Hibernate Validator is the reference implementation.

Adding the Hibernate Validator dependency

Let's start by adding Hibernate Validator to our `pom.xml` project:

```
<dependency>
  <groupId>org.hibernate</groupId>
  <artifactId>hibernate-validator</artifactId>
  <version>5.0.2.Final</version>
</dependency>
```

Defining simple validations on the bean

The Bean Validation API specifies the number of validations that can be specified on attributes on the beans. Take a look at the following listing:

```
@Size(min = 6, message = "Enter at least 6 characters")
private String name;

@Size(min = 6, message = "Enter at least 6 characters")
private String userId;

@Size(min = 8, message = "Enter at least 8 characters")
private String password;

@Size(min = 8, message = "Enter at least 8 characters")
private String password2;
```

One important thing to note is as follows:

- `@Size(min = 6, message = "Enter at least 6 characters")` : This specifies that the field should at least have six characters. If the validation does not pass, the text from the message attribute is used as a validation error message.

Other validations that can be performed using Bean Validation are as follows:

- @NotNull: This should not be null.
- @Size(min =5, max = 50): This indicates a maximum size of 50 characters and a minimum size of 5 characters.
- @Past: This should be a date in the past.
- @Future: This should be a future date.
- @Pattern: This should match the regular expression provided.
- @Max: This represents the maximum value for the field.
- @Min: This represents the minimum value for the field.

Now, let's focus on getting the controller method to validate the form on submits. The complete method listing is as follows:

```
@RequestMapping(value = "/create-user-with-validation", method =
RequestMethod.POST)
    public String addTodo(@Valid User user, BindingResult result) {

    if (result.hasErrors()) {
      return "user";
     }

    logger.info("user details " + user);

    return "redirect:list-users";

}
```

Some important things to observe are as follows:

- public String addTodo(@Valid User user, BindingResult result): When the @Valid annotation is used, Spring MVC validates the bean. The result of the validation is made available in the BindingResult instance result.
- if (result.hasErrors()): This checks whether there are any validation errors.
- return "user": If there are any validation errors, we send the user back to the user page.

We need to enhance `user.jsp` to show the validation messages in the event of validation errors. The complete list for one of the fields is shown here. Other fields have to be similarly updated:

```
<fieldset>
  <form:label path="name">Name</form:label>
  <form:input path="name" type="text" required-"required" />
  <form:errors path="name" cssClass="text-warning"/>
</fieldset>
```

`<form:errors path="name" cssClass="text-warning"/>`: This is the Spring form tag to display the errors related to the field name specified in the path. We can also assign the CSS class used to display the validation error.

Implementing custom validations

More complex custom validations can be implemented using the `@AssertTrue` annotation. The following list an example method added to the `User` class:

```
@AssertTrue(message = "Password fields don't match")
private boolean isValid() {
   return this.password.equals(this.password2);
}
```

`@AssertTrue(message = "Password fields don't match")` is the message to be shown if validation fails.

Any complex validation logic with multiple fields can be implemented in these methods.

An overview of Spring MVC

Now that we've looked at the implementation of a few basic flows with Spring MVC, we will switch our attention to understanding how these flows work. How does the magic happen with Spring MVC?

Understanding the important features

When working with the different flows, we looked at some of the important features of the Spring MVC Framework. These include the following:

- It has loosely coupled architecture with well-defined, independent roles for each of the objects.
- They are highly flexible controller method definitions. Controller methods can have a varied range of parameters and return values. This gives the programmer the flexibility to choose the definition that meets their needs.
- It allows the reuse of domain objects as form-backing objects and reduces the need to have separate form objects.
- There are built-in tag libraries (Spring and `spring-form`) with localization support.
- The model uses a `HashMap` with key-value pairs. It allows integration with multiple View technologies.
- There is flexible binding. Type mismatches while binding can be handled as validation errors instead of runtime errors.
- There is a MockMVC Framework to unit test controllers.

Working with Spring MVC

Key components in the Spring MVC architecture are shown in the following diagram:

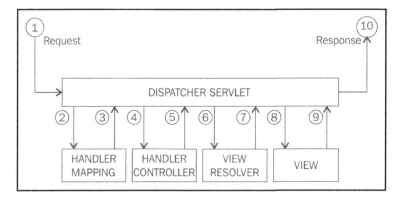

Let's look at an example flow and understand the different steps involved in executing the flow. We will take flow **4**, returning `ModelAndView` as the specific example. The URL of flow **4** is `http://localhost:8080/welcome-model-view`. The different steps are detailed as follows:

1. The browser issues a request to a specific URL. `DispatcherServlet` is the FrontController, handling all requests. So, it receives the request.

2. **DISPATCHER SERVLET** looks at the URI (in the example, `/welcome-model-view`) and needs to identify the right controller to handle it. To help find the right controller, it talks to the handler mapping.

3. Handler mapping returns the specific handler method (in the example, the `welcome` method in `BasicModelViewController`) that handles the request.

4. `DispatcherServlet` invokes the specific handler method (`public ModelAndView welcome(ModelMap model)`).

5. The handler method returns the Model and View. In this example, the `ModelAndView` object is returned.

6. `DispatcherServlet` has the logical View name (from `ModelAndView`; in this example, it is `welcome-model-view`). It needs to figure out how to determine the physical View name. It checks whether there are any View resolvers available. It finds the View resolver that was configured (`org.springframework.web.servlet.view.InternalResourceViewResolver`). It calls the View resolver, giving it the logical View name (in this example, `welcome-model-view`) as the input.

7. View resolver executes the logic to map the logical View name to the physical View name. In this example, `welcome-model-view` is translated into `/WEB-INF/views/welcome-model-view.jsp`.

8. `DispatcherServlet` executes the View. It also makes the Model available to the View.

9. View returns the content to be sent back to `DispatcherServlet`.

10. `DispatcherServlet` sends the response back to the browser.

Important concepts behind Spring MVC

Now that we have completed an example with Spring MVC, we are ready to understand the important concepts behind Spring MVC.

RequestMapping

As we've discussed in earlier examples, `RequestMapping` is used to map a URI to a Controller or a Controller method. It can be done at class and/or method levels. An optional method parameter allows us to map the method to a specific request method (`GET`, `POST`, and so on).

Examples of request mapping

A few examples in the upcoming sections illustrate the variations.

Example 1

In the following example, there is only one `RequestMapping` method in the `showPage` method. The `showPage` method will be mapped to `GET`, `POST`, and any other request types for the `/show-page` URI:

```
@Controller
public class UserController {
  @RequestMapping(value = "/show-page")
  public String showPage() {
    /* Some code */
  }
}
```

Example 2

In the following example, there is a method defined on `RequestMapping`, `RequestMethod.GET`. The `showPage` method will be mapped only to the `GET` request for the `/show-page` URI. All other request method types would throw a *method not supported* exception:

```
@Controller
public class UserController {
  @RequestMapping(value = "/show-page" , method =
  RequestMethod.GET)
  public String showPage() {
    /* Some code */
  }
}
```

Example 3

In the following example, there are two `RequestMapping` methods—one in the class and the other in the method. A combination of both `RequestMapping` methods is used to determine the URI. The `showPage` method will be mapped only to the `GET` request for the `/user/show-page` URI:

```
@Controller
@RequestMapping("/user")
public class UserController {
  @RequestMapping(value = "/show-page" , method =
  RequestMethod.GET)
  public String showPage() {
    /* Some code */
  }
}
```

RequestMapping methods – supported method arguments

The following are some of the types of arguments that are supported in Controller methods with `RequestMapping`:

Argument Type/Annotation	Use
`java.util.Map` / `org.springframework.ui.Model` / `org.springframework.ui.ModelMap`	This acts as the model (MVC) that will be the container for values that are exposed to the view.
Command or form objects	This is used to bind request parameters to beans. There is support for validation as well.
`org.springframework.validation.Errors` / `org.springframework.validation.BindingResult`	This is the result of validating the command or form object (the form object should be the immediately preceding method argument).

@PreDestroy	On any spring bean, a pre-destroy method can be provided using the @PreDestroy annotation. This method is called just before a bean is removed from the container. It can be used to release any resources that are held by the bean.
@RequestParam	This is the annotation to access specific HTTP request parameters.
@RequestHeader	This is the annotation to access specific HTTP request headers.
@SessionAttribute	This is the annotation to access attributes from the HTTP session.
@RequestAttribute	This is the annotation to access specific HTTP request attributes.
@PathVariable	The annotation allows access to variables from the URI template, /owner/{ownerId}. We will look at this in detail when we discuss microservices.

RequestMapping methods – supported return types

The RequestMapping methods support a varied range of return types. Thinking conceptually, a request mapping method should answer two questions:

- What's the View?
- What's the model that the View needs?

However, with Spring MVC, the View and model need not be explicitly declared at all times:

- If a View is not explicitly defined as part of the return type, then it is implicitly defined.
- Similarly, any model object is always enriched, as detailed in the following rules.

Spring MVC uses simple rules to determine the exact View and model. A couple of important rules are listed as follows:

- **Implicit enriching of the Model**: If a model is part of the return type, it is enriched with command objects (including results from the validation of the command objects). In addition, the results of methods with the `@ModelAttribute` annotations are also added to the model.
- **Implicit determination of the View**: If a view name is not present in the return type, it is determined using `DefaultRequestToViewNameTranslator`. By default, `DefaultRequestToViewNameTranslator` removes the leading and trailing slashes as well as the file extension from the URI; for example, `display.html` becomes `display`.

The following are some of the return types that are supported on Controller methods with `RequestMapping`:

Return Type	What happens?
`ModelAndView`	The object includes a reference to the model and the View name.
`Model`	Only Model is returned. The View name is determined using `DefaultRequestToViewNameTranslator`.
`Map`	This is a simple map to expose a model.
`View`	This is a View with a model implicitly defined.
`String`	This is a reference to a View name.

Exploring View resolution

Spring MVC provides a very flexible View resolution. It provides multiple View options:

- There is integration with JSP and, Freemarker.
- There are multiple View resolution strategies. A few of them are listed as follows:
  - `XmlViewResolver`: View resolution based on an external XML configuration.

- `ResourceBundleViewResolver`: View resolution based on a property file.
- `UrlBasedViewResolver`: This direct mapping of the logical View name to a URL.
- `ContentNegotiatingViewResolver`: This delegates to other View resolvers based on the accept request header.
- `InternalResourceViewResolver` : This is a subclass of `UrlBasedViewResolver`. It provides support for servlets and JSPs along with `JstlView` and `TilesView`.

- There is support for chaining of View resolvers with the explicitly defined order of preference.
- It provides direct generation of XML, JSON, and Atom using content negotiation.

Configuring the JSP View resolver

The following example shows the commonly used approach to configure a JSP View resolver using `InternalResourceViewResolver`. The physical View name is determined using the configured prefix and suffix for the logical View name using `JstlView`:

```
<bean id="jspViewResolver" class=
  "org.springframework.web.servlet.view.
  InternalResourceViewResolver">
  <property name="viewClass"
    value="org.springframework.web.servlet.view.JstlView"/>
  <property name="prefix" value="/WEB-INF/jsp/"/>
  <property name="suffix" value=".jsp"/>
</bean>
```

There are other approaches using property and XML files for mapping.

Configuring Freemarker

Freemarker is one of the popular Java templating engines. We can use Freemarker in Spring applications to generate your View.

The following example shows the typical approach used to configure a Freemarker View resolver.

First, the `freemarkerConfig` bean is used to load the Freemarker templates:

```xml
<bean id="freemarkerConfig"
  class="org.springframework.web.servlet.view.
  freemarker.FreeMarkerConfigurer">
  <property name="templateLoaderPath" value="/WEB-
  INF/freemarker/"/>
</bean>
```

The following bean definition shows how to configure a Freemarker View resolver:

```xml
<bean id="freemarkerViewResolver"
 class="org.springframework.web.servlet.view.
 freemarker.FreeMarkerViewResolver">
   <property name="cache" value="true"/>
   <property name="prefix" value=""/>
   <property name="suffix" value=".ftl"/>
</bean>
```

As with JSP, the View resolution can be defined using properties or an XML file.

Exploring handler mappings and interceptors

In the version before Spring 2.5 (before there was support for annotations), the mapping between a URL and a controller (also called a handler) was expressed using something called a handler mapping. It is almost a historical fact today. The use of annotations eliminated the need for explicit handler mapping.

`HandlerInterceptors` can be used to intercept requests to handlers (or **controllers**). Sometimes, you would want to do some processing before and after a request. You might want to log the content of the request and response, or you might want to find out how much time a specific request took.

There are two steps in creating `HandlerInterceptor`:

1. Define the `HandlerInterceptor`.
2. Map the `HandlerInterceptor` to the specific handlers to be intercepted.

Defining a HandlerInterceptor

The following are the methods you can override in `HandlerInterceptorAdapter`:

- `public boolean preHandle(HttpServletRequest request, HttpServletResponse response, Object handler)`: This is invoked before the handler method is invoked.
- `public void postHandle(HttpServletRequest request, HttpServletResponse response, Object handler, ModelAndView modelAndView)`: This is invoked after the handler method is invoked.
- `public void afterCompletion(HttpServletRequest request, HttpServletResponse response, Object handler, Exception ex)`: This is invoked after the request processing is complete.

The following example implementation shows how to create `HandlerInterceptor`. Let's start by creating a new class that extends `HandlerInterceptorAdapter`:

```
public class HandlerTimeLoggingInterceptor extends
HandlerInterceptorAdapter {
```

The `preHandle` method is invoked before the handler is called. Let's place an attribute on the request, indicating the start time of the handler invocation:

```
@Override
public boolean preHandle(HttpServletRequest request,
  HttpServletResponse response, Object handler) throws Exception {
  request.setAttribute(
  "startTime", System.currentTimeMillis());
  return true;
}
```

The `postHandle` method is invoked after the handler is called. Now, let's place an attribute on the request, indicating the end time of the handler invocation:

```
@Override
public void postHandle(HttpServletRequest request,
HttpServletResponse response, Object handler,
ModelAndView modelAndView) throws Exception {
    request.setAttribute(
    "endTime", System.currentTimeMillis());
  }
```

The `afterCompletion` method is invoked once the request processing is complete. We will identify the time spent in the handler, using the attributes that we set in the request earlier:

```
@Override
public void afterCompletion(HttpServletRequest request,
HttpServletResponse response, Object handler, Exception ex)
throws Exception {
  long startTime = (Long) request.getAttribute("startTime");
  long endTime = (Long) request.getAttribute("endTime");
  logger.info("Time Spent in Handler in ms : "
  + (endTime - startTime));
}
```

Mapping HandlerInterceptor to handlers

`HandlerInterceptors` can be mapped to specific URLs that you want to intercept. The following example shows an example XML context configuration. By default, the interceptor will intercept all handlers (controllers):

```
<mvc:interceptors>
  <bean class="com.mastering.spring.springmvc.
  controller.interceptor.HandlerTimeLoggingInterceptor" />
</mvc:interceptors>
```

We can configure precise URIs to be intercepted. In the following example, all handlers, except those with URI mapping starting with `/secure/`, are intercepted:

```
<mvc:interceptors>
  <mapping path="/**"/>
  <exclude-mapping path="/secure/**"/>
  <bean class="com.mastering.spring.springmvc.
   controller.interceptor.HandlerTimeLoggingInterceptor" />
</mvc:interceptors>
```

Using model attributes

Common web forms contain a number of select boxes or radio buttons containing reference data—a list of states, a list of countries, and so on. These lists of values need to be available in the model so that the View can display the list. Such common things are typically populated in the model using methods that are marked with `@ModelAttribute` annotations.

There are two variations possible. In the following example, the method returns the object that needs to be put into the model:

```
@ModelAttribute
public List<State> populateStateList() {
  return stateService.findStates();
  }
```

The approach in this example is used to add multiple attributes to the model:

```
@ModelAttribute
public void populateStateAndCountryList() {
  model.addAttribute(stateService.findStates());
  model.addAttribute(countryService.findCountries());
  }
```

An important thing to note is that there is no limitation to the number of methods that can be marked with the @ModelAttribute annotation.

Model attributes can be made common across multiple controllers using controller advice. We will discuss controller advice later in this section.

Using session attributes

All of the attributes and values that have we discussed hitherto are used within a single request. However, there may be values, such as a specific web user configuration, that might not change across requests. These kinds of values will typically be stored in an HTTP session. Spring MVC provides a simple type-level (class-level) annotation, @SessionAttributes, to specify the attributes that would be stored in the session.

 You need to set both request scoped and session scoped attributes to your model. Session scoped attributes are marked with the @SessionAttributes annotation.

Take a look at the following example:

```
@Controller
@SessionAttributes("exampleSessionAttribute")
public class LoginController {
```

Putting an attribute in the session

Once we define an attribute in the @SessionAttributes annotation, it is automatically added to the session if the same attribute is added to the model.

In the preceding example, if we incorporate an attribute with the name exampleSessionAttribute in the model, it would be automatically stored in the session conversation state:

```
model.put("exampleSessionAttribute", sessionValue);
```

Another option is to create a method annotated with @ModelAttribute:

```
@ModelAttribute("exampleSessionAttribute")
public User populateUser() {
    //Your logic to create the sessionValue
    return sessionValue;
}
```

exampleSessionAttribute will be populated in the session.

Reading an attribute from the session

This value can be accessed in other controllers by first specifying the @SessionAttributes annotation at a type level:

```
@Controller
@SessionAttributes("exampleSessionAttribute")
public class SomeOtherController {
```

The value of the session attribute will be made available directly to all model objects. So, it can be accessed from the model:

```
Value sessionValue =(Value)model.get("exampleSessionAttribute");
```

Removing an attribute from the session

It is important to remove values from the session when they are no longer needed. There are two ways in which we can remove values from the session conversational state. The first way is demonstrated in the following snippet. It uses the removeAttribute method available in the WebRequest class:

```
@RequestMapping(value="/some-method",method = RequestMethod.GET)
public String someMethod(/*Other Parameters*/
WebRequest request, SessionStatus status) {
  status.setComplete();
  request.removeAttribute("exampleSessionAttribute",
  WebRequest.SCOPE_SESSION);
   //Other Logic
}
```

This example shows the second approach using the cleanUpAttribute method in SessionAttributeStore:

```
@RequestMapping(value = "/some-other-method",
method = RequestMethod.GET)
public String someOtherMethod(/*Other Parameters*/
SessionAttributeStore store, SessionStatus status) {
  status.setComplete();
  store.cleanupAttribute(request, "exampleSessionAttribute");
  //Other Logic
}
```

Understand the need for InitBinders

Typical web forms have dates, currencies, and amounts. The values in the forms need to be bound to the form-backing objects. Customization of how binding happens can be introduced using the @InitBinder annotation.

Customization can be effected in a specific controller or a set of controllers using Handler Advice. This example shows how to set the default date format to use for form binding:

```
@InitBinder
protected void initBinder(WebDataBinder binder) {
  SimpleDateFormat dateFormat = new SimpleDateFormat("dd/MM/yyyy");
  binder.registerCustomEditor(Date.class, new CustomDateEditor(
  dateFormat, false));
}
```

Implementing common features using the @ControllerAdvice annotation

Some of the functionality we defined at the controller level can be common across the application. For example, we may want to use the same date format across the application. So, @InitBinder, which we defined earlier, can be applied across the application. How do we achieve that? @ControllerAdvice helps us to make the functionality common across all RequestMapping by default.

For example, consider the Controller advice example listed here. We use an @ControllerAdvice annotation on the class and define the method with @InitBinder in this class. By default, the binding defined in this method is applicable to all request mappings:

```
@ControllerAdvice
public class DateBindingControllerAdvice {
  @InitBinder
  protected void initBinder(WebDataBinder binder) {
    SimpleDateFormat dateFormat = new
    SimpleDateFormat("dd/MM/yyyy");
    binder.registerCustomEditor(Date.class,
    new CustomDateEditor(
      dateFormat, false));
    }
}
```

Controller advice can also be used to define common model attributes (@ModelAttribute) and common exception handling (@ExceptionHandler). All you need to do is to create methods marked with appropriate annotations. We will discuss exception handling in the next section.

A quick look at Spring MVC advanced features

In this section, we will discuss advanced features related to Spring MVC, including the following:

- How do we implement generic exception handling for the web application?
- How do we internationalize messages?

- How do we expose static content and integrate with frontend frameworks such as Bootstrap?
- How do we secure our web application with Spring Security?

Implementing exception handling

Exception handling is one of the critical parts of any application. It is very important to have a consistent exception handling strategy across the application. One of the popular misconceptions is that only bad applications require exception handling. Nothing can be further from the truth. Even well-designed, well-written applications require good exception handling.

Before the emergence of Spring Framework, exception handling code was required across application code due to the wide use of checked exceptions. For example, most of the JDBC methods threw checked exceptions, requiring a try catch to handle the exception in every method (unless you would want to declare that the method throws a JDBC exception).

With Spring Framework, most of the exceptions were rendered unchecked exceptions. This made sure that, unless specific exception handling was needed, exception handling could be handled generically across the application.

In this section, we will look at a couple of example implementations of exception handling, as follows:

- Common exception handling across all controllers
- Specific exception handling for a controller

Common exception handling across controllers

Controller advice can also be used to implement common exception handling across controllers.

Take a look at the following code:

```
@ControllerAdvice
public class ExceptionController {
  private Log logger =
  LogFactory.getLog(ExceptionController.class);
  @ExceptionHandler(value = Exception.class)
  public ModelAndView handleException
  (HttpServletRequest request, Exception ex) {
      logger.error("Request " + request.getRequestURL()
```

```
        + " Threw an Exception", ex);
        ModelAndView mav = new ModelAndView();
        mav.addObject("exception", ex);
        mav.addObject("url", request.getRequestURL());
        mav.setViewName("common/spring-mvc-error");
        return mav;
    }
}
```

Some things to note are as follows:

- `@ControllerAdvice`: Controller Advice, by default, applies to all controllers.
- `@ExceptionHandler(value = Exception.class)`: Any method with this annotation will be called when an exception of the type or the sub-type of the class specified (`Exception.class`) is thrown in the controllers.
- `public ModelAndView handleException (HttpServletRequest request, Exception ex)`: The exception that is thrown is injected into the `Exception` variable. The method is declared with a `ModelAndView` return type to be able to return a model with the exception details and an exception View.
- `mav.addObject("exception", ex)`: The exception is added to the model so that the exception details can be shown in the view.
- `mav.setViewName("common/spring-mvc-error")`: This is the exception View.

Defining the error View

Whenever an exception happens, `ExceptionController` redirects the user to the `ExceptionController` spring-mvc-error View after populating the model with exception details. The following snippet shows the complete `/WEB-INF/views/common/spring-mvc-error.jsp` JSP:

```
<%@ taglib prefix="c" uri="http://java.sun.com/jsp/jstl/core"%>
<%@page isErrorPage="true"%>
<h1>Error Page</h1>
 URL: ${url}
<BR />
 Exception: ${exception.message}
<c:forEach items="${exception.stackTrace}"
   var="exceptionStackTrace">
   ${exceptionStackTrace}
</c:forEach>
```

Important elements to note include the following:

- URL: `${url}`: This shows the URL from the model.
- Exception: `${exception.message}`: This displays the exception message. The exception is populated in the model from ExceptionController.
- forEach around `${exceptionStackTrace}`: This displays the stack trace from exception handling specific to ExceptionController.

Creating specific exception handling in a Controller

In some situations, there is a need for specific exception handling in a Controller. This situation can easily be handled by implementing a method annotated with `@ExceptionHandler(value = Exception.class)`.

In case specific exception handling is required only for a specific exception, the specific Exception class can be provided as the value for the value attribute of the annotation.

Internationalizing your application

When we develop applications, we would want them to be usable in multiple locales. You would want the text that is shown to the user to be customized based on the location and language of the user. This is called **internationalization**. Internationalization, i18n, is also called **localization**.

It can be implemented using two approaches:

- SessionLocaleResolver
- CookieLocaleResolver

In the case of SessionLocaleResolver, the locale chosen by the user is stored in the user session and, therefore, is valid for the user session only. However, in the case of CookieLocaleResolver, the locale chosen is stored as a cookie.

Setting up the message bundle

First, let's set up a message bundler. The code snippet from the Spring context is as follows:

```
<bean id="messageSource" class= "org.springframework.context.support.
ReloadableResourceBundleMessageSource">

    <property name="basename" value="classpath:messages" />
    <property name="defaultEncoding" value="UTF-8" />

</bean>
```

Important elements to note include the following:

- `class="org.springframework.context.support.ReloadableResourceBundleMessageSource"`: This configures a reloadable resource bundle. It supports the reloading of properties through the `cacheSeconds` setting.
- `<property name="basename" value="classpath:messages" />`: This configures the loading of properties from `messages.properties` and `messages_{locale}.properties file`. We will discuss the locale soon.

Now, let's configure a couple of property files and make them available in the `src/main/resources` folder.

The following code snippets show the filename and the content of each file.

The content of the `message_en.properties` file is shown in the following snippet:

```
welcome.caption=Welcome in English
```

The content of the `message_fr.properties` file is shown in the following snippet:

```
welcome.caption=Bienvenue - Welcome in French
```

We can display the message from the message bundle in a View using the `spring:message` tag:

```
<spring:message code="welcome.caption" />
```

Configuring SessionLocaleResolver

There are two parts to configuring `SessionLocaleResolver`. The first one is to configure a `localeResolver` bean. The second one is to configure an interceptor to handle the change in the locale:

```
        <bean id="springMVCLocaleResolver"
class="org.springframework.web.servlet.i18n.SessionLocaleResolver">
            <property name="defaultLocale" value="en" />
        </bean>

        <mvc:interceptors>
          <bean id="springMVCLocaleChangeInterceptor"
class="org.springframework.web.servlet.i18n.LocaleChangeInterceptor">
            <property name="paramName" value="language" />
          </bean>
        </mvc:interceptors>
```

The following definitions explain the workings of the preceding code block:

- `<property name="defaultLocale" value="en" />`: By default, the `en` locale is used.
- `<mvc:interceptors>`: `LocaleChangeInterceptor` is configured as a `HandlerInterceptor`. It would intercept all of the handler requests and check for the locale.
- `<property name="paramName" value="language" />`: `LocaleChangeInterceptor` is configured to use a request parameter name called language to indicate the locale. So, any URL of the `http://server/uri?language={locale}` format would trigger a change in the locale.
- If you append `language=en` to any URL, you would be using `en` locale for the duration of the session. If you append `language=fr` to any URL, then you would be using a `French` locale.

Configuring CookieLocaleResolver

We use `CookieLocaleResolver` in the following example:

```xml
<bean id="localeResolver"
class="org.springframework.web.servlet.i18n.CookieLocaleResolver">

    <property name="defaultLocale" value="en" />
    <property name="cookieName" value="userLocaleCookie"/>
    <property name="cookieMaxAge" value="7200"/>

</bean>
```

The following definitions explain the workings of the preceding code block:

- `<property name="cookieName" value="userLocaleCookie"/>`: The name of the cookie stored in the browser is `userLocaleCookie`.
- `<property name="cookieMaxAge" value="7200"/>`: The lifetime of the cookie is 2 hours (7200 seconds).
- Since we are using `LocaleChangeInterceptor` from the previous example, if you append `language=en` to any URL, you would be using the `en` locale for a duration of 2 hours (or until the locale is changed). If you append `language=fr` to any URL, then you would be using a `French` locale for 2 hours (or until the locale is changed).

Serving static resources

Most teams today have separate teams delivering frontend and backend content. The frontend is developed with modern JavaScript frameworks, such as AngularJS, and Backbone. Backend is built through web applications or REST services based on frameworks such as Spring MVC.

With this evolution in frontend frameworks, it is very important to find the right solutions to version and deliver frontend static content.

The following are some of the important features provided by the Spring MVC framework:

- They expose static content from folders in the web application root.
- They enable caching.
- They enable `gzip` compression of static content.

Exposing static content

Web applications typically have a lot of static content. Spring MVC provides options to expose static content from folders on the web application root, as well as locations on the classpath. The following snippet shows that content within war can be exposed as static content:

```
<mvc:resources
    mapping="/resources/**"
    location="/static-resources/"/>
```

Elements to note include the following:

- location="/static-resources/": The location specifies the folders inside war or the classpath that you would want to expose as static content. In this example, we want to expose all of the content in the static-resources folder inside the root of war as static content. We can specify multiple comma-separated values to expose multiple folders under the same external facing URI.
- mapping="/resources/**": The mapping specifies the external facing URI path. So, a CSS file named app.css inside the static resources folder can be accessed using the /resources/app.css URI.

The complete Java configuration for the same configuration is shown here:

```
@Configuration
@EnableWebMvc
public class WebConfig extends WebMvcConfigurerAdapter {

  @Override
  public void addResourceHandlers (ResourceHandlerRegistry registry) {
    registry
      .addResourceHandler("/static-resources/**")
      .addResourceLocations("/static-resources/");
  }
}
```

Caching static content

Caching for static resources can be enabled for improved performance. The browser would cache the resources served for the specified time period. The cache-period attribute or the setCachePeriod method can be used to specify the caching interval (in seconds) based on the type of configuration used. The following snippets show the details.

This is the Java configuration:

```
registry
   .addResourceHandler("/resources/**")
   .addResourceLocations("/static-resources/")
   .setCachePeriod(365 * 24 * 60 * 60);
```

This is the XML configuration:

```
<mvc:resources
    mapping="/resources/**"
    location="/static-resources/"
    cache-period="365 * 24 * 60 * 60"/>
```

The `Cache-Control: max-age={specified-max-age}` response header will be sent to the browser.

Enabling gzip compression of static content

Compressing a response is a simple way to make web applications faster. All modern browsers support `gzip` compression. Instead of sending the full static content file, a compressed file can be sent as a response. The browser will decompress and use the static content.

The browser can specify that it can accept the compressed content with a request header. If the server supports it, it can deliver the compressed content—again, marked with a response header.

A request header sent from the browser is as follows:

Accept-Encoding: gzip, deflate

A response header sent from the web application is as follows:

Content-Encoding: gzip

The following snippet shows how to add a `gzip` resolver to deliver compressed static content:

```
registry
  .addResourceHandler("/resources/**")
  .addResourceLocations("/static-resources/")
  .setCachePeriod(365 * 24 * 60 * 60)
  .resourceChain(true)
  .addResolver(new GzipResourceResolver())
  .addResolver(new PathResourceResolver());
```

The following definitions explain the workings of the preceding code block:

- `resourceChain(true)`: We would want to enable `gzip` compression, but would want to fall back to delivering the full file if the full file was requested. So, we use resource chaining (chaining of resource resolvers).
- `addResolver(new PathResourceResolver())`: `PathResourceResolver`: This is the default resolver. It resolves based on the resource handlers and locations configured.
- `addResolver(new GzipResourceResolver())`: `GzipResourceResolver`: This enables `gzip` compression when requested.

Integrating Spring MVC with Bootstrap

One of the approaches to using Bootstrap in a web application is to download the JavaScript and CSS files and make them available in their respective folders. However, this would mean that, every time there is a new version of Bootstrap, we would need to download and make it available as part of the source code. The question is this—is there a way that we can introduce Bootstrap or any other static (JS or CSS) libraries using dependency management such as Maven?

The answer is yes, using WebJars. WebJars are client-side JS or CSS libraries packaged into JAR files. We can use Java build tools (Maven or Gradle) to download and make them available to the application.

Now, let's use Bootstrap WebJar and include it in our web application. The steps involved are as follows:

- Add Bootstrap WebJars as a Maven dependency.
- Configure the Spring MVC resource handler to deliver static content from WebJar.
- Use Bootstrap resources (CSS and JS) in the JSP.

Defining Bootstrap WebJar as a Maven dependency

Let's add the following to the `pom.xml` file:

```
<dependency>
    <groupId>org.webjars</groupId>
    <artifactId>bootstrap</artifactId>
    <version>3.3.6</version>
</dependency>
```

Configuring the Spring MVC resource handler to deliver WebJar static content

This is very simple. We need to add the following mapping to the spring context:

```
<mvc:resources mapping="/webjars/**" location="/webjars/"/>
```

With this configuration, `ResourceHttpRequestHandler` makes the content from WebJars available as static content.

As discussed in the section on static content, we can specifically cache a period if we want to cache the content.

Using Bootstrap resources in JSP

We can add Bootstrap resources just like other static resources in the JSP:

```
<script src= "webjars/bootstrap/3.3.6/js/bootstrap.min.js">
</script>

<link
    href="webjars/bootstrap/3.3.6/css/bootstrap.min.css"
    rel="stylesheet">
```

Unit testing Spring MVC applications – basic flows

Earlier in this chapter, we created six simple flows to understand Spring MVC. In this section, let's write simple unit tests for these six flows. The flows are listed as follows:

- **Flow 1**: Controller without a View; serving content on its own
- **Flow 2**: Controller with a View (a JSP)
- **Flow 3**: Controller with a View and using `ModelMap`
- **Flow 4**: Controller with a View and using `ModelAndView`
- **Flow 5**: Controller for a simple form
- **Flow 6**: Controller for a simple form with validation

Unit testing is a very important part of developing maintainable applications. Before we start with the unit tests, we need to do a little bit of setting up.

We will be using the Spring MVC Mock framework to unit test the controllers that we will write in this chapter. We will add in a dependency on the Spring test framework to use the Spring MVC Mock framework:

```
<dependency>
  <groupId>org.springframework</groupId>
  <artifactId>spring-test</artifactId>
  <scope>test</scope>
</dependency>
```

Flow 1 – simple controller flow without View

Let's start by unit testing the simplest flow, showing text output from a Spring MVC controller on screen.

Here is a screenshot of how this would appear on screen when the http://localhost:8080/welcome URL is hit on the browser:

We would want to do something similar in a unit test. We will invoke the /welcome URI and assert for the correct response.

The approach we will be taking involves the following steps:

1. Setting up the controller to test
2. Writing the test method

Setting up the controller to test

The controller we want to test is BasicController. The convention to create a unit test is a class name with the Test suffix . We will create a test class named BasicControllerTest.

The basic setup is shown as follows:

```
public class BasicControllerTest {

    private MockMvc mockMvc;

    @Before
    public void setup() {
        this.mockMvc = MockMvcBuilders.standaloneSetup(new
BasicController()).build();
    }
}
```

The following definitions explain the workings of the preceding code block:

- `mockMvc`: This variable can be used across different tests. So, we define an instance variable of the `MockMvc` class.
- `@Before setup`: This method is run before every test in order to initialize `MockMvc`.
- `MockMvcBuilders.standaloneSetup(new BasicController()).build()`: This line of code builds a `MockMvc` instance. It initializes `DispatcherServlet` to serve requests to the controller(s) configured, `BasicController`, in this instance.

Writing the Test method

The complete `Test` method is shown in the following code:

```
@Test
public void basicTest() throws Exception {
    this.mockMvc
        .perform(
                get("/welcome")
.accept(MediaType.parseMediaType("application/html;charset=UTF-8")))
        .andExpect(status().isOk())
        .andExpect(content().contentType("application/html;charset=UTF-8"))
        .andExpect(content().string("Welcome to Spring MVC"));
}
```

The following definitions explain the workings of the preceding code block:

- `MockMvc mockMvc.perform`: This method executes the request and returns an instance of `ResultActions` that allows chaining calls. In this example, we are chaining the `andExpect` calls to check expectations.

- `get("/welcome").accept(MediaType.parseMediaType("application/html;charset=UTF-8"))`: This creates an HTTP `get` request accepting a response with the media type, `application/html`.

- `andExpect`: This method is used to check expectations. This method will fail the test if the expectation is not met.

- `status().isOk()`: This uses `ResultMatcher` to check whether the response status is that of a successful request, `200`.

- `content().contentType("application/html;charset=UTF-8")`: This uses `ResultMatcher` to check whether the content type of the response is as specified.

- `content().string("Welcome to Spring MVC")`: This uses `ResultMatcher` to check whether the response content contains the specified string.

Flow 2 – simple controller flow with a View

Now, let's shift our attention to unit testing flow 2, which uses a view—JSP. Here is a screenshot of how this would appear on screen when the URL is hit:

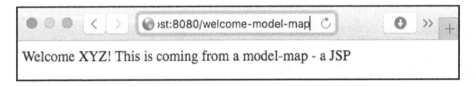

In this unit test, we want to set up `BasicViewController`, execute a `get` request to `/welcome-view`, and check whether the View name returned is `welcome`.

 A standalone setup of the `MockMvc` framework creates the bare minimum infrastructure required by `DispatcherServlet`. If provided with a View resolver, it can execute View resolution. However, it would not execute the View. So, during a unit test with the standalone setup, we cannot verify the content of the View. However, we can check whether the correct View is being delivered.

 In a future section, we will discuss how to execute the integration test, including the rendering of View.

As far as this test is concerned, we restrict our purview to verifying the View name.

Setting up the controller to test

This step is very similar to the previous flow. We want to test `BasicViewController`. We instantiate `MockMvc` using `BasicViewController`. We also configure a simple View resolver:

```
public class BasicViewControllerTest {

    private MockMvc mockMvc;

    @Before
    public void setup() {
        this.mockMvc = MockMvcBuilders
                        .standaloneSetup(new BasicViewController())
                        .setViewResolvers(viewResolver())
                        .build();
    }

    private ViewResolver viewResolver() {
        InternalResourceViewResolver viewResolver = new
InternalResourceViewResolver();
        viewResolver.setViewClass(JstlView.class);
        viewResolver.setPrefix("/WEB-INF/jsp/");
        viewResolver.setSuffix(".jsp");
        return viewResolver;
    }
}
```

We are setting up the `ViewResolver` method in the `viewResolver` method and using it to build to a `MockMvc` object.

Writing the Test method

The complete `Test` method is shown as follows:

```
@Test
public void testWelcomeView() throws Exception {
    this.mockMvc
    .perform(get("/welcome-view")
.accept(MediaType.parseMediaType("application/html;charset=UTF-8")))
    .andExpect(view().name("welcome"));
}
```

A number of important elements to note include the following:

- `get("/welcome-model-view")`: This executes the `get` request to the specified URL.
- `view().name("welcome")`: This uses `ResultMatcher` to check whether the View name returned is as specified.

Flow 3 – controller redirecting to a View with Model

Here is a screenshot of how flow 3 looks on the browser:

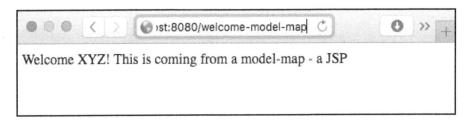

In this unit test, we want to set up `BasicModelMapController`, execute a `get` request to `/welcome-model-map`, and check whether the model has the expected attribute and whether the expected View name is returned.

Setting up the controller to test

This step is very similar to the previous flow. We instantiate MockMVC with `BasicModelMapController`:

```
this.mockMvc = MockMvcBuilders.standaloneSetup
  (new BasicModelMapController())
  .setViewResolvers(viewResolver()).build();
```

Writing the Test method

The complete `Test` method is shown in the following code:

```
@Test
public void basicTest() throws Exception {
  this.mockMvc
```

```
    .perform(
    get("/welcome-model-map")
    .accept(MediaType.parseMediaType
    ("application/html;charset=UTF-8")))
    .andExpect(model().attribute("name", "XYZ"))
    .andExpect(view().name("welcome-model-map"));
}
```

A number of important elements to note include the following:

- `get("/welcome-model-map")`: This executes a `GET` request to the specified URL.
- `model().attribute("name", "XYZ")`: `ResultMatcher` checks whether the model contains the specified attribute, `name`, with the specified value, `XYZ`.
- `view().name("welcome-model-map")`: `ResultMatcher` checks whether the View name returned is as specified.

Flow 4 – controller redirecting to a View with ModelAndView

We will skip discussing unit testing for this flow as it is similar to *Flow 3 – controller redirecting to a View with Model*. We would need to check whether the expected View name is returned.

Flow 5 – controller redirecting to a View with a form

We will discuss unit testing for *Flow 5* in combination with *Flow 6* in the next section.

Flow 6 – adding validation to the previous flow

In *Flow 5* and *Flow 6*, we created a simple form with fields and validations. We will focus on unit testing the validation errors. We will write a test for an empty form, which triggers four validation errors.

Controller setup

The controller setup is very simple:

```
this.mockMvc = MockMvcBuilders.standaloneSetup(
                            new
    UserValidationController()).build();
```

The Test method

The complete `Test` method is listed as follows:

```
@Test
public void basicTest_WithAllValidationErrors() throws Exception {
    this.mockMvc
        .perform(
            post("/create-user-with-validation")
.accept(MediaType.parseMediaType("application/html;charset=UTF-8")))
        .andExpect(status().isOk())
        .andExpect(model().errorCount(4))
        .andExpect(model().attributeHasFieldErrorCode("user", "name",
"Size"));
    }
```

The following definitions explain the workings of the preceding code block:

- `post("/create-user-with-validation")`: This creates an HTTP POST request to the specified URI. Since we are not passing any request parameters, all attributes are null. This will trigger validation errors.
- `model().errorCount(4)`: This checks whether there are four validation errors on the model.
- `model().attributeHasFieldErrorCode("user", "name", "Size")`: This checks whether the `user` attribute has a `name` field with the validation error named `Size`.

Writing integration tests for Spring MVC controllers

In the earlier section, we wrote unit tests for controllers—ones that only load up the specific controllers that are being tested.

The other kind of tests we can write are basic integration tests—launching up the entire application—that is, the entire Spring context.

We will focus on testing *Flow 1*. The following example launches the entire Spring context, launching all controllers:

```
@RunWith(SpringRunner.class)
@WebAppConfiguration
@ContextConfiguration("file:src/main/webapp/WEB-INF/user-web-
context.xml")
public class BasicControllerSpringConfigurationIT {

    private MockMvc mockMvc;

    @Autowired
    private WebApplicationContext wac;

    @Before
    public void setup() {
      this.mockMvc = MockMvcBuilders.webAppContextSetup
                                (this.wac).build();
    }
}
```

The following definitions explain the workings of the preceding code block:

- `@RunWith(SpringRunner.class)`: `SpringRunner` helps us to launch a Spring context.
- `@WebAppConfiguration`: This is used to launch a web app context with Spring MVC.
- `@ContextConfiguration("file:src/main/webapp/WEB-INF/user-web-context.xml")`: This specifies the location of the Spring context XML.
- `this.mockMvc = MockMvcBuilders.webAppContextSetup(this.wac).build()`: In the earlier examples, we used a standalone setup. However, in this example, we want to launch the entire web app. Hence, we use `webAppContextSetup`.

The execution of the test is very similar to how we did it in earlier tests. It is shown in the following code:

```
@Test
public void basicTest() throws Exception {
    this.mockMvc
        .perform(get("/welcome")
.accept(MediaType.parseMediaType("application/html;charset=UTF-8")))
```

```
        .andExpect(status().isOk())
        .andExpect(content().string("Welcome to Spring MVC"));
  }
```

We make a call to `/welcome` and check whether the content is as expected.

Spring Security

Security is a critical component of every application. Authentication is the process of establishing a user's identity. Authentication involves verifying that the user is who they claim to be. Typically, a user ID/password combination is used for authentication.

Authorization is the act of checking whether the user has access to perform a specific action.

- Can the user view a page?
- Can the user edit a page?
- Can the user delete a page?

A best practice is to enforce authentication and authorization on every page in the application. User credentials and their authorizations should be verified before executing any request on a web application.

Spring Security provides a comprehensive security solution for Java EE enterprise applications. While providing great support to Spring-based (and Spring MVC-based) applications, it can be integrated with other frameworks as well.

The following list highlights some of the vast range of authentication mechanisms that Spring Security supports:

- **Form-based authentication**: Simple integration for basic applications
- **LDAP**: Typically used in most Enterprise applications
- **Java Authentication and Authorization Service (JAAS)**: Authentication and authorization standard; part of Java EE standard specification
- Container-managed authentication
- Custom authentication systems

In this chapter, we will focus on Spring Security from the perspective of a web application.

Let's consider a simple example to enable Spring Security on the simple web application. We will use an in-memory configuration.

The steps involved are as follows:

1. Add the Spring Security dependency.
2. Configure the interception of all requests.
3. Configure Spring Security.
4. Add the logout functionality.

Adding the Spring Security dependency

We will start by adding the Spring Security dependencies to pom.xml:

```
<dependency>
  <groupId>org.springframework.security</groupId>
  <artifactId>spring-security-web</artifactId>
</dependency>

<dependency>
  <groupId>org.springframework.security</groupId>
  <artifactId>spring-security-config</artifactId>
</dependency>
```

The dependencies incorporated are spring-security-web and spring-security-config.

Configuring a filter to intercept all requests

The best practice when implementing security is to validate all incoming requests. We would want our security framework to look at the incoming request, authenticate the user, and allow the action to be performed only if the user has access to perform the operation. We will make use of a filter to intercept and validate the request. The following example shows more details.

We want to configure Spring Security to intercept all requests to a web application. We will use a filter, DelegatingFilterProxy, which delegates to a Spring-managed bean, FilterChainProxy:

```
<filter>
  <filter-name>springSecurityFilterChain</filter-name>
  <filter-class>
    org.springframework.web.filter.DelegatingFilterProxy
  </filter-class>
</filter>

<filter-mapping>
  <filter-name>springSecurityFilterChain</filter-name>
  <url-pattern>/*</url-pattern>
</filter-mapping>
```

Now, all requests to our web application will go through the filter. However, we have not yet configured anything related to security. Let's use a simple Java configuration example:

```
@Configuration
@EnableWebSecurity
public class SecurityConfiguration extends
    WebSecurityConfigurerAdapter {

  @Autowired
  public void configureGlobalSecurity (AuthenticationManagerBuilder
auth)
      throws Exception {
    auth
     .inMemoryAuthentication()
     .withUser("firstuser").password("password1")
     .roles("USER", "ADMIN");
  }
  @Override
  protected void configure(HttpSecurity http)throws Exception {
    http
      .authorizeRequests()
      .antMatchers("/login").permitAll()
      .antMatchers("/*secure*/**")
      .access("hasRole('USER')")
      .and().formLogin();
  }
}
```

The following definitions explain the workings of the preceding code block:

- `@EnableWebSecurity`: This annotation enables any `Configuration` class to contain the definition of Spring configuration. In this specific instance, we override a couple of methods to provide our specific Spring MVC configuration.
- `WebSecurityConfigurerAdapter`: This class provides a base class to create a Spring configuration (`WebSecurityConfigurer`).
- `protected void configure(HttpSecurity http)`: This method provides the security needs for different URLs.
- `antMatchers("/*secure*/**").access("hasRole('USER')")`: You need the role of `USER` to access any URL containing the `secure` sub-string.
- `antMatchers("/login").permitAll()`: This permits access to the login page to all users.
- `public void configureGlobalSecurity(AuthenticationManagerBuilder auth)`: In this example, we are using in-memory authentication. This can be used to connect to a database (`auth.jdbcAuthentication()`), or LDAP (`auth.ldapAuthentication()`), or a custom authentication provider (created extending `AuthenticationProvider`).
- `withUser("firstuser").password("password1")`: This configures an in-memory valid user ID and password combination.
- `.roles("USER", "ADMIN")`: This assigns roles to the user.

When we try to access any secure URLs, we will be redirected to a login page. Spring Security provides ways of customizing the login page, as well as the redirection. Only authenticated users with the correct roles will be allowed to access the secured application pages.

Logout

Spring Security provides features to enable a user to log out and be redirected to a specified page. The URI of the `LogoutController` is typically mapped to the `logout` link in the UI. The complete listing of `LogoutController` is as follows:

```
@Controller
public class LogoutController {

    @RequestMapping(value = "/secure/logout", method = RequestMethod.GET)
    public String logout(HttpServletRequest request, HttpServletResponse response) {
```

```
        Authentication auth =
SecurityContextHolder.getContext().getAuthentication();

        if (auth != null) {
            new SecurityContextLogoutHandler()
                    .logout(request, response, auth);
            request.getSession().invalidate();
          }

        return "redirect:/secure/welcome";

      }

    }
```

The following definitions explain the workings of the preceding code block:

- `if (auth != null)`: If there is a valid authentication, end the session.
- `new SecurityContextLogoutHandler().logout(request, response, auth)`: `SecurityContextLogoutHandler` performs a logout by removing the authentication information from `SecurityContextHolder`.
- `return "redirect:/secure/welcome"`: This redirects to the secure welcome page.

Summary

In this chapter, we discussed the basics of developing web applications with Spring MVC.

We used six example flows with Spring MVC to learn the important concepts related to developing web applications.

We learned about the key components of Spring MVC architecture—`DispatcherServlet`, Controllers, Views, and View Resolvers. `DispatcherServlet` acts as the FrontController—routing the requests to appropriate controllers and views as they arrive.

We also discussed how to manage user states using sessions and learned how to implement exception handling and internationalization for web applications. We also learned to secure our applications with Spring Security.

Spring MVC can also be used to build REST services. We will discuss that and more related to REST services in the subsequent chapters.

In the next chapter, we will get started with Spring Boot. We will learn the need for Spring Boot and how Spring Boot helps you to get started with developing Spring applications in less than five minutes.

Further reading

- Spring official website: `https://spring.io/`
- Spring MVC documentation: `https://docs.spring.io/spring/docs/current/spring-framework-reference/web.html`
- Spring Getting Started guides: `https://spring.io/guides`

Getting Started with Spring Boot

4

In the previous chapter, we created a web application with Spring MVC. Creating a new application with Spring framework involves a number of steps. You need to decide on the frameworks to use, and then you need to configure the frameworks and integrate them. Before you build your first use case, you need to set up a number of technical features—exception handling, application configuration, and so on.

But how about having all these for free when we create a new application?

Spring Boot aims to solve the problem of starting off quickly with a new application. In this chapter, we will understand the capabilities Spring Boot brings to the table. We will answer the following questions:

- Why Spring Boot?
- What are the features that Spring Boot provides?
- What is auto configuration?
- What is Spring Boot not?
- What happens in the background when you use Spring Boot?
- How do you use **SPRING INITIALIZR** to create new Spring Boot projects?
- How do you monitor applications using Spring Boot?
- What is the Spring Boot Actuator?
- How can you become productive with Spring Boot?

Technical requirements

The following are the requirements for this chapter:

- Your favorite IDE, Eclipse
- Java 8+
- Maven 3.x
- Internet connectivity

The GitHub link for this chapter can be found at `https://github.com/PacktPublishing/` `Mastering-Spring-5.1/tree/master/Chapter04`.

What is Spring Boot?

First of all, let's start by clearing up a few misconceptions regarding Spring Boot:

- Spring Boot is not a code generation framework. It does not generate any code.
- Spring Boot is neither an application server nor a web server. It provides good integration with different ranges of applications and web servers.
- Spring Boot does not implement any specific frameworks or specifications.

These questions still remain:

- What is Spring Boot?
- Why is it one of the best options available in terms of building Java applications today?

To answer these questions, let's build a quick example. Let's consider an example application that you want to quickly prototype.

Steps involved in building a quick prototype for an application

Let's say we want to build an application with Spring MVC and use JPA (with Hibernate as the implementation) to connect to the database.

Let's consider the steps in setting up such an application:

1. Decide which versions of Spring MVC, JPA, and Hibernate to use.
2. Set up a Spring context to wire all the different layers together.
3. Set up a web layer with Spring MVC (including Spring MVC configuration):
   - Configure beans for `DispatcherServlet`, `handler`, `resolvers`, view resolvers, and so on
4. Set up Hibernate in the data layer:
   - Configure beans for `SessionFactory`, data source, and so on
5. Decide and implement how to store your application configuration, which varies between different environments.
6. Decide how you would want to perform your unit testing.
7. Decide and implement your transaction management strategy.
8. Decide and implement how to implement security.
9. Set up your logging framework.
10. Decide and implement how you want to monitor your application in production.
11. Decide and implement a metrics management system to provide statistics about the application.
12. Decide and implement how to deploy your application to a web or application server.

 At least a few of the steps have to be completed before we can start with building our business logic—and this might take a few weeks at the least.

When we build an application, we want to make a quick start. All the preceding steps will not make it easy to develop an application. And that's the problem Spring Boot aims to solve.

Spring Boot allows developers to focus on the business logic behind their microservice. It aims to take care of all the nitty-gritty technical details involved in developing microservices.

Primary goals of Spring Boot

The primary goals of Spring Boot are as follows:

- To allow you to get off the ground quickly with Spring-based projects.
- Be opinionated. Make default assumptions based on common usage. Provide configuration options to handle deviations from defaults.
- To provide a wide range of non-functional features out of the box.
- To avoid using code generation and avoid using a lot of XML configuration.

Understanding Spring Boot's non-functional features

A few of the non-functional features provided by Spring Boot are as follows:

- Default handling of versioning and configuration of a wide range of frameworks, servers, and specifications
- Default options for application security
- Default application metrics, with options to extend
- Basic application monitoring using health checks
- Multiple options for externalized configuration

Building a Hello World application with Spring Boot

We will start by building our first Spring Boot application in this chapter. We will use Maven to manage dependencies.

The following steps are involved in starting up with a Spring Boot application:

1. Configure `spring-boot-starter-parent` in your `pom.xml` file.
2. Configure the `pom.xml` file with the required starter projects.
3. Configure `spring-boot-maven-plugin` to be able to run the application.
4. Create your first Spring Boot `launch` class.

Creating pom.xml with spring-boot-starter-parent

Let's start with a simple pom.xml file with spring-boot-starter-parent:

```xml
<project xmlns="http://maven.apache.org/POM/4.0.0"
 xmlns:xsi="http://www.w3.org/2001/XMLSchema-instance"
 xsi:schemaLocation="http://maven.apache.org/POM/4.0.0
 http://maven.apache.org/xsd/maven-4.0.0.xsd">
<modelVersion>4.0.0</modelVersion>
<groupId>com.mastering.spring</groupId>
<artifactId>springboot-example</artifactId>
<version>0.0.1-SNAPSHOT</version>
<name>First Spring Boot Example</name>
<packaging>war</packaging>
<parent>
    <groupId>org.springframework.boot</groupId>
    <artifactId>spring-boot-starter-parent</artifactId>
    <version>2.1.1.RELEASE</version>
</parent>

<properties>
    <java.version>1.8</java.version>
</properties>

<repositories>
 <repository>
    <id>spring-milestones</id>
    <name>Spring Milestones</name>
    <url>https://repo.spring.io/milestone</url>
    <snapshots>
      <enabled>false</enabled>
    </snapshots>
 </repository>
</repositories>

<pluginRepositories>
 <pluginRepository>
    <id>spring-milestones</id>
    <name>Spring Milestones</name>
    <url>https://repo.spring.io/milestone</url>
      <snapshots>
        <enabled>false</enabled>
      </snapshots>
  </pluginRepository>
  </pluginRepositories>

</project>
```

The first question is this—why do we need `spring-boot-starter-parent`?

The `spring-boot-starter-parent` dependency contains the default versions of Java to use, the default versions of dependencies that Spring Boot uses, and the default configuration of the Maven plugins.

 The `spring-boot-starter-parent` dependency is the parent POM providing dependency and plugin management for Spring Boot-based applications.

Now, let's look at some of the code inside `spring-boot-starter-parent` to obtain a deeper understanding of `spring-boot-starter-parent`.

Understanding spring-boot-starter-parent

The `spring-boot-starter-parent` dependency inherits from `spring-boot-dependencies`, which is defined at the top of the POM. The following code snippet shows an extract from `spring-boot-starter-parent`:

```
<parent>
  <groupId>org.springframework.boot</groupId>
  <artifactId>spring-boot-dependencies</artifactId>
  <relativePath>../../spring-boot-dependencies</relativePath>
</parent>
```

`spring-boot-dependencies` provides default dependency management for all the dependencies that Spring Boot uses. The following code shows the different versions of various dependencies that are configured in `spring-boot-dependencies`:

```
<activemq.version>5.15.8</activemq.version>
<aspectj.version>1.9.2</aspectj.version>
<ehcache.version>2.10.6</ehcache.version>
<elasticsearch.version>6.4.3</elasticsearch.version>
<gson.version>2.8.5</gson.version>
<h2.version>1.4.197</h2.version>
<hazelcast.version>3.11</hazelcast.version>
<hibernate.version>5.3.7.Final</hibernate.version>
<hibernate-validator.version>6.0.13.Final</hibernate-validator.version>
<hsqldb.version>2.4.1</hsqldb.version>
<htmlunit.version>2.33</htmlunit.version>
<jackson.version>2.9.7</jackson.version>
<jersey.version>2.27</jersey.version>
<jetty.version>9.4.12.v20180830</jetty.version>
<junit.version>4.12</junit.version>
```

```
<junit-jupiter.version>5.3.2</junit-jupiter.version>
<mockito.version>2.23.4</mockito.version>
<selenium.version>3.14.0</selenium.version>
<servlet-api.version>4.0.1</servlet-api.version>
<spring.version>5.1.3.RELEASE</spring.version>
<spring-amqp.version>2.1.2.RELEASE</spring-amqp.version>
<spring-batch.version>4.1.0.RELEASE</spring-batch.version>
<spring-hateoas.version>0.25.0.RELEASE</spring-hateoas.version>
<spring-restdocs.version>2.0.2.RELEASE</spring-restdocs.version>
<spring-security.version>5.1.2.RELEASE</spring-security.version>
<spring-ws.version>3.0.4.RELEASE</spring-ws.version>
<tomcat.version>9.0.13</tomcat.version>
<xml-apis.version>1.4.01</xml-apis.version>
```

If we want to override a specific version of a dependency, we can do that by providing a property with the correct name in the pom.xml file of our application. The following code snippet shows an example of configuring a specific version of Mockito:

```
<properties>
  <mockito.version>1.10.20</mockito.version>
</properties>
```

The following are some of the other things that are defined in spring-boot-starter-parent:

- The default Java version, <java.version>1.8</java.version>.
- The default configuration for Maven plugins:
    - maven-failsafe-plugin
    - maven-surefire-plugin
    - git-commit-id-plugin

Compatibility between different versions of frameworks is one of the major problems that's faced by developers.

How do I find the latest Spring Session version that is compatible with a specific version of Spring? The usual answer would be to read the documentation.

However, if we use Spring Boot, this is made simple by spring-boot-starter-parent. If we want to upgrade to a newer Spring version, all we need to do is find the spring-boot-starter-parent dependency for that Spring version.

Once we upgrade our application to use that specific version of `spring-boot-starter-parent`, we would have all the other dependencies upgraded to the versions that are compatible with the new Spring version. Hence, this is one less problem for developers to handle, which is something that always makes me happy.

Configuring pom.xml with starter projects

One of the first steps of building applications with Spring Boot is to identify the appropriate starter projects. You might be wondering: what are starter projects? Let's get started.

Understanding starter projects

Starters are simplified dependency descriptors that are customized for different purposes. This sounds somewhat technical, so let's break it down.

Let's consider one of the most popular starter projects, called Spring Boot Starter Web (`spring-boot-starter-web`). It is used to build web applications, including RESTful APIs, with Spring and Spring MVC frameworks.

Spring Boot Starter Web (`spring-boot-starter-web`) comes built in with all the frameworks that are typically used to build web applications:

- Spring MVC
- Compatible versions of `jackson-databind` (for binding) and `hibernate-validator` (for form validation)
- `spring-boot-starter-tomcat` (starter project for Tomcat)

The following code snippet shows some of the dependencies that are configured in `spring-boot-starter-web`:

```xml
<dependencies>
  <dependency>
    <groupId>org.springframework.boot</groupId>
    <artifactId>spring-boot-starter</artifactId>
  </dependency>
  <dependency>
    <groupId>org.springframework.boot</groupId>
    <artifactId>spring-boot-starter-tomcat</artifactId>
  </dependency>
  <dependency>
    <groupId>org.hibernate</groupId>
```

```
        <artifactId>hibernate-validator</artifactId>
    </dependency>

    <dependency>
        <groupId>com.fasterxml.jackson.core</groupId>
        <artifactId>jackson-databind</artifactId>
    </dependency>

    <dependency>
        <groupId>org.springframework</groupId>
        <artifactId>spring-web</artifactId>
    </dependency>

    <dependency>
        <groupId>org.springframework</groupId>
        <artifactId>spring-webmvc</artifactId>
    </dependency>

</dependencies>
```

For the web application that we would like to build, we also want to do some good unit testing and deploy it on Tomcat. The following snippet shows the different starter dependencies that we would need. We would need to add this to our pom.xml file:

```
<dependencies>

    <dependency>
        <groupId>org.springframework.boot</groupId>
        <artifactId>spring-boot-starter-web</artifactId>
    </dependency>

    <dependency>
        <groupId>org.springframework.boot</groupId>
        <artifactId>spring-boot-starter-test</artifactId>
        <scope>test</scope>
    </dependency>

    <dependency>
        <groupId>org.springframework.boot</groupId>
        <artifactId>spring-boot-starter-tomcat</artifactId>
        <scope>provided</scope>
    </dependency>

</dependencies>
```

We added three starter projects:

- We've already discussed `spring-boot-starter-web`. This provides us with the frameworks that are required to build a web application with Spring MVC.
- The `spring-boot-starter-test` dependency provides the following test frameworks that are needed for unit testing:
  - **JUnit**: The basic unit test framework
  - **Mockito**: For mocking
  - **Hamcrest, AssertJ**: For readable asserts
  - **Spring Test**: A unit testing framework for Spring context-based applications
- `spring-boot-starter-tomcat` is the starter for using Tomcat as the embedded servlet container. It is included by default for running web applications. We include it explicitly for clarity.

We now have our `pom.xml` file configured with the starter parent and the required starter projects. Now, let's add `spring-boot-maven-plugin`, which will allow us to run Spring Boot applications.

Configuring spring-boot-maven-plugin

When we build applications using Spring Boot, there are a couple of situations that are possible:

- We want to run the applications in place without building a JAR or a WAR.
- We want to build a JAR and a WAR for later deployment.

The `spring-boot-maven-plugin` dependency provides capabilities for both of the preceding situations. The following snippet shows how we can configure `spring-boot-maven-plugin` in an application:

```
<build>
 <plugins>
  <plugin>
    <groupId>org.springframework.boot</groupId>
    <artifactId>spring-boot-maven-plugin</artifactId>
  </plugin>
 </plugins>
</build>
```

The `spring-boot-maven-plugin` dependency provides several goals for a Spring Boot application. The most popular goal is run (this can be executed as `mvn spring-boot:run` on the command prompt from the root folder of the project).

Creating your first Spring Boot launch class

The following class explains how to create a simple Spring Boot launch class. It uses the static run method from the `SpringApplication` class, as shown in the following code snippet:

```
package com.mastering.spring.springboot;

import org.springframework.boot.SpringApplication;
import org.springframework.boot.autoconfigure.SpringBootApplication;
import org.springframework.context.ApplicationContext;
@SpringBootApplication
public class Application {

    public static void main(String[] args){
        ApplicationContext ctx =
SpringApplication.run(Application.class,args);
    }

}
```

The preceding code is a simple Java `main` method executing the static `run` method on the `SpringApplication` class.

Understanding the SpringApplication class

The `SpringApplication` class can be used to Bootstrap and launch a Spring application from a Java `main` method.

The following are the steps that are typically performed when a Spring Boot application is bootstrapped:

1. Create an instance of Spring's `ApplicationContext`.
2. Enable the functionality to accept command-line arguments and expose them as Spring properties.
3. Load all the Spring beans as per the configuration.

Requirements for the @SpringBootApplication annotation

The `@SpringBootApplication` annotation is a shortcut for three annotations:

- `@Configuration`: This indicates that this is a Spring application context configuration file.
- `@EnableAutoConfiguration`: This enables auto configuration, an important feature of Spring Boot. We will discuss auto configuration later in a separate section.
- `@ComponentScan`: This enables scanning for Spring beans in the package of this class and all its subpackages.

Running our Hello World application

We can run the Hello World application in multiple ways. Let's start running it with the simplest option—running as a Java application. In your IDE, right-click on the application **class** and run it as a **Java Application**. The following screenshot shows some of the log from running our `Hello World` application:

```
  |
 /\\ /___'_ _ _(_)_ __ __ _ \ \ \ \
( ( )\___ | '_ | '_| | '_ \/ _` | \ \ \ \
 \\/  ___)| |_)| | | | | || (_| |  ) ) ) )
  '  |____| .__|_| |_|_| |_\__, | / / / /
 =========|_|==============|___/=/_/_/_/
 :: Spring Boot ::        (v2.1.1.RELEASE)

2019-01-08 12:12:40.966  INFO 4535 --- [           main] c.m.spring.springboot.Application        : Starting Application on Rangas-MacBook-Pro.local with PID 4535 (
2019-01-08 12:12:40.975  INFO 4535 --- [           main] c.m.spring.springboot.Application        : No active profile set, falling back to default profiles: default
2019-01-08 12:12:45.463  INFO 4535 --- [           main] o.s.b.w.embedded.tomcat.TomcatWebServer  : Tomcat initialized with port(s): 8080 (http)
2019-01-08 12:12:45.591  INFO 4535 --- [           main] o.apache.catalina.core.StandardService   : Starting service [Tomcat]
2019-01-08 12:12:45.591  INFO 4535 --- [           main] org.apache.catalina.core.StandardEngine  : Starting Servlet Engine: Apache Tomcat/9.0.13
2019-01-08 12:12:45.619  INFO 4535 --- [           main] o.a.catalina.core.AprLifecycleListener   : The APR based Apache Tomcat Native library which allows optimal
2019-01-08 12:12:45.975  INFO 4535 --- [           main] o.a.c.c.C.[Tomcat].[localhost].[/]       : Initializing Spring embedded WebApplicationContext
2019-01-08 12:12:45.975  INFO 4535 --- [           main] o.s.web.context.ContextLoader            : Root WebApplicationContext: initialization completed in 4766 ms
2019-01-08 12:12:46.866  INFO 4535 --- [           main] o.s.s.concurrent.ThreadPoolTaskExecutor  : Initializing ExecutorService 'applicationTaskExecutor'
2019-01-08 12:12:47.872  INFO 4535 --- [           main] o.s.b.w.embedded.tomcat.TomcatWebServer  : Tomcat started on port(s): 8080 (http) with context path ''
2019-01-08 12:12:47.891  INFO 4535 --- [           main] c.m.spring.springboot.Application        : Started Application in 8.056 seconds (JVM running for 9.112)
application
```

The following are some key things to note:

- The Tomcat server is launched on port `8080`—`Tomcat started on port(s): 8080 (http)`.
- `DispatcherServlet` is configured. This means that the Spring MVC Framework is ready to accept requests – `Mapping servlet: 'dispatcherServlet' to [/]`.

- Four filters—`characterEncodingFilter`, `hiddenHttpMethodFilter`, `httpPutFormContentFilter`, and `requestContextFilter`—are enabled by default.
- The default error page is configured—`Mapped "{[/error]}" onto public org.springframework.http.ResponseEntity<java.util.Map<java.lang.String, java.lang.Object>> org.springframework.boot.autoconfigure.web.BasicErrorController .error(javax.servlet.http.HttpServletRequest)`.
- WebJars are auto configured. As we discussed in `Chapter 3`, *Building Web Applications with Spring MVC*, WebJars enable dependency management for static dependencies such as Bootstrap and query – `Mapped URL path [/webjars/**] onto handler of type [class org.springframework.web.servlet.resource.ResourceHttpRequestHandler]`.

The following screenshot shows the current application layout. We have just two files, `pom.xml` and `Application.java`:

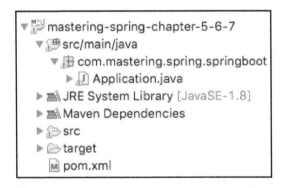

With a simple `pom.xml` file and one Java class, we were able to launch the Spring MVC application, with all the preceding functionality described. The most important thing about Spring Boot is to understand what happens in the background. Understanding the preceding startup log is the first. Let's look at the Maven dependencies to obtain a deeper picture.

The following screenshot shows some of the dependencies that are configured with the basic configuration in the `pom.xml` file that we created:

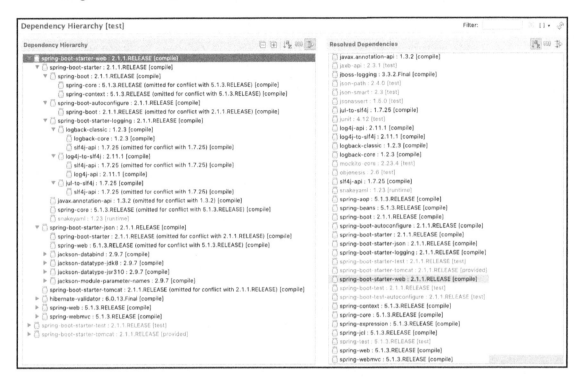

 As you can see, Spring Boot brings in different versions of different dependencies. To understand the dependencies and the versions that are included with a specific version of Spring boot, look at the `pom.xml` file in **spring-boot-dependencies**. Here's an example: `https://github.com/spring-projects/spring-boot/blob/master/spring-boot-project/spring-boot-dependencies/pom.xml`.

Spring Boot performs a lot of magic. Once you have the application configured and running, I recommend that you play around with it to gain a deeper understanding that will be useful when you are debugging problems.

 As Spiderman says, *with great power, comes great responsibility*. This is absolutely true in the case of Spring Boot. In the future, the developers who work best with Spring Boot will be the ones who understand what happens in the background—dependencies and auto configuration.

Understanding the magic of AutoConfiguration

To understand auto configuration further, let's expand our application class and include a few more lines of code:

```
ApplicationContext ctx = SpringApplication.run(Application.class,
  args);
String[] beanNames = ctx.getBeanDefinitionNames();
Arrays.sort(beanNames);

for (String beanName : beanNames) {
  System.out.println(beanName);
}
```

We get all the beans that are defined in the Spring application context and print their names. When `Application.java` is run as a Java program, it prints the list of beans, as shown in the following output:

```
application
basicErrorController
//Truncated
characterEncodingFilter
conventionErrorViewResolver
defaultServletHandlerMapping
defaultViewResolver
//Truncated
jacksonObjectMapper
jacksonObjectMapperBuilder
//Truncated
mvcValidator
mvcViewResolver
propertySourcesPlaceholderConfigurer
//Truncated
stringHttpMessageConverter
viewResolver
```

Some important elements to consider are as follows:

- Where are these beans defined?
- How are these beans created?

That's the magic of Spring auto configuration.

Whenever we add a new dependency to a Spring Boot project, Spring Boot auto configuration automatically tries to configure the beans based on the dependency.

For example, when we add a dependency to `spring-boot-starter-web`, the following beans are auto-configured:

- `basicErrorController`, and `handlerExceptionResolver`: Basic exception handling. This shows a default error page when an exception occurs.
- `beanNameHandlerMapping`: Used to resolve paths to a handler (controller).
- `characterEncodingFilter`: Provides default character encoding UTF-8.
- `dispatcherServlet`: DispatcherServlet is the Front Controller in Spring MVC applications.
- `jacksonObjectMapper`: Translates objects to JSON and JSON to objects in REST services.
- `messageConverters`: The default message converters to convert from objects into XML or JSON, and vice versa.
- `multipartResolver`: Provides support to upload files in web applications.
- `mvcValidator`: Supports the validation of HTTP requests.
- `viewResolver`: Resolves a logical view name to a physical view.
- `propertySourcesPlaceholderConfigurer`: Supports the externalization of application configuration.
- `requestContextFilter`: Defaults the filter for requests.
- `restTemplateBuilder`: Used to make calls to REST services.
- `tomcatEmbeddedServletContainerFactory`: Tomcat is the default embedded servlet container for Spring Boot-based web applications.

In the next section, we'll look at some of the starter projects and the auto configuration they provide.

Exploring Spring Boot starter projects

The following table shows some of the important starter projects provided by Spring Boot:

Starter	Description
`spring-boot-starter-web-services`	This is a starter project to develop XML-based web services.
`spring-boot-starter-web`	This is a starter project to build Spring MVC-based web applications or RESTful applications. It uses Tomcat as the default embedded servlet container.
`spring-boot-starter-activemq`	This supports message-based communication using JMS on ActiveMQ.

`spring-boot-starter-integration`	This supports the Spring Integration Framework, which provides implementations for Enterprise Integration Patterns.
`spring-boot-starter-test`	This provides support for various unit testing frameworks, such as JUnit, Mockito, and Hamcrest matchers.
`spring-boot-starter-jdbc`	This provides support for using Spring JDBC. It configures a Tomcat JDBC connection pool by default.
`spring-boot-starter-validation`	This provides support for the Java Bean Validation API. Its default implementation is hibernate-validator.
`spring-boot-starter-hateoas`	HATEOAS stands for Hypermedia as the Engine of Application State. RESTful services that use HATEOAS return links to additional resources that are related to the current context in addition to data.
`spring-boot-starter-jersey`	JAX-RS is the Java EE standard to develop REST APIs. Jersey is the default implementation. This starter project provides support to build JAX-RS-based REST APIs.
`spring-boot-starter-websocket`	HTTP is stateless. WebSockets allow you to maintain a connection between the server and the browser. This starter project provides support for Spring WebSockets.
`spring-boot-starter-aop`	This provides support for aspect-oriented programming. It also provides support for AspectJ for advanced aspect-oriented programming.
`spring-boot-starter-amqp`	With RabbitMQ as the default, this starter project provides message passing with AMQP.
`spring-boot-starter-security`	This starter project enables auto configuration for Spring Security.
`spring-boot-starter-data-jpa`	This provides support for Spring Data JPA. Its default implementation is Hibernate.
`spring-boot-starter`	This is a base starter for Spring Boot applications. It provides support for auto configuration and logging.
`spring-boot-starter-batch`	This provides support to develop batch applications using Spring Batch.
`spring-boot-starter-cache`	This is the basic support for caching using Spring Framework.
`spring-boot-starter-data-rest`	This is the support to expose REST services using Spring Data REST.

Up until now, we have set up a basic web application and understood some of the important concepts related to Spring Boot, including the following:

- `AutoConfiguration`
- Starter projects

- `spring-boot-maven-plugin`
- `spring-boot-starter-parent`
- The `@SpringBootApplication` **annotation**

In this section, we adopted the manual approach of creating a web application with Spring Boot.

Do you know that we could have autogenerated this application in a few simple steps? Let's look at that in the next section.

Getting started with SPRING INITIALIZR

Do you want to autogenerate Spring Boot projects? Do you want to quickly get started with developing your application?

SPRING INITIALIZR is the answer.

SPRING INITIALIZR is hosted at `http://start.spring.io`. The following screenshot shows how the website appears when you visit it:

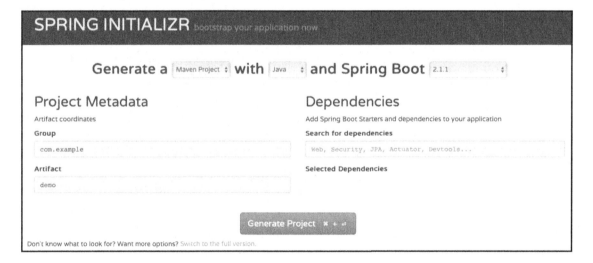

SPRING INITIALIZR provides a lot of flexibility in creating projects. You have options to do the following:

- Choose your build tool—Maven or Gradle.
- Choose the Spring Boot version you want to use.
- Configure a **Group ID** and **Artifact ID** for your component.
- Choose the starters (dependencies) that you want for your project. You can click on the link at the bottom of the screen, **Switch to the full version**, to see all the starter projects you can choose from.
- Choose how to package your component: JAR or WAR.
- Choose the Java version you want to use.
- Choose the JVM language you want to use.

The following screenshot shows some of the options **SPRING INITIALIZR** provides when you expand (click on the link) to the full version:

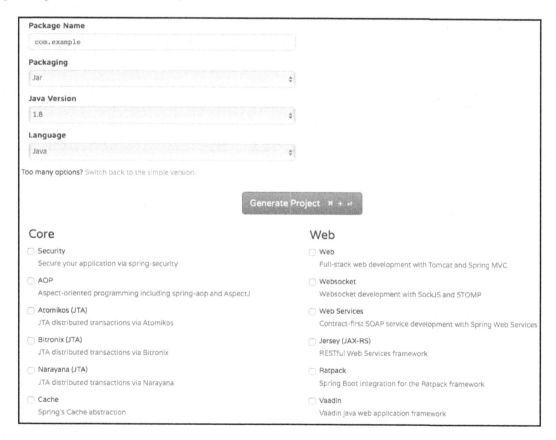

Creating your first SPRING INITIALIZR project

We will use the full version and enter the values, as follows:

Things to note include the following:

- **Build tool**: `Maven`.
- **Spring Boot version**: Choose the latest available.
- **Group**: `com.mastering.spring`.
- **Artifact**: `first-spring-initializr`.
- **Selected dependencies**: Choose `Web`, `JPA`, `Actuator`, `Dev Tools`. Type in each one of these in the textbox and press *Enter* to choose them. We will learn more about Actuator and Dev tools in the next section.
- **Java version**: `1.8`.

Go ahead and click on the **Generate Project** button. This will create a `.zip` file that you can download to your computer.

The following screenshot shows the structure of the project that's created:

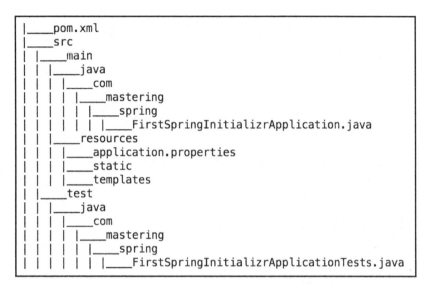

```
|_____pom.xml
|_____src
|  |_____main
|  |  |_____java
|  |  |  |_____com
|  |  |  |  |_____mastering
|  |  |  |  |  |_____spring
|  |  |  |  |  |_____FirstSpringInitializrApplication.java
|  |  |_____resources
|  |  |  |_____application.properties
|  |  |  |_____static
|  |  |  |_____templates
|  |_____test
|  |  |_____java
|  |  |  |_____com
|  |  |  |  |_____mastering
|  |  |  |  |  |_____spring
|  |  |  |  |  |_____FirstSpringInitializrApplicationTests.java
```

We will now import this project into our IDE. In Eclipse, you can perform the following steps:

1. Launch Eclipse.
2. Navigate to **File | Import**.
3. Choose the existing Maven projects.
4. Browse and select the folder that is the root of the Maven project (the one containing the `pom.xml` file).
5. Proceed with the defaults and click on **Finish**.

This will import the project into Eclipse. The following screenshot shows the structure of the project in Eclipse:

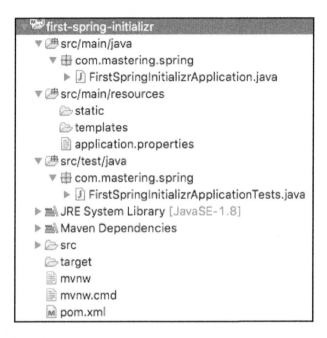

Now, let's look at some of the important files from the generated project.

Exploring pom.xml

The following snippet shows the dependencies that are declared:

```
<dependencies>

  <dependency>
    <groupId>org.springframework.boot</groupId>
    <artifactId>spring-boot-starter-web</artifactId>
  </dependency>

  <dependency>
    <groupId>org.springframework.boot</groupId>
    <artifactId>spring-boot-starter-data-jpa</artifactId>
  </dependency>

  <dependency>
    <groupId>org.springframework.boot</groupId>
```

```
        <artifactId>spring-boot-starter-actuator</artifactId>
    </dependency>

    <!-- Test dependency and DEV Tools removed for brevity-->

</dependencies>
```

A few other important observations are as follows:

- The packaging for this component is .jar.
- org.springframework.boot:spring-boot-starter-parent is declared as the parent POM.
- <java.version>1.8</java.version>: The Java version is 1.8.
- Spring Boot Maven Plugin (org.springframework.boot:spring-boot-maven-plugin) is configured as a plugin.

Understanding the FirstSpringInitializrApplication.java class

FirstSpringInitializrApplication.java is the launcher for Spring Boot:

```
package com.mastering.spring;

import org.springframework.boot.SpringApplication;
import org.springframework.boot.autoconfigure.SpringBootApplication;

@SpringBootApplication
public class FirstSpringInitializrApplication {

    public static void main(String[] args) {
        SpringApplication.run(FirstSpringInitializrApplication.class,
args);
    }

}
```

Looking at the tests – the FirstSpringInitializrApplicationTests class

`FirstSpringInitializrApplicationTests` contains the basic context that can be used to start writing the tests as we start developing the application:

```
package com.mastering.spring;
import org.junit.Test;
import org.junit.runner.RunWith;
import org.springframework.boot.test.context.SpringBootTest;
import org.springframework.test.context.junit4.SpringRunner;

@RunWith(SpringRunner.class)
@SpringBootTest
public class FirstSpringInitializrApplicationTests {

  @Test
  public void contextLoads() {
  }
}
```

The test uses `@SpringBootTest`, which is used to launch unit tests with Spring Boot Framework. It contains one unit test to check whether the context launches properly.

A quick peek into AutoConfiguration

Auto configuration is one of the most important features of Spring Boot. In this section, we will take a quick peek behind the scenes to understand how Spring Boot auto configuration works.

Most of the Spring Boot auto configuration magic comes from `spring-boot-autoconfigure-{version}.jar`. When we start any Spring Boot application, a number of beans get automatically configured. How does this happen?

The following screenshot shows an extract from `spring.factories` from `spring-boot-autoconfigure-{version}.jar`. We have filtered out some of the configurations in the interest of space:

```
spring.factories ⊠
31 org.springframework.boot.autoconfigure.data.jpa.JpaRepositoriesAutoConfiguration,\
32 org.springframework.boot.autoconfigure.data.mongo.MongoDataAutoConfiguration,\
33 org.springframework.boot.autoconfigure.data.mongo.MongoRepositoriesAutoConfiguration,\
34 org.springframework.boot.autoconfigure.data.neo4j.Neo4jDataAutoConfiguration,\
35 org.springframework.boot.autoconfigure.data.neo4j.Neo4jRepositoriesAutoConfiguration,\
36 org.springframework.boot.autoconfigure.data.solr.SolrRepositoriesAutoConfiguration,\
37 org.springframework.boot.autoconfigure.data.redis.RedisAutoConfiguration,\
38 org.springframework.boot.autoconfigure.data.redis.RedisRepositoriesAutoConfiguration,\
39 org.springframework.boot.autoconfigure.data.rest.RepositoryRestMvcAutoConfiguration,\
40 org.springframework.boot.autoconfigure.data.web.SpringDataWebAutoConfiguration,\
41 org.springframework.boot.autoconfigure.elasticsearch.jest.JestAutoConfiguration,\
42 org.springframework.boot.autoconfigure.freemarker.FreeMarkerAutoConfiguration,\
43 org.springframework.boot.autoconfigure.gson.GsonAutoConfiguration,\
44 org.springframework.boot.autoconfigure.h2.H2ConsoleAutoConfiguration,\
45 org.springframework.boot.autoconfigure.hateoas.HypermediaAutoConfiguration,\
46 org.springframework.boot.autoconfigure.hazelcast.HazelcastAutoConfiguration,\
47 org.springframework.boot.autoconfigure.hazelcast.HazelcastJpaDependencyAutoConfiguration,\
48 org.springframework.boot.autoconfigure.info.ProjectInfoAutoConfiguration,\
49 org.springframework.boot.autoconfigure.integration.IntegrationAutoConfiguration,\
50 org.springframework.boot.autoconfigure.jackson.JacksonAutoConfiguration,\
51 org.springframework.boot.autoconfigure.jdbc.DataSourceAutoConfiguration,\
52 org.springframework.boot.autoconfigure.jdbc.JdbcTemplateAutoConfiguration,\
53 org.springframework.boot.autoconfigure.jdbc.JndiDataSourceAutoConfiguration,\
54 org.springframework.boot.autoconfigure.jdbc.XADataSourceAutoConfiguration,\
55 org.springframework.boot.autoconfigure.jdbc.DataSourceTransactionManagerAutoConfiguration,\
56 org.springframework.boot.autoconfigure.jms.JmsAutoConfiguration,\
57 org.springframework.boot.autoconfigure.jmx.JmxAutoConfiguration,\
58 org.springframework.boot.autoconfigure.jms.JndiConnectionFactoryAutoConfiguration,\
59 org.springframework.boot.autoconfigure.jms.activemq.ActiveMQAutoConfiguration,\
60 org.springframework.boot.autoconfigure.jms.artemis.ArtemisAutoConfiguration,\
61 org.springframework.boot.autoconfigure.jms.hornetq.HornetQAutoConfiguration,\
62 org.springframework.boot.autoconfigure.flyway.FlywayAutoConfiguration,\
```

The preceding list of auto configuration classes is run whenever a Spring Boot application is launched. Let's take a quick look at one of them:

`org.springframework.boot.autoconfigure.web.WebMvcAutoConfiguration.`

Here's a small snippet:

```
@Configuration

@ConditionalOnWebApplication

@ConditionalOnClass(
```

```
          { Servlet.class, DispatcherServlet.class,
WebMvcConfigurerAdapter.class })

@ConditionalOnMissingBean(WebMvcConfigurationSupport.class)

@AutoConfigureOrder(Ordered.HIGHEST_PRECEDENCE + 10)

@AutoConfigureAfter(DispatcherServletAutoConfiguration.class)

public class WebMvcAutoConfiguration {
```

Some of the important points to note are as follows:

- `@ConditionalOnClass({ Servlet.class, DispatcherServlet.class, WebMvcConfigurerAdapter.class })`: This auto configuration is enabled if any of the classes mentioned are in the classpath. When we add a web starter project, we bring in dependencies with all these classes. Hence, this auto configuration will be enabled.

- `@ConditionalOnMissingBean(WebMvcConfigurationSupport.class)`: This auto configuration is enabled only if the application does not explicitly declare a bean of the `WebMvcConfigurationSupport.class` class.

- `@AutoConfigureOrder(Ordered.HIGHEST_PRECEDENCE + 10)`: This specifies the precedence of this specific auto configuration.

Let's look at another small snippet showing one of the methods from the same class:

```
@Bean
@ConditionalOnBean(ViewResolver.class)
@ConditionalOnMissingBean
    (name = "viewResolver", value =
ContentNegotiatingViewResolver.class)
   public ContentNegotiatingViewResolver viewResolver(BeanFactory
beanFactory) {

    ContentNegotiatingViewResolver resolver = new
ContentNegotiatingViewResolver();

    resolver.setContentNegotiationManager(beanFactory.getBean
(ContentNegotiationManager.class));
    resolver.setOrder(Ordered.HIGHEST_PRECEDENCE);

    return resolver;

}
```

View resolvers are one of the beans configured by the `WebMvcAutoConfiguration` class. The preceding snippet ensures that if a view resolver is not provided by the application, then Spring Boot automatically configures a default view resolver. Here are a few important points to note:

- `@ConditionalOnBean(ViewResolver.class)`: Create this bean if `ViewResolver.class` is on the classpath.
- `@ConditionalOnMissingBean(name = "viewResolver", value = ContentNegotiatingViewResolver.class)`: Create this bean if there are no explicitly declared beans of the `viewResolver` name and of the `ContentNegotiatingViewResolver.class` type.
- The remainder of the method is configured in the view resolver.

To summarize, all the auto configuration logic is executed at the start of a Spring Boot application. If a specific class (from a specific dependency or starter project) is available on the classpath, then the `AutoConfiguration` classes are executed. These auto configuration classes look at what beans are already configured. Based on the existing beans, they enable the creation of the default beans.

Externalizing application configuration

Applications are typically built once (in JAR or WAR) and then deployed into multiple environments. The following diagram shows some of the different environments to which an application can be deployed:

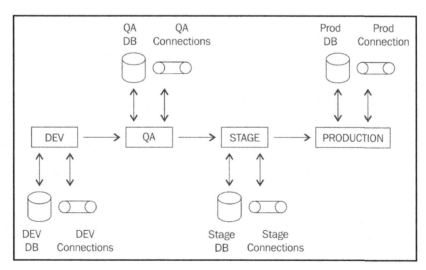

In each of the preceding environments, an application typically has the following:

- Connections to databases
- Connections to multiple services
- Specific environment configurations

It is good practice to externalize configurations that change between different environments into a configuration file or database.

Spring Boot provides a flexible, standardized approach for externalized configuration.

In this section, we will look at the following:

- How can properties from `application.properties` be used inside our services?
- How do type-safe configuration properties make application configuration a cakewalk?
- What kind of support does Spring Boot provide for **Spring Profiles**?
- How can you configure properties in `application.properties`?

Getting started with application.properties

In Spring Boot, `application.properties` is the default file from which configuration values are picked up. Spring Boot can pick the `application.properties` file from anywhere on the classpath. Typically, `application.properties` is located at `src\main\resources`, as shown in the following screenshot:

The following snippet shows how you can customize Spring Security using the configuration in `application.properties`:

```
security.basic.enabled=false
management.security.enabled=false
security.user.name=user-name
security.user.password=user-password
security.oauth2.client.clientId: clientId
security.oauth2.client.clientSecret: clientSecret
```

```
security.oauth2.client.authorized-grant-types:
authorization_code,refresh_token,password
security.oauth2.client.scope: openid
```

Similar to these, other Spring Boot starters, modules, and frameworks can be customized through configuration in `application.properties`.

In the next section, we'll look at some of the configuration options Spring Boot provides for these frameworks.

Customizing frameworks through application.properties

In this section, we will discuss some of the important things that can be configured through `application.properties`.

 For the complete list, refer to `https://docs.spring.io/spring-boot/docs/current-SNAPSHOT/reference/htmlsingle/#common-application-properties`.

Configuring logging

Some of the things that can be configured are as follows:

- The location of the logging configuration file
- The location of the log file
- Logging level

The following snippet shows a few examples:

```
# Location of the logging configuration file.
  logging.config=
# Log file name.
  logging.file=
# Configure Logging level.
# Example `logging.level.org.springframework=TRACE`
  logging.level.*=
```

Customizing the embedded server configuration

An embedded server is one of the most important features of Spring Boot. Some of the embedded server features that can be configured through application properties include the following:

- Server ports
- SSL support and configuration
- Access log configuration

The following snippet shows some of the embedded server features that can be configured through application properties:

```
# Path of the error controller.
server.error.path=/error
# Server HTTP port.
server.port=8080
# Enable SSL support.
server.ssl.enabled=
# Path to key store with SSL certificate
server.ssl.key-store=
# Key Store Password
server.ssl.key-store-password=
# Key Store Provider
server.ssl.key-store-provider=
# Key Store Type
server.ssl.key-store-type=
# Should we enable access log of Tomcat?
server.tomcat.accesslog.enabled=false
# Maximum number of connections that server can accept
server.tomcat.max-connections=
```

Configuring Spring MVC

Spring MVC can be extensively configured through `application.properties`. Listed here are some of the important configurations:

```
# Date format to use. For instance `dd/MM/yyyy`.
 spring.mvc.date-format=
# Locale to use.
 spring.mvc.locale=
# Define how the locale should be resolved.
 spring.mvc.locale-resolver=accept-header
# Should "NoHandlerFoundException" be thrown if no Handler is found?
 spring.mvc.throw-exception-if-no-handler-found=false
```

```
# Spring MVC view prefix. Used by view resolver.
  spring.mvc.view.prefix=
# Spring MVC view suffix. Used by view resolver.
  spring.mvc.view.suffix=
```

Configuring Spring starter security

Spring Security can be extensively configured through `application.properties`. The following examples show some of the important configuration options related to Spring Security:

```
# Set true to Enable basic authentication
  security.basic.enabled=true
# Provide a Comma-separated list of uris you would want to secure
  security.basic.path=/**
# Provide a Comma-separated list of paths you don't want to secure
  security.ignored=
# Name of the default user configured by spring security
  security.user.name=user
# Password of the default user configured by spring security.
  security.user.password=
# Roles granted to default user
  security.user.role=USER
```

Customizing data sources, JDBC, and JPA

Data sources, JDBC, and JPA can also be extensively configured through `application.properties`. Listed here are some of the important options:

```
# Fully qualified name of the JDBC driver.
  spring.datasource.driver-class-name=
# Populate the database using 'data.sql'.
  spring.datasource.initialize=true
# Name of the datasource.
  spring.datasource.name=testdb
# Login password of the database.
  spring.datasource.password=
# JDBC url of the database.
  spring.datasource.url=
# JPA - Initialize the schema on startup.
  spring.jpa.generate-ddl=false
# Enable logging of SQL statements.
  spring.jpa.show-sql=false
```

Looking at other configuration options

Some other elements that can be configured through `application.properties` are as follows:

- Profiles
- HTTP message converters (Jackson/JSON)
- Transaction management
- Internationalization

The following examples show some of the configuration options:

```
# Comma-separated list (or list if using YAML) of active profiles.
 spring.profiles.active=
# HTTP message conversion. jackson or gson
 spring.http.converters.preferred-json-mapper=jackson
# JACKSON Date format string. Example `yyyy-MM-dd HH:mm:ss`.
 spring.jackson.date-format=
# Default transaction timeout in seconds.
 spring.transaction.default-timeout=
# Perform the rollback on commit failures.
 spring.transaction.rollback-on-commit-failure=
# Internationalisation : Comma-separated list of basenames
 spring.messages.basename=messages
# Cache expiration for resource bundles, in sec. -1 will cache for ever
 spring.messages.cache-seconds=-1
```

The line before each of the configuration options listed here contains a comment explaining the configuration option.

Defining application-specific, custom-defined properties

Up until now, we have looked at using prebuilt properties provided by Spring Boot for various frameworks. In this section, we will look at creating our application-specific configuration, which that can also be configured in `application.properties`.

Let's consider an example—we want to be able to interact with an external service. We want to be able to externalize the configuration of the URL of this service. The following example shows how we would want to configure the external service in `application.properties`:

```
somedataservice.url=http://abc.service.com/something
```

We want to use the value of the `somedataservice.url` property in our data service. The following snippet shows how we can do that in an example data service:

```
@Component
public class SomeDataService {

  @Value("${somedataservice.url}")
  private String url;

  public String retrieveSomeData() {
    // TODO - Logic using the url and getting the data
   return "data from service";
  }

}
```

A couple of important things to note are as follows:

- `@Component public class SomeDataService`: The data service bean is managed by Spring because of the `@Component` annotation.
- `@Value("${somedataservice.url}")`: The value of `somedataservice.url` will be autowired into the `url` variable. The `url` value can be used in the `bean` methods.

Providing type-safe configuration through configuration properties

While the `@Value` annotation provides dynamic configuration, it also has several drawbacks:

- If we want to use three property values in a service, we would need to autowire them using `@Value` three times.
- The `@Value` annotations and the keys of the messages would be spread across the application. If we want to find the list of the configurable values in an application, we have to search through the application for `@Value` annotations.

Spring Boot provides a better approach to application configuration through the strongly typed `ConfigurationProperties` feature. This allows us to do the following:

- Have all the properties in a predefined bean structure.
- This bean would act as the centralized store for all application properties.
- The configuration bean can be autowired wherever application configuration is needed.

An example configuration bean is as follows:

```
@Component
@ConfigurationProperties("application")
public class ApplicationConfiguration {
    private boolean enableSwitchForService1;
    private String service1Url;
    private int service1Timeout;
    public boolean isEnableSwitchForService1() {
      return enableSwitchForService1;
    }
    public void setEnableSwitchForService1 (boolean
enableSwitchForService1) {
        this.enableSwitchForService1 = enableSwitchForService1;
    }

    public String getService1Url() {
     return service1Url;
    }

    public void setService1Url(String service1Url) {
     this.service1Url = service1Url;
    }

    public int getService1Timeout() {
      return service1Timeout;
    }

    public void setService1Timeout(int service1Timeout) {
        this.service1Timeout = service1Timeout;
    }

  }
```

A couple of important things to note are as follows:

- `@ConfigurationProperties("application")`: This is the annotation for an externalized configuration. We can add this annotation to any class to bind to external properties. `application` is used as a prefix while binding external configuration to this bean.
- We are defining multiple configurable values in the bean.
- Getters and setters are required since binding happens through Java bean's property descriptors.

The following snippet shows how the values for these properties can be defined in `application.properties`:

```
application.enableSwitchForService1=true

application.service1Url=http://abc-dev.service.com/somethingelse

application.service1Timeout=250
```

A couple of important things to note are as follows:

- `application`: The prefix is defined as part of `@ConfigurationProperties("application")` while defining the configuration bean.
- Values are defined by appending the prefix to the name of the property.

We can use configuration properties in other beans by autowiring `ApplicationConfiguration` into the bean:

```
@Component
public class SomeOtherDataService {

    @Autowired
    private ApplicationConfiguration configuration;

    public String retrieveSomeData() {

        // Logic using the url and getting the data
        System.out.println(configuration.getService1Timeout());

        System.out.println(configuration.getService1Url());

        System.out.println(configuration.isEnableSwitchForService1());

        return "data from service";
```

```
    }
  }
```

A couple of important things to note are as follows:

- `@Autowired private ApplicationConfiguration configuration`: `ApplicationConfiguration` is autowired into `SomeOtherDataService`.
- `configuration.getService1Timeout()`, `configuration.getService1Url()`, `configuration.isEnableSwitchForService1()`: These values can be accessed in bean methods using the getter methods on the configuration bean.

By default, any failure in binding externally configured values to the configuration properties bean would result in the failure of the server startup. This prevents problems that arise on account of misconfigured applications running in production.

Let's use the misconfigure service timeout to see what happens:

`application.service1Timeout=SOME_MISCONFIGURATION`

The application will fail to start up, generating the following error:

```
***************************
APPLICATION FAILED TO START
***************************
Description:
Binding to target
com.mastering.spring.springboot.configuration.ApplicationConfiguration@79d3
473e failed:

Property: application.service1Timeout
Value: SOME_MISCONFIGURATION
Reason: Failed to convert property value of type 'java.lang.String' to
required type 'int' for property 'service1Timeout'; nested exception is
org.springframework.core.convert.ConverterNotFoundException: No converter
found capable of converting from type [java.lang.String] to type [int]

Action:
Update your application's configuration
```

Creating profiles for different environments

Up until now, we've looked at how to externalize application configuration to a property file, `application.properties`. What we want to be able to do is have different values for the same property in different environments.

Profiles allow you to provide different configurations in different environments.

The following snippet shows how to configure an active profile in `application.properties`:

```
spring.profiles.active=dev
```

Once you have an active profile configured, you can define properties specific to that profile in `application-{profile-name}.properties`. For the `dev` profile, the name of the properties file would be `application-dev.properties`. The following example shows the configuration in `application-dev.properties`:

```
application.enableSwitchForService1=true
application.service1Url=http://abc-dev.service.com/somethingelse
application.service1Timeout=250
```

The values in `application-dev.properties` will override the default configuration in `application.properties` if the active profile is `dev`.

We can have configurations for multiple environments, as shown here:

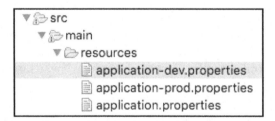

Configuring dynamic beans based on active profiles

Profiles can also be used to define different beans or different bean configurations in different environments. All of the classes marked with `@Component` or `@Configuration` can also be marked with an additional `@Profile` annotation to specify the profile in which the bean or configuration is enabled.

Let's consider an example. An application needs different caches enabled in different environments. In the dev environment, it uses a very simple cache. In production, we would want to use a distributed cache. This can be implemented using profiles.

The following bean shows the configuration enabled in a dev environment:

```
@Profile("dev")
@Configuration
public class DevSpecificConfiguration {

  @Bean
  public String cache() {
    return "Dev Cache Configuration";
  }

}
```

The following bean shows the configuration enabled in a production environment:

```
@Profile("prod")
@Configuration
public class ProdSpecificConfiguration {

  @Bean
  public String cache() {
    return "Production Cache Configuration - Distributed Cache";
  }

}
```

Based on the active profile configured, the respective configuration is picked up. Note that we aren't really configuring a distributed cache in this example. We are returning a simple string to illustrate that profiles can be used to implement these kinds of variations.

Other options for providing application configuration

Up until now, the approaches we took to configure application properties involved using the key-value pairs from either application.properties or application-{profile-name}.properties.

Spring Boot provides a number of other ways to configure application properties.

Listed here are some of the important ways of providing application configuration:

- Command-line arguments
- Creating a system property with the name; SPRING_APPLICATION_JSON, and including the JSON configuration
- ServletConfig init parameters
- ServletContext init parameters
- Java System properties (System.getProperties())
- Operating system environment variables
- Profile-specific application properties outside .jar, somewhere in the classpath of the application (application-{profile}.properties)
- Profile-specific application properties packaged inside your .jar (application-{profile}.properties and YAML variants)
- Application properties outside .jar
- Application properties packaged inside .jar

 More information can be found in the Spring Boot documentation at http://docs.spring.io/spring-boot/docs/current-SNAPSHOT/reference/htmlsingle/#boot-features-external-config.

The approaches at the top of this list have higher priority than those at the bottom of the list. For example, if a command-line argument with the name spring.profiles.active is provided when launching the application, it would override any configuration provided through application.properties because command-line arguments have higher preference.

This provides great flexibility in determining how you would want to configure your application in different environments.

Exploring the YAML configuration

Spring Boot also supports **YAML** in configuring your properties.

YAML is an abbreviation for *YAML Ain't Markup Language*. It is a human-readable structured format. YAML is commonly used for configuration files.

To understand the basic syntax of YAML, look at the following example
(`application.yaml`). This shows how our application configuration can be specified in
YAML:

```
spring:
   profiles:
      active: prod
security:
   basic:
      enabled: false
   user:
      name=user-name
      password=user-password
oauth2:
   client:
      clientId: clientId
      clientSecret: clientSecret
      authorized-grant-types: authorization_code, refresh_token, password
      scope: openid
application:
   enableSwitchForService1: true
   service1Url: http://abc-dev.service.com/somethingelse
   service1Timeout: 250
```

As you can see, the YAML configuration is much more readable
than `application.properties`, as it allows better grouping of properties.

Another advantage of YAML is that it allows you to specify the configuration for multiple
profiles in a single configuration file. The following snippet shows an example of this:

```
application:
  service1Url: http://service.default.com
---
spring:
  profiles: dev
  application:
    service1Url: http://service.dev.com
---
spring:
   profiles: prod
   application:
    service1Url: http://service.prod.com
```

In this example, `http://service.dev.com` will be used in the `dev` profile, and
`http://service.prod.com` will be used in the `prod` profile. In all other
profiles, `http://service.default.com` will be used as the service URL.

Understanding embedded servers

One of the important concepts associated with Spring Boot is embedded servers.

Let's understand the difference between traditional Java web application deployment and this new concept known as *embedded server*.

Understanding traditional Java application deployment

Traditionally, with Java web applications, we build a **Web Application Archive (WAR)**, or **Enterprise Application Archive (EAR)**, and deploy them in servers. Before we can deploy a WAR on the server, we need a web server or an application server installed on the server. The application server would be on top of the Java instance installed on the server. So, we need Java and an application (or web server) installed on the machine before we can deploy our application.

The following diagram shows an example of an installation in Linux:

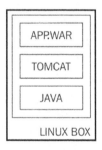

Understanding embedded servers

Spring Boot brings in the concept of embedded servers, where the web server is part of the application deployable—JAR. To deploy applications using embedded servers, it is sufficient if Java is installed on the server.

The following diagram shows an example installation:

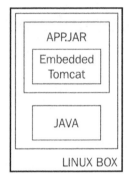

When we build any application with Spring Boot, the default is to build a JAR. With `spring-boot-starter-web`, the default embedded server is Tomcat.

When we use `spring-boot-starter-web`, a few Tomcat-related dependencies can be seen in the Maven dependencies section. These dependencies will be included as part of the application deployment package:

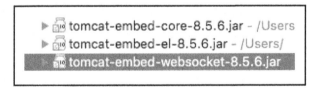

To deploy the application, we need to build a JAR. We can build a JAR using the following command:

```
mvn clean install
```

The following screenshot shows the structure of the JAR that was created.

`BOOT-INF\classes` contains all application-related class files (from `src\main\java`), as well as the application properties from `src\main\resources`:

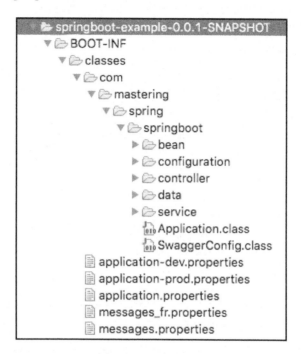

`BOOT-INF\lib` contains all the JAR dependencies of the application. Tomcat-specific JARs enable the launch of an embedded Tomcat service when the application is run as a Java application. Because of this, a Java installation is sufficient to deploy this application on a server.

Switching to Jetty and Undertow embedded servers

The following screenshot shows the changes that are required in order to switch to using the Jetty embedded server:

```xml
<dependency>
    <groupId>org.springframework.boot</groupId>
    <artifactId>spring-boot-starter-web</artifactId>
    <exclusions>
        <exclusion>
            <groupId>org.springframework.boot</groupId>
            <artifactId>spring-boot-starter-tomcat</artifactId>
        </exclusion>
    </exclusions>
</dependency>

<dependency>
    <groupId>org.springframework.boot</groupId>
    <artifactId>spring-boot-starter-jetty</artifactId>
</dependency>
```

All that we need to do is exclude the Tomcat starter dependency in `spring-boot-starter-web` and include the dependency in `spring-boot-starter-jetty`.

You can now see a number of Jetty dependencies in the Maven dependencies section. The following screenshot shows a few of the Jetty-related dependencies:

```
▶ jetty-servlets-9.3.14.v20161028.jar - /U
▶ jetty-continuation-9.3.14.v20161028.jar
▶ jetty-http-9.3.14.v20161028.jar - /Users
▶ jetty-util-9.3.14.v20161028.jar - /Users/
▶ jetty-io-9.3.14.v20161028.jar - /Users/
▶ jetty-webapp-9.3.14.v20161028.jar - /U
▶ jetty-xml-9.3.14.v20161028.jar - /Users/
▶ jetty-servlet-9.3.14.v20161028.jar - /Us
▶ jetty-security-9.3.14.v20161028.jar - /U
▶ jetty-server-9.3.14.v20161028.jar - /Us
```

Switching to Undertow is equally as easy. Use `spring-boot-starter-undertow` instead of `spring-boot-starter-jetty`:

```
<dependency>
    <groupId>org.springframework.boot</groupId>
    <artifactId>spring-boot-starter-undertow</artifactId>
</dependency>
```

Building a traditional WAR file instead of using a JAR

Spring Boot also provides the option of building a traditional WAR file instead of using a JAR.

First, we need to change our packaging in `pom.xml` to `war`:

```
<packaging>war</packaging>
```

We want to prevent the Tomcat server from being embedded as a dependency in the WAR file. We can do this by modifying the dependency on the embedded server (Tomcat, in the following example) to have a scope of provided. The following snippet shows the exact details:

```
<dependency>
    <groupId>org.springframework.boot</groupId>
    <artifactId>spring-boot-starter-tomcat</artifactId>
    <scope>provided</scope>
</dependency>
```

When you build the WAR file, Tomcat dependencies are not included. We can use this WAR to deploy on an application server, such as WebSphere or Weblogic, or a web server, such as Tomcat.

Using developer tools to improve productivity

Spring Boot provides tools that can improve the experience of developing Spring Boot applications. One of these is Spring Boot developer tools.

To use Spring Boot developer tools, we need to include a dependency:

```
<dependencies>
  <dependency>
    <groupId>org.springframework.boot</groupId>
    <artifactId>spring-boot-devtools</artifactId>
    <optional>true</optional>
  </dependency>
</dependencies>
```

Spring Boot developer tools, by default, disables the caching of view templates and static files. This allows a developer to see the changes as soon as they make them.

Another important feature is the automatic restart when any file in the classpath changes. Hence, the application automatically restarts in the following scenarios:

- When we make a change to a controller or a service class
- When we make a change to the property file

The advantages of Spring Boot developer tools are as follows:

- The developer doesn't need to stop and start the application each time. The application is automatically restarted as soon as there is a change.
- The restart feature in Spring Boot developer tools is intelligent. It only reloads the actively developed classes. It does not reload the third-party JARs (using two different class-loaders). Thereby, the restart when something in the application changes is much faster compared to cold-starting an application.

Enabling live reload on a browser

Another useful Spring Boot developer tools feature is **live reload**. You can download a specific plugin for your browser from `http://livereload.com/extensions/`.

You can enable live reload by clicking on the button in the browser. The button in the Safari browser is shown in the following screenshot. It's in the top-left corner, next to the address bar:

If there are code changes being made on the pages or services that are shown in the browser, they are auto-refreshed with new content. There is no longer any need to hit that refresh button!

Using Spring Boot Actuator for application monitoring

When an application is deployed in production, we want to know about the following:

- We want to know immediately whether a service goes down or is very slow.
- We want to know immediately whether any of the servers don't have sufficient free space or memory.

This is called **application monitoring**.

Spring Boot Actuator provides a number of production-ready monitoring features.

We will add Spring Boot Actuator by adding a simple dependency:

```xml
<dependency>
    <groupId>org.springframework.boot</groupId>
    <artifactId>spring-boot-starter-actuator</artifactId>
</dependency>
```

As soon as the actuator is added to an application, it enables a number of endpoints. The actuator endpoint (`http://localhost:8080/actuator`) acts as a discovery for all other endpoints.

By default, only health and info URLs are enabled. The following snippet shows the response when we execute a GET request to `http://localhost:8080/actuator`:

```
{
    "_links": {
        "self": {
            "href": "http://localhost:8080/actuator",
            "templated": false
```

```
        },
        "health": {
            "href": "http://localhost:8080/actuator/health",
            "templated": false
        },
        "health-component-instance": {
            "href":
"http://localhost:8080/actuator/health/{component}/{instance}",
            "templated": true
        },
        "health-component": {
            "href": "http://localhost:8080/actuator/health/{component}",
            "templated": true
        },
        "info": {
            "href": "http://localhost:8080/actuator/info",
            "templated": false
        }
    }
}
```

You can enable all actuator URLs by configuring the property in
`application.properties`:

```
management.endpoints.web.exposure.include=*
```

The following snippet shows the response when we execute a GET request to
`http://localhost:8080/actuator`:

```
{
    "_links": {
        "self": {
            "href": "http://localhost:8080/actuator",
            "templated": false
        },
        "beans": {
            "href": "http://localhost:8080/actuator/beans",
            "templated": false
        },
        "health": {
            "href": "http://localhost:8080/actuator/health",
            "templated": false
        },
        "configprops": {
            "href": "http://localhost:8080/actuator/configprops",
            "templated": false
        },
        "env": {
```

```
            "href": "http://localhost:8080/actuator/env",
            "templated": false
        },
        "info": {
            "href": "http://localhost:8080/actuator/info",
            "templated": false
        },
        "heapdump": {
            "href": "http://localhost:8080/actuator/heapdump",
            "templated": false
        },
        "threaddump": {
            "href": "http://localhost:8080/actuator/threaddump",
            "templated": false
        },
        "metrics": {
            "href": "http://localhost:8080/actuator/metrics",
            "templated": false
        }
    }
}
```

 Some of the URLs are removed for the sake of brevity.

Using the HAL browser to browse actuator endpoints

Actuator exposes a number of endpoints exposing a lot of data. To be able to visualize the information better, we will add a HAL browser to our application:

```
<dependency>
    <groupId>org.springframework.data</groupId>
    <artifactId>spring-data-rest-hal-browser</artifactId>
</dependency>
```

Spring Boot Actuator exposes REST APIs around all the data that's captured from the Spring Boot application and environment. The **HAL BROWSER** enables visual representations around the Spring Boot Actuator API:

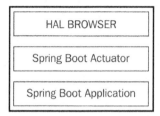

You can launch **HAL BROWSER** by using the `http://localhost:8080/` URL. You will see a screen similar to the following:

We can start browsing the Actuator API by typing in the URI for the actuator (/actuator) in the explorer and clicking **Go**. A screenshot of the screen is shown here:

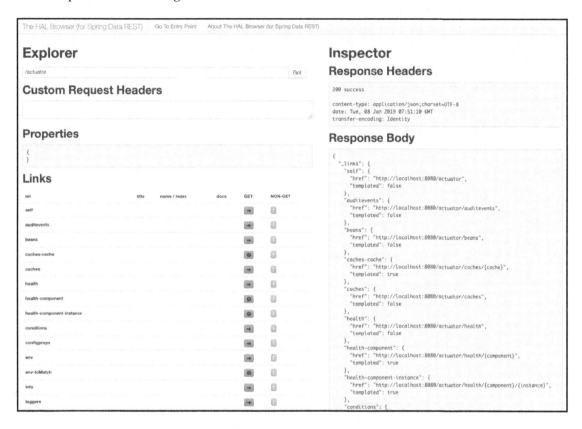

Now, let's browse all the information that's exposed by the actuator as part of different endpoints through the HAL browser.

Looking at application configuration

The `configprops` endpoint provides information about configuration options that can be configured through application properties. It is basically a collated list of all `@ConfigurationProperties`. The following screenshot shows the configuration props in the HAL browser:

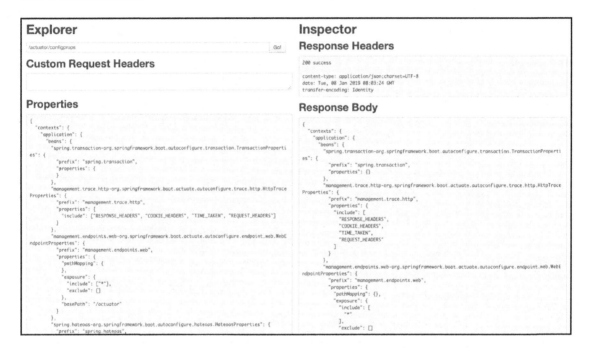

To illustrate a known example, the following section from the service response shows the configuration options that are available for Spring MVC:

```
"spring.mvc-
org.springframework.boot.autoconfigure.web.servlet.WebMvcProperties": {
        "prefix": "spring.mvc",
        "properties": {
          "contentnegotiation": {
            "favorPathExtension": false,
            "favorParameter": false,
            "mediaTypes": {
            }
          },
          "servlet": {
            "path": "/",
            "loadOnStartup": -1
          },
          "staticPathPattern": "/**",
          "dispatchOptionsRequest": true,
          "dispatchTraceRequest": false,
          "ignoreDefaultModelOnRedirect": true,
          "logResolvedException": false,
          "async": {
          },
          "view": {
          },
          "localeResolver": "ACCEPT_HEADER",
          "pathmatch": {
            "useSuffixPattern": false,
            "useRegisteredSuffixPattern": false
          },
          "throwExceptionIfNoHandlerFound": false
        }
    }
```

 To provide configuration for Spring MVC, we combine the prefix with the path in properties. For example, to configure loadOnStartup, we use a property with the name spring.mvc.servlet.loadOnStartup.

Getting environment details

The **environment (env)** endpoint provides information about the operating system, JVM installation, classpath, system environment variables, and the values that have been configured in various application properties files. The following screenshot shows the environment endpoint in the HAL browser:

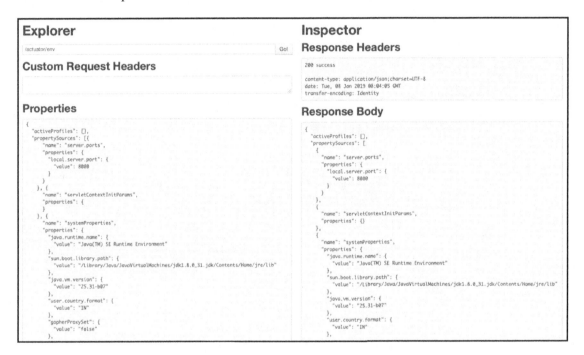

An extract from the response from the `/actuator/env` service is shown here. It shows a few system details, as well as the details from application configuration:

```
{ "name": "systemProperties",
    "properties": {
      "java.runtime.name": {
        "value": "Java(TM) SE Runtime Environment"
      },
      "sun.boot.library.path": {
        "value":
"/Library/Java/JavaVirtualMachines/jdk1.8.0_31.jdk/Contents/Home/jre/lib"
      },
      "path.separator": {
        "value": ":"
      },
      "java.vm.name": {
```

```
      "value": "Java HotSpot(TM) 64-Bit Server VM"
    },
    "sun.os.patch.level": {
      "value": "unknown"
    },
```

Some of the content has been removed for the sake of brevity.

Monitoring application health

The health service provides the status of the application. The following screenshot shows the service being executed from the HAL browser:

Getting mapping information

The mappings endpoint provides information about different service endpoints that are exposed from the application:

- URI
- Request methods
- Bean
- Controller methods exposing the service

Mappings provide a collated list of all `@RequestMapping` paths. An extract from the response of the `/actuator/mappings` endpoint is shown here. We can see the mappings of the different actuator methods:

```
        {
                "handler": "Actuator web endpoint 'health'",
                "predicate": "{GET /actuator/health, produces
[application/vnd.spring-boot.actuator.v2+json || application/json]}",
                "details": {
                  "handlerMethod": {
                    "className":
"AbstractWebMvcEndpointHandlerMapping.OperationHandler",
                    "name": "handle",
                    "descriptor":
"(Ljavax/servlet/http/HttpServletRequest;Ljava/util/Map;)Ljava/lang/Object;
"
                  },
                  "requestMappingConditions": {
                    "consumes": [],
                    "headers": [],
                    "methods": ["GET"],
                    "params": [],
                    "patterns": ["/actuator/health"],
                    "produces": [{
                        "mediaType": "application/vnd.spring-
boot.actuator.v2+json",
                        "negated": false
                    }, {
                        "mediaType": "application/json",
                        "negated": false
                    }]
                  }
                }
        }
```

Some of the content has been removed for the sake of brevity.

Debugging with the bean configuration

The beans endpoint provides the details about the beans that are loaded into the Spring context. This is useful in debugging any problems related to Spring context.

An extract from the response of the `/actuator/beans` endpoint is as follows:

```
    "beanNameViewResolver": {
            "aliases": [],
            "scope": "singleton",
            "type":
"org.springframework.web.servlet.view.BeanNameViewResolver",
            "resource": "class path resource
[org/springframework/boot/autoconfigure/web/servlet/error/ErrorMvcAutoConfi
guration$WhitelabelErrorViewConfiguration.class]",
            "dependencies": []
        },
"viewResolver": {
        "aliases": [],
        "scope": "singleton",
        "type":
"org.springframework.web.servlet.view.ContentNegotiatingViewResolver",
        "resource": "class path resource
[org/springframework/boot/autoconfigure/web/servlet/WebMvcAutoConfiguration
$WebMvcAutoConfigurationAdapter.class]",
        "dependencies":
["org.springframework.beans.factory.support.DefaultListableBeanFactory@7071
94ba"]
        },
"messageConverters": {
        "aliases": [],
        "scope": "singleton",
        "type":
"org.springframework.boot.autoconfigure.http.HttpMessageConverters",
        "resource": "class path resource
[org/springframework/boot/autoconfigure/http/HttpMessageConvertersAutoConfi
guration.class]",
        "dependencies": []
     },
"jsonComponentModule": {
        "aliases": [],
```

```
        "scope": "singleton",
        "type": "org.springframework.boot.jackson.JsonComponentModule",
        "resource": "class path resource
[org/springframework/boot/autoconfigure/jackson/JacksonAutoConfiguration.cl
ass]",
        "dependencies": []
    },
```

You can see the following details for all the beans that are loaded up by the Spring application context:

- The name of the bean and its aliases
- The scope of the bean
- The type of bean
- The exact location of the class from which this bean is created
- Dependencies of the bean

Exploring important metrics

The metrics endpoint shows some of the important metrics pertaining to the following:

- Server: Free memory, processors, uptime, and so on
- JVM: Details about the heap, threads, garbage collection, sessions, and so on
- Responses provided by application services

An extract from the response of the `/actuator/metrics` endpoint is as follows:

```
{
    "names":[
        "jvm.memory.max",
        "jvm.threads.states",
        "http.server.requests",
        //Lot of other values
        "tomcat.global.received",
        "process.uptime",
        "tomcat.sessions.rejected",
        "process.cpu.usage",
        //Lot of other values
        "process.start.time"
    ]
}
```

The metrics service returns the list of metrics. To get a specific metric value, you would need to use the `/actuator/metrics/{METRIC-NAME}` URI. `{METRIC-NAME}` should be replaced by the appropriate name from the preceding response.

For example, the `/actuator/metrics/jvm.memory.max` URI will return the following response:

```
{
  "name": "jvm.memory.max",
  "description": "The maximum amount of memory in bytes that can be used
for memory management",
  "baseUnit": "bytes",
  "measurements": [{
      "statistic": "VALUE",
      "value": 5600444415
    }],
  "availableTags": [{
      "tag": "area",
      "values": ["heap", "nonheap"]
    }, {
      "tag": "id",
      "values": ["Compressed Class Space", "PS Survivor Space", "PS Old
Gen", "Metaspace", "PS Eden Space", "Code Cache"]
    }]
}
```

Getting debug information about AutoConfiguration

Auto configuration is one of the most important features of Spring Boot. The `AutoConfiguration` endpoint (`/actuator/conditions`) exposes the details related to auto configuration. It shows both positive matches and negative matches, with details about why a particular auto configuration succeeded or failed.

The following extract shows some of the positive matches from the response:

```
"positiveMatches": {
  "AuditAutoConfiguration#auditListener": [
  {
    "condition": "OnBeanCondition",
    "message": "@ConditionalOnMissingBean (types:
    org.springframework.boot.actuate.audit.
    listener.AbstractAuditListener; SearchStrategy: all) did not find
    any beans"
```

```
  }
],
"AuditAutoConfiguration#authenticationAuditListener": [
{
  "condition": "OnClassCondition",
  "message": "@ConditionalOnClass found required class
  'org.springframework.security.authentication.
  event.AbstractAuthenticationEvent'"
},
```

The following extract shows some of the negative matches from the response:

```
"negativeMatches": {
  "CacheStatisticsAutoConfiguration.
  CaffeineCacheStatisticsProviderConfiguration": [
{
  "condition": "OnClassCondition",
  "message": "@ConditionalOnClass did not find required class
  'com.github.benmanes.caffeine.cache.Caffeine'"
}
],
  "CacheStatisticsAutoConfiguration.
  EhCacheCacheStatisticsProviderConfiguration": [
{
  "condition": "OnClassCondition",
  "message": "@ConditionalOnClass did not find required classes
  'net.sf.ehcache.Ehcache',
  'net.sf.ehcache.statistics.StatisticsGateway'"
}
],
```

All of these details are very useful in order to debug auto configuration.

Debugging

Three of the actuator endpoints are useful when debugging problems:

- /application/heapdump: This provides a heap dump.
- /application/httptrace: This provides a trace of the last few requests that were serviced by the application.
- /application/threaddump: This provides a thread dump.

You can shut down a Spring Boot application by using the actuator shutdown feature. You can enable the shutdown feature by using `management.endpoints.web.exposure.include=*` and `management.endpoint.shutdown.enabled=true`. You can execute a shutdown using the appropriate `curl` command, that is, `curl -X POST your_host:your_port/actuator/shutdown`.

Other information that can be obtained from the actuator includes loggers, caches, and scheduled tasks.

Summary

Spring Boot makes developing Spring-based applications easy. It allows us to create production-ready applications very quickly.

In this chapter, we started by understanding that Spring Boot is not a code generation framework. It is not a web server or application server. We built a `hello world` Spring Boot application to understand all the auto configuration that Spring Boot provides. We understood how to use different Spring Boot starters to get started with a wide variety of projects.

We used **SPRING INITIALIZR** to create Spring Projects. With **SPRING INITIALIZR**, we can easily choose from the different Spring Boot starters that are available and create a new project using Spring and Spring Boot framework in minutes.

In this chapter, we understood the different external configuration options provided by Spring Boot. We looked at a variety of embedded servers options—Tomcat, Jetty, and Undertow. Then, we explored how to monitor our application in production using Spring Boot Actuator.

At the end of the chapter, is we looked at the features that make a developer more productive—Spring Boot developer tools and live reload.

In the next chapter, we will explore another important facet of Spring Boot. Spring Boot makes learning Spring easier. We will use Spring Boot to quickly set up projects and learn how to execute a number of advanced things with Spring framework—aspect-oriented programming, scheduling, and scripting.

Digging Deeper into the Spring Framework

5

The Spring Framework aims to provide solutions to problems that are faced by enterprise applications.

In this chapter, we will start by understanding cross-cutting concerns and learn about the best practices of implementing cross-cutting concerns using **aspect-oriented programming (AOP)** with Spring and AspectJ.

Enterprises have simple tasks that need to be executed on a regular basis. Spring provides scheduling features that enable the execution of bean methods at regular intervals. Due to this, we will look at how you can schedule your tasks with the Spring `@Scheduled` annotation.

Scripting helps us change the application behavior at runtime. The JSR 223 API makes it easy to run scripts in Java. You can evaluate scripts written in dynamic languages such as Groovy and JavaScript. Spring provides features to integrate and execute dynamic scripts. In this chapter, we will look at the basics of scripting and how it can be integrated into Spring projects.

This chapter answers the following questions:

- What are cross-cutting concerns?
- What is AOP?
- What is the important terminology related to AOP?
- How can you implement AOP with Spring and AspectJ?
- What is scheduling?
- How can you schedule tasks with the Spring Framework?
- What is scripting?
- How can you integrate scripting into Spring applications?

Technical requirements

The following are the software and hardware requirements for this chapter:

- Your favorite IDE, Eclipse.
- This chapter is compatible with Java 8, 9, 10, 11, and 12.
- Maven 3.x.
- Internet connectivity.

The code on GitHub is available at `https://github.com/PacktPublishing/Mastering-Spring-5.1/tree/master/Chapter05`

Exploring AOP with Spring and AspectJ

Layered applications have a number of cross-cutting concerns. AOP with Spring and AspectJ is one of the preferred options to implement cross-cutting concerns.

Let's understand the terminology—cross-cutting concerns and AOP—and the solutions—Spring and AspectJ.

Exploring cross-cutting concerns and AOP

Spring applications are built with a layered architecture. Typically, applications have a web layer, a business layer, and a data layer. Each layer has its own concerns and implements them well with the following features:

- The web layer focuses on consumers of the application—offering a REST API or a user interface.
- The business layer focuses on the business logic.
- The data layer focuses on integration with databases and external applications.

Applications also have features that cut across multiple layers:

- Logging
- Security
- Performance tracing

These concerns that cut across layers are called **cross-cutting concerns**.

The question to ask is this: which layer should these cross-cutting concerns be implemented in?

Implementing them in each layer would make them difficult to maintain.

Ideally, you would want to implement the cross-cutting concerns in one place and apply them across multiple layers. The programming paradigm that allows you to do that is called AOP.

Understanding important AOP terminology

Let's consider a simple example. We have an application that has three layers—web, business, and data. We want to log every call that is made to every method in each layer.

Let's look at some of the key terminology that's used in AOP with respect to the previous example:

- The feature that we want to implement is to log a method call. This is called **advice**.
- Where do you want to apply this feature? To every method in web, business, and data layers. How do you identify these methods? You would need to define a **PointCut**. A PointCut identifies which methods advice should be applied to.
- The combination of a PointCut and advice is called an aspect. That's the reason why this programming paradigm is called AOP.

Understanding weaving

Once we define a PointCut (identifies which methods needed to be advised) and advice (what needs to be done), the AOP framework needs to modify the code so that the advice is applied to all the methods that match the PointCut. This process is called weaving.

There are three kinds of weaving:

- **Compile-Time Weaving**: The input is your source code, while the output is a compiled class with weaving.
- **Binary Weaving**: This is done after the code is compiled. The input is compiled class files or, jar files, while the output is either compiled classes or jars with weaving.
- **Runtime Weaving**: Weaving is done just before the class is loaded into JVM.

Compile-time weaving provides better performance than runtime weaving, but comes with greater complications since you would need an extra weaving step during compilation.

AOP frameworks

AspectJ is the most popular AOP framework for Java. AspectJ provides compile-time weaving. We can add the AspectJ compiler to our build process to do the weaving.

Spring AOP provides integration with AspectJ and a few basic AOP features of its own, and also Spring AOP does runtime weaving. It is simpler to use, but you can only intercept method calls on Spring beans.

Spring AOP does not aim to compete with AspectJ. Choosing between Spring AOP and AspectJ depends on your context.

If you are working with Spring beans and want to intercept method calls on Spring beans, then Spring AOP is sufficient. If you want to intercept method calls on objects that are not managed by the Spring container, you will need to use the complete AOP framework—AspectJ.

Getting hands-on with AOP

To use AOP with Spring Boot, the starter we would use is `spring-boot-starter-aop`:

```
<dependency>
 <groupId>org.springframework.boot</groupId>
 <artifactId>spring-boot-starter-aop</artifactId>
</dependency>
```

Some of the key dependencies that `spring-boot-starter-aop` brings in are as follows:

```
<dependency>
    <groupId>org.springframework</groupId>
    <artifactId>spring-aop</artifactId>
    <version>5.1.6.RELEASE</version>
    <scope>compile</scope>
</dependency>
<dependency>
    <groupId>org.aspectj</groupId>
    <artifactId>aspectjweaver</artifactId>
    <version>1.9.2</version>
    <scope>compile</scope>
</dependency>
```

spring-boot-starter-aop adds dependencies on spring-aop and aspectjweaver. We will see how spring-aop and aspectjweaver help us implement AOP in the next section.

Setting up a simple business scenario

Let's consider a simple shopping application. A shopping service checks the stock and places any orders. We want to be able to intercept all the calls using AOP and log information about them.

StockDao is a component that helps us check the stock:

```
@Component
public class StockDao {

    private Logger logger = LoggerFactory.getLogger(this.getClass());

    public Stock retrieveStock() {
        // Logic Goes Here
        logger.info("Returning a dummy value");
        return new Stock(20);
    }
}
```

Stock is a simple Java data class:

```
public class Stock {
    private int quantity;

    public Stock(int quantity) {
        super();
        this.quantity = quantity;
    }
}
```

`OrderDao` is a component that helps us place an order:

```
@Component
public class OrderDao {

    private Logger logger = LoggerFactory.getLogger(this.getClass());

    public void placeOrder(int value) {
        // Logic Goes Here
        logger.info("Placed Order - {}", value);
    }

}
```

`ShoppingService` has business logic. `StockDao` and `OrderDao` are autowired into `ShoppingService`:

```
@Service
public class ShoppingService {

    private Logger logger = LoggerFactory.getLogger(this.getClass());

    @Autowired
    private StockDao stockDao;

    @Autowired
    private OrderDao orderDao;

}
```

The `checkAndPlaceOrder` method checks the stock and places the order when stock is available:

```
public void checkAndPlaceOrder() {
    int availableQuantity = stockDao.retrieveStock().getQuantity();
    logger.info("Retrieved Stock - {}", availableQuantity);
    if (availableQuantity > 0) {
        orderDao.placeOrder(availableQuantity);
    }
}
```

Let's start with intercepting the method calls and logging the parameters that are passed to them.

Identifying the PointCut

The first step is to identify the PointCut.

Consider this example: execution(*
com.mastering.spring.ch03aopwithspring.*Dao.*(..)).

As we discussed previously, a PointCut is an expression that identifies which method calls to intercept.

In the previous example, we want to intercept all method executions within the com.mastering.spring.ch03aopwithspring package, with class names matching the *Dao pattern. OrderDao and StockDao would match this pattern; therefore, the PointCut identifies all method calls to OrderDao and StockDao.

Defining the aspect

The next step is to define the aspect class.

AspectJ provides a number of interception points for method calls, including the following:

- @Before: Before executing a method.
- @After: After executing a method. This executed even if the method throws an exception.
- @AfterReturning: After successful execution of a method.
- @AfterThrowing: After a method call which resulted in an exception being thrown.
- @Around: Take complete control of method execution. We will talk about this a little later.

We want to log all the parameters before executing the method; therefore, we would use the @Before annotation to define the interception point.

We would start with defining a BeforeMethodAspect class. We use the @Aspect and @Configuration annotations to specify that this class contains Spring configuration for an aspect:

```
@Aspect
@Configuration
public class BeforeMethodAspect {
```

We can define the method with `@Before` and use the previously discussed PointCut to intercept all `*Dao` calls:

```
@Before("execution(* com.mastering.spring.ch03aopwithspring.*Dao.*(..))")
public void before(JoinPoint joinPoint) {
    logger.info(" Before executing a method {}", joinPoint);
    logger.info(" Arguments passed are {}", joinPoint.getArgs());
}
```

An important concept to understand is `JoinPoint`.

`JoinPoint` is the runtime result of AOP. A specific instance where the PointCut matches and advice is being executed is called `JoinPoint`.

You can get the details of the method—the name and arguments—by using `JoinPoint`. In the previous snippet, we are using `joinPoint.getArgs()` to get the arguments that were passed to the method.

The result of the execution of the previous aspect is as follows:

```
dAspect$$EnhancerBySpringCGLIB$$91f21e3d : Before executing a method
execution(Stock
com.mastering.spring.ch03aopwithspring.StockDao.retrieveStock())
dAspect$$EnhancerBySpringCGLIB$$91f21e3d : Arguments passed are {}
dAspect$$EnhancerBySpringCGLIB$$91f21e3d : Before executing a method
execution(void
com.mastering.spring.ch03aopwithspring.OrderDao.placeOrder(int))
dAspect$$EnhancerBySpringCGLIB$$91f21e3d : Arguments passed are 20
```

You can see that we are intercepting method calls to `StockDao` and `OrderDao` and printing the arguments. Here are a couple of things to note:

- You can use the `execution(* com.mastering.spring.ch03aopwithspring.*.*(..))` PointCut to match every method call in the `com.mastering.spring.ch03aopwithspring` package.
- `@Before` interceptions are also used for implementing validations. You can use it to validate the arguments or validate access for method calls in specific sets of classes.

Let's look at examples of other interception points.

Understanding @After advice

@After advice is executed following the execution of the method in two scenarios:

- Method executed successfully
- Method threw an exception

Here, is an example implementation of @After advice:

```
@Aspect
@Configuration
public class AfterMethodAspect {

    private Logger logger = LoggerFactory.getLogger(this.getClass());

    @After("execution(*
com.mastering.spring.ch03aopwithspring.*Dao.*(..))")
    public void after(JoinPoint joinPoint) {
        logger.info(" After executing a method {}", joinPoint);
        logger.info(" Arguments passed are {}", joinPoint.getArgs());

    }

}
```

Implementing @After advice is very similar to implementing @Before advice. The result of the execution is as follows:

```
dAspect$$EnhancerBySpringCGLIB$$f7765220 : After executing a method
execution(Stock
com.mastering.spring.ch03aopwithspring.StockDao.retrieveStock())
dAspect$$EnhancerBySpringCGLIB$$f7765220 : Arguments passed are {}
dAspect$$EnhancerBySpringCGLIB$$f7765220 : After executing a method
execution(void
com.mastering.spring.ch03aopwithspring.OrderDao.placeOrder(int))
dAspect$$EnhancerBySpringCGLIB$$f7765220 : Arguments passed are 20
```

You can see that the advice is executed after both method calls on StockDao and OrderDao.

Understanding @AfterReturning advice

@AfterReturning advice is executed when a method successfully completes execution. This allows us to process the return value of successful execution.

An implementation of `@AfterReturning` is as follows:

```
@Aspect
@Configuration
public class AfterReturningMethodAspect {

    private Logger logger = LoggerFactory.getLogger(this.getClass());

    @AfterReturning(value = "execution(*
com.mastering.spring.ch03aopwithspring.*Dao.*(..))",
        returning = "result")
    public void afterReturning(JoinPoint joinPoint, Object result) {
        logger.info(" After returning from a method {}", joinPoint);
        logger.info(" Arguments passed are {}", joinPoint.getArgs());
        logger.info(" Value returned is {}", result);
    }

}
```

From the preceding code, we can understand the following:

- `@AfterReturning(value="execution(*
  com.mastering.spring.ch03aopwithspring.*Dao.*(..))", returning
  = "result")`: In addition to specifying the PointCut, we add `returning =
  "result"` to indicate the name of the variable to represent the return value from
  the method.
- `public void afterReturning(JoinPoint joinPoint, Object result)`:
  We added `Object result` as a method parameter to allow printing of the
  return value from the method execution.

Here's the result of the execution:

```
dAspect$$EnhancerBySpringCGLIB$$798ca1f0 : After returning from a method
execution(Stock
com.mastering.spring.ch03aopwithspring.StockDao.retrieveStock())
dAspect$$EnhancerBySpringCGLIB$$798ca1f0 : Arguments passed are {}
dAspect$$EnhancerBySpringCGLIB$$798ca1f0 : Value returned is Stock
[quantity=20]
dAspect$$EnhancerBySpringCGLIB$$798ca1f0 : After returning from a method
execution(void
com.mastering.spring.ch03aopwithspring.OrderDao.placeOrder(int))
dAspect$$EnhancerBySpringCGLIB$$798ca1f0 : Arguments passed are 20
dAspect$$EnhancerBySpringCGLIB$$798ca1f0 : Value returned is null
```

You can see that the `Stock [quantity=20]` return value is printed for the `retrieveStock` method. However, the `placeOrder` method returns `void`; therefore, `null` is printed.

Understanding @Around advice

`@Around` advice can be used to do something before and after the method execution.

For example, let's say we wanted to track how much time a method took to execute. We would want to be able to start a timer before the method is executed, execute the method, and stop the timer.

An example of `@Around` advice is as follows:

```
public class CalculateMethodExecutionTimeAspect {

    private Logger logger = LoggerFactory.getLogger(this.getClass());

    @Around(value = "execution(*
com.mastering.spring.ch03aopwithspring.*Dao.*(..))")
    public Object calculateMethodExecutionTime(ProceedingJoinPoint
proceedingJoinPoint) throws Throwable {
        long start = System.currentTimeMillis();
        Object retVal = proceedingJoinPoint.proceed();
        long duration = System.currentTimeMillis() - start;
        logger.info("Method {} took {} ms to execute", proceedingJoinPoint,
duration);
        return retVal;
    }
}
```

Important observations include the following:

- The parameter to `calculateMethodExecutionTime` is of the `ProceedingJoinPoint` type. `ProceedingJoinPoint` exposes the `proceed` method to support `@Around` advice.
- We start a timer with `long start = System.currentTimeMillis()`.
- We execute the method and capture the return value using `Object retVal = proceedingJoinPoint.proceed()`.
- We calculate method execution time using `long duration = System.currentTimeMillis() - start`.

The result of executing the code is as follows:

```
meAspect$$EnhancerBySpringCGLIB$$2ac1ace : Method execution(Stock
com.mastering.spring.ch03aopwithspring.StockDao.retrieveStock()) took 22 ms
to execute
meAspect$$EnhancerBySpringCGLIB$$2ac1ace : Method execution(void
com.mastering.spring.ch03aopwithspring.OrderDao.placeOrder(int)) took 22 ms
to execute
```

PointCut best practices

Up until now, we have been using several PointCuts. One of the problems with having a number of aspects is the proliferation of PointCuts across the application.

One of the best practices is to have a central class to define all the PointCuts.

An example of this is as follows:

```
public class JoinPointConfiguration {

    @Pointcut("execution(*
com.mastering.spring.ch03aopwithspring.OrderDao.*(..))")
    public void orderDaoExecution() {}

    @Pointcut("execution(*
com.mastering.spring.ch03aopwithspring.StockDao.*(..))")
    public void stockDaoExecution() {}

    @Pointcut("execution(*
com.mastering.spring.ch03aopwithspring.business.*.*(..))")
    public void allBusinessLayerMethods() {}

    @Pointcut("execution(*
com.mastering.spring.ch03aopwithspring.data.*.*(..))")
    public void allDataLayerMethods() {}

}
```

We are defining methods to represent specific PointCuts. You can use these method names to represent PointCuts when defining advices. For example, the @Around advice can now be defined as follows:

```
@Around("com.mastering.spring.ch03aopwithspring.JoinPointConfiguration.allD
ataLayerMethods()")
```

The preceding approach ensures that PointCuts are specified at one location and can easily be maintained.

You can use `&&` to combine PointCuts, as the following code shows with an example of `JoinPointConfiguration`. This PointCut method would match methods from business and data layers:

```
@Pointcut("allBusinessLayerMethods() && allDataLayerMethods()")
public void methodsFromBusinessAndDataLayers(){}
```

Defining custom AOP annotations

In all the examples until now, we have identified methods so that we can apply advice when we're using execution PointCuts.

We can also define custom annotations and use annotation PointCuts to identify methods to apply the advice to.

For example, let's say you found out that there are few specific methods running slowly and you wanted to add advice for detailed logging on them.

One of the implementation approaches is to create a `@LogEverything` annotation, use the annotation on the methods you want to trace in detail, and define a PointCut matching the annotation.

Defining an annotation is easy:

```
@Target(ElementType.METHOD)
@Retention(RetentionPolicy.RUNTIME)
public @interface LogEverything {
}
```

We can use `@LogEverything` on methods that we want to trace, as follows:

```
@LogEverything
public void placeOrder(int value) {
```

Before we are able to run the previous example, we need to define the PointCut and advice.

Let's define a common `JoinPointConfiguration` method for the PointCut. Notice that instead of `execution`, we are using `@annotation` in the PointCut:

```
@Pointcut("@annotation(com.mastering.spring.ch03aopwithspring.LogEverything
)")
public void logEverythingAnnoation(){}
```

Let's define an `@Around` aspect for logging, as follows. This code is similar to what we did earlier. You can log more details as per your requirements:

```
@Aspect
@Configuration
public class LogEverythingAspect {

    private Logger logger = LoggerFactory.getLogger(this.getClass());

@Around("com.mastering.spring.ch03aopwithspring.JoinPointConfiguration.logE
verythingAnnoation()")
    public Object calculateMethodExecutionTime(ProceedingJoinPoint
proceedingJoinPoint) throws Throwable {
        logger.info("Method {} started execution", proceedingJoinPoint);
        logger.info("Method {} arguments are {}", proceedingJoinPoint,
proceedingJoinPoint.getArgs());
        Object retVal = proceedingJoinPoint.proceed();
        logger.info("Method {} completed execution ", proceedingJoinPoint);
        return retVal;
    }
}
```

The result of executing the preceding code is as follows:

```
gAspect$$EnhancerBySpringCGLIB$$57feda03 : Method execution(void
com.mastering.spring.ch03aopwithspring.OrderDao.placeOrder(int)) started
execution
gAspect$$EnhancerBySpringCGLIB$$57feda03 : Method execution(void
com.mastering.spring.ch03aopwithspring.OrderDao.placeOrder(int)) arguments
are [20]
//Other Log
gAspect$$EnhancerBySpringCGLIB$$57feda03 : Method execution(void
com.mastering.spring.ch03aopwithspring.OrderDao.placeOrder(int)) completed
execution
```

You can see that we added the complete logging around this method execution.

You can add `@LogEverything` to all the methods you want to be able to trace completely.

Scheduling tasks with Spring

Enterprises have simple tasks that would be run on a regular schedule. Spring provides scheduling features that enable the execution of bean methods at regular intervals.

Scheduling tasks with @Scheduled

Let's look at how you can schedule your tasks with the Spring @Scheduled annotation.

Consider the bean that's defined as follows:

```
@Component
public class Task {

    private static final Logger log = LoggerFactory.getLogger(Task.class);

    @Scheduled(fixedRate = 10000)
    public void execute() {
        log.info("The time is now {}", new Date());
    }
}
```

Make sure that scheduling is enabled by adding @EnableScheduling on the Spring Boot application class:

```
@EnableScheduling
public class TaskSchedulingApplication implements CommandLineRunner {
```

Once the bean has been managed by the Spring container, @Scheduled(fixedRate = 10000) ensures that the execute method is run once every 10000 ms:

```
[ scheduling-1] c.mastering.spring.taskscheduling.Task : The time is now
Thu Apr 25 14:15:29 IST [ scheduling-1]
c.mastering.spring.taskscheduling.Task : The time is now Thu Apr 25
14:15:39 IST 2019
[ scheduling-1] c.mastering.spring.taskscheduling.Task : The time is now
Thu Apr 25 14:15:49 IST 2019
[ scheduling-1] c.mastering.spring.taskscheduling.Task : The time is now
Thu Apr 25 14:15:59 IST 2019
[ scheduling-1] c.mastering.spring.taskscheduling.Task : The time is now
Thu Apr 25 14:16:09 IST 2019
```

You can customize @Schedule further with annotation attributes:

- You can use fixedDelay=10000 to indicate that the task has to be run 10000 ms after the completion of the previous task. Instead of saying that we want to run a task every 10 seconds, we are asking fixedDelay=10000 to run the task, wait for 10 seconds, and run it again.
- You can use initialDelay=20000 to specify an initial delay before the task is run for the first time.
- You can also use cron="*/8 * * * * MON"—a Unix cron expression—to specify intervals.

Running tasks asynchronously using @Async

You can also trigger tasks asynchronously using the @Async annotation. Consider the following example:

```
@Component
public class AsyncTask {

    private Logger logger = LoggerFactory.getLogger(this.getClass());

    @Async
    void doThisAsynchronously() {
        IntStream.range(1, 100).forEach(x - > logger.info("AsyncTask {}",
x));
    }

}
```

When doThisAsynchronously is called on the bean, it will always be executed asynchronously.

Before using @Async, we need to ensure that @EnableAsync is added to our Spring Boot application class:

```
@EnableAsync
public class TaskSchedulingApplication implements CommandLineRunner {
```

Consider the following code to trigger doThisAsynchronously:

```
@Autowired
private AsyncTask asyncTask;
@Override
public void run(String...args) throws Exception {
    asyncTask.doThisAsynchronously();
    IntStream.range(1, 100).forEach(x - >
logger.info("TaskSchedulingApplication {}", x));
}
```

We are autowiring AsyncTask in and implementing the run method of
CommandLineRunner to trigger doThisAsynchronously, in parallel with other code.

You can see that the code runs asynchronously. You can also see that there are logs related
to TaskSchedulingApplication before AsyncTask completes execution:

```
[ task-1] c.m.spring.taskscheduling.AsyncTask : AsyncTask 86
[ task-1] c.m.spring.taskscheduling.AsyncTask : AsyncTask 87
[ main] plication$$EnhancerBySpringCGLIB$$3ed9f7 :
TaskSchedulingApplication 1
[ task-1] c.m.spring.taskscheduling.AsyncTask : AsyncTask 88
//More log
//More log
[ main] plication$$EnhancerBySpringCGLIB$$3ed9f7 :
TaskSchedulingApplication 2
```

Returning values from @Async methods

You can also return values from @Async methods. To be able to do that, we use Future.
Consider the doThisAsynchronouslyAndReturnAValue method, which is defined as
follows, in the AsyncTask class. We are making it return Future using new
AsyncResult<>(sum):

```
@Async
Future < Long > doThisAsynchronouslyAndReturnAValue() {
    IntStream.range(1, 100).forEach(x - > logger.info("AsyncTask With
Return Value {}", x));
    long sum = IntStream.range(1, 100).sum();
    return new AsyncResult < > (sum);
}
```

We can run the `doThisAsynchronouslyAndReturnAValue` method from the `TaskSchedulingApplication` class. When we call the method, we get `Future<Long>` `futureValue` as the result. We can let the method continue executing asynchronously. When you need the result of the execution of the method, you can call `futureValue.get()`. This will cause the calling thread to wait for the `doThisAsynchronouslyAndReturnAValue` method to complete execution and return a value:

```
@Override
public void run(String...args) throws Exception {
    asyncTask.doThisAsynchronously();
    Future < Long > futureValue =
asyncTask.doThisAsynchronouslyAndReturnAValue();
    IntStream.range(1, 100).forEach(x - >
logger.info("TaskSchedulingApplication {}", x));
    logger.info("Sum is {}", futureValue.get());

}
```

Understanding task executors

As we start executing tasks asynchronously, it is important to understand the task executors running these tasks.

The Java executor framework is used to manage Java threads. Similarly, Spring task executors are used to run Spring tasks.

The default task executor that's used by the Spring Framework is `SimpleAsyncTaskExecutor`. The default number of concurrent threads for `SimpleAsyncTaskExecutor` is unlimited. `SimpleAsyncTaskExecutor` does not reuse earlier threads; therefore, it is not ideal for scenarios involving a huge number of short-lived tasks.

A good alternative is `ThreadPoolTaskExecutor`. It allows you to specify `corePoolSize` and `maxPoolSize`.

Here's a simple example of `ThreadPoolTaskExecutor` with `corePoolSize` set to 3 and `maxPoolSize` set to 10:

```
ThreadPoolTaskExecutor threadPoolTaskExecutor = new
ThreadPoolTaskExecutor();
threadPoolTaskExecutor.setCorePoolSize(3);
threadPoolTaskExecutor.setMaxPoolSize(10);
```

You can configure a Spring bean for ThreadPoolTaskExecutor as follows:

```
@Configuration
class ThreadPoolConfigurer implements AsyncConfigurer {

    @Override
    public Executor getAsyncExecutor() {
        ThreadPoolTaskExecutor threadPoolTaskExecutor = new
ThreadPoolTaskExecutor();
        threadPoolTaskExecutor.setCorePoolSize(3);
        threadPoolTaskExecutor.setMaxPoolSize(10);
        threadPoolTaskExecutor.initialize();
        return threadPoolTaskExecutor;
    }

}
```

We are creating a simple Spring Configuration class with a method returning the Executor class. Make sure that you initialize the threadPoolTaskExecutor instance before returning it.

In this section, we looked at how the Spring Framework helps us to schedule and run tasks asynchronously.

Scripting with the Spring Framework

Scripting helps applications change behavior at runtime. JSR 223 makes it easy to execute dynamic language scripts in Java.

We will start by executing simple examples of JavaScript and Groovy code from Java.

Spring provides features for integrating and executing dynamic scripts. We will look at the basics of scripting and how they can be integrated into Spring projects in this section.

JSR 223 – scripting for the JavaTM platform

JSR 223 defines the API for embedding scripts from dynamic languages into Java.

The important interfaces are ScriptEngineManager, ScriptEngine, and Bindings.

ScriptEngineManager **allows you to create instances of** ScriptEngine. **You can bind parameters to pass to** ScriptEngines **using** Bindings.

Oracle JVM includes JavaScript engines from Java 6. From Java 8, the JavaScript engine that's included is Nashorn.

Executing JavaScript code in Java

Let's start with trying to execute some JavaScript code by using the built-in Nashorn script engine.

We are passing a string value as bindings and executing a JavaScript print(str) statement using ScriptEngine:

```
public class JavaScriptCode {

    public static void main(String[] args) throws ScriptException {
        final ScriptEngineManager scriptEngineManager = new
ScriptEngineManager();
        final ScriptEngine scriptEngine =
scriptEngineManager.getEngineByName("Nashorn");
        final Bindings bindings = scriptEngine.createBindings();
        bindings.put("str", "Let's pass from Java to JavaScript");
        scriptEngine.eval(" print(str)", bindings);
    }

}
```

The output of the preceding code is as follows:

```
Let's pass from Java to JavaScript
```

You can see that we are able to easily execute JavaScript code.

Executing Groovy code in Java

Groovy is one of the most popular dynamic JVM languages. Executing Groovy code in Java is equally simple. We are using ScriptEngine. println str is the Groovy syntax for printing a String:

```
public class GroovyCode {

    public static void main(String[] args) throws ScriptException {
```

```
        final ScriptEngineManager scriptEngineManager = new
ScriptEngineManager();
        final ScriptEngine scriptEngine =
scriptEngineManager.getEngineByName("Groovy");
        final Bindings bindings1 = scriptEngine.createBindings();
        bindings1.put("str", "Let's pass from Java to Groovy");
        scriptEngine.eval(" println str", bindings1);
    }


}
```

Here's the result of executing the code:

```
Let's pass from Java to Groovy
```

To run the previous code, make sure that you have Groovy installed locally and that you have included Groovy jars in the class path.

Here's an example of how to run it from the command prompt:

```
java -cp ".:/usr/local/opt/groovy/libexec/lib/*"
com.mastering.spring.taskscheduling.dynamic.GroovyCode
```

Executing Groovy code in Spring enterprise applications

Spring makes it easy to define classes and objects in multiple dynamic languages and use them as Spring-managed beans.

Spring supports Groovy and languages supported by JSR 223, such as JRuby.

Each of the languages has separate `lang` elements—`<lang:jruby/>` for JRuby and `<lang:groovy/>` for Groovy—to allow us to create Spring beans.

Consider the following example. We are using `lang:groovy` to create a bean with a `planet` ID for the `script.groovy` script. You can create inline scripts as well, but we'll talk about this later:

```
//dynamic-beans.xml

<beans xmlns="http://www.springframework.org/schema/beans"
 xmlns:xsi="http://www.w3.org/2001/XMLSchema-instance"
 xmlns:lang="http://www.springframework.org/schema/lang"
 xsi:schemaLocation="http://www.springframework.org/schema/beans
 http://www.springframework.org/schema/beans/spring-beans-4.1.xsd
```

```
http://www.springframework.org/schema/lang
http://www.springframework.org/schema/lang/spring-lang-2.0.xsd">

<lang:groovy id="planet" script-source="classpath:script.groovy"/>

</beans>
```

`script.groovy` contains an implementation of a `planet` interface:

```
import com.mastering.spring.dynamic.scripting.Planet
class Earth implements Planet {
    public long getDistanceFromSun() {
        return 100000000
    }
}
```

A `Planet` interface has a simple method, `getDistanceFromSun`:

```
public interface Planet {
    long getDistanceFromSun();
}
```

The following code shows how you can launch up a Spring Boot application to test the Spring bean that was created from the Groovy script. `@ImportResource(value = { "classpath:dynamic-beans.xml" })` ensures that the dynamic beans that are defined are loaded. We are implementing `CommandLineRunner` to ensure that our code runs at application startup. We are autowiring `planet` and calling `planet.getDistanceFromSun()` in the run method:

```
@SpringBootApplication
@ImportResource(value = {
    "classpath:dynamic-beans.xml"
})
public class DynamicScriptingApplication implements CommandLineRunner {

    private Logger logger = LoggerFactory.getLogger(this.getClass());

    @Autowired
    private Planet planet;

    @Override
    public void run(String...args) throws Exception {
        logger.info("{}", planet.getDistanceFromSun());
    }
```

The result of the preceding execution is as follows:

```
2019-04-25 14:27:23.629 INFO 25639 --- [ main]
ication$$EnhancerBySpringCGLIB$$2fb04251 : 100000000
```

You can see that we are able to execute a Groovy script from the Spring application.

The Groovy script can be outside the application as well —anywhere in the classpath. This gives us the flexibility of modifying the Groovy script without changing the application's deployable unit.

Inlining Groovy code into Spring context XML

Let's look at an example of directly writing Groovy code in Spring context XML. We are defining a bean—its ID is `inlineBean`—with `lang:inline-script` , which contains the Groovy code:

```
<lang:groovy id="inlineBean">
 <lang:inline-script>
 import com.mastering.spring.dynamic.scripting.SecretMessenger
 class DummyMessenger implements SecretMessenger {
    String key
 }
 </lang:inline-script>
 <lang:property name="key" value="SECRET_KEY" />
</lang:groovy>
```

The interface definition is as follows:

```
public interface SecretMessenger {
   String getKey();
}
```

We can enhance `DynamicScriptingApplication` to autowire `SecretMessenger` and call `messenger.getKey()` in the `run` method:

```
public class DynamicScriptingApplication implements CommandLineRunner {

    @Autowired
    private SecretMessenger messenger;

    @Override
    public void run(String...args) throws Exception {
        logger.info("{}", messenger.getKey());
    }
```

The result is as follows:

```
2019-04-25 14:27:23.632 INFO 25639 --- [ main]
ication$$EnhancerBySpringCGLIB$$2fb04251 : SECRET_KEY
```

Summary

Cross-cutting concerns such as logging and security are some of the most important features of well-developed applications.

In this chapter, we have understood why cross-cutting concerns are best developed using AOP. We have understood the basic concepts of AOP—PointCuts, advice, and weaving.

Then, we looked at the popular options for implementing AOP with the Spring Framework—Spring AOP and AspectJ. We learned that Spring AOP is recommended when you want to weave around Spring beans. For more complex features, AspectJ is the framework to use.

Afterwards, we looked at examples of implementing different advice with Spring AOP—@Before, @Around, @After, and @AfterReturning. We understood the best practice in defining PointCuts, which is creating a common PointCut class. Then, we learned to implement a custom AOP annotation in order to identify methods where advice has to be applied to.

Next, we explored the different options that the Spring Framework provides to schedule your tasks. We also learned how to run our tasks in parallel with @Async. We also explored an important task executor—ThreadPoolTaskExecutor.

Then, we looked at how you can execute JavaScript and Groovy scripts with the Spring Framework, with the important JSR 223 interfaces—ScriptEngineManager, ScriptEngine, and Bindings.

At the end of this chapter, we learned how to schedule tasks and execute dynamic scripts with the Spring Framework.

In the next chapter, we will start our journey toward building great REST API and Full Stack applications with Spring Boot.

Section 2: Building a REST API and Full Stack Applications with Spring

2

In the last decade, application architectures have continuously evolved toward full stack applications with a REST API as a backend.

In this section, we will learn how to build great REST APIs with Spring Boot. We will add all-important REST API features, including unit testing and security. We will build a basic full stack application integration with the REST API.

The following chapters are covered in this section:

- Chapter 6, *Building REST APIs with Spring Boot*
- Chapter 7, *Unit Testing REST API with Spring Boot*
- Chapter 8, *Securing REST API with Spring Security*
- Chapter 9, *Full Stack App with React and Spring Boot*
- Chapter 10, *Managing Data with Spring Data*

Building REST APIs with Spring Boot

6

In the previous chapter, we looked at the basics of Spring Boot. In this chapter, we'll focus on building great **Representational State Transfer** (**REST**) APIs with Spring Boot.

Applications do not live alone. They talk to each other. Applications can be built in a wide range of languages—Java, C#, JavaScript, and more. How do we get these to talk to others? Web services is the answer. Initially, XML-based web services using **Simple Object Access Protocol** (**SOAP**) were the order of the day. In the last few years, web services built in the REST style have become popular.

In this chapter, we will answer the following questions:

- What is REST?
- Why is REST popular today?
- How do you build REST APIs with Spring Boot?
- What are the different request methods—`GET`, `POST`, and so on—and when do you use them?
- How do you provide great exception handling and validations for your REST API?
- How do you provide documentation for your REST API?
- How do you implement advanced features for your REST API, such as **Hypermedia as the Engine of Application State** (**HATEOAS**), caching, and internationalization?
- How do you deploy your REST API to the cloud?

Understanding REST

REST is basically an architectural style for the web. REST specifies a set of constraints. These constraints ensure that clients (service consumers and browsers) can interact with servers in flexible ways.

First, let's understand some common terminology:

- **Server**: Service provider. Exposes services that can be consumed by clients.
- **Client**: Service consumer. Could be a browser or another system.
- **Resource**: Any information can be a resource: a person, an image, a video, or a product you want to sell.
- **Representation**: A specific way in which a resource can be represented. For example, the product resource can be represented using JSON, XML, or HTML. Different clients might request different representations of the resource.

Some of the important REST constraints are listed as follows:

- **Client-server**: There should be a server (service provider) and a client (service consumer). This enables loose coupling and independent evolution of the server and client as new technologies emerge.
- **Stateless**: Each service should be stateless. Subsequent requests should not depend on some data from a previous request being temporarily stored. Messages should be self-descriptive.
- **Uniform interface**: Each resource has a resource identifier. In the case of web services, we use this **Uniform Resource Identifier (URI)**, for example—`/users/Jack/todos/1`. In this example URI, `Jack` is the name of the user, and `1` is the ID of the todo we would want to retrieve.
- **Cacheable**: The service response should be cacheable. Each response should indicate whether it is cacheable.
- **Layered system**: The consumer of the service should not assume a direct connection to the service provider. Since requests can be cached, the client might be getting the cached response from a middle layer.
- **Manipulation of resources through representations**: A resource can have multiple representations. It should be possible to modify the resource through a message with any of these representations.
- **HATEOAS**: The consumer of a RESTful application should know about only one fixed service URL. All subsequent resources should be discoverable from the links included in the resource representations.

An example response with the HATEOAS link is shown here. This is the response to a request to retrieve all todos:

```
{
"_embedded":{
"todos":[
        {
            "user":"Jill",
            "desc":"Learn Hibernate",
            "done":false,
            "_links":{
              "self":{
                    "href":"http://localhost:8080/todos/1"
                },
                "todo":{
                    "href":"http://localhost:8080/todos/1"
                }
            }
        }
    ]
},
"_links":{
    "self":{
        "href":"http://localhost:8080/todos"
    },
    "profile":{
        "href":"http://localhost:8080/profile/todos"
    },
    "search":{
        "href":"http://localhost:8080/todos/search"
    }
  }
}
```

The preceding response includes links to the following:

- Specific todos (`http://localhost:8080/todos/1`)
- Search resource (`http://localhost:8080/todos/search`)

If the service consumer wants to do a search, it has the option of taking the search URL from the response and sending the search request to it. This would reduce coupling between the service provider and the service consumer.

The initial services we develop will not be adhering to all of these constraints. As we move on to the next chapters, we will introduce you to the details of these constraints and add them to the services to make them more RESTful.

Designing your first REST API

In this chapter, we'll focus on building a REST API for managing your todos. We would want to provide APIs to retrieve, update, add, and delete todo information. We will start with understanding the best practices in designing REST APIs. We will decide on the URIs that we would want to use for different operations.

Deciding on request methods and URIs for REST API operations

One of the best practices of REST services is to use the appropriate HTTP request method based on the action we perform. In the services we exposed until now, we've used the GET method since we focused on services that read data.

The following table shows the appropriate HTTP request methods based on the operations that we perform:

HTTP Request Method	Operation
GET	Read—retrieve details for a resource
POST	Create—create a new item or resource
PUT	Update/replace
PATCH	Update/modify a part of the resource
DELETE	Delete

Let's quickly map the services that we want to create to the appropriate request methods:

- **Retrieving a list of todos for a given user**: This is READ. We will use GET. We will use a /users/{name}/todos URI. One more good practice is to use plurals for static things in the URI—users, todo, and so on. This results in more readable URIs.

- **Retrieving details for a specific todo**: Again, we will use GET. We will use a /users/{name}/todos/{id} URI. You can see that this is consistent with the previous URI that we decided for the list of todos.

- **Creating a todo for a user**: For the create operation, the suggested HTTP request method is POST. To create a new todo, we will post to the following URI: /users/{name}/todos. The body of the request will contain the details of the todo.

- **Deleting a todo**: For the delete operation, the suggested HTTP request method is DELETE. The URI to identify a todo is the same as the URI for retrieving todo details: /users/{name}/todos/{id}.
- **Updating a todo:** For the update operation, the suggested HTTP request method is PUT. To update an existing todo, we will do a PUT request to /users/{name}/todos/{id}. The body of the request will contain the details of the todo.

Understanding the high-level approach for creating APIs

Spring Boot makes it easy to develop REST APIs. To understand the basic features of Spring Boot (URI mapping, path variables, generating JSON responses, and more), we will create a couple of Hello World services. Once we are comfortable with creating basic services with Spring Boot, we will start creating the GET, POST, PUT, and DELETE operations for the todo REST API.

Creating a Hello World API with Spring Boot

Let's start by taking small steps toward building the complete API. We will start with creating a simple Hello World REST service that returns a welcome message.

Creating an API that returns a Hello World string

Let's start by creating a simple @RESTController method that returns a string:

```
@RestController
public class BasicController {

  @GetMapping("/welcome")
  public String welcome() {
    return "Hello World";
  }

}
```

A few important things to note are as follows:

- `@RestController`: The `@RestController` annotation provides a combination of `@ResponseBody` and `@Controller` annotations. This is typically used to create REST controllers.
- `@GetMapping("welcome")`: `@GetMapping` is a shortcut for `@RequestMapping(method = RequestMethod.GET)`. This annotation is a readable alternative. The method with this annotation would handle a GET request to the `welcome` URI.

If we run `Application.java` as a Java application, it would start up the embedded Tomcat container. We can launch `http://localhost:8080/welcome` in the browser, as shown in the following screenshot:

Creating a REST API that returns a welcome JSON response

In the previous request, we returned a string as the response. Now, let's create an API that returns a proper JSON response.

To be able to return a JSON response, we would need to create a **Plain Old Java Object (POJO)** to hold the response structure. We will create a simple POJO `WelcomeBean` class with a member field called message and one argument constructor, as shown in the following code snippet:

```
package com.mastering.spring.springboot.bean;

public class WelcomeBean {
  private String message;

    public WelcomeBean(String message) {
      super();
      this.message = message;
```

```
    }

  public String getMessage() {
    return message;
  }
}
```

Take a look at the following method. It returns a simple `WelcomeBean` class initialized with a message—"Hello World":

```
@GetMapping("/welcome-with-object")
public WelcomeBean welcomeWithObject() {

  return new WelcomeBean("Hello World");

}
```

Executing a request

Let's send a test request and see what response we get. The following screenshot shows the output:

localhost:8080/welcome-with-object

{"message":"Hello World"}

The response for the `http://localhost:8080/welcome-with-object` URL is as follows:

```
{"message":"Hello World"}
```

 The question that needs to be answered is this—how does the `WelcomeBean` object that we returned get converted into JSON? It's the magic of Spring Boot auto-configuration. If Jackson is on the classpath of an application, instances of the default object to JSON (and vice versa) converters are autoconfigured by Spring Boot.

Creating a welcome message with a name path variable

Path variables are used to bind values from the URI to a variable on the controller method. Let's consider an example—`/welcome-with-parameter/name/Ranga`. In this URI, `Ranga` is a value. I want to be able to map `Ranga` to a variable in the request method.

The following code example shows how we can use path variables and customize the name in the welcome message:

```
@GetMapping("/welcome-with-parameter/name/{name}")
public WelcomeBean welcomeWithParameter(@PathVariable String name) {

        return new WelcomeBean(String.format("Hello World, %s!", name));

}
```

A few important things to note are as follows:

- `@GetMapping("/welcome-with-parameter/name/{name}")`: `{name}` indicates that this value will be the variable. We can have multiple variable templates in a URI.
- `welcomeWithParameter(@PathVariable String name)`: `@PathVariable` ensures that the variable value from the URI is bound to the variable name.
- `String.format(helloWorldTemplate, name)`: A simple string format to replace `%s` in the template with the name.

Executing a request

Let's send a test request and see what response we get. The following screenshot shows the output:

localhost:8080/welcome-with-parameter/name/Buddy

```
{"message":"Hello World, Buddy!"}
```

The response for the
`http://localhost:8080/welcome-with-parameter/name/Buddy` URL is as follows:

```
{"message":"Hello World, Buddy!"}
```

As expected, the name in the URI is used to form the message in the response.

Creating a todo REST API

Here, we will focus on creating REST services for a basic todo management system. We will create services for the following:

- Retrieving a list of todos for a given user
- Retrieving details for a specific todo
- Creating a todo
- Deleting a todo
- Updating todo details

Before creating the REST API for todos, we will start by setting up the beans and services.

Setting up beans and services

To be able to retrieve and store the details of a todo, we need a `Todo` bean and a service to retrieve and store the details.

Let's create a `Todo` bean:

```java
public class Todo {
  private int id;
  private String user;

  private String desc;

  private Date targetDate;
  private boolean isDone;

  public Todo() {}

  public Todo(int id, String user, String desc,
  Date targetDate, boolean isDone) {
    super();
    this.id = id;
```

```
        this.user = user;
        this.desc = desc;
        this.targetDate = targetDate;
        this.isDone = isDone;
    }


    //ALL Getters
}
```

We have a created a simple `Todo` bean with the ID, the name of the user, the description of the todo, the todo target date, and an indicator for the completion status. We have added a constructor and getters for all the fields.

Let's add `TodoService` now. To keep things simple, this service does not talk to the database. It maintains an in-memory array list of todos. This list is initialized using a static initializer:

```
@Service
public class TodoService {

    private static List<Todo> todos = new ArrayList<Todo>();

    private static int todoCount = 3;

    static {
        todos.add(new Todo(1, "Jack", "Learn Spring MVC", new Date(),
false));
        todos.add(new Todo(2, "Jack", "Learn Struts", new Date(), false));
        todos.add(new Todo(3, "Jill", "Learn Hibernate", new Date(), false));
    }
```

Some of the important methods are as follows:

```
    public List<Todo> retrieveTodos(String user) {
        //returns all todos for a given users
    }

    public Todo addTodo(String name, String desc, Date targetDate, boolean
isDone) {
        //logic for adding a todo
    }

    public Todo retrieveTodo(int id) {
        //retrieve a todo
    }

    public Todo update(Todo todo) {
        //update a todo
```

```
    }

    public Todo deleteById(int id) {
        //delete a todo
    }
}
```

Now that we have the service and the bean ready, we can create our first service to retrieve a list of todos for a user.

Retrieving a todo list

We will create a new `RestController` annotation called `TodoController`. The code for the `retrieveTodos` method is as follows:

```
@RestController
public class TodoController {

  @Autowired
  private TodoService todoService;

  @GetMapping("/users/{name}/todos")
  public List<Todo> retrieveTodos(@PathVariable String name) {
    return todoService.retrieveTodos(name);
  }

}
```

A couple of things to note are as follows:

- We are autowiring the todo service using the `@Autowired` annotation.
- We use the `@GetMapping` annotation to map the GET request for the `"/users/{name}/todos"` URI to the `retrieveTodos` method.

Executing the service

Let's send a test request and see what response we get. The following screenshot shows the output:

The response for the `http://localhost:8080/users/Jack/todos` URL is as follows:

```
[
    {
        "id":1,
        "user":"Jack",
        "desc":"Learn Spring MVC",
        "targetDate":"2019-01-08T12:42:42.337+0000",
        "done":false
    },
    {
        "id":2,
        "user":"Jack",
        "desc":"Learn Struts",
        "targetDate":"2019-01-08T12:42:42.337+0000",
        "done":false
    }
]
```

Since we are returning a list of todos, we have an array of todos sent back as a response.

Retrieving details for a specific Todo

First of all, we want to identify the todo to retrieve the details. We will do that by adding the todo `id` as a path variable.

The details can be seen in the following method:

```
@GetMapping(path = "/users/{name}/todos/{id}")
public Todo retrieveTodo(@PathVariable String name,
                                    @PathVariable int id) {

    return todoService.retrieveTodo(id);

}
```

A couple of things to note are as follows:

- The URI that's mapped is `/users/{name}/todos/{id}`.
- We have two path variables defined for `name` and `id`.

Executing the service

Let's send a test request and see what response we get, as shown in the following screenshot:

The response for the `http://localhost:8080/users/Jack/todos/1` URL is as follows:

```
{
    "id":1,
    "user":"Jack",
    "desc":"Learn Spring MVC",
    "targetDate":"2019-01-08T12:42:42.337+0000",
    "done":false
}
```

Adding a Todo

We will now add the method to create a new `Todo`. The HTTP method to be used for creation is `Post`. We will post to a `"/users/{name}/todos"` URI:

```
@PostMapping("/users/{name}/todos")
ResponseEntity<?> add( @PathVariable String name,
                                        @RequestBody Todo todo) {

  Todo createdTodo = todoService.addTodo(name, todo.getDesc(),

  todo.getTargetDate(), todo.isDone());

  if (createdTodo == null) {
     return ResponseEntity.noContent().build();
  }

  URI location = ServletUriComponentsBuilder.fromCurrentRequest()

  .path("/{id}").buildAndExpand(createdTodo.getId()).toUri();

   return ResponseEntity.created(location).build();

}
```

A few things to note are as follows:

- `@PostMapping("/users/{name}/todos")`: The `@PostMapping` annotation maps the `add()` method to the HTTP request with a POST method.
- `ResponseEntity<?> add(@PathVariable String name, @RequestBody Todo todo)`: An HTTP post request should ideally return the URI to the created resources. We use `ResourceEntity` to do this. `@RequestBody` binds the body of the request directly to the bean.
- `ResponseEntity.noContent().build()`: This is used to inform us that the creation of the resource failed.
- `ServletUriComponentsBuilder.fromCurrentRequest().path("/{id}").buildAndExpand(createdTodo.getId()).toUri()`: Forms the URI for the created resource that can be returned in the response.
- `ResponseEntity.created(location).build()`: Returns a status of 201(CREATED) with a link to the resource that was created.

Introducing Postman – a REST API client

We will use the **Postman** app to interact with the REST services. You can install it from the website, `https://www.getpostman.com/`. It is available on Windows and Mac. A Google Chrome plugin is also available.

If you are on Mac, you might want to try the `Paw` application as well.

The following screenshot shows us sending of a simple `GET` request using Postman:

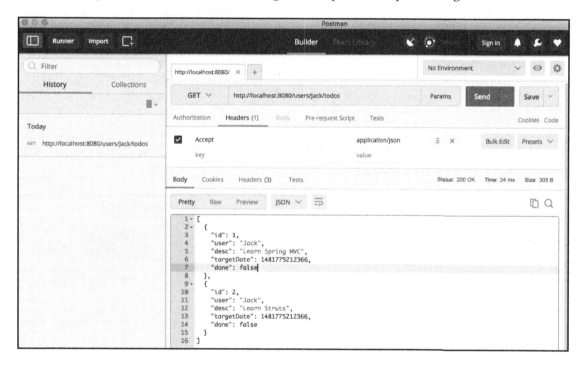

Executing the POST service using Postman

To create a new `Todo` using `POST`, we need to include the JSON for the `Todo` in the body of the request.

Let's consider an example—we want to create a new `Todo` for `Jack to Learn Spring Boot`.

Some important details are listed here:

- We would need to send a POST request to the following
  URI: `http://localhost:8080/users/Jack/todos`.
- The body of the request contains JSON; therefore, we would need to send a
  request header—`Content-Type:application/json`.

The complete request details are as follows:

```
Header
Content-Type:application/json

Body
  {
    "user": "Jack",
    "desc": "Learn Spring Boot",
     "done": false
  }
```

The following screenshot shows how we can use the Postman app to create the request, and
the response after executing the request:

A few important things to note are as follows:

- We are sending a POST request; therefore, we choose POST from the top-left dropdown.
- To send the Todo JSON as part of the body of the request, we select the **raw** option in the **Body** tab (highlighted with a blue dot). We choose the content type as JSON (application/json).
- Once the request has been successfully executed, you can see the status of the request in the bar in the middle of the screen: **Status: 201 Created**.
- The location is http://localhost:8080/users/Jack/todos/5. This is the URI of the newly created todo that is received in the response.

Updating a Todo

We will now add the method for updating the details of an existing Todo. The HTTP method to be used for updating a resource is PUT. We will post to a "/users/{name}/todos/{id}" URI:

```
@PutMapping("/users/{name}/todos/{id}")
public ResponseEntity<Todo> updateTodo(@PathVariable String name,
@PathVariable int id,
    @RequestBody Todo todo) {

  todoService.update(todo);

  return new ResponseEntity<Todo>(todo, HttpStatus.OK);

}
```

A few things to note are as follows:

- @PutMapping("/users/{name}/todos/{id}"): @PutMapping annotations map the update() method to the HTTP request with a PUT method.
- public ResponseEntity<Todo> updateTodo(@PathVariable String name, @PathVariable int id, @RequestBody Todo todo): An HTTP PUT request should ideally return the content of the updated resource. We use ResourceEntity to do this. @RequestBody binds the body of the request directly to the bean.

Executing the PUT service using Postman

To update a `Todo` using `PUT`, we need to include the JSON for the `Todo` in the body of the request.

Let's consider an example—we want to update the `Todo` with ID 1 belonging to Jack.

Some important details are listed here:

- We would need to send a `PUT` request to the following URI: `http://localhost:8080/users/Jack/todos/1`.
- The body of the request contains JSON; therefore, we would need to send a request header—`Content-Type:application/json`.

The complete request details are as follows:

```
Header
Content-Type:application/json

Body
{
    "id"   : 1,
    "user": "Jack",
    "desc": "Learn Spring MVC & More",
    "done": false
}
```

The following screenshot shows how we can use the Postman app to create the request:

The following is the screenshot of the response after executing the request:

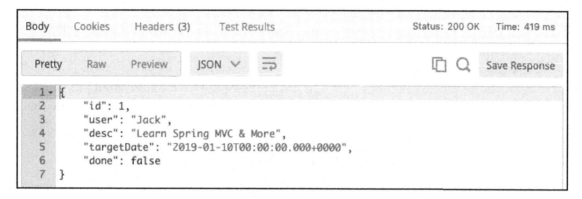

A few important things to note are as follows:

- We are sending a PUT request; therefore, we choose PUT from the top-left dropdown.
- To send the Todo JSON as part of the body of the request, we select the **raw** option in the **Body** tab (highlighted with a blue dot). We choose the content type as JSON (application/json).
- Once the request is successfully executed, you can see the status of the request in the bar in the middle of the screen: **Status: 200 Ok**.

Deleting a Todo

We will now add the method to delete the details of an existing Todo. The HTTP method to be used for deleting a resource is DELETE. We will map the following URI: "/users/{name}/todos/{id}". The method is as follows:

```
@DeleteMapping("/users/{name}/todos/{id}")
public ResponseEntity<Void> deleteTodo(@PathVariable String name,
@PathVariable int id) {

    Todo todo = todoService.deleteById(id);

    if (todo != null) {
        return ResponseEntity.noContent().build();
    }

    return ResponseEntity.notFound().build();
}
```

A few things to note are as follows:

- `@DeleteMapping("/users/{name}/todos/{id}")`:
  The `@PutMapping` annotation maps the `deleteById()` method to the HTTP request with a `DELETE` method.
- `public ResponseEntity<Void> deleteTodo(@PathVariable String name, @PathVariable int id)`: An HTTP `DELETE` method should ideally return a status of `No Content` if successful. We use `ResourceEntity` to do this.

Executing the DELETE service using Postman

Let's consider an example—we want to delete the todo with ID 1 belonging to Jack. We need to send a `DELETE` request to the following URI: `http://localhost:8080/users/Jack/todos/1`.

The following screenshot shows how we can use the Postman app to create the request:

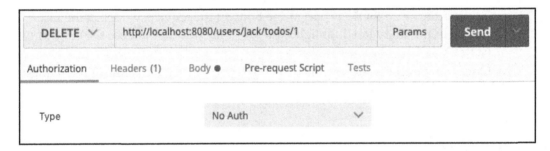

The following is the screenshot of the response after executing the request:

A couple of important things to note are as follows:

- We are sending a DELETE request; therefore, we choose DELETE from the top-left dropdown.
- Once the request is successfully executed, you can see the status of the request in the bar in the middle of the screen: **Status: 204 No Content**.

In this section, we looked at defining a REST API, exposing all the typical **Create, Read, Update, and Delete (CRUD)** operations that are performed on resources. In the subsequent sections, we will implement exception handling, validation, and more advanced features for the todo REST API.

Implementing exception handling for REST APIs

Exception handling is one of the most important parts of developing web services. When something goes wrong, we want to return a good description of what went wrong to the service consumer. You would not want the service to crash without returning anything useful to the service consumer.

Spring Boot provides good default exception handling. We will start by looking at the default exception handling features provided by Spring Boot before moving on to customizing them.

Understanding Spring Boot default exception handling

To understand the default exception handling provided by Spring Boot, let's start with firing a request to a nonexistent URL.

What happens when a resource doesn't exist?

Let's send a GET request to http://localhost:8080/non-existing-resource using a header (**Content-Type:application/json**).

The following screenshot shows the response when we execute the request:

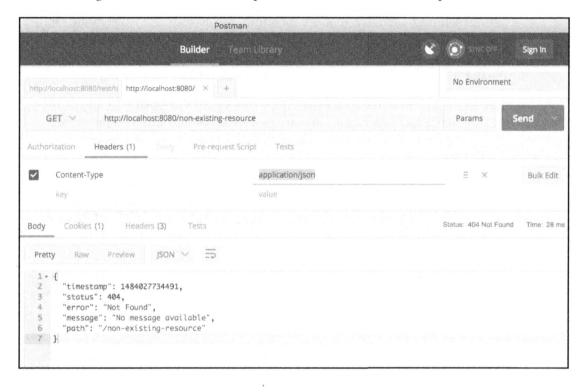

The response is shown in the following code snippet:

```
{
    "timestamp": 1484027734491,
    "status": 404,
    "error": "Not Found",
    "message": "No message available",
    "path": "/non-existing-resource"
}
```

A couple of important things to note are as follows:

- The response header has an HTTP status of **404 Not Found**.
- Spring Boot returns a valid JSON message as a response, with the message stating that the resource is not found.

What happens when service code throws a runtime exception?

Let's create a resource that throws an exception and send a GET request to it in order to understand how the application reacts to runtime exceptions.

Let's create a dummy service that throws an exception. The following code snippet shows a simple service:

```
@GetMapping(path = "/users/dummy-service")
public Todo errorService() {

    throw new RuntimeException("Some Exception Occured");

}
```

A couple of important things to note are as follows:

- We are creating a GET service with the following URI: /users/dummy-service.
- The service throws RuntimeException. We chose RuntimeException to be able to create the exception easily. We can easily replace it with a custom exception if needed.

Let's fire a GET request to the preceding service at http://localhost:8080/users/dummy-service using Postman. The response is shown in the following code:

```
{
    "timestamp": 1484028119553,
    "status": 500,
    "error": "Internal Server Error",
    "exception": "java.lang.RuntimeException",
    "message": "Some Exception Occured",
    "path": "/users/dummy-service"
}
```

A couple of important things to note are as follows:

- The response header has an HTTP status of 500 Internal server error.
- Spring Boot also returns the message with which the exception is thrown.

As we can see in the preceding two examples, Spring Boot provides good default exception handling.

In the next section, we will focus on understanding how the application reacts to custom exceptions.

What happens when the service method throws a custom exception?

Let's create a custom exception and throw it from a service. Take a look at the following code:

```
public class TodoNotFoundException extends RuntimeException {
  public TodoNotFoundException(String msg) {
    super(msg);
  }
}
```

It's a very simple piece of code that defines TodoNotFoundException.

Now, let's enhance our TodoController class to throw TodoNotFoundException when a todo with a given ID is not found:

```
@GetMapping(path = "/users/{name}/todos/{id}")
public Todo retrieveTodo(@PathVariable String name,
                                  @PathVariable int id) {

  Todo todo = todoService.retrieveTodo(id);

  if (todo == null) {
    throw new TodoNotFoundException("Todo Not Found");
   }

  return todo;

}
```

If todoService returns a null todo, we throw TodoNotFoundException.

When we execute the service with a GET request to a nonexistent todo (http://localhost:8080/users/Jack/todos/222), we get the response that's shown in the following code snippet:

```
{
  "timestamp": 1484029048788,
  "status": 500,
  "error": "Internal Server Error",
  "exception":
```

```
      "com.mastering.spring.springboot.bean.TodoNotFoundException",
      "message": "Todo Not Found",
      "path": "/users/Jack/todos/222"
  }
```

As we can see, a clear exception response is sent back to the service consumer.

 However, there is one thing that can be improved further—the response status. When a resource is not found, it is recommended that you return a `404 Not Found` status. We will look at how to customize the response status in the next section.

Customizing the exception response

Now, let's look at how to customize the preceding exception and return the proper response status with a customized message.

The following steps are involved:

1. Defining the structure of exception response.
2. Defining global exception handling advice.

Defining the exception response structure

Let's create a bean to define the structure of our custom exception message.

We have created the following simple exception response bean with an auto-populated timestamp and a few additional properties, namely messages and details:

```java
public class ExceptionResponse {

  private Date timestamp = new Date();
  private String message;
  private String details;

  public ExceptionResponse(String message, String details) {
    super();
    this.message = message;
    this.details = details;
  }

  public Date getTimestamp() {
    return timestamp;
  }
```

```
public String getMessage() {
  return message;
}

public String getDetails() {
  return details;
}

}
```

When `TodoNotFoundException` is thrown, we want to return a response using the `ExceptionResponse` bean.

Defining custom exception handling advice for TodoNotFoundException

When `TodoNotFoundException` occurs anywhere in the application, we want to return a response adhering to the structure of `ExceptionResponse`.

We can do that by creating a controller advice extending the default exception handling mechanism in Spring Boot. The following code shows the details for handling `TodoNotFoundException.class`:

```
@ControllerAdvice
@RestController
public class RestResponseEntityExceptionHandler
                extends  ResponseEntityExceptionHandler {

    @ExceptionHandler(TodoNotFoundException.class)
    public final ResponseEntity<ExceptionResponse>
                    todoNotFound(TodoNotFoundException ex) {

        ExceptionResponse exceptionResponse =
                new ExceptionResponse(  ex.getMessage(),
                            "Any details you would want to add");

        return new ResponseEntity<ExceptionResponse>
                (exceptionResponse, new HttpHeaders(),
                                    HttpStatus.NOT_FOUND);

    }

}
```

Some important things to note are as follows:

- `RestResponseEntityExceptionHandler extends ResponseEntityExceptionHandler`: We are extending `ResponseEntityExceptionHandler`, which is the base class provided by Spring MVC for centralized exception handling when it comes to `ControllerAdvice` classes.
- `@ExceptionHandler(TodoNotFoundException.class)`: This defines that the method to follow will handle the specific exception of `TodoNotFoundException.class`. Any other exceptions for which custom exception handling is not defined will follow the default exception handling provided by Spring Boot.
- `ExceptionResponse exceptionResponse = new ExceptionResponse(ex.getMessage(), "Any details you would want to add")`: This creates a custom exception response.
- `new ResponseEntity<ExceptionResponse>(exceptionResponse, new HttpHeaders(), HttpStatus.NOT_FOUND)`: This is the definition to return a `404 Not Found` response with the custom exception we defined earlier.

When we execute the service with a `GET` request to a nonexistent todo (`http://localhost:8080/users/Jack/todos/222`), we get the following response:

```
{
  "timestamp": 1484030343311,
  "message": "Todo Not Found",
  "details": "Any details you would want to add"
}
```

Defining global default exception handling advice for all other exceptions

If you want to create a generic exception message for all exceptions, we can add a method to `RestResponseEntityExceptionHandler` with the `@ExceptionHandler(Exception.class)` annotation.

The following code snippet shows how we can do this:

```
@ExceptionHandler(Exception.class)
public final ResponseEntity<ExceptionResponse> todoNotFound(Exception ex) {
    //Customize and return the response
}
```

Any exception for which a custom exception handler is not defined will be handled by the previous method.

Mapping response statuses for different scenarios

One of the important things to focus on with REST services is the response status of an error response. The following table shows the scenarios and the error response statuses to use:

Situation	Response Status
The request body does not meet the API specification. It does not contain enough details or contains validation errors.	400 BAD REQUEST
Authentication or authorization failure.	401 UNAUTHORIZED
The user cannot perform the operation due to various factors, such as exceeding limits.	403 FORBIDDEN
The resource does not exist.	404 NOT FOUND
The unsupported operation, for example, trying POST on a resource where only GET is allowed.	405 METHOD NOT ALLOWED
Error on a server. Ideally, this should not happen. The consumer would not be able to fix this.	500 INTERNAL SERVER ERROR

In this section, we looked at the default exception handling provided by Spring Boot and how we can customize it further to suit our needs. Next, we will explore HATEOAS in more detail.

Exploring HATEOAS

HATEOAS is one of the constraints of the REST application architecture.

Let's consider a situation where a service consumer is consuming numerous services from a service provider. The easiest way to develop this kind of system is to have the service consumer store the individual resource URIs of every resource they need from the service provider. However, this would create a tight coupling between the service provider and the service consumer. Whenever any of the resource URIs change on the service provider, the service consumer needs to be updated.

Consider a typical web application. Let's say I navigate to my bank account details page. Almost all banking websites would show links to all the transactions that are possible on my bank account on the screen so that I can easily navigate using the link.

What if we can bring a similar concept to RESTful services so that the service returns not only the data about the requested resource, but also provides details of other related resources?

HATEOAS brings this concept of displaying related links for a given resource to RESTful services. When we return the details of a specific resource, we also return links to operations that can be performed on the resource, as well as links to related resources. If a service consumer can use the links from the response to perform transactions, then I wouldn't need to hardcode all the links.

An example response with a HATEOAS link is shown here. This is the response to the /todos request in order to retrieve all todos:

```
{
  "_embedded" : {
    "todos" : [ {
      "user" : "Jill",
      "desc" : "Learn Hibernate",
      "done" : false,
    "_links" : {
    "self" : {
            "href" : "http://localhost:8080/todos/1"
            },
        "todo" : {
            "href" : "http://localhost:8080/todos/1"
            }
        }
    } ]
  },
  "_links" : {
```

```
  "self" : {
          "href" : "http://localhost:8080/todos"
          },
  "profile" : {
          "href" : "http://localhost:8080/profile/todos"
          },
  "search" : {
          "href" : "http://localhost:8080/todos/search"
          }
    },
  }
```

In the preceding output, the following links are included:

- **Specific** `todos` (`http://localhost:8080/todos/1`)
- **Search resources** (`http://localhost:8080/todos/search`)

If the service consumer wants to do a search, it has the option of taking the search URL from the response and sending the search request to it. This would reduce coupling between the service provider and the service consumer.

Sending HATEOAS links in response

Now that we understand what HATEOAS is, let's look at how we can use it to send links related to a resource in the response.

Spring Boot starter HATEOAS

Spring Boot has a specific starter for HATEOAS called `spring-boot-starter-hateoas`. We need to add it to the `pom.xml` file.

The following code snippet shows the `dependency` block:

```
<dependency>
  <groupId>org.springframework.boot</groupId>
  <artifactId>spring-boot-starter-hateoas</artifactId>
</dependency>
```

One of the important dependencies that's included as part of `spring-boot-starter-hateoas` is `spring-hateoas`, which provides the HATEOAS features, is as follows:

```
<dependency>
  <groupId>org.springframework.hateoas</groupId>
  <artifactId>spring-hateoas</artifactId>
</dependency>
```

Let's enhance the `retrieveTodo` resource (`/users/{name}/todos/{id}`) to return a link to retrieve all `todos` (`/users/{name}/todos`) in the response:

```
@GetMapping(path = "/users/{name}/todos/{id}")
public Resource<Todo> retrieveTodo(
@PathVariable String name, @PathVariable int id) {

    Todo todo = todoService.retrieveTodo(id);
    if (todo == null) {
        throw new TodoNotFoundException("Todo Not Found");
    }

    Resource<Todo> todoResource = new Resource<Todo>(todo);

    ControllerLinkBuilder linkTo =
linkTo(methodOn(this.getClass()).retrieveTodos(name));

    todoResource.add(linkTo.withRel("parent"));

    return todoResource;

}
```

Some important points to note are as follows:

- `ControllerLinkBuilder linkTo = linkTo(methodOn(this.getClass()).retrieveTodos(name))`: We want to get a link to the `retrieveTodos` method on the current class.
- `linkTo.withRel("parent")`: The relationship with the current resource is the parent.

The following snippet shows the response when a GET request is sent to
http://localhost:8080/users/Jack/todos/1:

```
{
  "id": 1,
  "user": "Jack",
  "desc": "Learn Spring MVC",
  "targetDate": 1484038262110,
  "done": false,
  "_links": {
          "parent": {
                  "href": "http://localhost:8080/users/Jack/todos"
          }
      }
}
```

The _links section will contain all the links. Currently, we have one link with the relation
parent and href as http://localhost:8080/users/Jack/todos.

 If you have problems executing the preceding request, try executing using
an Accept header—application/json.

HATEOAS is not something that is commonly used in most resources today; however, it
has the potential to be really useful in reducing the coupling between the service provider
and the consumer.

Implementing validation for REST APIs

A good service always validates data before processing it. In this section, we will look at the
Bean Validation API and use its reference implementation to implement validation in our
services.

The Bean Validation API provides a number of annotations that can be used to validate
beans. The *JSR 349* specification defines **Bean Validation API 1.1. Hibernate Validator** as
the reference implementation. Both are already defined as dependencies in the spring-
boot-web-starter project:

- hibernate-validator-5.2.4.Final.jar
- validation-api-1.1.0.Final.jar

We will create a simple validation for the `createTodo` service method.

Creating validations involves two steps:

1. Enabling validation on the controller method.
2. Adding validations on the bean.

Enabling validation on the controller method

It's very simple to enable validation on the controller method. The following snippet shows an example of this:

```
    @RequestMapping(method = RequestMethod.POST, path =
"/users/{name}/todos")
    ResponseEntity<?> add(@PathVariable String name
                                    @Valid @RequestBody Todo todo) {
```

The `@Valid(package javax.validation)` annotation is used to mark a parameter for validation. Any validation that is defined in the `Todo` bean is executed before the `add` method is executed.

Defining validations on the bean

Let's define a few validations on the `Todo` bean:

```
    public class Todo {
      private int id;

      @NotNull
      private String user;

      @Size(min = 9, message = "Enter atleast 10 Characters.")
      private String desc;
```

A couple of important points to note are as follows:

- `@NotNull`: Validates that the user field is not empty
- `@Size(min = 9, message = "Enter atleast 10 Characters.")`: Checks whether the `desc` field has at least nine characters

There are a number of other annotations that can be used to validate beans. The following are some of the Bean Validation annotations:

- `@AssertFalse`, `@AssertTrue`: For Boolean elements. Checks the annotated element.
- `@AssertFalse`: Checks for false.
- `@Assert`: Checks for true.
- `@Future`: The annotated element must be a date in the future.
- `@Past`: The annotated element must be a date in the past.
- `@Max`: The annotated element must be a number whose value must be lower or equal to the specified maximum.
- `@Min`: The annotated element must be a number whose value must be higher or equal to the specified minimum.
- `@NotNull`: The annotated element cannot be null.
- `@Pattern`: The annotated `{@code CharSequence}` element must match the specified regular expression. The regular expression follows the Java regular expression conventions.
- `@Size`: The annotated element size must be within the specified boundaries.

Documenting REST services using the OpenAPI Specification

Before a service provider can consume a service, they need a service contract. A service contract defines all the details about a service:

- How can I call the service?
- What is the URI of the service?
- What should the request format be?
- What kind of response should I expect?

There are multiple options to define a service contract for RESTful services. The most popular one in the last couple of years is **Swagger**. Swagger is gaining a lot of ground, with support from major vendors in the last couple of years. Swagger is now called **the OpenAPI Specification**. In this section, we will generate Swagger documentation for our services.

Generating a Swagger specification

One of the interesting developments in the last few years of RESTful services development is the evolution of tools that are used to generate service documentation (specification) from code. This ensures that the code and documentation are always in sync.

Springfox Swagger can be used to generate Swagger documentation from the RESTful services code. What's more, there is a wonderful tool called **Swagger UI** which, when integrated into the application, provides human-readable documentation.

The following code snippet shows how we can add both of these tools to the pom.xml file:

```
<dependency>
 <groupId>io.springfox</groupId>
 <artifactId>springfox-swagger2</artifactId>
 <version>2.4.0</version>
</dependency>

<dependency>
 <groupId>io.springfox</groupId>
 <artifactId>springfox-swagger-ui</artifactId>
 <version>2.4.0</version>
</dependency>
```

The next step is to add the configuration class to enable and generate Swagger documentation. The following snippet shows us how to do this:

```
@Configuration
@EnableSwagger2
public class SwaggerConfig {
  @Bean
  public Docket api() {
    return new Docket(DocumentationType.SWAGGER_2)
    .select()
    .apis(RequestHandlerSelectors.any())
    .paths(PathSelectors.any()).build();
  }
}
```

Some important points to note are as follows:

- @Configuration: Defines a Spring configuration file
- @EnableSwagger2: The annotation to enable Swagger support
- Docket: A simple builder class to configure the generation of Swagger documentation using the Swagger Spring MVC framework

- `new Docket(DocumentationType.SWAGGER_2)`: Configures Swagger 2 as the Swagger version to be used
- `.apis(RequestHandlerSelectors.any()).paths(PathSelectors.any())`: Includes all APIs and paths in the documentation

Exploring the Swagger specification

When we bring the server up, we can launch the API Docs URL (`http://localhost:8080/v2/api-docs`). The following screenshot shows some of the generated documentation:

Let's look at some of the generated documentation. Listed here is the documentation for retrieving the todos service:

```
"/users/{name}/todos": {
  "get": {
  "tags": [
        "todo-controller"
        ],
  "summary": "retrieveTodos",
  "operationId": "retrieveTodosUsingGET",
  "consumes": [
        "application/json"
        ],
  "produces": [
        "*/*"
        ],
  "parameters": [
        {
          "name": "name",
          "in": "path",
          "description": "name",
          "required": true,
          "type": "string"
        }
        ],
  "responses": {
  "200": {
        "description": "OK",
        "schema": {
               "type": "array",
               items": {
                   "$ref": "#/definitions/Todo"
                 }
               }
        },
  "401": {
          "description": "Unauthorized"
        },
  "403": {
          "description": "Forbidden"
        },
  "404": {
          "description": "Not Found"
        }
    }
  }
}
```

The service definition clearly defines the request and response of the service. Also defined are the different response statuses that the service can return in different situations.

The following code snippet shows the definition of the Todo bean:

```
"Resource«Todo»": {
  "type": "object",
  "properties": {
  "desc": {
          "type": "string"
        },
  "done": {
          "type": "boolean"
        },
  "id": {
          "type": "integer",
          "format": "int32"
      },
  "links": {
          "type": "array",
          "items": {
                  "$ref": "#/definitions/Link"
                }
          },
  "targetDate": {
              "type": "string",
              "format": "date-time"
          },
  "user": {
          "type": "string"
      }
    }
  }
```

This defines all the elements in the Todo bean, along with their formats.

Using the Swagger UI to navigate the Swagger documentation

Swagger UI (`http://localhost:8080/swagger-ui.html`) can also be used to look at the documentation. Swagger UI is enabled by the dependency (`io.springfox:springfox-swagger ui`) that was added in our `pom.xml` in the previous step.

Swagger UI (`http://petstore.swagger.io`) is also available online. We can visualize any Swagger documentation (including Swagger JSON) using the Swagger UI.

The following screenshot shows the list of controller-exposing services. When we click on any controller, it expands to show the list of request methods and URIs each controller supports:

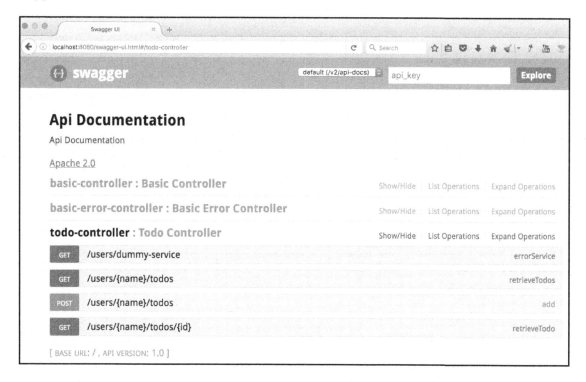

The following screenshot shows the details for the POST service to create a todo parameter for the user in Swagger UI:

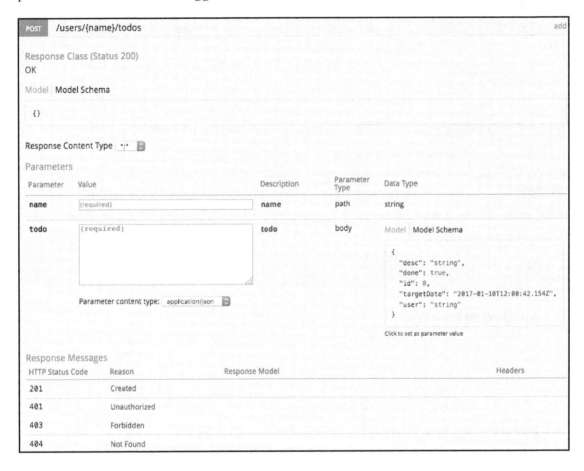

Some important things to note are as follows:

- **Parameters** show all the important parameters, including the request body.
- The **Parameter Type** body (for the `todo` parameter) shows the expected structure for the body of the request.
- The **Response Messages** sections show different HTTP status codes that are being returned by the service.

The Swagger UI provides an excellent way to expose service definitions for your API without a lot of additional effort.

Customizing the Swagger documentation using annotations

The Swagger UI also provides annotations so that you can further customize your documentation.

Listed here is some of the documentation for retrieving the `todos` service:

```
"/users/{name}/todos": {
  "get": {
  "tags": [
        "todo-controller"
        ],
  "summary": "retrieveTodos",
  "operationId": "retrieveTodosUsingGET",
  "consumes": [
          "application/json"
          ],
  "produces": [
            "*/*"
          ],
```

As you can see, the documentation that was generated is very raw. There are a number of things we can improve in the documentation to describe the services better. Here are a couple of examples:

- Provide a better summary.
- `produces` has a value of `*/*` in the preceding documentation. We can make `produces` more specific to indicate the response content type, that is, `application/json`.

Swagger provides annotations that we can add to our RESTful services in order to customize the documentation. Let's add a few annotations to the controller in order to improve the documentation:

```
@ApiOperation(
        value = "Retrieve all todos for a user by passing in his name",
        notes = "A list of matching todos is returned. Current pagination
        is not supported.",
        response = Todo.class,
        responseContainer = "List",
        produces = "application/json")
@GetMapping("/users/{name}/todos")
public List<Todo> retrieveTodos(@PathVariable String name) {

        return todoService.retrieveTodos(name);

}
```

A few important points to note are as follows:

- `@ApiOperation(value = "Retrieve all todos for a user by passing in his name")`: Produced in the documentation as a summary of the service
- `notes = "A list of matching todos is returned. Current pagination is not supported."`: Produced in the documentation as a description of the service
- `produces = "application/json"`: Customizes the `produces` section of the service documentation

Here is an extract of the documentation after the update:

```
get": {
    "tags": [
                "todo-controller"
            ],
    "summary": "Retrieve all todos for a user by passing in his
    name",
    "description": "A list of matching todos is returned. Current
    pagination is not supported.",
    "operationId": "retrieveTodosUsingGET",
    "consumes": [
                "application/json"
            ],
    "produces": [
                "application/json",
                "*/*"
            ],
```

Swagger provides a lot of other annotations to customize the documentation. Listed here are some of the important annotations:

- `@Api`: Marks a class as a Swagger resource
- `@ApiModel`: Provides additional information about Swagger models
- `@ApiModelProperty`: Adds and manipulates the data of a model property
- `@ApiOperation`: Describes an operation or an HTTP method against a specific path
- `@ApiParam`: Adds additional metadata for operation parameters
- `@ApiResponse`: Describes an example response of an operation
- `@ApiResponses`: A wrapper to allow a list of multiple `ApiResponse` objects
- `@Authorization`: Declares an authorization scheme to be used on a resource or an operation
- `@AuthorizationScope`: Describes an OAuth 2 authorization scope
- `@ResponseHeader`: Represents a header that can be provided as part of the response

Swagger provides a few Swagger definition annotations that can be used to customize high-level information about a group of services—contacts, licensing, and other general information. Listed here are some of the important ones:

- `@SwaggerDefinition`: Definition-level properties to be added to the generated Swagger definition
- `@Info`: General metadata for a Swagger definition
- `@Contact`: Properties to describe the person to be contacted for a Swagger definition
- `@License`: Properties to describe the license for a Swagger definition

Implementing internationalization for REST APIs

Internationalization (i18n) is the process of developing applications and services so that they can be customized for different languages and cultures around the world. It is also called **localization**. The goal of internationalization or localization is to build applications that can offer content in multiple languages and formats.

Spring Boot has built-in support for internationalization.

Let's build a simple service to understand how we can build internationalization in our APIs.

We need to add `LocaleResolver` and a message source to our Spring Boot application. The following code snippet should be included in `Application.java`:

```
@Bean
public LocaleResolver localeResolver() {

    SessionLocaleResolver sessionLocaleResolver = new
SessionLocaleResolver();
    sessionLocaleResolver.setDefaultLocale(Locale.US);
    return sessionLocaleResolver;

}

@Bean
public ResourceBundleMessageSource messageSource() {

    ResourceBundleMessageSource messageSource = new
ResourceBundleMessageSource();
    messageSource.setBasenames("messages");
    messageSource.setUseCodeAsDefaultMessage(true);
    return messageSource;

}
```

Some important things to note are as follows:

- `sessionLocaleResolver.setDefaultLocale(Locale.US)`: We're setting a default locale of `Locale.US`.
- `messageSource.setBasenames("messages")`: We're setting the base name of the message source as `messages`. If we are in `fr` locale (France), we would use messages from `message_fr.properties`. If a message is not available in `message_fr.properties`, it would be searched for in the default `message.properties`.
- `messageSource.setUseCodeAsDefaultMessage(true)`: If a message is not found, then the code is returned as the default message.

Let's configure the messages in the respective files. Let's start with `messages.properties`. The messages in this file would act as the defaults:

```
welcome.message=Welcome in English
```

Let's also configure `messages_fr.properties`. The messages in this file would be used for the locale. If a message is not present here, then the defaults from `messages.properties` will be used:

```
welcome.message=Welcome in French
```

Let's create a service that returns a specific message using the locale specified in the `"Accept-Language"` header:

```
@GetMapping("/welcome-internationalized")
public String msg(@RequestHeader(value = "Accept-Language",
                                         required = false) Locale
locale) {
    return messageSource.getMessage("welcome.message", null,
    locale);
}
```

Here are a couple of things to note:

- `@RequestHeader(value = "Accept-Language", required = false)
  Locale locale`: The locale is picked up from the `Accept-Language` request header. It is not required. If a locale is not specified, the default locale is used.
- `messageSource.getMessage("welcome.message", null, locale)`:
  So, `messageSource` is autowired into the controller. We get the welcome message based on the given locale.

The following screenshot shows the response when the preceding service is called without specifying a default `Accept-Language` header:

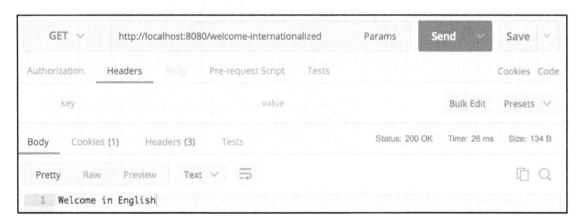

The default message from `messages.properties` is returned.

The following screenshot shows the response when the preceding service is called with `Accept-Language fr`:

The localized message from `messages_fr.properties` is returned.

In the preceding example, we customized the service to return localized messages based on the locale in the request. A similar approach can be used to internationalize all the services in a component.

Implementing caching for REST APIs

Caching data from services plays a crucial role in improving the performance and scalability of applications. In this section, we will look at the implementation options that Spring Boot provides.

Spring provides a caching abstraction based on annotations. We will start using Spring caching annotations. Later, we will introduce JSR 107 caching annotations and compare them with Spring abstractions.

Exploring a starter project for caching – spring-boot-starter-cache

Spring Boot provides a starter project for caching—`spring-boot-starter-cache`. Adding this to an application brings in all the dependencies to enable JSR 107 and Spring caching annotations. The following code snippet shows the dependency details for `spring-boot-starter-cache`. Let's add this to our `pom.xml` file:

```xml
<dependency>
  <groupId>org.springframework.boot</groupId>
  <artifactId>spring-boot-starter-cache</artifactId>
</dependency>
```

Enabling caching on the application

Before we can start using caching, we need to enable caching on the application. The following code snippet shows how we can enable caching:

```java
@EnableCaching
@SpringBootApplication
public class Application {
```

`@EnableCaching` would enable caching in a Spring Boot application.

Spring Boot automatically configures a suitable `CacheManager` framework to serve as a provider for the relevant cache. We will look at the details of how Spring Boot decides on the `CacheManager` framework a little later.

Caching data

Now that we have enabled caching, we can add the `@Cacheable` annotation to the methods where we want to cache the data. The following code snippet shows how to enable caching on `retrieveTodos`:

```java
@Cacheable("todos")
public List<Todo> retrieveTodos(String user) {
```

In the preceding example, the `todos` for a specific user are cached. On the first call to the method for a specific user, the `todos` will be retrieved from the service. On subsequent calls for the same user, the data will be returned from the cache.

Spring also provides conditional caching. In the following snippet, caching is only enabled if the specified condition is satisfied:

```
@Cacheable(cacheNames="todos", condition="#user.length < 10")
public List<Todo> retrieveTodos(String user) {
```

Spring also provides additional annotations to evict data from the cache and add some custom data to cache. A few important ones are listed here:

- @CachePut: Used to explicitly add data to the cache
- @CacheEvict: Used to remove stale data from the cache
- @Caching: Allows multiple nested @Cacheable, @CachePut, and @CacheEvict annotations to be used on the same method

JSR-107 caching annotations

JSR-107 aims to standardize caching annotations. Listed here are some of the important JSR-107 annotations:

- @CacheResult: Similar to @Cacheable.
- @CacheRemove: Similar to @CacheEvict, @CacheRemove supports conditional eviction if an exception occurs.
- @CacheRemoveAll: Similar to @CacheEvict(allEntries=true), it is used to remove all the entries from the cache.

JSR-107 and Spring's caching annotations are fairly similar in terms of the features they offer. Either of them is a good choice. We lean slightly more toward JSR-107 because it's a standard. However, make sure you are not using both in the same project.

Understanding the auto-detection order of caching providers

When caching is enabled, Spring Boot auto-configuration starts looking for a caching provider. The following list shows the order in which Spring Boot searches for caching providers. The list is in order of decreasing preference:

- JCache (JSR-107) (EhCache 3, Hazelcast, Infinispan, and so on)
- EhCache 2.x
- Hazelcast

- Infinispan
- Couchbase
- Redis
- Caffeine
- Guava
- Simple

Deploying Spring Boot applications to the cloud

Spring Boot has great support for most popular cloud **Platform as a Service (PaaS)** providers.

Some of the popular ones are as follows:

- Cloud Foundry
- Heroku
- OpenShift
- **Amazon Web Services (AWS)**

In this section, we will focus on deploying our application to Cloud Foundry.

Deploying applications to Cloud Foundry

The Cloud Foundry Java buildpack has excellent support for Spring Boot. We can deploy standalone applications based on JAR's as well as the traditional Java EE WAR applications.

Cloud Foundry provides a Maven plugin to deploy applications:

```
<build>
    <plugins>
        <plugin>
            <groupId>org.cloudfoundry</groupId>
            <artifactId>cf-maven-plugin</artifactId>
            <version>1.1.2</version>
        </plugin>
    </plugins>
</build>
```

Before we can deploy our application, we need to configure the application with a target and a space to deploy the application to.

The following are the steps involved:

1. We need to create a Pivotal Cloud Foundry account at `https://account.run.pivotal.io/sign-up`.
2. Once we have an account, we can log in at `https://run.pivotal.io` to create an organization and space. Have the `org` and `space` details ready as we need them in order to deploy the application.

We can update the plugin with the configuration of `org` and `space`:

```
<build>
    <plugins>
        <plugin>
            <groupId>org.cloudfoundry</groupId>
            <artifactId>cf-maven-plugin</artifactId>
            <version>1.1.2</version>
            <configuration>
                <target>http://api.run.pivotal.io</target>
                <org>in28minutes</org>
                <space>development</space>
                <memory>512</memory>
                <env>
                    <ENV-VAR-NAME>prod</ENV-VAR-NAME>
                </env>
            </configuration>
        </plugin>
    </plugins>
</build>
```

We need to log in to Cloud Foundry using the Maven plugin on the Command Prompt or the Terminal:

```
mvn cf:login -Dcf.username=<<YOUR-USER-ID>> -Dcf.password=<<YOUR-PASSWORD>>
```

If everything is successful, you will see a message, as shown here:

```
[INFO] ------------------------------------------------------------------------
[INFO] Building Your First Spring Boot Example 0.0.1-SNAPSHOT
[INFO] ------------------------------------------------------------------------
[INFO]
[INFO] --- cf-maven-plugin:1.1.2:login (default-cli) @ springboot-for-
beginners-example ---
[INFO] Authentication successful
[INFO] ------------------------------------------------------------------------
```

```
[INFO] BUILD SUCCESS
[INFO] ------------------------------------------------------------
[INFO] Total time: 14.897 s
[INFO] Finished at: 2017-02-05T16:49:52+05:30
[INFO] Final Memory: 22M/101M
[INFO] ------------------------------------------------------------
```

Once you are able to log in, you can push the application to Cloud Foundry:

```
mvn cf:push
```

Once we execute this command, Maven will compile, run tests, build the application JAR or WAR, and then deploy it to the cloud:

```
[INFO] Building jar: /in28Minutes/Workspaces/SpringTutorial/springboot-for-
beginners-example-rest-service/target/springboot-for-beginners-
example-0.0.1-SNAPSHOT.jar
 [INFO]
 [INFO] --- spring-boot-maven-plugin:1.4.0.RELEASE:repackage (default) @
springboot-for-beginners-example ---
 [INFO]
 [INFO] <<< cf-maven-plugin:1.1.2:push (default-cli) < package @
springboot-for-beginners-example <<<
 [INFO]
 [INFO] --- cf-maven-plugin:1.1.2:push (default-cli) @ springboot-for-
beginners-example ---
 [INFO] Creating application 'springboot-for-beginners-example'
 [INFO] Uploading '/in28Minutes/Workspaces/SpringTutorial/springboot-for-
beginners-example-rest-service/target/springboot-for-beginners-
example-0.0.1-SNAPSHOT.jar'
 [INFO] Starting application
 [INFO] Checking status of application 'springboot-for-beginners-example'
 [INFO] 1 of 1 instances running (1 running)
 [INFO] Application 'springboot-for-beginners-example' is available at
'http://springboot-for-beginners-example.cfapps.io'
 [INFO] ------------------------------------------------------------
[INFO] BUILD SUCCESS
 [INFO] ------------------------------------------------------------
[INFO] Total time: 02:21 min
 [INFO] Finished at: 2017-02-05T16:54:55+05:30
 [INFO] Final Memory: 29M/102M
 [INFO] ------------------------------------------------------------
```

Once the application is up and running on the cloud, we can use the URL from the log to launch the application: http://springboot-for-beginners-example.cfapps.io.

`http://springboot-for-beginners-example.cfapps.io` is just an example. You can pick up the correct URL from the execution log that was shown previously.

You can find more information about the Java Build Pack of Cloud Foundry at `https://docs.run.pivotal.io/buildpacks/java/build-tool-int.html#maven`.

Summary

Spring Boot makes developing Spring-based applications easy. It allows us to create production-ready applications very quickly.

In this chapter, we looked at building awesome REST APIs with Spring Boot. We looked at some of the REST API best practices. Then, we implemented exception handling, caching, and internationalization for our REST API application. We also discussed the best practices of documenting REST services using Swagger. Finally, we learned how to deploy REST APIs to a cloud provider.

In the next chapter, we will focus on unit testing REST APIs, as well as providing tight security around our RESTful services by using Spring Security.

Unit Testing REST API with Spring Boot

In the last chapter, we looked at how Spring Boot makes it easy to develop REST APIs. We understood the basic features of Spring Boot by creating a couple of simple `Hello World` REST APIs. We created REST APIs for `GET`, `POST`, `PUT`, and `DELETE` operations for the `Todo` REST API.

In this chapter, let's focus on writing great unit and integration tests for the REST API when it is developed with Spring Boot.

Unit testing focuses on writing automated tests for the responsibilities of each method or a group of methods. Unit testing acts as a safety net against future defects. It helps to catch defects earlier.

In unit tests for REST APIs, we launch REST API controllers in isolation and then test them. We use the Spring Mock **Model, View and Controller (MVC)** framework to launch Spring contexts with only the web layer components, and we mock out all other dependencies.

Integration tests help us to test multiple layers of an application in combination. In integration tests, we launch the entire Spring context, including business and data components. We invoke the REST API, and assert the responses.

This chapter answers the following questions:

- How do you write unit tests for different REST API methods that have been implemented with Spring MVC?
- How can you launch Spring contexts for unit tests just for the web layer components, and using the Spring Mock MVC framework?
- How do you write integration tests for different REST API methods that have been implemented with Spring MVC?
- Why is Spring Boot Starter Test a great place to start when writing unit and integration tests?

Technical requirements

The following are the requirements for this chapter:

- Your favorite IDE, Eclipse
- Maven 3.x
- Java 8+
- Internet connectivity

The code on GitHub is available at `https://github.com/PacktPublishing/Mastering-Spring-5.1/tree/master/Chapter07`

Unit testing REST API with Spring Boot

In `Chapter 2`, *Dependency Injection and Unit Testing*, we wrote a few basic unit tests for Spring contexts. We saw how the Spring framework makes unit testing easy, by making components loosely coupled.

As we discussed in `Chapter 2`, *Dependency Injection and Unit Testing*, typical web applications are huge, and have thousands of classes and methods. Unit testing involves writing independent automated tests for individual classes and methods. Instead of testing the entire application once it is deployed, unit testing focuses on writing automated tests for the responsibilities of each class and each method.

Unit testing acts as a safety net against future defects. They help in catching defects earlier. Well-written tests act as a documentation of the code and functionality.

Spring and Spring Boot frameworks provide excellent support for writing great unit tests.

Let's start with the basic starter project provided by Spring Boot for unit testing.

Adding dependency on Spring Boot Starter Test

`spring-boot-starter-test` is the starter for writing unit tests with Spring Boot:

```
<dependency>
    <groupId>org.springframework.boot</groupId>
    <artifactId>spring-boot-starter-test</artifactId>
    <scope>test</scope>
</dependency>
```

`spring-boot-starter-test` brings in a number of important unit testing frameworks:

```xml
<dependency>
    <groupId>org.springframework</groupId>
    <artifactId>spring-test</artifactId>
</dependency>
<dependency>
    <groupId>com.jayway.jsonpath</groupId>
    <artifactId>json-path</artifactId>
</dependency>
<dependency>
    <groupId>junit</groupId>
    <artifactId>junit</artifactId>
</dependency>
<dependency>
    <groupId>org.assertj</groupId>
    <artifactId>assertj-core</artifactId>
</dependency>
<dependency>
    <groupId>org.mockito</groupId>
    <artifactId>mockito-core</artifactId>
</dependency>
<dependency>
    <groupId>org.hamcrest</groupId>
    <artifactId>hamcrest-core</artifactId>
</dependency>
<dependency>
    <groupId>org.skyscreamer</groupId>
    <artifactId>jsonassert</artifactId>
</dependency>
```

Let's take a quick look at these frameworks:

- **JUnit**: Most popular Java unit testing framework, provides the base structure for writing unit tests.
- **Spring Test** (`spring-test`): Brings in capabilities to write unit tests to launch spring contexts. Also provides a Mock MVC framework that can be used to unit test REST APIs.
- **Mockito** (`mockito-core`): Helps in writing unit testings using mocks.
- **AssertJ** (`assertj-core`): Helps you write simple, readable assertions; for example—`assertThat(numbersList).hasSize(15).contains(1, 2, 3).allMatch(x -> x < 100)`.
- **Hamcrest** (`hamcrest-core`): Another framework to write great assertions; for example—`assertThat("XYZ", containsString("XY"))`.

- **JSONPath** (`json-path`): Similar to XPath for XML, you can use JSONPath for identifying and unit testing elements in your JSON responses.
- **JSON Assert** (`JSONAssert`): JSON Assert allows us to specify an expected JSON, and use it to check for specific elements in the JSON response. We will use JSON Assert a little later in this chapter.

Unit tests for the BasicController API

We will start with writing unit tests for the `Hello World` service implemented in `BasicController`.

Setting up the basic unit test

When writing unit tests for the web layer, we want to focus on specific controllers, without worrying about the business and data layers.

The Spring Test framework provides the `@WebMvcTest` framework to create tests that focus just on the Spring MVC components. This annotation will disable all auto configuration that is unrelated to web MVCs. Some of the annotations that will be disabled include `@Component`, `@Service`, and `@Repository`.

The complete list of beans that will be scanned for by `@WebMvcTest` includes `@Controller`, `@ControllerAdvice`, `@JsonComponent`, `Converter`, `GenericConverter`, `Filter`, `WebMvcConfigurer`, and `HandlerMethodArgumentResolver`.

The following snippet shows the basic configuration that is needed to launch a web mock `mvc` test:

```
@RunWith(SpringRunner.class)
@WebMvcTest(value = BasicController.class, secure = false)
public class BasicControllerTest {
    @Autowired
    private MockMvc mvc;
```

Please note the following:

- `@RunWith(SpringRunner.class)`: `SpringRunner` is a shortcut to the `SpringJUnit4ClassRunner` class. This launches a simple Spring context for unit testing.

- `@WebMvcTest(BasicController.class)`: This annotation can be used along with `SpringRunner` to write simple tests for Spring MVC controllers. This will load only the beans that are annotated with Spring MVC-related annotations. In this example, we are launching a web MVC test context, with the `BasicController` class being tested.
- `@Autowired private MockMvc mvc`: Autowires the `MockMvc` bean that can be used to make requests.
- `secure = false`: We would not want to use security in our unit tests. A `secure = false` parameter on the `WebMvcTest` annotation disables Spring Security for the unit test.

Writing a unit test for the Hello World API returning a string

We would like to write a unit test for the `hello world` API, `http://localhost:8080/welcome`, which returns `"Hello World"`.

In the unit test, we want to send a `GET` request to the resource at `/welcome`, and check whether the response is as expected.

The following code shows a unit test:

```
@Test
public void welcome() throws Exception {
    mvc.perform(
            MockMvcRequestBuilders.get("/welcome")
            .accept(MediaType.APPLICATION_JSON))
        .andExpect(status().isOk())
        .andExpect(content().string(equalTo("Hello World")));
}
```

Here are a few key things to note:

- `mvc.perform(MockMvcRequestBuilders.get("/welcome").accept(MediaType.APPLICATION_JSON))`: Performs a request to `/welcome`, with the `Accept` header value, `application/json`
- `andExpect(status().isOk())`: Expects that the status of the response is `200` (success)
- `andExpect(content().string(equalTo("Hello World")))`: Expects that the content of the response is equal to `"Hello World"`

Writing a unit test for the Hello World API returning a JSON

In the previous test, the REST API returned a string. However, in the real world, the REST API typically returns JSON responses.

Let's consider the `http://localhost:8080/welcome-with-object` API. The `GET` request to it would return a JSON, as shown in the following snippet of code:

```
{"message":"Hello World"}
```

How do we assert a JSON response?

In this test, let's take a shortcut, and test for a substring:

```
@Test
public void welcomeWithObject() throws Exception {
    mvc.perform(
      MockMvcRequestBuilders.get("/welcome-with-object")
                            .accept(MediaType.APPLICATION_JSON))
        .andExpect(status().isOk())
        .andExpect(content().string(containsString("Hello World")));
}
```

This test is very similar to the earlier unit test, except that we are using `containsString` to check whether the content contains a `"Hello World"` substring. We will learn how to write proper JSON tests a little later in this chapter.

Writing a unit test for the Hello World API with a path parameter

Let's now look at writing a unit test for an API with a path parameter.

The response for the `http://localhost:8080/welcome-with-parameter/name/Buddy` URL is as follows:

```
{"message":"Hello World, Buddy!"}
```

In the unit test, we want to pass a name as part of the URI, and check whether the response contains the name. The following code shows how we can do that:

```
@Test
public void welcomeWithParameter() throws Exception {
    mvc.perform(
```

```
        MockMvcRequestBuilders.get("/welcome-with-
parameter/name/Buddy")
        .accept(MediaType.APPLICATION_JSON))
    .andExpect(status().isOk())
    .andExpect(content().string(containsString("Hello World, Buddy")));
}
```

Please note the following:

- `MockMvcRequestBuilders.get("/welcome-with-parameter/name/Buddy")`: This matches against the variable template in the URI. We pass in the name, `Buddy`.
- `.andExpect(content().string(containsString("Hello World, Buddy")))`: We expect the response to contain the message with the name.

Unit tests for the TodoController API

Until now, we have looked at writing simple unit tests for the Hello World REST API. It lays the foundation for writing unit tests for more complex REST APIs.

There are a couple of important things to focus on:

- How can we write better asserts for JSON responses instead of a simple substring comparison?
- How can we write unit tests for PUT, POST, and DELETE request methods?

Let's start with writing unit tests for the Todo REST API.

Setting up unit tests for the TodoController API

Let's start with setting up a simple unit test called `TodoControllerTest`. This is very similar to `BasicControllerTest`.

We are writing a unit test, so we want to test only the logic present in the `TodoController` class. We initialize a Mock MVC framework with only the `TodoController` class, using `@WebMvcTest(TodoController.class)`:

```
@RunWith(SpringRunner.class)
@WebMvcTest(value = TodoController.class, secure = false)
public class TodoControllerTest {

    @Autowired
```

```
    private MockMvc mvc;

    @MockBean
    private TodoService service;
```

One important addition is `@MockBean private TodoService service`. We are mocking out `TodoService` using the `@MockBean` annotation.

In test classes that are run with `SpringRunner`, the beans defined with `@MockBean` will be replaced by a mock—created using the Mockito framework.

Writing a unit test to retrieve all todos – the GET method

Let's start with writing a unit test to retrieve all todos—`http://localhost:8080/users/Jack/todos`. The following code is an example response:

```
[
  {
  "id":1,
  "user":"Jack",
  "desc":"Learn Spring MVC",
  "targetDate":"2019-01-08T12:42:42.337+0000",
  "done":false
  },
  {
  "id":2,
  "user":"Jack",
  "desc":"Learn Struts",
  "targetDate":"2019-01-08T12:42:42.337+0000",
  "done":false
  }
]
```

The REST API uses the `service.retrieveTodos` method to retrieve the `Todo` details for a user. In a unit test, we want to mock the service, and configure a mock response. We can do this using Mockito:

```
List < Todo > mockList = Arrays.asList(
    new Todo(1, "Jack", "Learn Spring MVC", new Date(), false),
    new Todo(2, "Jack", "Learn Struts", new Date(), false)
);
when(service.retrieveTodos(anyString()))
    .thenReturn(mockList);
```

When the `retrieveTodos` method is called, it will return a mock hardcoded response.

Here's the complete unit test:

```
@Test
public void retrieveTodos() throws Exception {
    //GIVEN
    List < Todo > mockList = Arrays.asList(
        new Todo(1, "Jack", "Learn Spring MVC", new Date(), false),
        new Todo(2, "Jack", "Learn Struts", new Date(), false)
    );

    when(service.retrieveTodos(anyString())).thenReturn(mockList);

    //WHEN
    MvcResult result = mvc.perform(
            MockMvcRequestBuilders.get("/users/Jack/todos")
          .accept(MediaType.APPLICATION_JSON))
        .andExpect(status().isOk()).andReturn();

    //THEN
    String expected = "[" + "{id:1,user:Jack,desc:\"Learn Spring
MVC\",done:false}" + "," +
        "{id:2,user:Jack,desc:\"Learn Struts\",done:false}" + "]";
    JSONAssert.assertEquals(expected,
result.getResponse().getContentAsString(), false);
}
```

You can see clear `Given`, `When`, `Then` parts in the preceding test. `Given` indicates the setup for the scenario being tested. `When` involves execution of the scenario. `Then` involves asserting or checking for the result. This is also called **Given-When-Then (GWT)**.

`JSONAssert` is a very useful framework that is used to perform asserts on JSON. It compares the response text with the expected value:

```
JSONAssert.assertEquals(expected,
result.getResponse().getContentAsString(), false)
```

The last parameter, `false`, indicates the use of a non-strict mode. In a non-strict mode, `JSONAssert` only compares the elements that are specified in the expected JSON string. If it is changed to true, then the expected string should exactly match the result.

Writing a unit test for retrieving a specific todo – the GET method

Writing a unit test for retrieving specific `Todo` details is very similar to the earlier method.

The response for the `http://localhost:8080/users/Jack/todos/1` URL is as follows:

```
{
  "id":1,
  "user":"Jack",
  "desc":"Learn Spring MVC",
  "targetDate":"2019-01-08T12:42:42.337+0000",
  "done":false
}
```

The following code shows the unit test:

```
@Test
public void retrieveTodo() throws Exception {
    Todo mockTodo = new Todo(1, "Jack", "Learn Spring MVC", new Date(),
false);
    when(service.retrieveTodo(anyInt())).thenReturn(mockTodo);
    MvcResult result = mvc
        .perform(MockMvcRequestBuilders.get("/users/Jack/todos/1")
            .accept(MediaType.APPLICATION_JSON))
        .andExpect(status().isOk()).andReturn();
    String expected = "{id:1,user:Jack,desc:\"Learn Spring
MVC\",done:false}";
    JSONAssert.assertEquals(expected,
            result.getResponse().getContentAsString(), false);
}
```

Please note the following:

- `when(service.retrieveTodo(anyInt())).thenReturn(mockTodo)`: We are mocking the `retrieveTodo` service method in order to return the mock todo.
- `MvcResult result = ..`: We are accepting the result of the request in a `MvcResult` variable in order to enable us to perform assertions on the response.
- `JSONAssert.assertEquals(expected, result.getResponse().getContentAsString(), false)`: Asserts whether the result is as expected.

Writing a unit test for creating a todo – the POST method

To create a new `Todo`, we need to send a `POST` request to the
`http://localhost:8080/users/Jack/todos` URI. We would need to send the `Todo`
content in the body of the request in JSON format.

Example request details are as follows:

```
Header
 Content-Type:application/json

Body
 {
 "user": "Jack",
 "desc": "Learn Spring Boot",
 "done": false
 }
```

In the unit test, we would want to call the `POST` method in the `/users/Jack/todos` URI,
and send the JSON content as the body. We would want to check whether the status of the
response is `CREATED`, and whether a header location with a new `Todo` location is part of the
response.

Here's the unit test:

```
@Test
public void createTodo() throws Exception {
    Todo mockTodo = new Todo(CREATED_TODO_ID, "Jack", "Learn Spring MVC",
new Date(), false);
    String todo = "{\"user\":\"Jack\",\"desc\":\"Learn Spring
MVC\",\"done\":\"false\"}";
    when(service.addTodo(anyString(), anyString(), isNull(), anyBoolean()))
        .thenReturn(mockTodo);
    mvc.perform(
            MockMvcRequestBuilders.post("/users/Jack/todos")
            .content(todo)
            .contentType(MediaType.APPLICATION_JSON))
        .andExpect(status().isCreated())
        .andExpect(header().string("location",
            containsString("/users/Jack/todos/" + CREATED_TODO_ID)));
}
```

Please note the following:

- `String todo = "{"user":"Jack","desc":"Learn Spring MVC","done":false}"`: The `Todo` content to post to the create todo service.
- `when(service.addTodo(anyString(), anyString(), isNull(), anyBoolean())).thenReturn(mockTodo)`: Mocks the service to return a dummy `Todo`.
- `MockMvcRequestBuilders.post("/users/Jack/todos").content(todo).contentType(MediaType.APPLICATION_JSON))`: Creates a `POST` method to a given URI with the given content type.
- `andExpect(status().isCreated())`: Expects that the status is created.
- `andExpect(header().string("location",containsString("/users/Jack/todos/" + CREATED_TODO_ID)))`: Expects that the header contains the location with the URI of the created resource.

Writing a unit test for creating a todo with validation errors

It is important to write unit tests for error scenarios. Invoking REST APIs can result in validation errors. The following example shows how we can unit test validations.

We are sending in a description of `"Learn"`—length 5. This will cause validation failure for the field description against the `@Size(min = 9, message = "Enter atleast 10 Characters.")` validation:

```
@Test
public void createTodo_withValidationError() throws Exception {
    Todo mockTodo = new Todo(CREATED_TODO_ID, "Jack",
        "Learn Spring MVC", new Date(), false);
    String todo =
"{\"user\":\"Jack\",\"desc\":\"Learn\",\"done\":\"false\"}";
    when(service.addTodo(anyString(), anyString(), isNull(), anyBoolean()))
        .thenReturn(mockTodo);
    MvcResult result = mvc
        .perform(
            MockMvcRequestBuilders.post("/users/Jack/todos")
            .content(todo)
            .contentType(MediaType.APPLICATION_JSON))
        .andExpect(status().is4xxClientError())
        .andReturn();
}
```

We are using `.andExpect(status().is4xxClientError())` to assert for validation error status.

Writing a unit test for updating a todo – the PUT method

Let's now shift our attention to writing a unit test for updating todo using the `PUT` method.

To update a todo, we would need to send a `PUT` request to the `http://localhost:8080/users/Jack/todos/1` URI:

The following code is an example of the request details:

```
Header
 Content-Type:application/json

Body
 {
 "id" : 1,
 "user": "Jack",
 "desc": "Learn Spring MVC More",
 "done": false
 }
```

The unit test for the previous request is as follows:

```
@Test
public void updateTodo() throws Exception {
    Todo mockTodo = new Todo(UPDATED_TODO_ID, "Jack",
        "Learn Spring MVC 5", new Date(), false);
    String todo = "{\"user\":\"Jack\",\"desc\":\"Learn Spring MVC
5\",\"done\":false}";
    when(service.update(mockTodo)).thenReturn(mockTodo);
    MvcResult result = mvc.perform(
            MockMvcRequestBuilders.put("/users/Jack/todos/" +
UPDATED_TODO_ID)
            .content(todo)
            .contentType(MediaType.APPLICATION_JSON))
        .andExpect(status().isOk()).andReturn();
    JSONAssert.assertEquals(todo,
        result.getResponse().getContentAsString(), false);
}
```

We are mocking the update method to return `mockTodo`, and to invoke the `PUT` method, `MockMvcRequestBuilders.put`. We are asserting for a successful response using `status().isOk()`. We are asserting the response content using `JSONAssert.assertEquals`.

Writing a unit test for deleting a todo – the DELETE method

To test the `DELETE` method, we need to send a `DELETE` request to the `http://localhost:8080/users/Jack/todos/1` URI, and assert for a response status of `NO_CONTENT`.

We can use `MockMvcRequestBuilders.delete` to send a `DELETE` request.

`status().isNoContent()` helps us to assert for the error status.

The complete unit test is as follows:

```
@Test
public void deleteTodo() throws Exception {
    Todo mockTodo = new Todo(1, "Jack", "Learn Spring MVC", new Date(),
false);
    when(service.deleteById(anyInt())).thenReturn(mockTodo);
    mvc.perform(
            MockMvcRequestBuilders.delete("/users/Jack/todos/" +
mockTodo.getId())
            .accept(MediaType.APPLICATION_JSON))
        .andExpect(status().isNoContent());
}
```

We can also unit test for the error scenario—trying to delete a todo that does not exist.

We make the mock return null by using `when(service.deleteById(anyInt())).thenReturn(null)`. We assert for a `404` response status using `status().isNotFound()`.

The complete unit test is as follows:

```
@Test
public void deleteTodo_error() throws Exception {
    when(service.deleteById(anyInt())).thenReturn(null);
    mvc.perform(
            MockMvcRequestBuilders.delete("/users/Jack/todos/1")
            .accept(MediaType.APPLICATION_JSON))
```

```
              .andExpect(status().isNotFound());
}
```

Let's move on to integration testing of REST APIs.

Integration testing REST API with Spring Boot

Spring Boot applications are built in multiple layers—web, business, and data, for example.

In unit tests, we test each of these layers independently. For example, we test the web controllers that mock out the business services. This ensures that we can test each of these components in isolation.

But how do you test that all these layers work well when combined together?

That's where we use integration tests, launching the entire Spring context with all the layers.

Typically, in automated integration tests, you do not want to rely on external dependencies. We would typically use an in-memory database, such as H2.

Let's start with writing a simple integration test for the `Hello World` API.

Writing integration tests for BasicController

In an integration test, we want to launch the embedded server with all the controllers and beans that are configured.

Spring Boot Test provides a `@SpringBootTest` annotation that can be used to quickly launch an integration test. You can also configure a `webEnvironment` annotation to specify the kind of test that you want to run:

- `MOCK`: To unit test controllers in a mock web environment. This is similar to what we did in our unit tests.
- `RANDOM_PORT`: Launch the entire web context, including other layers, in an embedded server on an available random port.

- DEFINED_PORT: **Similar to** RANDOM_PORT, except that you hardcode a port number.
- NONE: Loads up a Spring context without a web context.

In our integration test, we want to launch a web context, including other layers. We do not want to hardcode a port in our tests, as they could run on other servers, including a variety of build servers. Hardcoding ports can result in port conflicts, so we use RANDOM_PORT. This will ensure that the Spring Boot Test will use an available port wherever it runs.

The basic setup for an integration test with Spring Boot is as follows:

```
@RunWith(SpringRunner.class)
@SpringBootTest(classes = Application.class,
    webEnvironment = SpringBootTest.WebEnvironment.RANDOM_PORT)
public class BasicControllerIT {

    @Autowired
    private TestRestTemplate template;
```

TestRestTemplate is typically used in integration tests. It provides additional functionality on top of RestTemplate, which is especially useful in the integration test context. It does not follow redirects, therefore, we can assert a response location.

Writing an integration test for the Hello World API returning a string

In the first integration test, we want to call /welcome and check for the "Hello World" response.

Writing an integration test for this is simple:

```
@Test
public void welcome() throws Exception {
    ResponseEntity < String > response =
        template.getForEntity("/welcome", String.class);
    assertThat(response.getBody(),
        equalTo("Hello World"));
}
```

When we use `RANDOM_PORT` or `DEFINED_PORT`, and we use `@Autowired` to wire in `TestRestTemplate`, we get a fully configured `TestRestTemplate` with the port details. It is sufficient to specify a relative URL in order to execute a REST API—`"/welcome"`—as we do in `template.getForEntity("/welcome", String.class)`. We get a `String` response.

`assertThat(response.getBody(), equalTo("Hello World"))` asserts that the response body content is `"Hello World"`.

Writing an integration test for the Hello World API returning a JSON

Let's shift our focus to writing an integration test for a `REST` method, returning a JSON. `/welcome-with-object` returns the following response:

```
{"message":"Hello World"}
```

An example integration test is as follows:

```
@Test
public void welcomeWithObject() throws Exception {
    ResponseEntity < String > response =
        template.getForEntity("/welcome-with-object", String.class);
    assertThat(response.getBody(),
        containsString("Hello World"));
}
```

This method is similar to the earlier integration test, except that we are asserting for a substring using the `containsString` method.

We can also use `JSONAssert` to assert the JSON content. We will use `JSONAssert` in writing integration tests for the `Todo` REST API.

Writing an integration test for the Hello World API with a path parameter

The response for the `http://localhost:8080/welcome-with-parameter/name/Buddy` URL is as follows:

```
{"message":"Hello World, Buddy!"}
```

The integration test for the preceding method is very simple and is as follows:

```
@Test
public void welcomeWithParameter() throws Exception {
    ResponseEntity < String > response =
        template.getForEntity("/welcome-with-parameter/name/Buddy",
String.class);
    assertThat(response.getBody(),
        containsString("Hello World, Buddy"));
}
```

Please note the following:

- `"/welcome-with-parameter/name/Buddy"`: This matches against the variable template in the URI. We are passing in the name, `Buddy`.
- `assertThat(response.getBody(), containsString("Hello World, Buddy"))`: We expect the response to contain the message with the name.

Integration tests for the TodoController API

Until now, we have looked at simple integration tests for the `Hello World` REST API. It lays the foundation for writing unit tests for more complex REST APIs. Let's now shift our attention toward integration tests for the `Todo` REST API, using all other request methods.

Todo API integration testing setup

The code to perform integration testing in the `TodoController` class is shown in the following code snippet. It launches the entire Spring context, with all the beans defined. This test is very similar to the integration test for `BasicController`:

```
@RunWith(SpringJUnit4ClassRunner.class)
@SpringBootTest(classes = Application.class,
    webEnvironment = SpringBootTest.WebEnvironment.RANDOM_PORT)
public class TodoControllerIT {
    @Autowired
    private TestRestTemplate template;
```

Since the `Todo` REST API is secured using basic authentication, we would need to supply basic `auth` credentials to do the integration test.

The code that would be used to create the `auth` headers is as follows:

```java
HttpHeaders headers = createHeaders("user-name", "user-password");

HttpHeaders createHeaders(String username, String password) {
    return new HttpHeaders() {
        {
            String auth = username + ":" + password;
            byte[] encodedAuth = Base64.getEncoder().encode(
                auth.getBytes(Charset.forName("US-ASCII")));
            String authHeader = "Basic " + new String(encodedAuth);
            set("Authorization", authHeader);
        }
    };
}
```

Please note the following:

- `createHeaders("user-name", "user-password")`: This method creates Base64—encoded headers.
- `ResponseEntity<String> response = template.exchange("/users/Jack/todos", ;HttpMethod.GET,new HttpEntity<String>(null, headers), String.class)`: The key change here is the use of `HttpEntity` to supply the headers to the REST template.

Writing an integration test to retrieve all todos – the GET method

Writing an integration test to retrieve all todos is simple. Consider the following method:

```java
@Test
public void retrieveTodos() throws Exception {
    String expected = "[" + "{id:1,user:Jack,desc:\"Learn Spring
MVC\",done:false}" + "," +
        "{id:2,user:Jack,desc:\"Learn Struts\",done:false}" + "]";

    ResponseEntity < String > response = template.exchange(
        "/users/Jack/todos",
        HttpMethod.GET,
        new HttpEntity < String > (null, headers), String.class);
    JSONAssert.assertEquals(expected,
        response.getBody(), false);
}
```

This test is very similar to the integration test for `BasicController`, except for the fact that we are using `JSONAssert` to assert the response content.

Writing an integration test for creating a todo – the POST method

To create a todo, we need to send a `POST` request to the `http://localhost:8080/users/Jill/todos` URI, with a request body containing the todo content in JSON format.

Example request details are as follows:

```
Header
 Content-Type:application/json

Body
 {
 "user": "Jill",
 "desc": "Learn Hibernate",
 "done": false
 }
```

The following code is the complete integration test. We are creating a `Todo` object, and then using `template.postForLocation` to post the `Todo` content to the `/users/Jill/todos` URL:

```
@Test
public void addTodo() throws Exception {
    Todo todo = new Todo(-1, "Jill", "Learn Hibernate",
        new Date(), false);
    URI location = template
        .postForLocation("/users/Jill/todos", todo);
    assertThat(location.getPath(),
        containsString("/users/Jill/todos/5"));
}
```

Please note the following:

- `URI location = template.postForLocation("/users/Jill/todos", todo)`: `postForLocation` is a utility method that is especially useful in tests to create new resources. We are posting the todo to the given URI, and getting the location from the header.

- `assertThat(location.getPath(),`
  `containsString("/users/Jill/todos/4"))`: Asserts that the location
  contains the path to the newly created resource.

Writing an integration test for updating a todo – the PUT method

We would need to send a `PUT` request to the
`http://localhost:8080/users/Jill/todos/1` URI. The body of the request contains
the updated todo details in JSON format.

Example request details are as follows:

```
Header
 Content-Type:application/json

Body
 {
 "id" : 4,
 "user": "Jill",
 "desc": "Learn Spring MVC 5",
 "done": false
 }
```

This is the complete integration test:

```
@Test
public void updatedTodo() throws Exception {
    String expected = "{id:4,user:Jill,desc:\"Learn Spring MVC
5\",done:false}";
    Todo todo = new Todo(4, "Jill", "Learn Spring MVC 5", new Date(),
false);
    ResponseEntity < String > response = template
        .exchange("/users/Jill/todos/" + todo.getId(),
            HttpMethod.PUT,
            new HttpEntity < > (todo, headers), String.class);
    JSONAssert.assertEquals(expected, response.getBody(), false);
}
```

We are creating a `Todo` object, and then using `template.exchange` to send a `PUT` request
to the `/users/Jill/todos` URI. We are asserting the content of the response using
`JSONAssert.assertEquals`.

Writing an integration test for deleting a todo – the DELETE method

In the integration test for the DELETE method, let's try to delete the todo with an ID, 3, belonging to Jill.

We would need to send a DELETE request to /users/Jill/todos/3.

The integration test is as follows:

```
@Test
public void deleteTodo() throws Exception {
    ResponseEntity < String > response = template.exchange(
        "/users/Jill/todos/3",
        HttpMethod.DELETE,
        new HttpEntity < > (null, headers), String.class);
    assertEquals(HttpStatus.NO_CONTENT, response.getStatusCode());
}
```

We use template.exchange to execute the DELETE request. We assert the status of HttpStatus.NO_CONTENT.

Unit and integration testing best practices

With the evolution of architectures, the importance of unit testing is growing with time. Having great unit tests is no longer a luxury. It's a necessity that ensures that you are able to continuously improve code, and have a safety net to fall back on.

It's important to treat your unit test code equally with your production code.

At the most basic level, your unit tests should adhere to the *4 Principles of Simple Design*.

A software application is said to adhere to the *4 Principles of Simple Design* if it does the following:

1. **Runs all tests**: Unit tests are continuously written alongside source code and are run in continuous integration.
2. **Contains no duplication**: There is as less duplication as possible in your code.
3. **Expresses the intent of programmers**: The code is easy to understand. You make your tests readable by clearly highlighting the important values in the tests, and give good method names to your tests. Use frameworks such as Hamcrest Matchers, AssertJ, and JSON Path to write great assertions.

4. **Minimizes the number of classes and methods**: Each of the elements involved is as small as possible—methods, classes, packages, components, and applications. You can keep your unit tests small by writing one condition per test. Also, keep the scope of your unit test as small as possible—typically a method, at most; a group of methods.

Here are some of the best practices that are specific to unit tests:

- **Tests fail only when there is a problem with the production code**: If tests fail because of external dependency, for example, a change in the data in a database, the development team would lose confidence in the tests. Over a period of time, you would see that tests would rot, and the team would start ignoring test failures.
- **Tests should find all the important problems with the production code**: Try and write unit tests for all possible scenarios—including exceptions.
- **Tests should run quickly**: It's important that your test runs quickly. This would ensure that the developers are inclined to run tests often. This would also ensure that continuous integration builds run fast, and the developers get quick feedback. Launching a Spring context in a unit test is time-consuming. So, wherever possible, we prefer to run unit tests with mocking, without launching a Spring context.
- **Tests are run as often as possible**: Make sure that you run your tests in continuous integration. As soon as the code is committed to version control, a build should be triggered and the test run. This would ensure that you are taking maximum advantage of the great unit tests that your team is writing.

Summary

In this chapter, we focused on writing great unit and integration tests for a REST API that has been developed with Spring Boot.

We started with Spring Boot Starter Test, and got an overview of all the important unit testing frameworks that it provides.

We looked at several unit tests for REST APIs, focusing on the specific responsibility of a controller method. We used the Spring Mock MVC framework to launch Spring contexts with just the web layer components, and mock out all other dependencies.

We saw that great unit tests act as a safety net against future defects. They help in catching defects earlier.

Integration tests help us in testing multiple application layers together. We used @SpringBootTest with RANDOM_PORT to launch the entire Spring context, including business and data components. We used JSONAssert to write asserts on the JSON response.

At the end of the chapter, we looked at automation testing best practices. We learned that great tests adhere to the *4 Principles of Simple Design*. We learned that great tests run fast, do not have external dependencies, and run in continuous integration.

In the next chapter, let's turn our attention to securing our REST API with Spring Security. We will understand the different options that are available to authenticate and authorize your REST API consumers, including Basic Auth, JWT, and OAuth2.

Further reading

- Spring Unit Testing, available at https://docs.spring.io/spring/docs/current/spring-framework-reference/testing.html.
- Spring Boot Unit Testing, available at https://docs.spring.io/spring-boot/docs/current/reference/html/boot-features-testing.html.

8
Securing REST API with Spring Security

In the last few chapters, we built awesome REST APIs using Spring Boot, and added features such as versioning, exception handling, documentation, unit testing, and integration testing.

In this chapter, let's get started with the most important features that need to be considered when building REST APIs—authentication and authorization.

Spring Security is the framework of choice to secure web applications and REST APIs in the Java world—especially for applications built with Spring and Spring Boot.

Security is one of the important non-functional features in building your applications. You will need to take care to secure your application from the first day you start building it. In this chapter, let's learn about the basics of securing REST API—authentication and authorization. We will start with understanding how to integrate Spring Security into a Spring Boot REST API project, and how to understand all the auto-configuration that Spring Security Starter brings.

We will learn about the key building blocks behind Spring Security using the following:

- Filters
- Authentication managers, providers, and the UserDetailsService
- Access decision managers and action decision voters

After that, we will focus on securing your REST API with basic authentication. We will look at how to store user credentials in an in-memory data store, as well as in a database.

We will discuss the basics of OAuth, and use Spring Security OAuth to add OAuth authentication to our REST API. We will also learn the basics of **JSON Web Token (JWT)**, and how to use it with Spring Security OAuth.

Technical requirements

The following are the requirements for this chapter:

- Your favorite IDE, Eclipse
- Java 8+
- Maven 3.x
- Internet connectivity

The GitHub repository link for this chapter can be found at `https://github.com/PacktPublishing/Mastering-Spring-5.1/tree/master/Chapter08`

Security REST API with Spring Security

Spring Security is the most popular framework that is used to secure a REST API that has been developed in the Java world—typically with Spring and Spring Boot.

Spring Security provides authentication and authorization for REST APIs. It integrates well with multiple sources for user credentials, including databases and LDAP. Spring Security provides multiple authentication options, including basic security and JWT.

Let's start by gaining an understanding of the basics of security REST API.

Securing the REST API basics

Let's say we want to secure our `Todo` REST API. The first questions to ask would be the following:

- Who would be the users of our API?
- How do we identify a user?
- Where can we store the user's details?
- What are the different kinds of users?
- What actions can each type of user perform?

Authentication

Typically, we would identify a user using a user ID and a password. These are called user credentials. The process of checking the user credentials and determining whether it's a valid user for our API is called **authentication**.

Authentication – Is this a valid user?

Authorization

Once we authenticate the user, we need to decide what kind of actions they can perform.

The popular option is to have multiple roles associated with the API. We can have permissions for different API actions that are associated with the roles; for example:

- The user role can perform all actions on their todos—Read, Update, Delete, and Create.
- The support role can only view the todos—only Read is allowed.

The process of establishing whether the user has the right permissions to perform an action is called **authorization**.

Authorization – Is the valid user allowed to perform an action?

Implementing security for REST API

Every REST API request should be checked for authentication and authorization before being executed. REST APIs are implemented in the Java world using servlets and controllers. We want to ensure that the authorization and authentication are performed before the servlets and/or controllers are executed.

Filters provide this feature. Typically, we can execute filters before the API is executed. The following diagram shows a typical implementation approach:

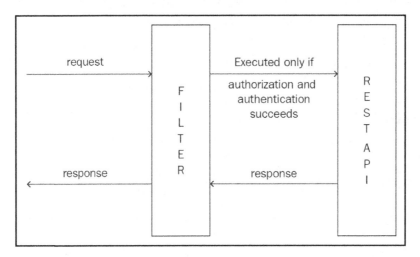

Here are the important steps:

- The REST API request is executed by providing the URL, request data, and user credentials.
- The filter checks for authentication—is it a valid user? Typically, user ID/password combination, or a token are used as credentials. After that, the filter checks for authorization—does the user have the right permissions?
- The REST API request is executed.

The preceding approach would ensure authentication and authorization are always performed before executing the request.

Until now, we have discussed a generic approach for securing REST APIs. Let's now shift our attention towards Spring Security.

Adding Spring Security to the Todo API

In the previous chapters, we created todo APIs. Let's look at quickly securing this API using Spring Security.

Spring Boot provides a starter for Spring Security—spring-boot-starter-security. We will start by adding Spring Security Starter to our pom.xml file.

Adding Spring Security Starter

Add the following dependency to your `pom.xml` file:

```
<dependency>
    <groupId>org.springframework.boot</groupId>
    <artifactId>spring-boot-starter-security</artifactId>
</dependency>
```

Spring Boot Starter security dependencies

The `spring-boot-starter-security` dependency brings in three important Spring Security dependencies:

- `spring-security-core`: Implements the core features of Spring Security
- `spring-security-config`: Provides the Spring Security namespace
- `spring-security-web`: Provides filters and other features needed to secure web applications

Here are the dependencies that are automatically included:

```
<dependency>
    <groupId>org.springframework.security</groupId>
    <artifactId>spring-security-config</artifactId>
</dependency>
<dependency>
    <groupId>org.springframework.security</groupId>
    <artifactId>spring-security-web</artifactId>
</dependency>
<dependency>
    <groupId>org.springframework.security</groupId>
    <artifactId>spring-security-core</artifactId>
</dependency>
```

Spring Boot Starter security auto-configuration

Spring Boot Starter Security does not only bring in the dependencies—but it also provides the auto-configuration of the Spring Security framework.

If we try to access any of the services now, we would get `Access Denied`.

When we send a request to `http://localhost:8080/users/Jack/todos`, an example of the response is shown in the following code snippet:

```
{
  "timestamp": "2019-05-03T11:49:29.464+0000",
  "status": 401,
  "error": "Unauthorized",
  "message": "Full authentication is required to access this resource",
  "path": "/users/Jack/todos"
}
```

The response status is `401 - Unauthorized`.

The default authentication approach that is auto-configured is called **basic authentication**.

Basic authentication is one of the simplest authentication mechanisms that is present with the HTTP protocol. When an API is protected with basic authentication, you need to send a basic authentication header to access the API. The basic authentication header is Base64, an encoded combination of the user ID and password.

You might be wondering—where are the user ID and password?

The default auto-configured user ID is `user`, and the default password is printed in the log at the server startup.

An example from the log is as follows:

```
Using default security password: 3fb5564a-ce53-4138-9911-8ade17b2f478
```

Underlined in the preceding code snippet is the default security password that is printed in the log.

We can use Postman to fire a request with basic authentication. The default **Username** is `user`, and we can pick up the underlined **Password** from the log.

The following diagram shows how basic authentication details can be sent, along with a request:

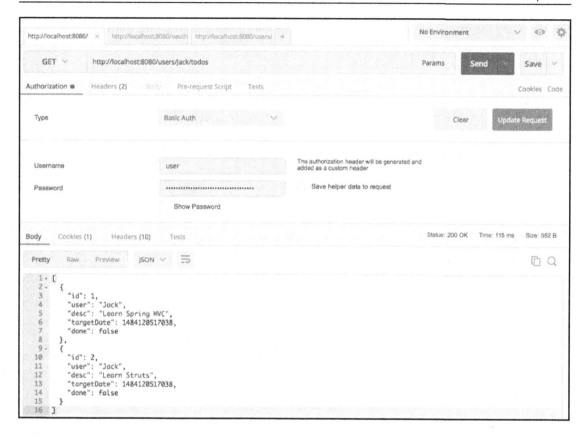

As you can see, authentication succeeds, and we get a proper response back.

We can configure the user ID and password of our choice in `application.properties`, as shown here:

```
spring.security.user.name=user-name
spring.security.user.password=user-password
```

Updating an integration test with basic authentication credentials

The integration test that we wrote for the REST API earlier will start failing because of invalid credentials.

Let's update the integration test to supply the basic authentication credentials:

```
private TestRestTemplate template = new TestRestTemplate();

HttpHeaders headers = createHeaders("user-name", "user-password");

HttpHeaders createHeaders(String username, String password) {
    return new HttpHeaders() {
        {
            String auth = username + ":" + password;
            byte[] encodedAuth = Base64.getEncoder()
                .encode(auth.getBytes(Charset.forName("US-ASCII")));
            String authHeader = "Basic " + new String(encodedAuth);
            set("Authorization", authHeader);
        }
    };
}
```

`createHeaders` creates a `Base64`-encoded basic authentication header. `HttpHeaders headers = createHeaders("user-name", "user-password")` sets up the `headers` variable with a basic authentication header.

We would need to send this header when executing the REST API request. The following code shows the updated test:

```
@Test
public void retrieveTodos() throws Exception {
    String expected = "[" +
        "{id:1,user:Jack,desc:\"Learn Spring MVC\",done:false}" + "," +
        "{id:2,user:Jack,desc:\"Learn Struts\",done:false}" + "]";
    ResponseEntity < String > response = template.exchange(
        createUrl("/users/Jack/todos"), HttpMethod.GET,
        new HttpEntity < String > (null, headers),
        String.class);
    JSONAssert.assertEquals(expected, response.getBody(), false);
}
```

We are using `template.exchange` to send the headers—`new HttpEntity<String>(null, headers)`.

Similar changes need to be performed on all other integration test methods in `BasicControllerIT` and `TodoControllerIT`.

Updating a unit test to disable security

In a unit test, we want to focus on the behavior of the controller. We do not want to test security in our unit tests.

The following code snippet shows how we can disable security for the unit test:

```
@RunWith(SpringRunner.class)
@WebMvcTest(value = TodoController.class, secure = false)
public class TodoControllerTest {
```

The key part is the `secure = false` parameter on the `WebMvcTest` annotation. This will disable Spring Security for the unit test.

Similar changes need to be performed on all other unit test classes, including `BasicControllerTest`.

A quick review of the chapter until now

In this chapter, we have seen how basic authentication is automatically configured when you add Spring Security to the REST API. We saw how to execute requests by providing basic authentication credentials.

Spring Security provides multiple options to configure user credentials—databases and LDAP.

Before we get there, let's focus on understanding what's happening in the background:

- What is being auto-configured when Spring Security is added to the project?
- How does Spring Security work?

Understanding Spring Security

To understand Spring Security, let's start by looking at the log to find out what's happening in the background.

Reviewing the log

Reviewing the log helps us to understand what's happening behind the screens. The following snippets are some of the important extracts from the log when you enable debug logging. You can see that `SecurityAutoConfiguration` is kicked off, and that `SecurityFilterAutoConfiguration` **auto-configures** `SecurityFilter`:

```
SecurityAutoConfiguration matched:
 - @ConditionalOnClass found required class
'org.springframework.security.authentication.DefaultAuthenticationEventPubl
isher'; @ConditionalOnMissingClass did not find unwanted class
(OnClassCondition)
SecurityFilterAutoConfiguration matched:
 - @ConditionalOnClass found required classes
'org.springframework.security.web.context.AbstractSecurityWebApplicationIni
tializer',
'org.springframework.security.config.http.SessionCreationPolicy';
@ConditionalOnMissingClass did not find unwanted class (OnClassCondition)
 - found ConfigurableWebEnvironment (OnWebApplicationCondition)
```

You can also see that a security filter chain is being configured. Also, in the log, is a list of filters that are part of the chain:

```
SecurityFilterAutoConfiguration#securityFilterChainRegistration matched:
 - @ConditionalOnBean (names: springSecurityFilterChain; SearchStrategy:
all) found bean 'springSecurityFilterChain' (OnBeanCondition)
2019-05-02 14:11:44.257 INFO 5053 - [ restartedMain]
o.s.s.web.DefaultSecurityFilterChain : Creating filter chain:
org.springframework.security.web.util.matcher.AnyRequestMatcher@1,
[org.springframework.security.web.context.request.async.WebAsyncManagerInte
grationFilter@47e122e9,
org.springframework.security.web.context.SecurityContextPersistenceFilter@5
df6d952,
org.springframework.security.web.header.HeaderWriterFilter@2cf48198,
org.springframework.security.web.csrf.CsrfFilter@1a6342c0,
org.springframework.security.web.authentication.logout.LogoutFilter@4e8861f
e,
org.springframework.security.web.authentication.UsernamePasswordAuthenticat
ionFilter@50951d86,
org.springframework.security.web.authentication.ui.DefaultLoginPageGenerati
ngFilter@6a8113f8,
org.springframework.security.web.authentication.www.BasicAuthenticationFilt
er@4dda8e9d,
org.springframework.security.web.savedrequest.RequestCacheAwareFilter@6a6c2
1f8,
org.springframework.security.web.servletapi.SecurityContextHolderAwareReque
stFilter@766e8466,
```

```
org.springframework.security.web.authentication.AnonymousAuthenticationFilt
er@55b96e7b,
org.springframework.security.web.session.SessionManagementFilter@1dd7e56d,
org.springframework.security.web.access.ExceptionTranslationFilter@489b0280
,
org.springframework.security.web.access.intercept.FilterSecurityInterceptor
@6bd7b76c]
```

Understanding Spring Security filters

In any security implementation, we use filters to ensure that requests are authenticated and authorized before being executed.

Spring Security uses a chain of filters to check for authentication and authorization before a request is authorized for execution.

Before Spring Boot, in order to enable Spring Security on a web project, we configured a filter chain in `web.xml`. With Spring Boot, this filter chain is auto-configured. We do not need to manually do it.

The configuration is as follows:

```
<filter>
  <filter-name>springSecurityFilterChain</filter-name>
  <filter-
class>org.springframework.web.filter.DelegatingFilterProxy</filter-class>
</filter>
<filter-mapping>
  <filter-name>springSecurityFilterChain</filter-name>
  <url-pattern>/*</url-pattern>
</filter-mapping>
```

The following diagram shows how the **Spring Security Filter Chain** sits before all requests:

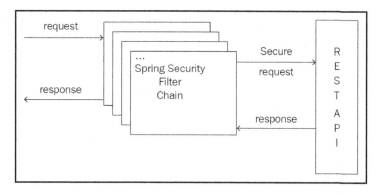

The **Spring Security Filter Chain** checks the authentication and authorization on every request. If a request does not have proper credentials or authorization, the request would be rejected, and an error would be thrown.

Here are some of the important filters that are executed in the filter chain:

- UsernamePasswordAuthenticationFilter: Performs authentication using the user credentials. Executed if the request is POST, and has user credentials.
- BasicAuthenticationFilter: Performs basic authentication. Executed if there is a basic authentication request header in the request.
- AnonymousAuthenticationFilter: If there are no authentication credentials in the request, this would create an anonymous user. Typically, anonymous users are allowed to execute requests for public API—an API that does not require authentication.
- ExceptionTranslationFilter: It does not provide additional security. It translates authentication exceptions to a suitable HTTP response.
- FilterSecurityInterceptor: Responsible for authorization decisions.

Here are some of the filters that provide auxiliary Spring Security features:

- HeaderWriterFilter: Writes security headers to the response—X-Frame-Options, X-XSS-Protection, and X-Content-Type-Options.
- CsrfFilter: Checks for **Cross-Site Request Forgery (CSRF)** protection.

Understanding authentication in Spring Security

In the previous section, we saw two examples of filters that provide authentication—BasicAuthenticationFilter and UsernamePasswordAuthenticationFilter. You can also add other filters for authentication. You can use DigestAuthenticationFilter for digest authentication.

User credentials might be stored in different kinds of data stores—LDAP, databases, or in-memory.

How do these filters authenticate against user credentials?

Consider this piece of code from BasicAuthenticationFilter:

```
Authentication authResult = this.authenticationManager
  .authenticate(authRequest);
SecurityContextHolder.getContext().setAuthentication(authResult);
```

It does two things:

- Calls `authenticationManager` to authenticate the request.
- If the request is successful, it sets the result to `SecurityContextHolder`. This result is visible to other filters down the chain, and also to the REST API implementation controllers.

Typical Spring Security authentication implementations work in a similar way to `BasicAuthenticationFilter`.

Understanding authentication managers

In the previous section, we saw that authentication filters typically delegate to **authentication managers**.

How do authentication managers work?

A high-level overview of how the default authentication manager works is shown in the following diagram:

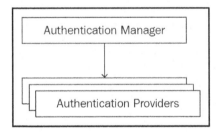

The default **Authentication Manager** (`ProviderManager`) talks with multiple authentication providers. Each authentication provider can talk to a `UserDetailsService` in order to retrieve and authenticate user details.

Here's the definition of the **Authentication Manager** interface:

```
public interface AuthenticationManager {
    Authentication authenticate(Authentication authentication)
    throws AuthenticationException;
}
```

Understanding provider managers

The default implementation of `AuthenticationManager` is `ProviderManager`:

```
public class ProviderManager implements AuthenticationManager
```

A `ProviderManager` typically depends on a number of list of authentication providers to check for authentication. It is sufficient if one of the authentication providers returns a successful authentication.

The following code shows an extract from `ProviderManager`:

```
for (AuthenticationProvider provider: getProviders()) {
    result = provider.authenticate(authentication);
    if (result != null) {
        copyDetails(authentication, result);
        break;
    }
}
```

Understanding authentication providers

You can have multiple `AuthenticationProvider` interfaces configured. Each authentication provider talks with a different data store or `api` authentication.

The `AuthenticationProvider` interface is shown here:

```
public interface AuthenticationProvider {
    Authentication authenticate(Authentication authentication)
    throws AuthenticationException;
    boolean supports(Class << ? > authentication);
}
```

You can have different `AuthenticationProvider` interfaces. One talking to a database; another to a LDAP. Typically, you will have one authentication provider talking to your user credentials database or your security `api`.

`DaoAuthenticationProvider` is one of the default implementations of `AuthenticationProvider`, provided by Spring Security. It talks to something called `UserDetailsService`, to retrieve the user details based on the username.

Implementing the UserDetailsService

`UserDetailsService` provides a single method that can be integrated with any of your authentication credential data stores:

```
public interface UserDetailsService {
    UserDetails loadUserByUsername(String username)
    throws UsernameNotFoundException;
}
```

`loadUserByUsername` should return `UserDetails`. The details of the `UserDetails` interface are as follows:

```
public interface UserDetails extends Serializable {
    Collection << ? extends GrantedAuthority > getAuthorities();
    String getPassword();
    String getUsername();
    boolean isAccountNonExpired();
    boolean isAccountNonLocked();
    boolean isCredentialsNonExpired();
    boolean isEnabled();
}
```

Spring Security also provides a default `UserDetailsService` service to talk to a relational database. It assumes a default schema. Two tables need to be created, adhering to a specific structure—`users` and `authorities`:

```
public class JdbcDaoImpl extends JdbcDaoSupport
implements UserDetailsService, MessageSourceAware {
    public static final String DEF_USERS_BY_USERNAME_QUERY
        = "select username,password,enabled " +
        "from users " + "where username = ?";
    public static final String DEF_AUTHORITIES_BY_USERNAME_QUERY
        = "select username,authority " +
        "from authorities " + "where username = ?";
    public static final String DEF_GROUP_AUTHORITIES_BY_USERNAME_QUERY
        = "select g.id, g.group_name, ga.authority " +
        "from groups g, group_members gm, group_authorities ga " +
        "where gm.username = ? " + "and g.id = ga.group_id " +
        "and g.id = gm.group_id";
}
```

You can also provide your own custom queries using the set methods in `JdbcDaoImpl`:

```
public void setAuthoritiesByUsernameQuery(String queryString)
public void setGroupAuthoritiesByUsernameQuery(String queryString)
public void setUsersByUsernameQuery(String usersByUsernameQueryString)
```

Managing users with a UserDetailsManager

Spring Security also provides default interfaces and implementations to support the management of users. You can create/delete/update users, and manage passwords using the UserDetailsManager interface. Details of the interface are as follows:

```
public interface UserDetailsManager extends UserDetailsService {
    void createUser(UserDetails user);
    void updateUser(UserDetails user);
    void deleteUser(String username);
    void changePassword(String oldPassword, String newPassword);
    boolean userExists(String username);
}
```

InMemoryUserDetailsManager and JdbcUserDetailsManager are a couple of default implementations of UserDetailsManager:

- InMemoryUserDetailsManager is typically used for testing purposes. It stores user details in-memory.
- JdbcUserDetailsManager provides a **Java Database Connectivity (JDBC)** implementation.

Understanding authentication extension points in Spring Security

You can customize the default auto-configured security that is provided by Spring Security Starter in multiple ways. Let's look at some of these options in this section.

Providing a custom implementation of the Use DetailsService

We can extend Spring Security by providing a custom implementation for UserDetailsService. The following example shows a hardcoded in-memory implementation:

```
@Service
public class InMemoryUserDetailsService implements UserDetailsService {

    static List < CustomizedUserDetails > inMemoryUserList = new ArrayList
< > ();
```

```
    static {
        inMemoryUserList.add(new CustomizedUserDetails(1 L, "mastering-
spring-inmemory", "{noop}dummy", "ROLE_USER_2"));
    }

    @Override
    public UserDetails loadUserByUsername(String username) throws
UsernameNotFoundException {

        Optional < CustomizedUserDetails > findFirst =
inMemoryUserList.stream()
            .filter(user - >
user.getUsername().equals(username)).findFirst();

        if (!findFirst.isPresent()) {
            throw new
UsernameNotFoundException(String.format("USER_NOT_FOUND '%s'.", username));
        }

        return findFirst.get();
    }

}
```

We are creating an in-memory user list—inMemoryUserList. Now, loadUserByUsername checks the username against the in-memory list, and returns an instance of CustomizedUserDetails—an implementation of UserDetails. A few details about CustomizedUserDetails are shown here:

```
public class CustomizedUserDetails implements UserDetails {

    private final Long id;
    private final String username;
    private final String password;
    private final Collection << ? extends GrantedAuthority > authorities;

    public CustomizedUserDetails(Long id, String username, String password,
String role) {
        //Constructor
    }
```

We can also integrate with a database, and implement UserDetailsService. The following example shows a UserDetailsService implementation talking to a Spring data JPA-configured userRepository:

```
@Service
public class DatabaseUserDetailsService implements UserDetailsService {
```

```
    @Autowired
    private UserRepository userRepository;

    @Override
    public UserDetails loadUserByUsername(String username) throws
UsernameNotFoundException {
        User user = userRepository.findByUsername(username);

        if (user == null) {
            throw new
UsernameNotFoundException(String.format("USER_NOT_FOUND '%s'.", username));
        }

        return new CustomizedUserDetails(user.getId(), user.getUsername(),
user.getPassword(), user.getRole());
    }
}
```

Extending the web security configurer adapter to configure a global authentication manager

Another option for extending the default security configuration is to extend `WebSecurityConfigurerAdapter`. Now, `WebSecurityConfigurerAdapter` provides the base implementation of the Spring Security configuration, which can be easily extended.

You can provide a global authentication manager implementation by creating a bean for `AuthenticationManager`, and overriding `configureGlobal` in order to configure it.

An example implementation is shown here:

```
@Configuration
public class SpringSecurityConfiguration extends
WebSecurityConfigurerAdapter {

    @Bean
    @Override
    public AuthenticationManager authenticationManagerBean() throws
Exception {
        return super.authenticationManagerBean();
    }

    @Autowired
    public void configureGlobal(AuthenticationManagerBuilder auth) throws
Exception {
```

```
auth.inMemoryAuthentication().withUser("user1").password("{noop}user1-
password").roles("ADMIN");
auth.inMemoryAuthentication().withUser("user2").password("{noop}user2-
password").roles("USER");
    }
```

In the preceding example, we are configuring in-memory authentication with two users—user1 and user2.

 {noop} is to specify that no encoder is used. Spring security also supports BCryptPasswordEncoder, StandardPasswordEncoder (uses SHA-256 hashing with 1024 iterations), and Pbkdf2PasswordEncoder.

We can also provide a local authentication manager by overriding the configure(AuthenticationManagerBuilder auth) method in WebSecurityConfigurerAdapter, as shown here:

```
@Override
protected void configure(AuthenticationManagerBuilder auth) throws
Exception {
    auth.inMemoryAuthentication().withUser("user3")
        .password("{noop}user3-password").roles("ADMIN");
    auth.inMemoryAuthentication().withUser("user4")
        .password("{noop}user4-password").roles("USER");
}
```

In the previous example, we configured an in-memory authentication with two users—user3 and user4.

Using the web security configurer adapter to configure web security

We can override configure(WebSecurity web) in order to configure URLs that do not need authorization and authentication.

An example implementation is shown here:

```
@Override
public void configure(WebSecurity webSecurity) throws Exception {
    webSecurity.ignoring().antMatchers(HttpMethod.POST, "/auth")
        .antMatchers(HttpMethod.OPTIONS, "/**")
        .and().ignoring()
        .antMatchers(HttpMethod.GET, "/");
}
```

The previous configuration does not carry out any authentication or authorization on the following:

- All options requests
- The GET requests to the "/" root URL
- The POST requests to the /auth URL

Understanding authorization in Spring Security

Authorization involves verifying whether the authenticated user has the right permissions to perform the requested action on the resource.

FilterSecurityInterceptor is typically the last filter that is executed in the Spring Security Filter Chain. One of its important responsibilities is checking for authorization.

FilterSecurityInterceptor extends AbstractSecurityInterceptor—where the actual authorization checks are implemented.

Consider the following snippet:

```
this.accessDecisionManager.decide(authenticated, object, attributes);
```

Using access decision manager to support authorization

You can see that AccessDecisionManager is used to make the access decision.

The following diagram shows how AccessDecisionManager works:

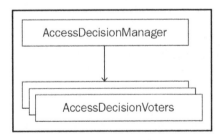

AccessDecisionManager talks with multiple AccessDecisionVoter implementations.

Each voter chooses one of three results:

- ACCESS_GRANTED: A positive vote
- ACCESS_ABSTAIN: Not participating in the vote
- ACCESS_DENIED: A negative vote

There are three default implementations of AccessDecisionManager:

- AffirmativeBased: Provides access even if one of the voters returns a positive vote.
- ConsensusBased: Decides access based on the majority vote. If the positive votes are greater than the negative votes, access is granted. If positive and negative votes are equal, access is decided based on a configured flag, allowIfEqualGrantedDeniedDecisions.
- UnanimousBased: Access is denied even if one voter casts a negative vote. If there are no positive votes, the access decision is based on a configured flag, allowIfAllAbstainDecisions.

The interface for AccessDecisionManager is as follows:

```
public interface AccessDecisionManager {

    void decide(Authentication authentication, Object object,
        Collection < ConfigAttribute > configAttributes)
    throws AccessDeniedException, InsufficientAuthenticationException;

}
```

Each AccessDecisionManager has a logic similar to this. They talk to all the AccessDecisionVoter, and make a decision:

```
for (AccessDecisionVoter voter: getDecisionVoters()) {
    int result = voter.vote(authentication, object, configAttributes);
    //Other Logic
}
```

The interface for AccessDecisionVoter is shown in the following code. As discussed earlier, each voter returns one of the three statuses—ACCESS_GRANTED , ACCESS_ABSTAIN, or ACCESS_DENIED:

```
public interface AccessDecisionVoter < S > {

    boolean supports(ConfigAttribute attribute);
```

```
    boolean supports(Class << ? > clazz);

    int vote(Authentication authentication, S object,
        Collection < ConfigAttribute > attributes);
}
```

The following screenshot shows the different implementations of `AccessDecisionVoter`:

Some of the important implementations are as follows:

- `RoleVoter`: Votes based on the role of the user. Does the user role have access to the requested resource?
- `AuthenticatedVoter`: Votes based on the authentication status of the user. Is the user anonymous, is the user already authenticated, or are they a *remember me* user?
- `Jsr250Voter`: Votes based on JSR-250 annotations. We will talk about JSR-250 a little later.

Understanding authentication extension points in Spring Security

There are different extension points in Spring Security that can be used to configure authorizations. Let's look at some of the important ones in this section.

Using the web security configurer adapter to configure HTTP security

We can override `configure(HttpSecurity http)` in `WebSecurityConfigurerAdapter` in order to configure the URL patterns and roles that are needed to access them:

```
@Override
protected void configure(HttpSecurity http) throws Exception {
    http.authorizeRequests()
        .anyRequest().authenticated()
        .antMatchers("/admin/**").hasRole("ADMIN")
        .antMatchers("/users/**").hasRole("USER")
        .antMatchers("/login").permitAll();
}
```

The `http.authorizeRequests()` signature is as follows:

```
public
ExpressionUrlAuthorizationConfigurer<HttpSecurity>.ExpressionInterceptUrlRe
gistry authorizeRequests()
```

`ExpressionUrlAuthorizationConfigurer` allows you to configure URL-based authorization for your REST API.

Here is a quick overview of the preceding implementation. By default, all URLs are protected (`.anyRequest().authenticated()`). Only users with the `"ADMIN"` role can access URLs starting with `/admin` (`.antMatchers("/admin/**").hasRole("ADMIN")`). Similarly, only users with the `"USER"` role can access URLs starting with `/users`. All users can access `/login`.

Spring Security also provides a concept of `Authority`, which is very similar to `Role`. For all practical purposes, an `Authority` of `ROLE_ADMIN` is the same as a `Role` of `ADMIN`. The `ROLE_` prefix automatically gets added to a role.

A role is just an authority with a special `ROLE_` prefix.

The following methods can also be used to specify the required roles and authorities:

- `hasAnyRole`: Access is allowed only if the user has at least one of the roles specified.
- `hasAuthority`: Access is allowed if the user has specified authority.
- `hasAnyAuthority`: Access is allowed only if the user has at least one of the authorities specified.

Providing secured annotations on service methods

Spring Security, starting from version 2.0, provides a simple option to secure your service layer methods using a `@Secured` annotation.

You need `@EnableGlobalMethodSecurity` on a Spring configuration class in order to enable method-level security:

```
@EnableGlobalMethodSecurity(securedEnabled = true)
@SpringBootApplication
public class SpringSecurityApplication {
```

You can use `@Secured` to check for a role before executing the service method:

```
@Secured("ROLE_ADMIN")
 public List<User> retrieveAllUsers() {
 // Your code
 }
```

`@Secured` allows you to specify multiple roles. Method execution is allowed if the user has any of the specified roles:

```
@Secured({"ROLE_ADMIN", "ROLE_USER"})
 public User retrieveUser(String userName) {
 // Your code
 }
```

Providing JSR-250 annotations on service methods

JSR-250 also provides a few standard annotations that can be used for specifying method security. Spring Security, starting at version 3.0, supports these annotations.

You can enable JSR-250 by using the `jsr250Enabled = true` annotation in `@EnableGlobalMethodSecurity`:

```
@EnableGlobalMethodSecurity(jsr250Enabled = true)
@SpringBootApplication
public class SpringSecurityApplication {
```

`@RolesAllowed` is the JSR-250 annotation that is equivalent to `@Secured`:

```
@RolesAllowed("ROLE_ADMIN")
 public List<User> retrieveAllUsers() {
 // Your code
 }
```

`@RolesAllowed` allows **multiple roles** to be specified. Method execution is allowed if the user has any of the specified roles:

```
@RolesAllowed({"ROLE_ADMIN", "ROLE_USER"})
 public User retrieveUser(String userName) {
 // Your code
 }
```

Using Spring Security pre and post annotations

Spring Security pre and post annotations allow even more complex authorization checks to be carried before securing methods.

You can enable pre and post annotations by using the `prePostEnabled = true` annotation on `@EnableGlobalMethodSecurity`:

```
@EnableGlobalMethodSecurity(prePostEnabled = true)
@SpringBootApplication
public class SpringSecurityApplication {
```

The following code adds `PreAuthorize` to the method in order to check for user roles. You can specify a **Spring Expression Language (SpEL)**, expression to check for authorization before executing the method:

```
@PreAuthorize("hasRole('ROLE_ADMIN') or hasRole('ROLE_USER')")
 public User retrieveUser(String userName) {
 // Your code
 }
```

You can access principal and authentication objects from security contexts in EL expressions.

The following example checks whether the value of the parameter name is the same as the principal's username:

```
@PreAuthorize("#name == authentication.principal.username")
```

`PostAuthorize` allows you to execute checks after method execution. You can also use the return value from a method using `returnObject`:

```
@PostAuthorize("returnObject.name == authentication.principal.username")
```

Implementing security best practices with Spring Security

Spring Security, by default, enables a number of security best practices in web applications and REST APIs:

- It prevents CSRF attacks.
- It provides protection from session fixation problems.
- It automatically adds headers to the response to make it secure.
- It specifies HTTP strict transport security if the request is HTTPs:
    - Adds cache control headers
    - Adds cross-site protection headers
    - Prevents clickjacking by adding X-Frame-Options headers

 Clickjacking is used by hackers to get confidential information, by tricking a user to do something different (an insecure link or a button) from what they think they are doing.

Spring Security makes it easy to implement authentication and authorization for your REST API, by providing easy extension points, and implementing several security best practices out of the box.

Exploring OAuth2 authentication

OAuth is a protocol that provides flows in order to exchange authorization and authentication information between a range of web-enabled applications and services. It enables third-party applications to get restricted access to user information from a service, for example, Facebook, Twitter, or the GitHub repository.

Before we go into the details, it would be useful to review the terminology that is typically associated with OAuth2 authentication.

Let's consider an example. We want to enable third-party applications to access the `Todo` API that we created. Our API might have data belonging to thousands of users. We cannot give blanket access to the third party with user permissions.

OAuth2 enables users to grant third-party application access to their data available with the `Todo` API.

Here are some of the important players in a typical OAuth2 exchange:

- **Resource owner**: The resource owner is the owner of the data—the user of the `Todo` API. The resource owner decides how much of the information that is available with our API can be made available to the third-party application.
- **Resource server**: This is the actual resource that is being provided access to—the `Todo` API.
- **Client**: This is the third-party application that wants to integrate with the `Todo` API application.
- **Authorization server**: This is the server that provides the OAuth Service.
- **Client credentials**: Each third-party application has credentials that identifies itself to the OAuth Server. These are called client credentials.

Understanding OAuth2 high-level flow

Let's dig deeper into OAuth and gain an understanding of the two typical flows in OAuth authentication:

- Authorization Grant Flow
- Resource Access Flow

Exploring Authorization Grant Flow

During this flow, the user provides access to their information from the `Todo` API to a third-party application. Here are the steps involved:

- Third-party application requests access to a specific user for the `Todo` API.
- The OAuth Server asks the user for permissions that they would want to allow the third-party application.
- User grants permissions for the third-party application to access their details in the `Todo` API. This is called an authorization grant.

Resource Access Flow

During this flow, the third-party application accesses information from the Todo API, providing the required authentication and authorization details to the OAuth Server. Here are the steps involved:

- Third-party application provides its client credentials and user authorization grants to the authorization server, in order to get access to the Todo API.
- If the authentication is successful, the authorization server responds with an access token. Otherwise, the Authorization Grant Flow would start again.
- Third-party application calls the Todo API (the resource server) that is providing the access token. If the access token is valid, the resource server returns the details of the resource. Otherwise, it receives an error.

Creating the OAuth2 Server

OAuth2 for Spring Security (spring-security-oauth2) is the module to provide OAuth2 support to Spring Security. We will add it as a dependency in our pom.xml file:

```
<dependency>
  <groupId>org.springframework.security.oauth</groupId>
  <artifactId>spring-security-oauth2</artifactId>
  <version>2.0.10.RELEASE</version>
</dependency>
```

Typically, an authorization server would be a different server from the application where the API is exposed. To keep things simple, we will make our current API server act both as the resource server and as the authorization server.

Setting up the authorization server

An authorization server should have the following:

- A store for user credentials—user authentication and authorization for the Todo API.
- A store for third-party application credentials—also called client credentials.

An authorization server provides a URI where third-party applications can provide their client credentials and user authorization, in order to get an access token. Third-party applications can use this to talk to the resource API—the Todo API.

Configuring the user credentials for REST API

We will use an in-memory store. The following snippet shows the configuration of a couple of users with different roles:

```
@Configuration
public class SpringSecurityConfiguration extends
WebSecurityConfigurerAdapter {

    @Autowired
    public void configureGlobal(AuthenticationManagerBuilder auth) throws
Exception {
        auth.inMemoryAuthentication()
          .withUser("user1").password("{noop}user1-
password").roles("ADMIN");
        auth.inMemoryAuthentication()
          .withUser("user2").password("{noop}user2-
password").roles("USER");
    }

}
```

We are configuring a couple of users for the API—user1 and user2.

Configuring the authorization server with third-party client credentials

To enable the authorization server with OAuth2, we need to add
@EnableAuthorizationServer:

```
@Configuration
 @EnableAuthorizationServer // Open the authentication Server
 public class AuthorizationServerConfig implements
AuthorizationServerConfigurer {
```

We implement AuthorizationServerConfigurer in order to configure the authorization server.

We can override the configure(ClientDetailsServiceConfigurer clients) method in order to configure third-party client credentials. In the following example, we are hardcoding an in-memory store:

```
@Override
public void configure(ClientDetailsServiceConfigurer clients) throws
Exception {
    clients.inMemory().withClient("YourClientID")
        .secret("{noop}TopSecretClientPassword")
        .authorizedGrantTypes("authorization_code", "refresh_token",
```

```
"password")
        .scopes("openid");
}
```

`YourClientID` is the client ID. `TopSecretClientPassword` is the password. We are enabling three grant types. Grant types are the permissions that a third-party application can request from a user of the REST API.

Obtaining an access token

To get an access token, we call the authorization server token API (`http://localhost:8080/oauth/token`), providing the client authentication details in the basic authentication mode, and the user credentials as part of the form data. The following screenshot shows how we can configure the client authentication details in the basic authentication mode:

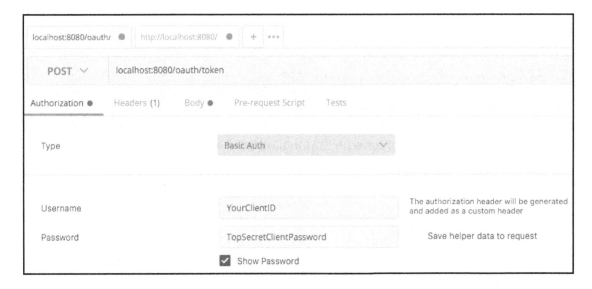

The following screenshot shows how to configure the user authentication details as part of the POST parameters:

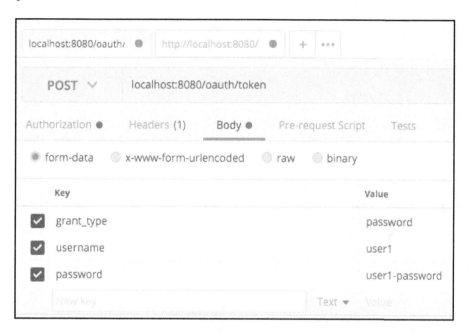

When we execute the request, we get a response similar to the one shown in the following code snippet:

```
{
"access_token": "08480948-2139-4d20-9504-5389a47c16ce",
"token_type": "bearer",
"refresh_token": "81bfc160-a04c-4e59-bf2f-66e183d9ede8",
"expires_in": 43199,
"scope": "openid"
}
```

Here are a couple of important details:

- access_token: The client application can use the access token to authenticate further API calls. However, the access token will expire, typically in a very short time period.
- refresh_token: The client application can submit a new request to the authentication server with refresh_token to get a new access_token.

Setting up the resource server

We would need to set up the `Todo` API application to act as a resource server.

We use the `@EnableResourceServer` annotation in order to enable the application to be a resource server:

```
@Configuration
@EnableResourceServer
public class ResourceServerConfig extends ResourceServerConfigurerAdapter {
```

We extend `ResourceServerConfigurerAdapter` in order to configure authorizations on the resource server resources:

```
@Override
public void configure(HttpSecurity http) throws Exception {
    http.anonymous().disable()
        .authorizeRequests()
        .antMatchers("/users/**").access("hasRole('USER')")
        .and().exceptionHandling()
        .accessDeniedHandler(new OAuth2AccessDeniedHandler());
}
```

In the previous code, we are configuring that all requests to URIs that match the `/users/**` pattern should have a role of `USER`. We are also configuring the error handler, in case access is denied by the OAuth Server.

Next, we need to configure a resource ID, and declare it as stateless, as the REST API does not have any state:

```
private static final String RESOURCE_ID = "resource_id";

@Override
public void configure(ResourceServerSecurityConfigurer resources) {
    resources.resourceId(RESOURCE_ID).stateless(false);
}
```

Executing the request using the access token

Once we have `access_token`, we can execute the request using `access_token`, as shown in the following screenshot:

As you can see in the preceding sreenshot, we provide the access token in the request header called **Authorization**. We use the value of `"Bearer {access_token}"`. Authentication succeeds, and we get the expected resource details.

Updating the integration test

We will now update our integration test in order to provide the OAuth2 credentials. The following test highlights the important changes:

```java
private OAuth2RestTemplate getOAuthTemplate() {
    ResourceOwnerPasswordResourceDetails resource
                    = new ResourceOwnerPasswordResourceDetails();
    resource.setUsername("user2");
    resource.setPassword("user2-password");
    resource.setAccessTokenUri(createURL("/oauth/token"));
    resource.setClientId("YourClientID");
    resource.setClientSecret("TopSecretClientPassword");
    resource.setGrantType("password");
    OAuth2RestTemplate oauthTemplate
        = new OAuth2RestTemplate(resource, new
DefaultOAuth2ClientContext());
    return oauthTemplate;
}
```

Some important things to note are as follows:

- `ResourceOwnerPasswordResourceDetails resource = new ResourceOwnerPasswordResourceDetails()`: We set up `ResourceOwnerPasswordResourceDetails` with the user credentials and the client credentials.
- `resource.setAccessTokenUri(createUrl("/oauth/token"))`: Configures the URL of the authentication server.
- `OAuth2RestTemplate oauthTemplate = new OAuth2RestTemplate(resource,new DefaultOAuth2ClientContext())`: `OAuth2RestTemplate` is an extension of `RestTemplate`, which supports the OAuth2 protocol.

The following code shows the updated test using the `getOAuthTemplate` method:

```
@Test
public void welcome() throws Exception {
    ResponseEntity < String > response = getOAuthTemplate()
        .getForEntity(createURL("/welcome"), String.class);
    // ResponseEntity<String> response = template.getForEntity("/welcome",
    // String.class);
    assertThat(response.getBody(), equalTo("Hello World"));
}
```

Similar changes are needed in all other tests.

Spring Boot and Spring Security make it easy to implement OAuth2. In this quick section, we enabled our users to grant access to their `Todo` data to third-party applications, by implementing OAuth2 with Spring Boot and Spring Security.

Authentication with JWT

We have been using basic authentication in previous sections. The primary problem with basic authentication is that there is no expiration time for the authentication header. If a hacker is able to obtain the basic authentication header, they would be able to use it until you change your password. The other problem is that the basic authentication header only contains authentication information. It does not have any provision for authorizations, or adding user details.

There were a number of custom attempts to design a token-based authentication system to simplify communication between systems. The idea is to use some kind of an encryption algorithm to create a secure token with user authorizations and user details.

Over a period of time, we evolved it into a standard called **JWT**.

Introducing JWT

A JWT token is an encrypted token that contains user details, user authorization, and a few custom application-specific details.

An example JWT token is as follows:

```
eyJhbGciOiJIUzUxMiIsInR5cCI6IkpXVCJ9.eyJzdWIiOiIxMjM0NTY3ODkwIiwibmFtZSI6Ik
pvaG4gRG9lIiwiYWRtaW4iOnRydWUsImlhdCI6MTUxNjIzOTAyMiwiY3VzdG9tIjoidmFsdWUif
Q.AcXCIdAbFhpFM2w9LpB86aJKg3NMRWDXJmxO7v_eM22ZmVpT0A0W8NEntu4G2syp03L23h2Et
46yir96eTBiog
```

This JWT token is an encrypted value using a simple algorithm. We will look at how this token is created a little later.

A JWT token is a combination of three things:

- JWT payload
- JOSE header
- JWT signing and token creation

JWT payload

Here are some of the important details that are represented in the previous token. This is also called the JWT payload:

```
{
 "sub": "1234567890",
 "name": "John Doe",
 "admin": true,
 "iat": 1516239022,
 "custom": "value"
 }
```

A few details in the previous JSON are standard. These are called reserved claims:

- sub: Subject—whose details does the JWT token contain?
- iat: Issued at time—when was the JWT token created?
- name: Full name.

A full list of reserved claims can be found at `https://www.iana.org/assignments/jwt/jwt.xhtml#claims`.

The JSON token also contains a few custom claims. These are added as needed for your specific case:

- `admin`: Is the user an administrator?
- `custom`: A custom value.

JOSE header

A **JOSE** (short for **JSON object signing and encryption**) header contains the algorithm that is used for signing, and the type of token (which is JWT).

A variety of encryption algorithms can be used with JWT. Here are some of the algorithms from JWT Specification at `https://tools.ietf.org/html/rfc7518#section-3`:

- `HS256`: Uses HMAC with SHA-256
- `HS512`: Uses HMAC with SHA-512
- `RS256`: Uses RSASSA-PKCS1-v1_5 with SHA-256
- `RS512`: Uses RSASSA-PKCS1-v1_5 with SHA-512

An example JOSE header using HS512 is shown here:

```
{
 "alg": "HS512",
 "typ": "JWT"
 }
```

JWT signing and token creation

The algorithm for creating the JWT token is shown here:

```
HMACSHA512(
 base64UrlEncode(header) + "." +
 base64UrlEncode(payload), "your-512-bit-secret")
```

`HMACSHA512` is the encryption algorithm that we chose. The header and payload are Base64-encoded, and are separated by a dot (`.`).

A 512-bit secret (also called a secret key or a private key) is used to encrypt and create the JSON.

The secret is also used when decrypting the token.

You can play with the payload and different JWT signing algorithms on the website: `https://jwt.io`. The following screenshot shows the interface that is offered:

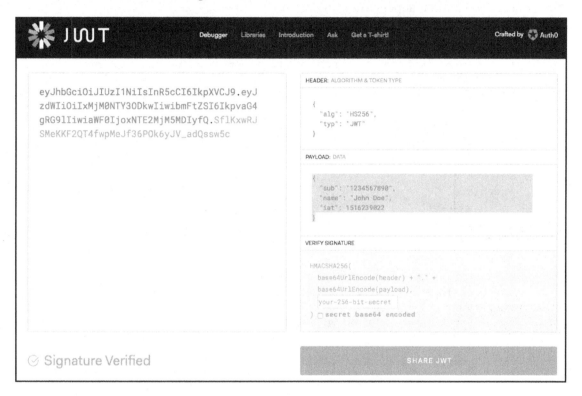

Using JWT for REST API authentication

Typically, using a JWT for REST API authentication involves two steps:

- Obtaining the token by providing the user details
- Sending the token along with the REST API requests

Typically, on the login page of a web application, we get the user credentials. We can send a POST request with the user credentials to the JWT authentication URL (for example, /auth), in order to receive a JWT token.

In all the subsequent REST API requests, the JWT token will be sent in the authorization header.

Using JWT with OAuth2

Let's enhance the earlier implementation of OAuth2 in order to use a JWT token.

We would need to add a dependency on `spring-security-jwt`:

```xml
<dependency>
 <groupId>org.springframework.security</groupId>
 <artifactId>spring-security-jwt</artifactId>
 <version>1.0.9.RELEASE</version>
 </dependency>
```

We can update the authentication server configuration in order to use the JWT token store:

```java
@Override
public void configure(AuthorizationServerEndpointsConfigurer endpoints)
throws Exception {
    endpoints
.tokenStore(tokenStore()).accessTokenConverter(accessTokenConverter())
        .authenticationManager(this.authenticationManager);
}

@Bean
public JwtAccessTokenConverter accessTokenConverter() {
    JwtAccessTokenConverter converter = new JwtAccessTokenConverter();
    converter.setSigningKey("abcdefgh");
    converter.setVerifierKey("abcdefgh");
    return converter;
}

@Bean
public TokenStore tokenStore() {
    return new JwtTokenStore(accessTokenConverter());
}
```

Here are some of the important details to consider:

- `JwtAccessTokenConverter`: Translates from/to JWT to/from OAuth authentication details.
- `converter.setSigningKey("abcdefgh")`: We are using `abcdefgh` as the secret key. This is needed on the OAuth Server in order to sign the token.
- `converter.setVerifierKey("abcdefgh")`: We are using `abcdefgh` as the verifier key. This is needed by the resource server in order to verify the token.
- `endpoints.tokenStore(tokenStore()).accessTokenConverter(accessTokenConverter())`: Configures the endpoints to use the token store, and to access the token converter.

In the previous example, we used symmetric keys, that is, the same signing and verifier keys. We can also use asymmetric private and public key combinations. We can use a keytool to generate a private, or a public key combination.

To get an access token, we call the authorization server token API (`http://localhost:8080/oauth/token`); providing the client authentication details in the basic authentication mode, and the user credentials as part of the form data:

```
{
 "access_token":
"eyJhbGciOiJIUzI1NiIsInR5cCI6IkpXVCJ9.eyJleHAiOjE1NTY5OTkxMzIsInVzZXJfbmFtZ
SI6InVzZXIyIiwiYXV0aG9yaXRpZXMiOlsiUk9MRV9VU0VSIl0sImp0aSI6IjVkNWJhMTIwLWM0
ODUtNDM2Ni1hNGViLWVhOWI0NzM1YTdmNCIsImNsaWVudF9pZCI6IllvdXJDbGllbnRJRCIsInN
jb3BlIjpbIm9wZW5pZCJdfQ.RFRjTU9RJNmUDTH7QedgqNRzsGRVakyvrcFkPZEcIuE",
 "token_type": "bearer",
 "refresh_token":
"eyJhbGciOiJIUzI1NiIsInR5cCI6IkpXVCJ9.eyJ1c2VyX25hbWUiOiJ1c2VyMiIsInNjb3BlI
jpbIm9wZW5pZCJdLCJhdGkiOiI1ZDViYTEyMC1jNDg1LTQzNjYtYTRlYi1lYTliNDczNWE3ZjQi
LCJleHAiOjE1NTk1NDc5MzIsImF1dGhvcml0aWVzIjpbIlJPTEVfVVNFUiJdLCJqdGkiOiI1MmI
1ZDEzMC1mOGE0LTRjNDgtYmU2OS00NTQwMTVlYWRlMzAiLCJjbGllbnRfaWQiOiJZb3VyQ2xpZW
50SUQifQ.DZhDZeZyqFKJ6HXMr6zc9DWDc5Dn2BqYCwTAlXgWewA",
 "expires_in": 43199,
 "scope": "openid",
 "jti": "5d5ba120-c485-4366-a4eb-ea9b4735a7f4"
 }
```

We can use `access_token` in the authorization header when executing REST API requests.

Summary

In this chapter, we started by learning the basics of securing web applications. We learned that filters are typically used to authenticate and authorize the request, before executing the REST API.

We discussed the basics of how Spring Security works. We learned that Spring Security uses a chain of security filters in order to perform authentication and authorization. We also looked at some of the filters.

`UsernamePasswordAuthenticationFilter` and `BasicAuthenticationFilter` are used for authentication. One of the key responsibilities of `FilterSecurityInterceptor` is to make authorization decisions.

We learned about the role that the authentication manager plays in authenticating your REST API request. The default implementation of the authentication manager, (ProviderManager), talks with multiple authentication providers (which typically use the UserDetailsService) in order to retrieve and authenticate user details.

We learned about the role that AccessDecisionManager plays in making authorization decisions. An AccessDecisionManager talks with multiple AccessDecisionVoter, which can give a positive or a negative vote. We looked at the different types of access decision managers—AffirmativeBased (at least one positive vote), ConsensusBased (go with the majority), and UnanimousBased (all votes should be positive).

We looked at the extension points that are provided by Spring Security to configure authentication and authorization with WebSecurityConfigurerAdapter.

We discussed OAuth and extended our REST API application to act as the OAuth Server and a resource server.

At the end of the chapter, we were introduced to JWT, and we extended our OAuth application to use JWT tokens.

This was a wonderful journey through a very important Spring framework—Spring Security.

In the next chapter, let's shift our attention toward full-stack applications. We will look at getting started with using React and Spring Boot, in order to build a full-stack application.

Further reading

- *Spring Security*, available at https://docs.spring.io/spring-security/site/docs/current/reference/htmlsingle/.
- *Spring Security OAuth2 Developers Guide*, available at https://projects.spring.io/spring-security-oauth/docs/oauth2.html.
- *JWT*, available at https://jwt.io.

Full Stack App with React and Spring Boot

9

In the last chapter, we focused on securing our RESTful API. We understood how Spring Security works and played with different kinds of authentication—Basic Auth, OAuth, and JWT.

In this chapter, let's shift our attention to full stack applications.

According to the StackOverflow 2019 survey (available at: `https://insights.stackoverflow.com/survey/2019`), full-stack developers have a higher salary. React, along with the Spring Framework, are loved by developers. That's why most developers today want to be full stack developers.

In this chapter, let's learn what full stack development is and understand why it is getting popular. We will create a simple frontend application with one of the popular frontend frameworks—React—and integrate it with a Spring Boot backend. We will learn about the various challenges that you face when doing full stack development.

Full stack development and React have huge ecosystems of their own and deserve a book on their own. The idea behind this chapter is to give you a quick 10,000-foot view so that you can start exploring them on your own.

This chapter answers the following questions:

- What is full stack development?
- Why is full stack development getting popular?
- What are the different full stack framework options?
- How do you create a frontend react application?
- What are the important react concepts that a beginner to React should understand?

- What are the typical challenges in integrating React applications with a RESTful API?
- How do you call RESTful API from the frontend?
- How do you provide security credentials and call a secure RESTful API with basic authentication and JWT?

Technical requirements

The following are some of the frameworks and tools you will need to make the best use of this chapter:

- Your favorite IDEs, Eclipse, and Visual Studio Code
- Node 8+
- Java 8+
- Maven 3.x
- NPM 5.6+
- Internet connectivity

The code on GitHub is available at `https://github.com/PacktPublishing/Mastering-Spring-5.1/tree/master/Chapter09`

Understanding full stack architecture

The shift towards full stack architecture is one of the important architecture trends in the last few years.

During the last decade, the World has become increasingly mobile and today we are writing a host of IoT applications. Businesses need to support a variety of mobile and IoT applications in addition to your web applications.

How do we ensure that we can build a variety of applications with a simple architecture?

Enter full stack architecture.

Full stack architecture involves developing frontend applications integrated with RESTful APIs. The following diagram shows the high-level architecture:

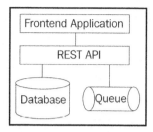

The key parts of the architecture are the frontend application and RESTful API. The RESTful API talks to a backend database or another application over a queue to provides its features.

We learned the basics of RESTful APIs in the previous chapters. We used Spring Boot to create a `Todo` RESTful API. Other popular options with which to create RESTful APIs include Node.js (JavaScript) and Python (Django). With a RESTful API, you expose resources that you can perform different actions with.

Frontend applications are static applications developed with JavaScript, HTML, and CSS, which run in your browser. Popular frameworks include Angular, React, and Vue.js. In this chapter, we will use React to create the frontend application. Frontend applications provide the user interface for users and invoke the RESTful API in response to user actions.

Understanding the need for full stack architecture

But you might be wondering—Why do we need a full stack architecture?

As we discussed earlier, our world has become increasingly mobile and businesses are developing a myriad of applications encompassing web, mobile, and IoT. This gives rise to a few questions:

- Should applications be completely isolated?
- How do we ensure that the same business logic is used in all applications? To phrase it differently: how do we ensure that the business logic is not duplicated across different applications and is easily maintainable?
- How do we create new kind of application easily?

Full stack architecture evolved as a solution to these potential problems. The following diagram shows how you can develop a variety of applications using full stack architecture:

You build a common RESTful API that represents the business logic of your application. As your needs expand, you can create a variety of applications consuming the RESTful API:

- Web applications that can run on the browser using frontend frameworks such as React and Angular
- Mobile applications that can run on mobile with React Native, Android, or other iOS frameworks
- IoT applications that can integrate with IoT devices

 IoT (short for **Internet of Things**): There are a number of devices that can talk to the internet today including your household appliances such as televisions, washing machines, and refrigerators. All of these devices come under the umbrella of IoT.

Full stack applications are built using a frontend application talking to a RESTful API. You can create mobile and IoT applications on top of the RESTful API. Hence, full stack applications are easily extensible.

Introducing React

React is an open-source JavaScript framework. It was developed by Facebook and is now open source. It helps you to develop web and mobile applications. React is popular because of the following reasons:

- Developing React applications is simple. Once you understand the basics—components, JSX, state, and props—you can easily develop your own React applications.
- React is not a complete **SPA** (**Single Page Application**) framework. It does a few things and does them very well.

- React is not all or nothing. You don't need to create a new application to use React. React can be integrated into existing web/mobile applications.
- React is highly performant. With features such as a virtual DOM, React manages updates to the **DOM (Document Object Model)** very efficiently.

Now that we have a quick overview of React, let's get an overview of important React concepts—components and JSX.

Components of a frontend application

Any frontend application has multiple parts—a header, footer, and menu. Good frameworks allow you to build individual parts separately and integrate them into an application. This ensures that the individual parts are reusable. React calls these building blocks components.

In a typical React application, you have separate components for header, footer, menu, and each of the individual pages. The following diagram shows a high-level overview:

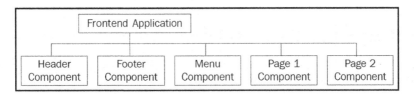

In React, we can build components also for individual elements present in a specific part of the screen. For example, if you are building a page listing all of your friends, you can have a component called **Friend Component**, which displays details of a single friend. The list-friends component can loop around all friends and display them using the **Friend Component**. The **Friend Component** can be reused on other pages.

In React, a component represents a screen element that can be reused across multiple pages.

We will create components and learn to display them in the next section on JSX.

JSX

Components display information on the browser. The language of the web is HTML. So, how do we combine components with data to display them on the screen?

Enter JSX. You can think of it as a JavaScript extension. JSX allows you to combine JavaScript and HTML. Consider the following JavaScript code:

```
const name = 'Ranga'
const page = <h1>Hello World, {name}</h1>
```

The example shows the creation of an h1 Hello World tag using some data stored in the name variable. The page is displayed as follows:

> **Hello World, Ranga**

<h1>Hello World, {name}</h1> is a JSX expression. We are using the value from the name variable using {name}.

Combining JSX and components

We will learn how to create a project using create-react-app in the next section. For now, focus on understanding JSX and components.

Creating a Header component

For easy maintenance and a better application structure, we create a header as a component. The following example shows creating the header component and using it to display the page:

```
const name = 'Ranga'

function Header(props) {
    return <h1>Hello World, {props.name}</h1>
}

const page = <div className="container">
                <Header name={name}/>
             </div>
```

We are creating a `function Header(props)` function, returning the JSX for the header. We are including the header component in the page JSX expression by using `<Header name={name}/>`. name here is called `prop`. `prop` is a parameter we want to pass to the component. `function Header(props)` uses the name parameter using `{props.name}`.

The display does not change, but we now have a reusable component for `Header`.

Creating a Footer component

Let's create a `Footer` component and include it on the page:

```
function Footer(props) {
    return <footer>Copyright {props.name}</footer>
}

const page = <div className="container">
                    <Header name={name}/>
                    <Footer name={name}/>
                 </div>
```

We are now creating a `Footer` component and including it on the page. You can see how easy it is to use JSX and components. The page is displayed as shown:

Hello World, Ranga

Copyright Ranga

Creating a Todo component

Now that we have created a footer, let's move on and use another component in this project to enhance it. Let's create a `Todo` component and include it on the page:

```
const todo = "Learn React"

function Todo(props) {
    return <>
                    You want to:
                    <ul><li>{props.desc}</li></ul>
            </>
 }

const page = <div className="container">
               <Header name={name}/>
```

```
        <Todo desc={todo}/>
        <Footer name={name}/>
    </div>
```

Creating a `Todo` component is simple. One new feature is the use of `<>` `</>`. A JSX expression has to be enclosed in a single parent tag. Since we have to return multiple elements, we are using a JSX fragment (`<>` `</>`) to enclose multiple elements.

The page is displayed as follows:

> **Hello World, Ranga**
>
> You want to:
>
> - Learn React
>
> Copyright Ranga

Building your first React application

Now that we have had a quick introduction to components and JSX, let's use `create-react-app` to create our first React application. `create-react-app` helps you to quickly create React projects adhering to most popular frontend standards.

Using create-react-app

To use `create-react-app`, you will need NPM version 5.2+. You can install the latest version of Node.js from `https://nodejs.org/en/download/` and you should have `npm` installed.

1. Launch a Terminal or Command Prompt. The command to create a new application is as follows:

    ```
    npx create-react-app react-todo-app
    ```

    `react-todo-app` is the name that we give to our application.

2. The following screenshot shows the command execution in progress:

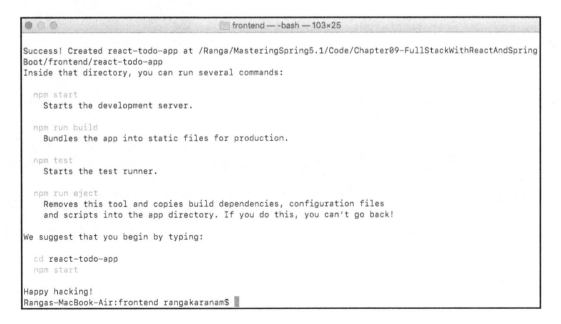

```
● ● ●          frontend — npm • node /usr/local/bin/npx create-react-app react-todo-app — 57×18
Rangas-MacBook-Air:frontend rangakaranam$ npx create-reac
t-app react-todo-app
npx: installed 91 in 9.204s

Creating a new React app in /Ranga/MasteringSpring5.1/Cod
e/Chapter09-FullStackWithReactAndSpringBoot/frontend/reac
t-todo-app.

Installing packages. This might take a couple of minutes.
Installing react, react-dom, and react-scripts...

^[[B((         )) :. loadDep:safe-buffer: sill reso
^[[B((         )) .: loadDep:safe-buffer: sill reso
^[[B((         )) :  fetchMetadata: sill resolveWit
^[[B((         )) .: fetchMetadata: sill resolveWit
^[[B((         )) ": fetchMetadata: sill resolveWit
^[[B^[[B((      )) : diffTrees: sill install ge
((              )) ∵ finalize:fsevents: sill finalize
```

3. When the installation completes, you should see a success screen similar to the following:

```
● ● ●                    🗖 frontend — -bash — 103×25
Success! Created react-todo-app at /Ranga/MasteringSpring5.1/Code/Chapter09-FullStackWithReactAndSpring
Boot/frontend/react-todo-app
Inside that directory, you can run several commands:

  npm start
    Starts the development server.

  npm run build
    Bundles the app into static files for production.

  npm test
    Starts the test runner.

  npm run eject
    Removes this tool and copies build dependencies, configuration files
    and scripts into the app directory. If you do this, you can't go back!

We suggest that you begin by typing:

  cd react-todo-app
  npm start

Happy hacking!
Rangas-MacBook-Air:frontend rangakaranam$ ▌
```

4. You can cd into the `react-todo-app` folder using `cd react-todo-app/` and run the `npm start` command, as shown in the following screenshot:

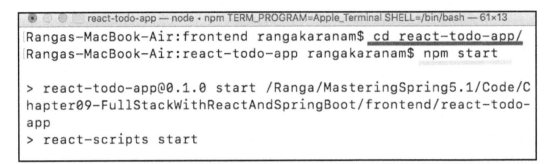

5. You should see the application launch, as shown in the following screenshot:

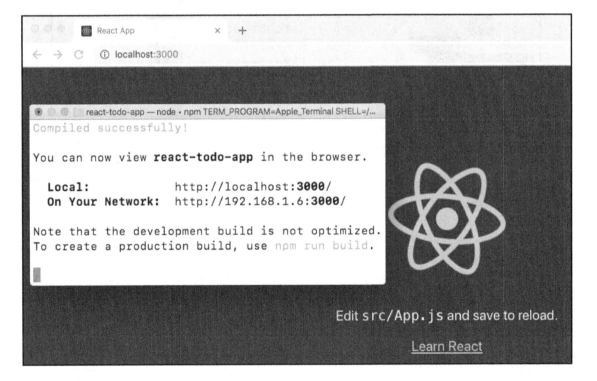

`create-react-app` and `npm start` might take a few minutes if this is the first time you are creating a react application.

Congratulations! You are up and running with a React application.

Importing a React application into Visual Studio Code IDE

We will use Visual Studio Code as the IDE for building a React application with JavaScript. You can download and install Visual Studio Code from `https://code.visualstudio.com/download`.

Visual Studio Code is an awesome IDE for editing frontend applications. It is lightweight, easy to learn, and highly performant. You can open the React project we created in Visual Studio Code by using `File > Open > Navigate to the react-todo-app folder`. Visual Studio Code should open up as shown in the following screenshot (I've expanded the `public` and `src` folders to show their content):

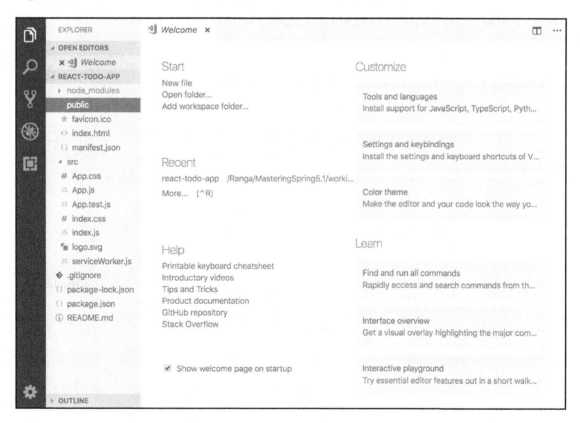

Quick introduction to the folder structure

Here's a quick introduction to the different folders and files present in the project:

- `public/index.html`: This is the initial HTML page that is loaded into the browser. This loads up the React framework and launches the root component.
- `src`: This folder contains all of the React source code.
- `App.js` and `App.css`: These contain the code for the `App` component—which is also called the `Root` component as this is first React component that is loaded into the HTML page.
- `package.json`: This contains a list of frameworks used in the project. This is similar to Maven's `pom.xml`. Just like Maven downloads dependencies listed in `pom.xml`, npm downloads the frameworks defined in `package.json`. These frameworks are downloaded into the `node_modules` folder.

Initializing the React framework

Now that we understand the folder structure, let's understand how React is initialized.

`package.json` contains important dependencies for React. When we run `npm start`, React is downloaded into `node_modules` and made available to the project. The following is an extract from `package.json`:

```
"dependencies": {
 "react": "^16.8.6",
 "react-dom": "^16.8.6",
 "react-scripts": "3.0.0"
 },
```

In the previous snippet, `react` refers to the core React library and `react-dom` to the library used to render React applications in a DOM-based browser.

`public/index.html` defines a root element with the `root` ID:

```
<div id="root"></div>
```

In `src/index.js`, we use `ReactDOM` to display the `App` component in the `root` element:

```
ReactDOM.render(<App />, document.getElementById('root'));
```

Let's update the `App` component in `App.js` to display something simpler:

```
function App() {
  return (<h1>Todo Application</h1>);
}
```

When you save this, you see that the browser refreshes automatically and shows the following screenshot:

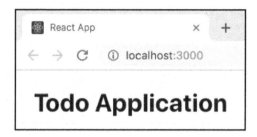

Creating a Todo component

Let's start by creating a component to represent the `Todo` page. Let's call it `TodoComponent`.

In the previous section, we used a function to create a `React` component. You can also build more complex components using classes. These are called `class` components. They can have more complex logic than `Function` components. The code for `TodoComponent` is shown here:

```
import React, { Component } from 'react';

class TodoComponent extends Component {
    render() {
        return (<div>Todos</div>);
    }
}

export default TodoComponent;
```

We make `TodoComponent` extend `Component` and implement the `render` method to return the basic JSX. We export `TodoComponent` to enable its use in other components.

Let's enhance `App.js` to use `TodoComponent`:

```
import TodoComponent from './TodoComponent'

......

function App() {
    return (
    <>
        <h1>Todo Application</h1>
        <TodoComponent />
    </>
    );
}
```

We added `TodoComponent` using `<TodoComponent/>`. The page is displayed as follows:

Adding basic Todo management features

Let's start by creating a `Todo` form with a textbox to enter a description and add a button to add `todo` to the list:

```
render() {
    return (
        <div>
            <form>
                <input placeholder="What do you want to learn today?">
                </input>
                <button type="submit">add</button>
            </form>
        </div>
    );
}
```

When you add a `todo` description and click the **add** button, we want to add the `todo` and show the list of `todos` in the page.

How do we store the list of todos?

The list of `todos` changes as we add and delete `todos`. So, we represent a list of `todos` as part of the state of the component. The moving parts of the component are identified as part of its state. We add `state` with an empty list of `todos` to our component:

```
state = {
    todos: []
}
```

We can also update the `todo` component `render` method to loop around `todos` in the state and display them in a list:

```
render() {
    return (
        <div>
            <form>
                <input placeholder="What do you want to learn today?">
                </input>
                <button type="submit">add</button>
                <ul>
                    {
                        this.state.todos.map(
                            todo => <li key={todo.id}>{todo.desc}</li>
                        )
                    }
                </ul>
            </form>
        </div>

    );
}
```

The `this.state.todos.map` method loops around all `todos` and creates a `li` element for each of them.

When the user clicks **add todo**, we want to add `todo` to `todos` in `state`. We can add an event on the `onSubmit` form. `this.addTodo` will be defined in `TodoComponent`:

```
<form onSubmit={this.addTodo}>
```

To get the value of the `todo` textbox in `TodoComponent`, we add a reference to `this._todoTextElement`:

```
<input ref={ (todoRef) => this._todoTextElement = todoRef}
                    placeholder="What do you want to learn today?">
```

The constant is defined as follows:

```
const HARDCODED_USER_NAME = 'Jack'
```

The `addTodo` method is as follows:

```
addTodo(e) {

    var newTodo = {
        desc: this._todoTextElement.value,
        id: -1,
        targetDate: new Date(),
        user: HARDCODED_USER_NAME
    };

    this.setState((prevState) => {
        return {
            todos: prevState.todos.concat(newTodo)
        };
    });

    this._todoTextElement.value = "";

    e.preventDefault();
}
```

We are creating a new todo with a few hardcoded details and the description of `todo` is picked up from `_todoTextElement` using `desc: this._todoTextElement.value`.

To update the list of `todos`, we need to update the state. In React, you update `state` by using the `setState` method and providing the new values. We are using the previous state and concatenating the new todo:

```
this.setState((prevState) => {
    return {
        todos: prevState.todos.concat(newTodo)
    };
});
```

After that, we make the text element empty and prevent the from being submitted:

```
this._todoTextElement.value = "";
e.preventDefault();
```

In the `addTodo` method, we use `this` to refer to the current object. To enable `this`, we need to do a simple bind in the constructor—`this.addTodo = this.addTodo.bind(this)`:

```
constructor(props) {
    super(props);
    this.addTodo = this.addTodo.bind(this);
}
```

When you refresh the page, you should be able to enter a description and click **add todos**. You can add multiple todos. The page is displayed as follows:

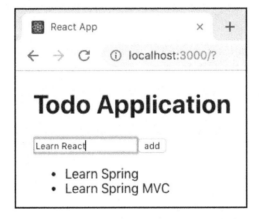

Validations

The `todo` description field does not have any validations as of now. Let's add a validation and a validation message if the user enters no description. As usual, we start to add an `error` flag to `state`. By default, it is `false`:

```
state = {
    todos: [],
    error: false
}
```

In the `addTodo` method, let's check the value of the text element and update the state if the text element has an empty value. We are setting the `error` flag to `true`:

```
addTodo(e) {

    if (this._todoTextElement.value === "") {

        this.setState((prevState) => {
            return {
                error: true
            };
        });

        this.preventFormFromReload(e);

        return
    }
    //REST OF THE CODE
}
```

 Only the important methods are shown in the code. For the complete code, refer to the GitHub repository: `https://github.com/PacktPublishing/Mastering-Spring-5.1/tree/master/Chapter09`.

We are setting the flag for `error` in `state`. We want to display the error in the screen if there is an error.

We can add the message display to the `render()` method:

```
{this.state.error
            <div className="alert alert-warning">Please enter a
description</div>}
```

This is a specific JSX syntax. If `this.state.error` is true, the message is shown.

We will add the `bootstrap` framework to `App.css` to style the page and remove all other styling:

```
@import url(https://unpkg.com/bootstrap@4.1.0/dist/css/bootstrap.min.css)
```

 The complete code for TodoComponent can be found at https://github.com/PacktPublishing/Mastering-Spring-5.1/blob/master/Chapter09/frontend/react-todo-app/src/components/TodoComponent.jsx.

Loading Todos from the API with the axios framework

We want to start using the API to fetch the todo details and use the API to insert a todo. Axios is a popular framework that is used to make RESTful API calls from React applications. Some important features of the axios framework are as follows:

- Making RESTful API calls from the browser
- Request and response interception
- Transformation of JSON data
- Protection against XSRF attacks

You can stop the todo React application and add axios by executing the npm add axios command at the Command Prompt. package.json reflects the new framework added in—axios:

```
"dependencies": {
 "axios": "^0.18.0",
 "react": "^16.8.6",
 "react-dom": "^16.8.6",
 "react-scripts": "3.0.0"
 },
```

Make sure that you start the app again to use the new framework.

Let's start by populating the initial list of todos from the RESTful API. We will create a TodoDataService class to interact with the RESTful API using axios. The implementation for the GET call to get todo details for a user—http://localhost:8080/users/Jack/todos—is shown in the following:

```
import axios from 'axios'

const TODO_API_ROOT = 'http://localhost:8080'

class TodoDataService {
    retrieveAllTodos(name) {
        return axios.get(`${TODO_API_ROOT}/users/${name}/todos`);
    }
}

export default new TodoDataService()
```

We are doing axios.get to the URL to execute a GET request. We are creating new TodoDataService() and exporting it for use from TodoComponent. In TodoComponent, we want to call retrieveAllTodos when the page loads.

React defines a number of life cycle methods for components. The most important among them is componentDidMount, which is called as soon as a component is mounted onto the page.

The implementation is shown in the following:

```
componentDidMount() {
    this.refreshTodos();
}

refreshTodos() {
    TodoDataService.retrieveAllTodos(HARDCODED_USER_NAME)
        .then(
            response => {
                this.setState((prevState) => {
                    return {
                        todos: response.data
                    };
                });
```

```
        }
      )
}
```

We are calling `retrieveAllTodos` and using the response to update `todos` in `state` using the `setState` method:

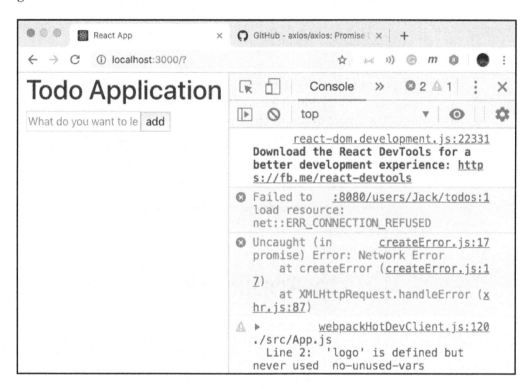

If you see an error as shown in the preceding screenshot, make sure that you start the backend RESTful API. We are using the unsecured RESTful API we developed in `Chapter 06`, *Building REST APIs with Spring Boot*, to start off.

When you launch up the RESTful API and refresh the browser again, you will see an error:

```
Access to XMLHttpRequest at 'http://localhost:8080/users/Jack/todos' from
origin 'http://localhost:3000' has been blocked by CORS policy: No 'Access-
Control-Allow-Origin' header is present on the requested resource.
```

Spring Boot, by default, provides **CORS (Cross-Origin Request)** protection. It does not allow API requests from other origins or URLs.

To enable requests from the frontend, we need to allow cross-origin requests from `http://localhost:3000`—the URL of the React application. We can do that using the `@CrossOrigin` annotation:

```
@RestController
@CrossOrigin("http://localhost:3000")
public class TodoController {
```

You might want to pick up the `http://localhost:3000` URL from the application's configuration instead of hardcoding. This will help us have different URLs across different environments.

When you restart the RESTful API and reload the todo application in the browser, you see the todos from API on the screen. The page is displayed as follows:

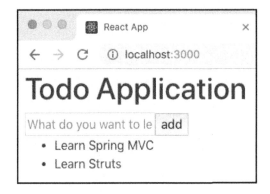

You can see the details of the RESTful API call made by the frontend application in the browser **Network** tab:

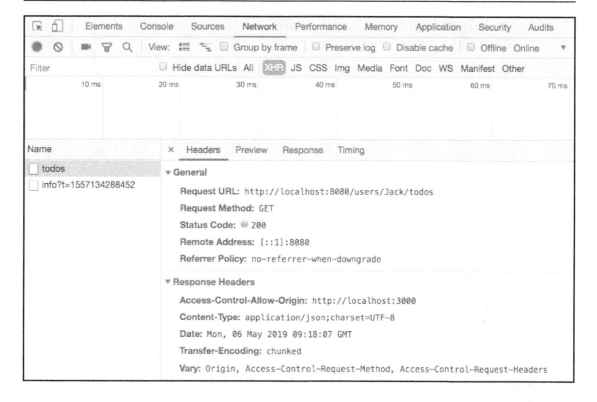

Adding todos invoking the RESTful API

When a user adds a todo, let's call the POST method on the Todo API to add the todo to the backend:

1. Let's start by adding a method to TodoDataService to create a todo:

```
class TodoDataService {

    createTodo(name, todo) {
        return axios.post(`${TODO_API_ROOT}/users/${name}/todos`,
    todo);
    }
}
```

The axios.post method sends a POST request to the API with the todo details.

2. We can add a call to `createTodo` in the `addTodo(e)` method of
   `TodoComponent`:

```
TodoDataService.createTodo(HARDCODED_USER_NAME, newTodo)
    .then(
        response => {
            console.log(response);
        }
    )
```

When the response comes back, we log it into the console.

3. When we add a todo, `"Learn React"`, it is added both to the frontend and
   backend. You can see the details of the `POST` RESTful API call in the browser
   Network tab:

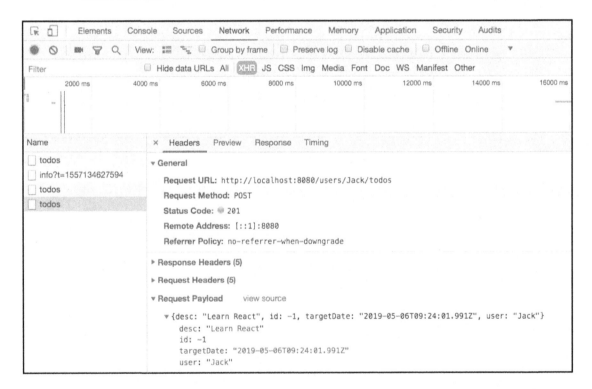

In the last few sections, we developed a simple React application. In the following section,
let's see how to interact with a secured API.

Authentication

RESTful APIs should always be secured. The typical flow for frontend applications to talk to secure REST APIs is similar irrespective of the authentication method used:

- Step 1: When a user logs in, call the authentication API and get a token or a key.
- Step 2: For each subsequent RESTful API call, use the token or key as part of the authorization header.

Basic authentication

For basic authentication, the RESTful API typically exposes an authentication endpoint returning whether the authentication is successful. When a user tries to log in, we can call the API to create a basic authentication header as follows:

```
executeBasicAuthenticationService(user, pwd) {
    return axios.get('/basicauth',
        { headers: { authorization: 'Basic ' + window.btoa(user + ":" +
pwd) } })
}
```

We are making a GET request to the authentication URL with the authorization header added in. If the response to the preceding call is 200, then we can set up an axios interceptor to add the authorization header onto every subsequent RESTful API call:

```
this.setupAxiosInterceptors('Basic ' + window.btoa(user + ":" + pwd))

setupAxiosInterceptors(basicAuthHeader) {

    axios.interceptors.request.use(
        (config) => {
            config.headers.authorization = basicAuthHeader
            return config
        }
    )
}
```

axios.interceptors.request.use configures an interceptor. config.headers.authorization = basicAuthHeader adds an authorization header.

The interceptor adds the header on all subsequent RESTful API calls.

JWT token-based authentication

For JWT authentication, the RESTful API typically exposes an authentication endpoint, returning a token if the authentication is successful. When a user tries to log in, we can call the API and get the token:

```
executeJwtService(user, pwd) {
    return axios.post('/authenticate', {
        user,
        pwd
    })
}
```

We are making a POST request to the authentication URL with the user and password in the request body.

If the request is successful, we can take the token from the response and use it to set up axios interceptors to use the token with every subsequent RESTful API call:

```
this.setupAxiosInterceptors(this.setupJWTToken(token))

setupJWTToken(token) {
 return 'Bearer ' + token
 }
```

The algorithm for implementing authentication is simple. Capture the token at user login and use it with every subsequent RESTful API call.

Summary

In this chapter, we learned the basics of full stack architecture. We created a React application interacting with a RESTful API created with Spring Boot. We learned the basics of React—components, JSX, state, and props. We learned how to create and integrate React components.

Finally, we looked at how to integrate React frontends with APIs secured with basic authentication and JWT.

Full stack development with React and Spring Boot is complex and deserves a book on its own. We hope this introduction will help you to start your journey into full stack development.

In the next chapter, we will look at how to integrate with relational and big data databases using Spring Data.

Further reading

- React—Getting Started: `https://reactjs.org/docs/getting-started.html`
- Create React App: `https://github.com/facebook/create-react-app`
- Axios: `https://github.com/axios/axios`

10
Managing Data with Spring Data

In previous chapters, we looked at building web applications and REST APIs with Spring Boot. We discussed advanced Spring Boot features, such as externalized configuration, monitoring, embedded servers, and deploying to the cloud.

In this chapter, let's turn our attention to data. In the last few years, there has been a rapid evolution in our understanding of where we store our data and how we store data in databases.

There are a number of new database options today.

With a variety of data stores in play, how we interact with these data stores is becoming even more important. While **Java Persistence APIs (JPAs)** made it easy to communicate with relational databases, Spring Data aims to bring in a common approach to talk to a wider variety of data stores—relational or otherwise.

The following are some of the questions we will answer during this chapter:

- What is Spring Data?
- What are the aims of Spring Data?
- How do you talk to a relational database using Spring Data and Spring Data JPAs?
- How do you talk to a non-relational database such as MongoDB using Spring Data?

Technical requirements

The following software is required for this chapter:

- Your favorite IDE, Eclipse
- Java 8+
- Maven 3.x
- Internet connectivity

The code on GitHub is available at `https://github.com/PacktPublishing/Mastering-Spring-5.1/tree/master/Chapter10`

Challenges with a variety of data stores

A decade ago, relational databases using SQL queries were the default choice as a data store. Oracle, MySQL, SQL Server, and DB2 were some of the most popular relational database options.

However, in the last few years, we saw the evolution of a variety of data stores that are providing alternatives to traditional databases. Typically, they are grouped under the term **NoSQL**. Other databases related to **big data** have also become more popular in the last few years. While there is no agreed definition of big data, there are a few shared characteristics:

- **Unstructured data**: There is no specific structure to the data.
- **Large volumes**: Typically, more volume than that can be processed by traditional databases, for example, log streams, Facebook posts, and Tweets.
- **Easily scalable**: Typically provides options to scale horizontally and vertically.

Hadoop, Cassandra, and MongoDB are among the most popular NoSQL options.

Ideally, we would like one approach to talk to a variety of data stores. This would help us keep things simple and maintainable. However, different approaches are needed to talk to different data stores. In fact, there are multiple approaches—including **Java Database Connectivity (JDBC)** and JPAs—and frameworks to talk to just the relational databases.

How do we get a common approach to talk to data stores? That's the problem Spring Data aims to solve.

In the next section, let's take relational databases as an example and explore the options when it comes to interacting with relational databases.

Communicating with relational databases

The most basic API provided by Java EE to talk to a relational database is JDBC. JDBC is used to talk to relational databases from the first version of Java EE. JDBC is based on using SQL queries to manipulate data. The following is an example of typical JDBC code:

```
PreparedStatement st = null;
st = conn.prepareStatement(INSERT_TODO_QUERY);
st.setString(1, bean.getDescription());
st.setBoolean(2, bean.isDone());
st.execute();
```

Typical JDBC code contains the following:

- The query (or stored procedure) to execute
- The code to set parameters for query into statement objects
- The code to liquidate `ResultSet` (the result of executing the query) into beans

Typical enterprise projects involved thousands of lines of JDBC code. JDBC code is cumbersome to write and maintain; however, two frameworks became popular in an effort to provide an additional layer on top of JDBC:

- **myBatis** (earlier called **iBatis**): MyBatis removes the need for manually writing code to set parameters and retrieve results. It provides simple XML or annotation-based configuration to map Java POJOs to a database.
- **Hibernate**: Hibernate is an **Object Relational Mapping** (**ORM**) framework. An ORM framework helps you to map your objects to tables in relational databases. The great thing about Hibernate is that developers do not need to write queries manually. Once the relationships between the objects and tables are mapped, Hibernate uses the mappings to create queries and populate/retrieve data.

Java EE came up with an API called a JPA that was roughly defined based on the popular ORM implementation at that time—the Hibernate framework. Hibernate (since 3.4.0.GA) supports/implements JPAs.

Introducing Spring Data

Data storage options are multiplying by the day. There are a plethora of NoSQL databases providing multiple approaches to access data. Even something as common as a relational database has multiple approaches to access data. Identifying the right data access approach and implementing it adds to the complexity of application development. How about having something in common?

Spring Data aims to solve this problem; it aims to provide a consistent model—another level of abstraction to access data from different kinds of data stores.

Some of the important Spring Data features are listed as follows:

- Easy integration with multiple data stores through various repositories
- The ability to parse and form queries based on repository method names
- Providing the default CRUD functionality
- Basic support for auditing, such as **created by user** and **last changed by user**
- Powerful integration with Spring
- Great integration with Spring MVC to expose REST controllers through **Spring Data Rest**

Spring Data is an umbrella project made up of a number of modules. A few of the important Spring Data modules are listed as follows:

- **Spring Data Commons**: Defines the common concepts for all Spring Data modules: repository and query methods
- **Spring Data JPA**: Provides easy integration with JPA repositories
- **Spring Data MongoDB**: Provides easy integration with MongoDB: a document-based data store
- **Spring Data REST**: Provides the functionality to expose Spring Data repositories as REST services with minimal code
- **Spring Data for Apache Cassandra**: Provides easy integration with Cassandra
- **Spring for Apache Hadoop**: Provides easy integration with Hadoop

In this chapter, we will take an in-depth look at the common concepts behind Spring Data, repository, and query methods.

Understanding Spring Data Commons

Spring Data Commons provides the basic abstractions behind Spring Data modules. It defines the common interfaces and patterns that are used across Spring Data implementations. We will use Spring Data JPA as an example to illustrate these abstractions.

Some of the important interfaces in Spring Data Commons are listed as follows:

```
Repository<T, ID extends Serializable>

CrudRepository<T, ID extends Serializable> extends Repository<T, ID>

    PagingAndSortingRepository<T, ID extends Serializable> extends
CrudRepository<T, ID>
```

Exploring the Repository interface

Repository is the core interface of Spring Data. Any class that interacts with the database using Spring Data should implement this interface. It is a **marker interface**.

Exploring the CrudRepository interface

The CrudRepository interface defines the basic Create, Read, Update, and Delete methods. The important methods in CrudRepository are shown in the following code:

```
public interface CrudRepository<T, ID extends Serializable>extends
Repository<T, ID> {

    <S extends T> S save(S entity);

    findOne(ID primaryKey);

    Iterable<T> findAll();

    Long count();

    void delete(T entity);

    boolean exists(ID primaryKey);

    // ... more functionality omitted.

}
```

Exploring the PagingAndSortingRepository interface

The `PagingAndSortingRepository` interface defines methods that provide the functionality to divide the `ResultSet` into pages as well as sort the results:

```
public interface PagingAndSortingRepository<T, ID extends Serializable>
                                                        extends
    CrudRepository<T, ID> {

        Iterable<T> findAll(Sort sort);

        Page<T> findAll(Pageable pageable);

    }
```

In summary, Spring Data Commons defines common interfaces irrespective of the data store. The `CrudRepository` interface exposes the basic CRUD methods. The `PagingAndSortingRepository` interface extends `CrudRepository` and adds capabilities to sort and paginate results.

In the next couple of sections, we will use these common abstractions (or interfaces) to simplify communicating with relational and NoSQL databases. We will use Spring Data JPA to communicate with relational database and Spring Data MongoDB to communicate with an example NoSQL database.

Connecting to relational databases using Spring Data JPA

Spring Data Common provides the base interfaces for Spring Data modules. Spring Data JPA provides implementations for talking to relational databases using JPAs. The important interfaces and implementations are as follows:

- `JpaRepository` is the JPA-specific repository interface:

```
public interface JpaRepository<T, ID extends Serializable>
                    extends PagingAndSortingRepository<T, ID>,
    QueryByExampleExecutor<T>
```

- `SimpleJpaRepository` is the default implementation of the `CrudRepository` interface for JPAs:

```
public class SimpleJpaRepository<T, ID extends Serializable>
                            implements JpaRepository<T, ID>,
JpaSpecificationExecutor<T>
```

Understanding Spring Data JPA with an example

Let's set up a simple project to understand the different concepts related to Spring Data Commons and Spring Data JPA.

The following are the steps involved:

1. Create a new project with `spring-boot-starter-data-jpa` as a dependency.
2. Add entities.
3. Add the `SpringBootApplication` class to run the application.
4. Create repositories.

Create a new project with a starter data JPA

We will create a simple Spring Boot Maven project using the following dependencies:

```xml
<dependency>
    <groupId>org.springframework.boot</groupId>
    <artifactId>spring-boot-starter-data-jpa</artifactId>
</dependency>
<dependency>
    <groupId>com.h2database</groupId>
    <artifactId>h2</artifactId>
    <scope>runtime</scope>
</dependency>

<dependency>
    <groupId>org.springframework.boot</groupId>
    <artifactId>spring-boot-starter-test</artifactId>
    <scope>test</scope>
</dependency>
```

`spring-boot-starter-data-jpa` is the Spring Boot starter project for Spring Data JPA.

Important dependencies that `spring-boot-starter-data-jpa` brings in are **Java Transaction APIs (JTAs)**, Hibernate Core, and Entity Manager (a default JPA implementation). Some of the other important dependencies are shown in the following screenshot:

We are using `H2` as an in-memory database and adding a dependency on `spring-boot-starter-test` for unit tests.

Defining entities

When we use JPAs, we define the `@Entity` classes that map to tables in the database. Let's define a couple of entities to use in our example. We will create a `Todo` entity. A simple example is shown as follows:

```
@Entity
public class Todo {

    @Id
    @GeneratedValue(strategy = GenerationType.AUTO)
    private Long id;
```

```
@ManyToOne(fetch = FetchType.LAZY)
@JoinColumn(name = "userid")
private User user;

private String title;

private String description;

private Date targetDate;

private boolean isDone;

public Todo() {// Make JPA Happy
}

}
```

Important things to note are as follows:

- `Todo` has a title, a description, a target date, and a completion indicator (`isDone`). The JPA needs a constructor.
- `@Entity`: The annotation specifies that the class is an entity.
- `@Id` specifies that ID is the primary key of the entity.
- `@GeneratedValue(strategy = GenerationType.AUTO)`: The `GeneratedValue` annotation is used to specify how the primary key is generated. In this example, we are using a strategy of `GenerationType.AUTO`. This indicates that we would want the persistence provider to choose the right strategy.
- `@ManyToOne(fetch = FetchType.LAZY)` indicates a many-to-one relationship between `User` and `Todo`. A `@ManyToOne` relationship is used on one side of the relationship. `FetchType.Lazy` indicates that the data can be lazily fetched.
- `@JoinColumn(name = "userid")`: The `JoinColumn` annotation specifies the name of the foreign key column.

The following snippet shows the `User` entity:

```
@Entity
public class User {

    @Id
    @GeneratedValue(strategy = GenerationType.AUTO)
    private Long id;

    private String userid;
```

```
        private String name;

        @OneToMany(mappedBy = "user")
        private List<Todo> todos;

        public User() {// Make JPA Happy
        }

        //Override toString method - Example code on github repository

    }
```

Important things to note are as follows:

- The user is defined as an entity with the `userid` and `name` attributes. The ID is the primary key, which is autogenerated.
- The `@OneToMany(mappedBy = "user")`: The `OneToMany` annotation is used on the many side of a many-to-one relationship. The `mappedBy` attribute indicates the property of the owner entity of the relationship.

Creating the SpringBootApplication class

Let's create a `SpringBootApplication` class to be able to run the Spring Boot application. The following snippet shows a simple example:

```
@SpringBootApplication
public class SpringDataJpaFirstExampleApplication {
  public static void main(String[] args) {
    SpringApplication.run(
            SpringDataJpaFirstExampleApplication.class, args);
  }
}
```

The following snippet shows some of the logs generated when we run `SpringDataJpaFirstExampleApplication` as a Java application:

```
HikariPool-1 - Starting...
HikariPool-1 - Start completed.

Processing PersistenceUnitInfo [
  name: default
  ...]
HHH000412: Hibernate Core {5.3.7.Final}
hibernate.properties not found
Hibernate Commons Annotations {5.0.4.Final}
```

```
HHH000400: Using dialect: org.hibernate.dialect.H2Dialect
HHH000476: Executing import script
'org.hibernate.tool.schema.internal.exec.ScriptSourceInputNonExistentImpl@2
5c1f5ee'
HHH000397: Using ASTQueryTranslatorFactory
Initialized JPA EntityManagerFactory for persistence unit 'default'
```

Some of the important observations are as follows:

- HHH000412: Hibernate Core {5.3.7.Final}: **The Hibernate framework is initialized.**
- HHH000400: Using dialect: org.hibernate.dialect.H2Dialect: **The H2 in-memory database is initialized.**

A lot of magic happened in the previous execution. Let's look at some of the important questions:

1. How does the Hibernate framework come into the picture even though we did not explicitly declare a dependency in pom.xml? Hibernate is one of the dependencies of the Spring Boot Starter JPAs, so it is the default JPA implementation used.
2. How is the H2 in-memory database used? In our dependencies, we included an H2 dependency with scope runtime. When Spring Boot Data JPA auto-configuration runs, it notices that we have not included any data source in our configuration (actually, we have no configuration at all). The Spring Boot Data JPA then tries to auto-configure an in-memory database. It sees H2 on the classpath, therefore, it initializes an in-memory H2 database.
3. What is the schema that is created? The following snippet shows the schema that is created based on the Entity classes and the relationships we declared. This is auto-created by Spring Boot Data JPA auto-configuration. Here's the user table:

```
create table user (
   id bigint generated by default as identity,
   name varchar(255),
   userid varchar(255),
   primary key (id)
)
```

Here's the todo table:

```
create table todo (
  id bigint generated by default as identity,
  description varchar(255),
  is_done boolean not null,
  target_date timestamp,
```

```
title varchar(255),
userid bigint,
primary key (id)
)

alter table todo
add constraint FK4wek61l9imiccm4ypjj5hfn2g
foreign key (userid) references user
```

The `todo` table has a foreign `userid` key for the user table.

Populating some data

To be able to test the repositories that we will create, we will populate some test data into these tables. All that we need to do is include the file called `data.sql` with the following statements in `src\main\resources`:

```
insert into user (id, name, userid)
 values (1, 'User Name 1', 'UserId1');

insert into user (id, name, userid)
 values (2, 'User Name 2', 'UserId2');

insert into user (id, name, userid)
 values (3, 'User Name 3', 'UserId3');

insert into user (id, name, userid)
 values (4, 'User Name 4', 'UserId4');

insert into todo (id, title, description, is_done, target_date, userid)
 values (101, 'Todo Title 1', 'Todo Desc 1', false, CURRENT_DATE(), 1);

insert into todo (id, title, description, is_done, target_date, userid)
 values (102, 'Todo Title 2', 'Todo Desc 2', false, CURRENT_DATE(), 1);

insert into todo (id, title, description, is_done, target_date, userid)
 values (103, 'Todo Title 3', 'Todo Desc 3', false, CURRENT_DATE(), 2);
```

These are simple `insert` statements. We are creating a total of four users—the first user has 2 todos, the second user has 1 todo, and the last two users have none.

> You can enable debug log to see the following logs using `logging.level.org.springframework.jdbc=DEBUG` in `application.properties`.

When you run `SpringDataJpaFirstExampleApplication` as a Java application again, you will see a few extra statements in the log:

```
ScriptUtils : Executing SQL script from URL
[file:/in28Minutes/Workspaces/SpringDataJPA-Preparation/Spring-Data-JPA-
Trial-Run/target/classes/data.sql]

ScriptUtils : Executed SQL script from URL
[file:/in28Minutes/Workspaces/SpringDataJPA-Preparation/Spring-Data-JPA-
Trial-Run/target/classes/data.sql] in 42 ms.
```

The `log` statements confirm that the data is being populated into the H2 in-memory database. Let's turn our attention to creating repositories to access and manipulate the data from the Java code.

Creating a simple repository

A custom repository can be created by extending the repository marker interface. In the following example, we extend the repository interface with two methods—`findAll` and `count`:

```java
import org.springframework.data.repository.Repository;
public interface TodoRepository extends Repository<Todo, Long> {

    Iterable<Todo> findAll();

    long count();

}
```

A few important things to note are as follows:

- `public interface TodoRepository extends Repository<Todo, Long>`: The `TodoRepository` interface extends the `Repository` interface. The two generic types indicate the entity being managed—`Todo`—and the type of the primary key—`Long`.
- `Iterable<Todo> findAll()`: Used to list all the todos. Note that the name of the method should match what's defined in `CrudRepository`.
- `long count()`: Used to find the count of all the todos.

Creating a unit test

Let's write a simple unit test to test whether we are able to access the `todo` data using `TodoRepository`. The following snippet shows the important details:

```java
@DataJpaTest
@RunWith(SpringRunner.class)
public class TodoRepositoryTest {

  @Autowired
  TodoRepository todoRepository;

  @Test
  public void check_todo_count() {

    assertEquals(3, todoRepository.count());

  }

}
```

A few important things to note are as follows:

- `@DataJpaTest`: The `@DataJpaTest` annotation is typically used along with `SpringRunner` in a JPA repository unit test. This annotation will enable only JPA-related auto-configuration. The test would use an in-memory database by default.
- `@RunWith(SpringRunner.class)`: A simple alias for `SpringJUnit4ClassRunner` is `SpringRunner`. It launches a Spring context.
- `@Autowired TodoRepository todoRepository`: Autowires `TodoRepository` to be used in the test.
- `assertEquals(3, todoRepository.count())`: Checks that the count returned is 3. Remember that we inserted three todos in `data.sql`.

 A word of caution—we are taking a shortcut to writing a unit test in the preceding example. Ideally, a unit test should not depend on data that was already created in the database. We will fix this in our future tests.

The `Extending Repository` interface helps us to expose selected methods in entities.

Create a repository extending the CrudRepository interface

We can extend CrudRepository to expose all create, read, update, and delete methods in an entity. The following snippet shows TodoRepository extending CrudRepository:

```
public interface TodoRepository extends CrudRepository<Todo, Long>
{
}
```

TodoRepository can be used to perform all methods exposed by the CrudRepository interface. Let's write a few unit tests to test some of these methods.

Testing using a unit test

The findById() method can be used to query using the primary key. The following snippet shows an example:

```
@Test
public void findOne() {
  Optional<Todo> todo = todoRepository.findById(101L);
  assertEquals("Todo Desc 1", todo.get().getDescription());
}
```

Optional represents a container object for an object that can be null. Some of the important methods in Optional are listed as follows:

- isPresent(): Checks whether Optional contains a non-null value
- orElse(): Default value if the object contained is null
- ifPresent(): Code in ifPresent is executed if the object contained is not null
- get(): To retrieve the contained object

The existsById() method can be used to check whether an entity with the given ID exists. The following example shows how it can be done:

```
@Test
public void exists() {
  assertFalse(todoRepository.existsById(105L));
  assertTrue(todoRepository.existsById(101L));
}
```

The deleteById() method is used to delete an entity with a specific ID. In the following example, we are deleting one of the todos items, reducing the available todo items from three to two:

```
@Test
public void delete() {
    todoRepository.deleteById(101L);
    assertEquals(2,todoRepository.count());
}
```

The deleteAll() method is used to delete all the entities managed by the specific repository. In the specific example here, all the todo items from the todo table are deleted:

```
@Test
public void deleteAll() {
    todoRepository.deleteAll();
    assertEquals(0,todoRepository.count());
}
```

The save() method can be used to update or insert an entity. The following example shows how the description of todos can be updated. The following test uses TestEntityManager to flush the data before retrieving it. TestEntityManager is autowired as part of the functionality of the @DataJpaTest annotation:

```
@Autowired
TestEntityManager entityManager;

@Test
public void save() {

    Todo todo = todoRepository.findById(101L).get();
    todo.setDescription("Todo Desc Updated");
    todoRepository.save(todo);

    entityManager.flush();

    Todo updatedTodo = todoRepository.findById(101L).get();

    assertEquals("Todo Desc Updated",updatedTodo.getDescription());
}
```

Creating a repository extending the PagingAndSortingRepository interface

PagingAndSortingRepository extends CrudRepository and provides methods in order to retrieve entities with pagination and a specified sort mechanism. Take a look at the following example:

```
    public interface UserRepository  extends
  PagingAndSortingRepository<User, Long> {
        }
```

Important things to note are as follows:

- public interface UserRepository extends PagingAndSortingRepository: The UserRepository interface extends the PagingAndSortingRepository interface.
- <User, Long>: Entities are of the User type and have an ID field of the Long type.

Exploring using unit tests

Let's write a few tests to use the sorting and pagination capabilities of UserRepository. The base of the test is very similar to TodoRepositoryTest:

```
    @DataJpaTest
    @RunWith(SpringRunner.class)
    public class UserRepositoryTest {
      @Autowired
      UserRepository userRepository;
      @Autowired
      TestEntityManager entityManager;
    }
```

Let's write a simple test to sort users and print users to the log:

```
    @Test
    public void testing_sort_stuff() {
      Sort sort = new Sort(Sort.Direction.DESC, "name")
      .and(new Sort(Sort.Direction.ASC, "userid"));
    Iterable<User> users = userRepository.findAll(sort);
    for (User user : users) {
      System.out.println(user);
      }
    }
```

Important things to note are as follows:

- new Sort(Sort.Direction.DESC, "name"): We would want to sort by name in descending order.
- and(new Sort(Sort.Direction.ASC, "userid")): The and() method is a conjunction method used to combine different sort configurations. In this example, we are adding a secondary criteria to sort by the user ID in the ascending order.
- userRepository.findAll(sort): The sort criteria are passed as a parameter to the findAll() method.

The output of the preceding test is shown as follows. The users are sorted in descending order by name:

```
User [id=4, userid=UserId4, name=User Name 4, todos=0]
User [id=3, userid=UserId3, name=User Name 3, todos=0]
User [id=2, userid=UserId2, name=User Name 2, todos=1]
User [id=1, userid=UserId1, name=User Name 1, todos=2]
```

The test for pageable is as follows:

```
@Test
public void using_pageable_stuff() {
  PageRequest pageable = new PageRequest(0, 2);
  Page<User> userPage = userRepository.findAll(pageable);
  System.out.println(userPage);
  System.out.println(userPage.getContent());
}
```

The output of the test is as follows:

```
Page 1 of 2 containing com.in28minutes.model.User instances
[User [id=1, userid=UserId1, name=User Name 1, todos=2],
User [id=2, userid=UserId2, name=User Name 2, todos=1]]
```

Important things to note are as follows:

- new PageRequest(0, 2): We are requesting the first page (index 0) and setting the size of each page to 2.
- userRepository.findAll(pageable): The PageRequest object is sent as a parameter to the findAll method.
- Page 1 of 2: The output shows that we are looking at the first page in a total of 2 pages.

A couple of important things to note about `PageRequest` are as follows:

- The `PageRequest` object has the `next()`, `previous()`, and `first()` methods to traverse the pages.
- The `PageRequest` constructor (`public PageRequest(int page, int size, Sort sort)`) also accepts a third parameter—Sort order.

Important methods in `Page` and its child interface, `Slice`, are listed as follows:

- `int getTotalPages()`: Returns the number of result pages
- `long getTotalElements()`: Returns the total number of elements in all pages
- `int getNumber()`: Returns the number of the current page
- `int getNumberOfElements()`: Returns the number of elements in the current page
- `List<T> getContent()`: Gets the content of the current slice (or page) as a list
- `boolean hasContent()`: Returns if the current slice has any elements
- `boolean isFirst()`: Returns if this is the first slice
- `boolean isLast()`: Returns if this is the last slice
- `boolean hasNext()`: Returns if there is a next slice
- `boolean hasPrevious()`: Returns if there is a previous slice
- `Pageable nextPageable()`: Gets access to the next slice
- `Pageable previousPageable()`: Gets access to the previous slice

Writing custom query methods

In the previous sections, we looked at the `CrudRepository` and `PagingAndSortingRepository` interfaces. We looked at the different methods that they provided by default; but Spring Data does not stop here. It defines a few patterns that allow you to define custom query methods. In this section, we will look at examples of some of the options that Spring Data provides to customize your query methods.

We will start with examples related to finding rows matching specific attribute values. The following example shows different methods in order to search for the `User` by their name:

```
public interface UserRepository
                extends PagingAndSortingRepository<User, Long> {

  List<User> findByName(String name);
  List<User> findByName(String name, Sort sort);
  List<User> findByName(String name, Pageable pageable);
```

```
Long countByName(String name);

Long deleteByName(String name);

List<User> removeByName(String name);
}
```

Important things to note are as follows:

- `List<User> findByName(String name)`: The pattern is `findBy` followed by the name of the attribute that you want to query by. The value of the attribute is passed in as a parameter.
- `List<User> findByName(String name, Sort sort)`: This method allows you to specify a specific sort order.
- `List<User> findByName(String name, Pageable pageable)`: This method allows the use of pagination.
- As well as find, we can also use read, query, or get to name the methods, for example, `queryByName` instead of `findByName`.
- Similar to `find..By`, we can use `count..By` to find the count, and `delete..By` (or `remove..By`) to delete records.

The following example shows how to search by attributes of a containing element:

```
List<User> findByTodosTitle(String title);
```

The user contains `Todos`. `Todo` has the `title` attribute. To create a method to search a user based on the title of the todo, we can create a method by the name `findByTodosTitle` in `UserRepository`.

The following examples show a few more variations that are possible with `findBy`:

```
public interface TodoRepository extends CrudRepository<Todo, Long> {

List<Todo> findByTitleAndDescription(String title, String description);

List<Todo> findDistinctTodoByTitleOrDescription(String title,
    String description);

List<Todo> findByTitleIgnoreCase(String title);

List<Todo> findByTitleOrderByIdDesc(String title);
List<Todo> findByIsDoneTrue();

}
```

Important things to note are as follows:

- `findByTitleAndDescription`: Multiple attributes can be used to query.
- `findDistinctTodoByTitleOrDescription`: Find distinct rows.
- `findByTitleIgnoreCase`: Illustrates the use of the `ignore` case.
- `findByTitleOrderByIdDesc`: Illustrates an example of specifying a specific sort order.

The following example shows how to find a specific subset of records using `find`:

```
public interface UserRepository
extends PagingAndSortingRepository<User, Long> {
  User findFirstByName(String name);
  User findTopByName(String name);
  List<User> findTop3ByName(String name);
  List<User> findFirst3ByName(String name);
}
```

Important things to note are as follows:

- `findFirstByName`, `findTopByName`: Queries for the first user
- `findTop3ByName`, `findFirst3ByName`: Finds the top three users

Writing custom JPQL queries

Spring Data JPA also provides options to write custom queries. The following snippet shows a simple example:

```
@Query("select u from User u where u.name = ?1")
List<User> findUsersByNameUsingQuery(String name);
```

Important things to note are as follows:

- `@Query`: The annotation to define queries for repository methods.
- `select u from User u where u.name = ?1`: **Java Persistence Query Language (JPQL)** query to be executed. `?1` represents the first parameter.
- `findUsersByNameUsingQuery`: When this method is called, the query specified is executed with the same name as the parameter.

Using named parameters

We can use named parameters to make the query more readable. The following snippet from `UserRepository` shows an example:

```
@Query("select u from User u where u.name = :name")
List<User> findUsersByNameUsingNamedParameters(@Param("name") String
name);
```

Important things to note are as follows:

- `select u from User u where u.name = :name`: Defines a named `"name"` parameter in the query.
- `findUsersByNameUsingNamedParameters(@Param("name") String name)`: The `@Param("name")` parameter defines the named parameter in the arguments list.

Using named queries

You can also define named queries on the entity itself. The following example shows how to define a named query on a `User` entity:

```
@Entity
@NamedQuery(name = "User.findUsersWithNameUsingNamedQuery",
            query = "select u from User u where u.name = ?1")
public class User {
```

To use this query in a repository, we would need to create a method with the same name as the named query. The following snippet shows the corresponding method in `UserRepository`:

```
List<User> findUsersWithNameUsingNamedQuery(String name);
```

Note that the name of the named query is `User.findUsersWithNameUsingNamedQuery`. Therefore, the name of the method in the repository should be `findUsersWithNameUsingNamedQuery`.

Executing native SQL queries

Spring Data JPA provides the option to execute native SQL queries as well. The following example demonstrates a simple native query in `UserRepository`:

```
@Query(value = "SELECT * FROM USERS WHERE u.name = ?1",
                                    nativeQuery - true)
List<User> findUsersByNameNativeQuery(String name);
```

Important things to note are as follows:

- `SELECT * FROM USERS WHERE u.name = ?1`: This is the native SQL query to be executed. Note that we are not referring to the `User` entity but are using the table name users in the query.
- `nativeQuery = true`: This attribute ensures that the query is executed as a native query.

Getting started with transaction management

When you write business logic, you would need to ensure that transactions are atomic.

For example, consider a transaction to transfer 100 dollars from your account to your friend's account. You want one of these end states:

- **Money transferred successfully**: Your account debited by 100 dollars. 100 dollars added to your friend's account.
- **Transaction failed**: No changes in account balances.

You don't want to be in a state where 100 dollars is deducted from your account but not added to your friend's account. This state is called an **inconsistent state**.

Transaction management aims to prevent you from getting into an inconsistent state.

Consider the following code example:

```
void performTransfer(Account from, Account to, BigDecimal amount) {
  from.debit(amount);
  to.credit(amount);
}
```

It involves two steps. If the second step, `to.credit(amount)`, fails, you will want the entire change to be rolled back.

Understanding the Spring @Transactional annotation

The Spring Framework provides a consistent and declarative approach for transaction management.

All that you need to do is to add `@Transactional` around the method to make it a single transaction:

```
@Transactional
void performTransfer(Account from, Account to, BigDecimal amount) {
```

`@Transactional` can be used at either a method or at a class level.

The following are some of the attributes you can specify on the `@Transactional` annotation:

- `propagation`: How does the transaction propagate? Should we continue an existing transaction, if one exists, or create a new transaction? The default is `Propagation.REQUIRED`.
- `readOnly`: Should the transaction be read-only?
- `noRollbackForClassName`: Which exceptions should not cause a rollback of a transaction?
- `rollbackForClassName`: Which exceptions should cause a rollback of a transaction?
- `timeout`: How long should we wait for a transaction to complete?
- `isolation`: What should be the isolation level for the transaction? The default is `Isolation.DEFAULT`.
- `transactionManager`: Identifies the transaction manager that manages this transaction.

Understanding Spring Boot auto-configuration for transactions

Spring Boot auto-configures a transaction manager based on the libraries in the classpath. Here are some of the transaction managers for single relational databases:

- `org.springframework.jdbc.datasource.DataSourceTransactionManager`: Can manage transactions for one JDBC database resource
- `org.springframework.orm.jpa.JpaTransactionManager`: Can manage transactions for one JPA database resource

JTA is a standard for managing transactions in Java applications. It defines a resource-neutral approach for managing transactions. JTA supports transactions across multiple resources—across databases, queues, or any other resources.

Spring Boot supports JTA and makes it easy to participate in distributed transactions with multiple resources. You can use an Atomikos or Bitronix-embedded transaction manager as the implementation by adding the appropriate starters—`spring-boot-starter-jta-atomikos` or `spring-boot-starter-jta-bitronix`.

Interacting with MongoDB using Spring Data

As we discussed in the introduction of the chapter, there are a variety of data stores that are providing alternatives to traditional databases. These are typically called the NoSQL databases.

In this section, we will connect to one of the most popular NoSQL databases—MongoDB—using Spring Data.

With Spring Data, interacting with a NoSQL database is very similar to talking to a relational database. The steps involved are very similar as well:

1. Setting up the dependency of Spring Data MongoDB
2. Creating a `Person` entity
3. Creating a `Person` repository
4. Writing a unit test to check whether we are good

Setting up the dependencies

 Follow the instructions at `http://docs.mongodb.org/manual/installation/` to install MongoDB onto your specific operating system.

To get started with connecting to MongoDB, include the dependency for the Spring Boot MongoDB starter in `pom.xml`:

```xml
<dependency>
        <groupId>org.springframework.boot</groupId>
        <artifactId>spring-boot-starter-data-mongodb</artifactId>
</dependency>
```

Creating a Person entity

Let's create a new `Person` entity class to store to MongoDB. The following snippet shows a `Person` class with an ID and a name:

```
public class Person {

    @Id
    private String id;

    private String name;

    public Person() {
    }

    public Person(String name) {
        super();
        this.name = name;
    }
}
```

Creating a Person repository

If we wanted to store the `Person` entities to MongoDB, we would need to create a new repository. The following snippet shows a MongoDB repository:

```
public interface PersonMongoDbRepository
                        extends MongoRepository<Person, String> {

    List<Person> findByName(String name);

    Long countByName(String name);

}
```

Important things to note are as follows:

- `PersonMongoDbRepository` extends `MongoRepository`:
  The `MongoRepository` interface is a MongoDB-specific repository interface.
- `MongoRepository<Person, String>`: We would want to store `Person` entities that have a key type of `String`.
- `List<Person> findByName(String name)`: A simple method to find a person by name.

Testing the repository in a unit test

We will write a simple unit test to test this repository. The code for the unit test is as follows:

```
@DataMongoTest
@RunWith(SpringRunner.class)
public class PersonMongoDbRepositoryTest {

        @Autowired
        PersonMongoDbRepository personRepository;

        @Test
        public void simpleTest(){

          personRepository.deleteAll();

          personRepository.save(new Person( "name1"));
          personRepository.save(new Person( "name2"));

          for (Person person : personRepository.findAll()) {
              System.out.println("Person 1: " + person);
          }

          System.out.println("Person 2: " +
personRepository.findByName("name1"));

          System.out.println("Person Count: "personRepository.count());
    }

    }
}
```

Some important things to note are as follows:

- Make sure that MongoDB is running when you run the test.
- @DataMongoTest: The DataMongoTest annotation is used in combination with SpringRunner for a typical MongoDB unit test. This disables auto-configuration for everything except things that are related to MongoDB.
- @Autowired PersonMongoDbRepository personRepository: Autowires the MongoDB repository in order for it to be tested.

All the code in the test is very similar to the code written for Spring Data JPAs. This is the beauty of Spring Data: it is one way to connect to a variety of data stores.

We saw that code for interacting with a big database such as MongoDB is made simple, and is very similar to how we talk with a relational database. That's the magic of Spring Data.

Using Spring Data REST to create REST APIs

Spring Data REST provides a very simple option to expose CRUD RESTful services around Spring Data repositories.

Some of the important features of Spring Data REST include the following:

- Exposing the REST APIs around Spring Data repositories.
- Support for pagination and filtering.
- Understanding query methods in Spring Data repositories and exposing them as search resources.
- Among the frameworks supported are JPAs, MongoDB, and Cassandra.
- Options to customize the resources are exposed by default.

 In this section, we will continue to enhance the code from the JPA example from the earlier section of this chapter, *Understanding Spring Data JPA with an example*.

We will start by including the Spring Boot Data REST starter in `pom.xml`:

```
<dependency>
<groupId>org.springframework.boot</groupId>
<artifactId>spring-boot-starter-data-rest</artifactId>
</dependency>
```

We can make `UserRepository` expose the REST service by adding a simple annotation, as shown in the following snippet:

```
@RepositoryRestResource(collectionResourceRel = "users", path ="users")
public interface UserRepository
extends PagingAndSortingRepository<User, Long> {
```

Important things to note are as follows:

- @RepositoryRestResource: The annotation used to expose a repository using REST
- collectionResourceRel = "users": The collectionResourceRel value to be used in the generated links
- path = "users": The path under which the resource has to be exposed

When we launch SpringDataJpaFirstExampleApplication as a Java application, the following can be seen in the log:

```
s.b.c.e.t.TomcatEmbeddedServletContainer : Tomcat initialized with port(s):
8080 (http)
o.s.b.w.servlet.ServletRegistrationBean : Mapping servlet:
'dispatcherServlet' to [/]
```

The preceding log shows that the Spring MVC DispatcherServlet is launched and ready to serve different request methods and URIs.

Exploring the GET method

When we send a GET request to http://localhost:8080/users, we get the response shown here. The response is edited to remove the details of UserId2, UserId3, and UserId4 for brevity:

```
{
  "_embedded" : {
  "users" : [ {
              "userid" : "UserId1",
              "name" : "User Name 1",
              "_links" : {
                "self" : {"href" : "http://localhost:8080/users/1"},
                "user" : {"href" : "http://localhost:8080/users/1"},
                "todos" : {"href" :
"http://localhost:8080/users/1/todos"}
              }
         } ]
    },
    "_links" : {
            "self" : {"href" : "http://localhost:8080/users"},
            "profile" : {"href" :
"http://localhost:8080/profile/users"},
            "search" : {"href" : "http://localhost:8080/users/search"}
    },
```

```
"page" : {
        "size" : 20,
        "totalElements" : 4,
        "totalPages" : 1,
        "number" : 0
        }
}
```

Exploring the POST method

The following screenshot shows how to fire a POST request to create a new user:

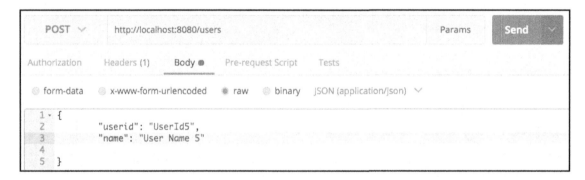

The following snippet shows the response:

```
{
   "userid": "UserId5",
   "name": "User Name 5",
   "_links": {
    "self": {
      "href": "http://localhost:8080/users/5"
        },
    "user": {
      "href": "http://localhost:8080/users/5"
        },
    "todos": {
      "href": "http://localhost:8080/users/5/todos"
      }
    }
}
```

The response contains the URI of the created resource—http://localhost:8080/users/5.

Using the search resource

Spring Data REST exposes search resources for other methods in the repository. For example, the `findUsersByNameUsingNamedParameters` method is exposed at `http://localhost:8080/users/search/findUsersByNameUsingNamedParameters?name=User%20Name%201`. The following snippet shows the response of a `GET` request to the preceding URL:

```
{
   "_embedded": {
       "users": [
               {
                   "userid": "UserId1",
                   "name": "User Name 1",
                   "_links": {
                     "self": {
                           "href":  "http://localhost:8080/users/1"
                           },
                       "user": {
                           "href": "http://localhost:8080/users/1"
                       },
                       "todos": {
                         "href":
   "http://localhost:8080/users/1/todos"
                       }
                   }
               }
           ]
       },
   "_links": {
     "self": {
         "href":"http://localhost:8080/users/search/
   findUsersByNameUsingNamedParameters?name=User%20Name%201"
       }
   }
}
```

Spring Data REST makes it easy to expose REST APIs around Spring Data repositories.

Summary

Spring Boot makes the development of Spring-based applications easy. Spring Data makes it easy to connect to different data stores.

In this chapter, we looked at Spring Data in depth.

We started by looking at Spring Data Commons, which provides the common interfaces and APIs that makes Spring Data easy—Repository, `CrudRepository`, and `PagingAndSortingRepository`.

We looked at connecting to a relational database using Spring Data JPA. We used an in-memory database, H2. We created a simple repository to perform CRUD operations. We implemented paging and sorting features. We learned how to create custom query methods and JPQL queries in a repository.

After that, we created a project connecting to a big data database, MongoDB, using Spring Data MongoDB. We saw that interacting with a big data database was no different from talking with a relational database.

That's the magic of Spring Data. It provides a consistent approach to talk to a variety of data stores.

As monolith applications grew bigger and more unmaintainable, a change was needed. In the next chapter, let's shift our attention toward microservice architectures.

3
Section 3: Cloud, Microservices, and Best Practices with Spring

The cloud, microservices, and reactive programming are buzzwords that have been used over the last few years.

In this section, we will understand the architectural evolution toward microservices, and learn how to implement microservices using Spring Cloud. We will discover reactive programming and look at the best practices in developing Spring applications.

The following chapters are covered in this section:

- Chapter 11, *Getting Started with Microservices*
- Chapter 12, *Building Microservices with Spring Boot and Spring Cloud*
- Chapter 13, *Reactive Programming*
- Chapter 14, *Spring Best Practices*
- Chapter 15, *Working with Kotlin in Spring*

11
Getting Started with Microservices

In the last decade, the Spring Framework has evolved into the most popular framework for developing Java Enterprise applications. The Spring Framework has made it easy to develop loosely coupled, testable applications. It has simplified the implementation of cross-cutting concerns.

The world today, however, is very different from a decade back. Over a period of time, applications grew into monoliths, which became difficult to manage, and the never-ending search for solutions to these challenges continues. The buzzwords in the recent past have been **microservices** and **cloud-native applications**.

In this chapter, we will look at the problems with **monolithic applications** and get introduced to the world of smaller, independently deployable components, which are known as microservices. We will explore the reasons why the world is moving toward microservices and cloud-native applications. We will also look at one of the important Spring projects—Spring Cloud—and the solutions that it offers regarding the challenges with microservices.

This chapter will cover the following topics:

- What are our goals when we develop applications?
- What are the challenges with monolithic applications?
- What are microservices?
- What are the advantages of microservices?
- What are the challenges with microservices?
- What are cloud-native applications?
- What are the Spring projects that help us in developing microservices and cloud-native applications?
- What is Spring Cloud?

Understanding the goals of application development

Before we move on to the concepts of microservices and cloud-native applications, let's take some time to understand the common goals that we have when we develop applications. Understanding these goals will help us understand why applications are moving toward microservices architecture.

 First of all, we should remember that the software industry is still a relatively young industry. One thing that's been a constant in my decade-and-a-half of experience with developing, designing, and architecting software is that things change. The requirements of today are not the requirements of tomorrow. Technology today is not the technology that we will use tomorrow. While we can try predicting what will happen in the future, we are often wrong.

One of the things we did during the initial decades of software development was to build software systems for the future. The design and architecture were made complex in preparation for future requirements.

During the last decade, with **agile** and **extreme programming**, the focus shifted to being **lean** and building good enough systems, adhering to basic principles of design. The focus has now shifted to evolutionary design.

 The thought process is this—*if a system has a good design for today's needs, and is continuously evolving and has good tests, it can easily be refactored to meet tomorrow's needs.*

While we do not know where we are heading, we do know that a big chunk of our goals when developing applications have not changed.

The key goals of software development, for a large number of applications, can be described with the statement, *speed and safety at scale*.

We will discuss each of these in elements in the next section.

Developing applications quickly – speed

The speed of delivering new requirements and innovations is increasingly becoming a key differentiator. It is not sufficient to develop (code and test) fast. It is important to deliver (to the production stage) quickly. It is now common knowledge that the best software organizations in the world deliver software to production multiple times every day.

The technology and business landscape is in a constant flux, and is constantly evolving. The key question is, *How fast can an application adapt to these changes?*

Some of the important changes in the technology and business landscape are highlighted here:

- New programming languages:
    - Go
    - Scala
    - Closure
- New programming paradigms:
    - Functional programming
    - Reactive programming
- New frameworks
- New tools:
    - Development
    - Code quality
    - Automation testing
    - Deployment
    - Containerization
- New processes and practices:
    - Agile
    - Test-driven development
    - Behavior-driven development
    - Continuous integration
    - Continuous delivery
    - DevOps
- New devices and opportunities:
    - Mobile
    - Cloud

Building dependable applications – safety

What is the use of speed without safety? Who would want to go in a car that can travel at 300 miles an hour, but has no proper safety features built in?

Let's consider a few characteristics of a safe application.

Reliability – does the application behave as expected?

Reliability is a measure of how accurately the system functions.

The key questions to ask are as follows:

- Is the system meeting its functional requirements?
- How many defects are leaked during different release phases?

Availability – is your application available all the time?

Most external client-facing applications are expected to be available round the clock. Availability is a measure of the percentage of time that your application is available to your end user.

Security – is your application secure?

The security of applications and data is critical to the success of organizations. There should be clear procedures for authentication (are you who you claim to be?), authorization (what access does a user have?), and data protection (is the data that is received or sent accurate? Is the data safe and not intercepted by unintended users?).

Performance – is your application quick enough?

If a web application does not respond within a couple of seconds, there is a very high chance that the user of your application will be disappointed. Performance usually refers to the ability of a system to provide an agreed-upon response time for a defined number of users.

High resilience – does your application react well to failures?

As applications become distributed, the probability of failures increases. How does the application react in the case of localized failures or disruptions? Can it provide basic operations without completely crashing?

The ability of an application to provide the bare minimum service levels in cases of unexpected failures is called resilience.

As more and more applications move toward the Cloud, the resilience of applications becomes more important.

Scalability – what is needed to support a drastic increase in application load?

Scalability is a measure of how an application would react when the resources at its disposal are scaled up. If an application supports 10,000 users with a given infrastructure, can it support at least 20,000 users with double the infrastructure?

If a web application does not respond within a couple of seconds, there is a very high chance that the user of your application will be disappointed.

In the world of the Cloud, the scalability of applications becomes even more important. It's difficult to guess how successful a start-up might be. Twitter or Facebook might not have expected such success when they were incubated. Their success, for a large measure, depends on how they were able to adapt to a multifold increase in their user base, without their performances being affected.

Challenges with monolithic applications

Over the last few years, in parallel to working with several small applications, I have had the opportunity to work on four different monolithic applications in varied domains—insurance, banking, and health care. All of these applications had very similar challenges. In this section, we will start by looking at the characteristics of monoliths, and then look at the challenges they bring in.

First of all, what is a monolith? An application with a lot of code—possibly with more than 100,000 lines of code.

For me, monoliths are those applications for which getting a release out to production is a big challenge.

Applications that fall into this category have a number of user requirements that are immediately needed, but these applications are able to do new feature releases once every few months. Some of these applications do feature releases once a quarter, but sometimes they are as little as twice a year.

Typically, monolithic applications may have some of these characteristics:

- **Large size**: Most monolithic applications have large code bases.
- **Large teams**: The team size could vary from 20 to 300.
- **Multiple ways of doing the same thing**: Since the team is huge, there is a communication gap. This results in multiple solutions for the same problem in different parts of the application.
- **Lack of automation testing**: Most of these applications have very few unit tests, and a complete lack of integration tests. These applications have a great dependency on manual testing.

Because of these characteristics, there are a number of challenges that are faced by monolithic applications.

Challenges in releasing updates – long release cycles

Making a code change in one part of the monolith may impact some other part of the monolith. Most code changes will need a complete regression cycle. This results in long release cycles.

Due to the lack of automation testing, these applications depend on manual testing to find defects. Taking the functionality live is a major challenge.

Difficulties with scaling up

Typically, most monolithic applications are not cloud-native, which means that they are not easy to deploy on the Cloud. They depend on manual installation and manual configuration. There is typically a lot of work put in by the operations team before a new application instance is added to the cluster. This makes scaling up and down a big challenge.

The other important challenge is large databases. Typically, monolithic applications have databases running into **terabytes** (**TB**). The database becomes the bottleneck when scaling up.

Difficulties with adapting new technologies

Most monolithic applications use old technologies. Adding new technologies to the monolith only makes it more complex to maintain. Architects and developers are reluctant to bring in any new technologies.

Difficulties with adapting new methodologies

New methodologies, such as **agile**, need small (four-seven team members), independent teams. The big questions with monoliths are these: How do we prevent teams from stepping on each other's toes? How do we create islands that enable teams to work independently? These are difficult challenges to solve.

Challenges in adapting modern development practices

Modern development practices, such as **test-driven development** (**TDD**) and **behavior-driven development** (**BDD**), need loosely coupled, testable architectures. If the monolithic application has tightly coupled layers and frameworks, it is difficult to unit test. It makes adapting modern development practices challenging.

Getting started with microservices

The challenges with monolithic applications lead to organizations searching for the silver bullet. How will we be able to make more features live more often?

Many organizations have tried different architectures and practices to find a solution.

In the last few years, a common pattern has emerged among all the organizations that have been successful in doing this. This resulted in an architectural style that became known as the **microservices architecture**.

> *"Many organizations have found that by embracing fine-grained microservice architectures, they can deliver software faster and embrace newer technologies."*

> *- Building Microservices, Sam Newman*

What is a microservice?

One of the principles that I love in software is to *keep it small*. This principle is applicable irrespective of what you are talking about—the scope of a variable, or the size of a method, class, package, or component. You should aim for all of these to be as small as possible.

Microservices are a simple extension of this principle. It's an architectural style that is focused on building small, capability-based, and independently deployable services.

There is no single accepted definition of a microservice. We will look at some of the popular definitions here:

> *"Microservices are small, autonomous services that work together"*

> *- Sam Newman, Thoughtworks*

> *"Loosely coupled service-oriented architecture with bounded contexts"*

> *- Adrian Cockcroft, Battery Ventures*

While there is no accepted definition for microservices, there are a few characteristics that are commonly featured in all definitions of microservice.

Before we look at the characteristics of microservices, we will try and understand the big picture—we will look at how monolith architectures compare with microservices architectures.

Understanding the big idea of microservice architecture

Most monolithic applications have a single deployable unit. Even if the monolith application is built using a modularized architecture with several components, it is finally deployed as a whole.

The following diagram shows an example of a monolithic application with three modules. These modules can either be technical modules or business capabilities. For example, in a shopping application, these modules could be login, search, and product recommendation modules:

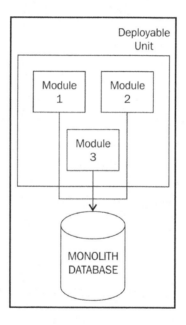

The consequence of having a single deployable unit is that any—even a very small—change in any of the modules would need the deployment of the entire monolith application.

The big idea of microservices architectures is to build smaller, independently deployable microservices. Instead of building the application as a single deployable component, each of the modules would be an independently deployable component. If there is a change in **MODULE 2**, you would only need to deploy **MODULE 2**.

The following diagram shows what the preceding monolith looks like when it's developed using a microservice architecture:

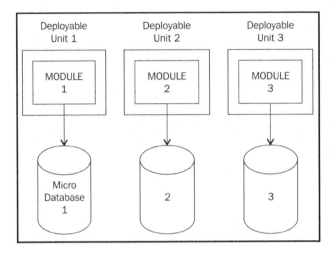

The following list highlights a few important things to note:

- Modules are identified based on business capabilities. The question to ask is, What is the responsibility of the module?
- Each module is independently deployable. In the following example, modules 1, 2, and 3 are separate deployable units. If there is a change in the business functionality of **MODULE 3**, we can individually build and deploy **MODULE 3**.
- It is recommended that each microservice has its own data store.

Understanding microservice characteristics

In the previous section, we looked at an example of the microservice architecture. An evaluation of the experiences of organizations that have been successful at adapting the microservices architectural style reveals that there are a few characteristics that are shared by teams and architectures. Let's look at some of them:

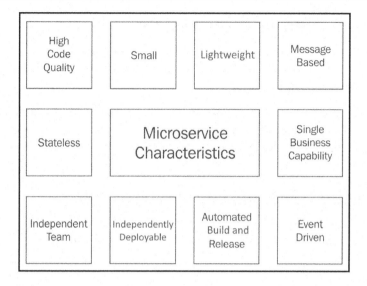

We will understand this diagram in more detail in the following sections.

Small and lightweight microservices

A good microservice provides business capabilities. Ideally, microservices should follow the single responsibility principle. Because of this, microservices are generally small in size. Typically, a rule of thumb that I use is that it should be possible to build and deploy a microservice within 5 minutes. If the building and deployment take any longer, it is likely that you are building a larger-than-recommended microservice.

Some examples of small and lightweight microservices are as follows:

- Product recommendation service
- Email notification service
- Shopping cart service

Interoperability with message-based communication

The key focus of microservices is on interoperability—communication between systems using diverse technologies. The best way to achieve interoperability is by using message-based communication.

Capability-aligned microservices

It is essential that microservices have a clear boundary. Typically, every microservice has a single identified business capability that it delivers well. Teams have found success in adapting the *Bounded Context* concept.

Essentially, for large systems, it is very difficult to create one domain model. The *Bounded Context* concept talks about splitting the system into different bounded contexts. Identifying the right bounded contexts is the key to success with microservice architecture.

Independently deployable microservices

Each microservice can be individually built and deployed. In the example we discussed earlier, modules 1, 2, and 3 can be independently built and deployed.

Stateless microservices

An ideal microservice does not have a state. It does not store any information between requests. All the information that's needed to create a response is present in the request.

Completely automated build and release process

Microservices have automated build and release processes. Take a look at the following diagram. It shows a simple build and release process for a microservice:

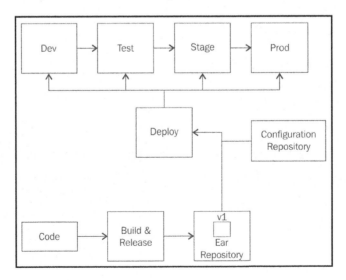

When a microservice is built and released, a version of the microservice is stored in the repository. The deploy tool has the capability of picking the right version of the microservice from the repository, matching it with the configuration that's needed for the specific environment (from the configuration repository), and deploying the microservice to a specific environment.

Some teams take it a step further and combine the microservice package with the underlying infrastructure that is needed to run the microservice. The deploy tool will replicate this image and match it with an environment-specific configuration to create an environment.

Adherence to event-driven architectures

Microservices are typically built with event-driven architectures. Let's consider a simple example. Whenever a new customer is registered, there are three things that need to be performed:

- Store customer information in the database
- Mail a welcome kit
- Send an email notification

Let's look at two different approaches to design this:

Approach 1 – The sequential approach

Let's consider three services—`CustomerInformationService`, `MailService`, and `EmailService`, which can provide the capabilities that we listed previously. We can create `NewCustomerService` using the following steps:

1. Call `CustomerInformationService` to save customer information in the database.
2. Call `MailService` to mail the welcome kit.
3. Call `EmailService` to send the email notification.

`NewCustomerService` becomes the central place for all business logic. Imagine if we have to do more things when a new customer is created. All that logic would start accumulating and would result in `NewCustomerService` becoming bloated.

Approach 2 – The event-driven approach

In this approach, we use a message broker. `NewCustomerService` will create a new event and post it to the message broker. The following diagram shows a high-level representation of this:

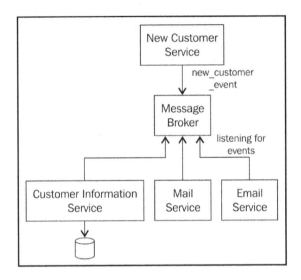

The three services—`CustomerInformationService`, `MailService`, and `EmailService`—will be listening on the message broker for new events. When they see the new customer event, they will process it and execute the functionality of that specific service.

The key advantage of the event-driven approach is that there is no centralized magnet for all business logic. Adding new functionality is easier. We can create a new service to listen for the event on the message broker. Another important thing to note is that we don't need to make changes to any of the existing services.

Independent teams developing and supporting microservices – DevOps

The team that's developing a microservice is typically independent. It contains all the skills that are needed to develop, test, and deploy a microservice. It is also responsible for supporting the microservice in production.

Understanding the advantages of microservice architectures

Microservices have several advantages. They help in keeping up with technology and getting solutions to your customers faster.

Faster time to market

The faster time to market is one of the key factors in determining the success of an organization.

Microservices architecture involves creating small, independently deployable components. Microservice enhancements are easier and less brittle, because each microservice focuses on a single business capability. All the steps in the process—building, releasing, deployment, testing, configuration management, and monitoring—are automated. Since the responsibility of a microservice is bounded, it is possible to write great automation unit and integration tests.

All these factors result in applications being able to react faster to customer needs.

Quick adaptation to technology evolution

There are new languages, frameworks, practices, and automation possibilities emerging every day. It is important that the application architectures provide the flexibility to adapt to emerging possibilities. The following diagram shows how different services are developed in different technologies:

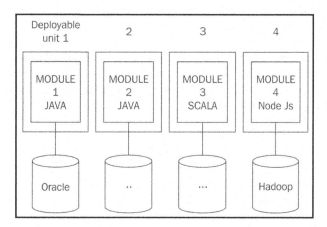

The microservice architecture involves creating small services. Within some boundaries, most organizations give the individual teams the technology to make some of the technology decisions. This allows teams to experiment with new technologies and innovate faster which, in turn, helps applications to adapt and stay in tune with the evolution of technology.

Ability to easily scale

The load on different parts of the application is typically very different. For example, in the case of a flight booking application, a customer usually searches multiple times before making a decision on whether to book a flight. The load on the search module would typically be many times more than the load on the booking module. The microservices architecture provides the flexibility of setting up multiple instances of the search service with a few instances of the booking service.

The following diagram shows how we can scale up specific microservices based on the load:

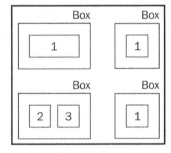

Microservices **2** and **3** share a single box (the deployment environment). Microservice **1**, which has more load, is deployed into multiple boxes.

Another example is the need for start-ups. When start-ups begin operating, they are typically unaware of the extent to which they might grow. What happens if the demand for applications grows very fast? If they adopt the microservice architecture, it allows them to scale better when the need arises.

Compatibility with current development methodologies

Development methodologies, such as agile, advocate small, independent teams. Since microservices are small, it is possible to build small teams around them. Teams are cross-functional, with end-to-end ownership of specific microservices.

The microservice architecture fits in very well with agile and other modern development methodologies.

Exploring microservice challenges

Microservice architecture has significant advantages. However, there are significant challenges, too. Deciding the boundaries of microservices is a challenging but important decision. Since microservices are small, and there would be hundreds of microservices in a large enterprise, having great automation and visibility is critical.

Increased need for automation

With microservice architecture, you are splitting up a large application into multiple microservices, and so the number of builds, releases, and deployments increases multifold. It would be very inefficient to have manual processes for these steps.

Test automation is critical in order to enable a faster time to market. Teams should be focused on identifying automation possibilities as they emerge.

Challenges in defining the boundaries of subsystems

Microservices should be intelligent. They are not weak CRUD services. They should model the business capability of the system. They own all the business logic in a bounded context. This being said, microservices should not be large, and deciding the boundaries of microservices is a challenge. Finding the right boundaries might be difficult on the first go. It is important that, as a team gains more knowledge about the business context, the knowledge flows into the architecture and new boundaries are determined. Generally, finding the right boundaries for microservices is an evolutionary process.

A couple of important points to note are as follows:

- Loose coupling and high cohesion are fundamental to any programming and architectural decisions. When a system is loosely coupled, changes in one part should not require a change in other parts.
- Bounded contexts represent autonomous business modules representing specific business capabilities.

Always think, "What capabilities are we providing to the rest of the domain?"

Increased need for visibility and monitoring

With microservices, one application is split into several microservices. To conquer the complexity that is associated with multiple microservices and asynchronous event-based collaboration, it is important to have great visibility.

Ensuring high visibility means each microservice should be monitored. Automated health management of the microservices becomes important.

The debugging of problems needs an insight into what's happening behind multiple microservices. Centralized logging with the aggregation of logs and metrics from different microservices is typically used. Mechanisms such as correlation IDs need to be used to isolate and debug issues.

Increased need for fault tolerance

Let's say we are building a shopping application. What happens if the recommendation microservice is down? How does the application react? Does it completely crash? Or will it let the customer shop? These kinds of situations happen more often as we adopt the microservices architecture.

As we make the services small, the chance that a service goes down increases. How the application reacts to these situations becomes an important question. In the previous example, a fault-tolerant application would show some default recommendations, while letting the customer shop.

As we move into microservices architecture, applications should be more fault-tolerant. Applications should be able to provide toned-down behavior when services are down.

Maintaining consistency across microservices

It is important to have a degree of consistency between microservices in an organization. Consistency between microservices enables similar development, testing, release, deployment, and operational processes across the organization. This allows different developers and testers to be productive when they move across teams. It is important not to be too rigid, and to have a degree of flexibility within limits, so as to not stifle innovation.

Establishing standardized shared capabilities (enterprise level)

Let's look at a few capabilities that have to be standardized at an enterprise level:

- **Hardware**: Which hardware do we use? Do we use the Cloud?
- **Code management**: Which version control system do we use? What are our practices in branching and committing code?
- **Build and deployment**: How do we build? Which tools do we use to automate deployment?
- **Data store**: What kind of data stores do we use?
- **Service orchestration**: How do we orchestrate services? What kind of message broker do we use?
- **Security and identity**: How do we authenticate and authorize users and services?
- **System visibility and monitoring**: How do we monitor our services? How do we provide fault isolation across the system?

Increased need for operations teams

As we move into a microservice world, there is a distinct shift in the responsibilities of the operations team. The responsibilities shift to identifying opportunities for automation compared to manual operations, such as executing releases and deployments.

With multiple microservices and an increase in communications across different parts of the system, the operations team becomes critical. It is important to involve operations as part of the team from the initial stages in order to allows them to identify solutions to make operations easier.

Understanding cloud-native applications

The Cloud is disrupting the world. A number of possibilities have emerged that were never possible before. Organizations are able to provision computing, network, and storage devices on demand. This has a high potential to reduce costs in a number of industries.

Consider the retail industry, where there are pockets of high demand (Black Friday, holiday season, and so on). Why should they pay for hardware throughout the year, when they could provision it on demand?

While we would like to benefit from the possibilities of the Cloud, these possibilities are limited by architectures and the nature of applications.

How do we build applications that can be easily deployed on the Cloud? That's where cloud-native applications come into the picture.

Cloud-native applications are those that can easily be deployed on the Cloud. These applications share a few common characteristics. We will begin by looking at the Twelve-Factor App—a combination of common patterns among cloud-native applications.

What is the Twelve-Factor App?

The Twelve-Factor App evolved from the experiences of engineers at Heroku. It is a list of patterns that are used in cloud-native application architectures.

It is important to note that an app here refers to a single deployable unit. Essentially, every microservice is an app (because each microservice is independently deployable).

Let's discuss the twelve factors, one by one.

Maintain one code base

Each app has one code base in revision control. There can be multiple environments where the app can be deployed. However, all of these environments use the code from a single code base. An example antipattern is building a single deployable from multiple code bases.

 Antipatterns are the opposite of design patterns. Antipatterns are bad practices and should be avoided when possible.

Explicit declaration of dependencies

All dependencies must be explicitly declared and isolated, making it easy to configure and change dependencies. Typical Java applications use build management tools such as Maven and Gradle to isolate and track dependencies.

The following screenshot shows typical Java applications that are managing their dependencies using Maven:

The following screenshot shows pom.xml, where the dependencies are managed for a Java application:

```
M  mastering-spring-chapter-3/pom.xml ⊠
42          </dependency>
43
44⊖        <dependency>
45              <groupId>org.springframework.security</groupId>
46              <artifactId>spring-security-web</artifactId>
47              <version>4.0.1.RELEASE</version>
48          </dependency>
49
50⊖        <dependency>
51              <groupId>org.springframework.security</groupId>
52              <artifactId>spring-security-config</artifactId>
53              <version>4.0.1.RELEASE</version>
54          </dependency>
55
56⊖        <dependency>
57              <groupId>org.hibernate</groupId>
58              <artifactId>hibernate-validator</artifactId>
59              <version>5.0.2.Final</version>
60          </dependency>
61
62⊖        <dependency>
63              <groupId>org.webjars</groupId>
64              <artifactId>bootstrap</artifactId>
65              <version>3.3.6</version>
66          </dependency>
67
68⊖        <dependency>
69              <groupId>org.webjars</groupId>
70              <artifactId>jquery</artifactId>
71              <version>1.9.1</version>
72          </dependency>
```

Application configuration stored in an environment

All applications have a configuration that varies from one environment to another. The configuration is found at multiple locations; application code, property files, databases, environment variables, **Java Naming and Directory Interface (JNDI)**, and system variables are a few examples.

A Twelve-Factor App should store configuration in the environment. While environment variables are recommended in order to manage configuration in a Twelve-Factor App, other alternatives, such as having a centralized repository for application configuration, should be considered for more complex systems.

Irrespective of the mechanism that's used, we recommend that you do the following:

- Manage configuration outside the application code (independent of the application's deployable unit)
- Use a standardized way of configuration

All dependencies are treated as backing services

A backing service is any service that an application accesses over the network—an external application, an external database, or an email server.

Applications should make no distinction between local services and backing services.

This makes applications loosely coupled. They can easily switch from a local service to an external service.

Clear separation between build, release, and run phases

The build, release, and run phases are described as follows. We should maintain a clear separation between all of these three phases:

- **Build**: Creates an executable bundle (EAR, WAR, or JAR) from code, as well as dependencies that can be deployed to multiple environments
- **Release**: Combines the executable bundle with a specific environment configuration to deploy in an environment
- **Run**: Runs the app in an execution environment using a specific release

The build and release phases are highlighted in the following diagram:

An antipattern is building separate executable bundles that are specific to each environment.

Applications do not store states – stateless

A Twelve-Factor App does not have a state. All the data that it needs is stored in a persistent store.

An antipattern is a sticky session.

All the services are exposed with port binding

A Twelve-Factor App exposes all the services using port binding. While it is possible to have other mechanisms to expose services, these mechanisms are implementation-dependent. Port binding gives full control of receiving and handling messages, irrespective of where an app is deployed.

Possibility to scale horizontally – concurrency

A Twelve-Factor App is able to achieve more concurrency by scaling out horizontally. Scaling vertically has its limits. Scaling out horizontally provides opportunities to expand without limits.

Each application instance is disposable

A Twelve-Factor App should promote elastic scaling. Hence, they should be disposable. They can be started and stopped when needed.

A Twelve-Factor App should do the following:

- Have a minimum startup time. A long startup time means a long delay before an application can take requests.
- Shut down gracefully.
- Handle hardware failures gracefully.

Achieving environmental parity – all environments are the same

All the environments, that is, development, test, staging, and production, should be similar. They should use the same processes and tools. With continuous deployment, they should have frequently had similar code. This makes finding and fixing problems easier.

Treating all logs as event streams

Visibility is critical to a Twelve-Factor App. Since applications are deployed on the Cloud and are automatically scaled, it is important that you have a centralized view of what's happening across different instances of the applications.

Treating all logs as streams enables the routing of the log stream to different destinations for viewing and archival purposes. This stream can be used to debug issues, perform analytics, and create alerting systems based on error patterns.

No distinction for admin processes

Twelve-Factor Apps treat administrative tasks (migrations, scripts, and so on) in a similar way to normal application processes.

In this section, we looked at the cloud-native application best practices—12 characteristics of the Twelve-Factor App. In the next section, we'll look at some of the Spring projects which help us build cloud-native applications.

Exploring Spring projects for microservices

As the world moves toward cloud-native applications and microservices, Spring projects are not far behind. There are a number of new Spring projects—Spring Boot and Spring Cloud, among others—which solve the problems of the emerging world.

Getting an overview of Spring Boot

We discussed Spring Boot extensively in earlier chapters. This section highlights the key role Spring Boot plays in microservice architectures.

In the era of monoliths, we had the luxury of taking the time to set up the frameworks for an application. However, in the era of microservices, we want to create individual components faster. The Spring Boot project aims to solve this problem.

 As the official website highlights, Spring Boot makes it easy to create standalone, production-grade, Spring-based applications that you can *just run*. We take an opinionated view of the Spring platform and third-party libraries so that you can get started with minimal fuss.

Spring Boot aims to take an opinionated view—basically making a lot of decisions for us—to developing Spring-based projects.

Getting started with Spring Cloud

Spring Cloud aims to provide solutions to some of the commonly encountered patterns when building systems on the Cloud:

- **Configuration management**: As we discussed in the *What is the Twelve-Factor App* section, managing configuration is an important part of developing cloud-native applications. Spring Cloud provides a centralized configuration management solution for microservices—Spring Cloud Config.
- **Service discovery**: Service discovery promotes loose coupling between services. Spring Cloud provides integration with popular service discovery options, such as Eureka, ZooKeeper, and Consul.

- **Circuit breakers**: Cloud-native applications must be fault-tolerant. They should be able to handle the failure of backing services gracefully. Circuit breakers play a key role in providing the default minimum service in case of failures. Spring Cloud provides integration with the Netflix Hystrix fault tolerance library.
- **API Gateway**: An API Gateway provides centralized aggregation, routing, and caching services. Spring Cloud provides integration with the API Gateway library, Netflix Zuul.

It is important to understand that Spring Cloud is not a single project. It is a group of subprojects aimed at solving the problems associated with applications that are deployed on the Cloud.

Some important Spring Cloud subprojects are as follows:

- **Spring Cloud Netflix**: Netflix is one of the early adopters of the microservice architecture. A number of internal Netflix projects were open sourced under the umbrella of Spring Cloud Netflix. Examples include Eureka, Hystrix, and Zuul.
- **Spring Cloud Config**: Enables centralized external configuration across different microservices across different environments.
- **Spring Cloud Bus**: Makes it easier to build the integration of microservices with a lightweight message broker.
- **Spring Cloud Sleuth**: Along with Zipkin, this provides distributed tracing solutions.
- **Spring Cloud Data Flow**: Provides capabilities for building orchestration around microservice applications. Provides a DSL, GUI, and REST API.
- **Spring Cloud Stream**: Provides a simple declarative framework to integrate Spring-based (and Spring Boot-based) applications with message brokers such as Apache Kafka or RabbitMQ.

A few things are common to all projects under the Spring Cloud umbrella:

- They solve some of the common problems with developing applications on the Cloud.
- They provide great integration with Spring Boot.
- They are typically configured with simple annotations.
- They make extensive use of auto-configuration.

Let's start exploring some of the Spring Cloud projects in depth.

Exploring Spring Cloud Netflix

Netflix is one of the first organizations to start making the switch from monolithic to microservice architectures. Netflix has been very open to documenting this experience. Some of the internal Netflix frameworks are open sourced under the umbrella of Spring Cloud Netflix.

Some of the important projects under the Spring Cloud Netflix umbrella are as follows:

- **Eureka**: The name provides service registration and discovery capabilities for microservices.
- **Hystrix**: Capabilities to build fault-tolerant microservices through circuit breakers. It also provides a dashboard.
- **Feign**: The declarative REST Client makes it easy to call services that are created with JAX-RS and Spring MVC.
- **Ribbon**: Provides client-side load balancing capabilities.
- **Zuul**: Provides typical API Gateway capabilities, such as routing, filtering, authentication, and security. It can be extended with custom rules and filters.

Summary

In this chapter, we discussed the problems with monolithic applications and how architectures evolved toward microservices. Organizations that adopt microservice architectures also need to make challenging decisions around the consistency of microservices, without affecting the innovation capabilities of the microservice teams—smaller applications means more builds, releases, and deployments. This is usually addressed using more automation; microservice architectures are built based on a large number of smaller, fine-grained services. There are challenges associated with managing the configuration and availability of these services; debugging issues become more difficult because of the distributed nature of the applications.

In order to reap the maximum benefits from microservice architectures, microservices should be cloud-native—easily deployable on the Cloud. We discussed the characteristics of Twelve-Factor Apps—patterns that are typically considered to be good practices in cloud-native applications.

We also discussed the solutions that Spring Cloud provides to commonly encountered patterns when building applications for the Cloud—managing configuration, service registration, service discovery, load balancing, fault tolerance, API Gateways, and distributed tracing across microservices.

In the next chapter, we'll get our hands dirty and implement solutions for all the problems we have discussed.

Further reading

- *Spring Microservices*, by Rajesh RV. Available at `https://www.packtpub.com/ application-development/spring-microservices`.

12
Building Microservices with Spring Boot and Spring Cloud

In the previous chapter, we were introduced to the concept of microservices.

In this chapter, we will implement microservices using projects under the umbrella of Spring Cloud. We will start by getting an overview of the microservices we will build.

We will explore managing microservices configuration with Spring Cloud Config, and understand how we can use Spring Cloud Bus to connect microservices with lightweight message brokers such as RabbitMQ, and use Spring Cloud Bus to automatically propagate configuration changes to all microservices.

Then, we will implement client-side load balancing for microservices with Ribbon, and understand the need for having a naming server, and implement a naming server with Eureka. Afterwards, will use an API gateway, Zuul, to implement one of the most common features in microservices—logging.

Finally, we will learn how to use Spring Cloud Sleuth and Zipkin to implement distributed tracing, and how to make our microservices fault-tolerant using Hystrix.

Let's get started on this incredible journey with microservices.

Technical requirements

The following are the requirements for this chapter:

- Your favorite IDE, Eclipse
- Java 8+
- Maven 3.x
- Internet connectivity

The GitHub link for this chapter is a follows: `https://github.com/PacktPublishing/ Mastering-Spring-5.1/tree/master/Chapter12`

Understanding the microservices we will build

To understand microservices concepts better, we will use an example-driven approach.

We will build two microservices that talk to each other—Microservice A and the Service Consumer. Microservice A exposes a random number service that is consumed by the Service Consumer microservice.

A few more details about each of these microservices are as follows:

- **Microservice A**: This is a simple microservice that exposes two services—one to retrieve a message from the configuration file and another random service that provide a list of five random numbers.
- **Service Consumer microservice**: This is a simple microservice that exposes a simple calculation service called the **add** service. The **add** service consumes the random service from **Microservice A** and adds the numbers up.

The following diagram shows the relationship between the microservices and the services that are exposed:

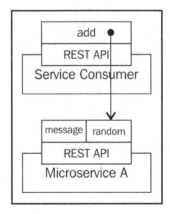

Let's get started by setting up these microservice examples. We will use **SPRING INITIALIZR** to quickly set them up.

Setting up Microservice A

Let's use **SPRING INITIALIZR** (`https://start.spring.io`) to get started with
Microservice A. This involves two steps, which are explained in the following sections.

Step 1 – initializing Microservice A using SPRING INITIALIZR

Choose **GroupId**, **ArtifactId**, and the frameworks, as shown in the following screenshot:

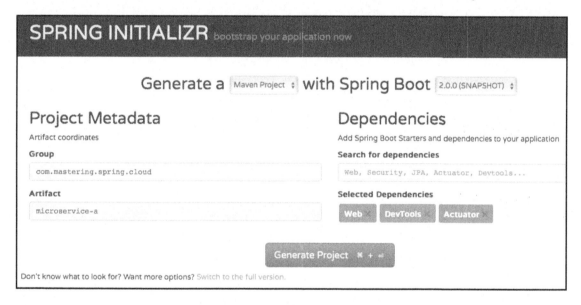

After importing the project into the IDE as a Maven project, let's configure a name for the
application in `application.properties`:

```
spring.application.name=microservice-a
```

Step 2 – creating the random list service in Microservice A

We want to create a simple service that returns five random numbers. An example response
from the service is shown here:

```
[5,6,6,4,992]
```

It should be easy to build a RESTful controller to return a list of five random numbers. The following snippet shows the implementation details:

```
@RestController
public class RandomNumberController {

    private Log log =
        LogFactory.getLog(RandomNumberController.class);

    @RequestMapping("/random")
    public List<Integer> random() {

        List<Integer> numbers = new ArrayList< >();

        for (int i = 1; i <= 5; i++) {
            numbers.add(generateRandomNumber());
        }

        log.info("Returning " + numbers);

        return numbers;

    }

    private int generateRandomNumber() {
        return (int) (Math.random() * 1000);
    }
}
```

Some important things to note are as follows:

- `@RequestMapping("/random") public List<Integer> random()`: This is a random service that returns a list of random numbers.
- `private int generateRandomNumber() {`: This generates random numbers between 0 and 1000.

The following snippet shows a sample response from the service at `http://localhost:8080/random`:

```
[666,257,306,204,992]
```

Building the Service Consumer microservice

Let's start setting up the Service Consumer microservice. Let's use **SPRING INITIALIZR** (`https://start.spring.io`) to initialize the microservice, as shown in the following screenshot:

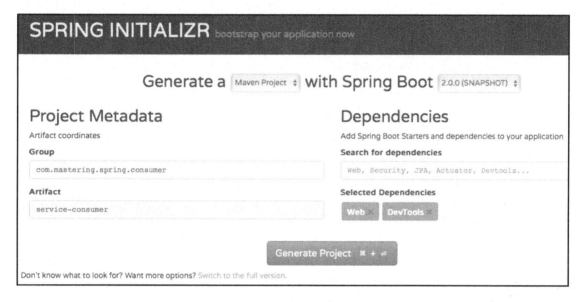

Let's configure `application.properties`, as shown in the following snippet:

```
spring.application.name=service-consumer
server.port=8100
```

We will use port `8100` to run the Service Consumer application. We also configured a name for the application.

Creating the method to consume the random list service (from Microservice A)

We want the Service Consumer microservice to invoke the service exposed from Microservice A—a random list service. The business logic we will implement in Service Consumer is to take the list of random numbers that are returned from Microservice A and add them up.

A simple implementation using `RestTemplate` is shown here:

```
@RestController
public class NumberAdderController {

    private Log log = LogFactory.getLog(NumberAdderController.class);

    @Value("${number.service.url}")
    private String numberServiceUrl;

    @RequestMapping("/add")
    public Long add() {
        long sum = 0;

        ResponseEntity<Integer[]> responseEntity
                        = new RestTemplate()
                                .getForEntity(numberServiceUrl,
    Integer[].class);

        Integer[] numbers = responseEntity.getBody();

        for (int number : numbers) {
            sum += number;
        }

        log.warn("Returning " + sum);

        return sum;
    }
}
```

Some important things to note are as follows:

- `@Value("${number.service.url}") private String numberServiceUrl`: We want the number service URL to be configurable in application properties.
- `@RequestMapping("/add") public Long add()`: This exposes a service at the URI, that is, `/add`. The `add` method calls the number service using `RestTemplate` and has the logic to sum the numbers that are returned in the response.

Let's configure `application.properties`, as shown in the following snippet:

```
spring.application.name=service-consumer
server.port=8100
number.service.url=http://localhost:8080/random
```

Some important things to note are as follows:

- `spring.application.name=service-consumer`: Configures a name for the Spring Boot application
- `server.port=8100`: Uses `8100` as the port for service consumer
- `number.service.url=http://localhost:8080/random`: Configures the number service URL for use in the `add` service

Testing the Service Consumer microservice

When the service is called at the `http://localhost:8100/add` URL, the following response is returned:

```
2890
```

The following is an extract from the log of Microservice A:

```
c.m.s.c.c.RandomNumberController : Returning [752, 119, 493, 871, 445]
```

The log shows that the random service from Microservice A returned 5 numbers. The `add` service in Service Consumer added them up and returned a result of `2890`.

Congratulations! We now have our example microservices ready. In the following steps, we will add Cloud-native features to these microservices.

Standardizing ports that are used for different microservices

In this chapter, we will create six different microservices applications and components. To keep things simple, we will use specific ports for specific applications.

The following table shows the ports that we would reserve for use by the different applications that are created in this chapter:

Microservice component	Port(s) used
Microservice A	8080 and 8081
Service Consumer microservice	8100
Config Server (Spring Cloud Config)	8888
Eureka server (Name server)	8761
Zuul API gateway server	8765
Zipkin Distributed Tracing Server	9411

We have two of our microservices ready. We are now ready to Cloud-enable our microservices.

Using recommended versions for Spring Boot and Spring Cloud

The world of microservices is still relatively new and evolving continuously. All of the examples in this chapter have been tested with the following versions. If you have problems, we recommend trying these versions:

- Spring Boot: 2.1.1. release
- Spring Cloud: Greenwich.RC2

The following snippet illustrates these details in `pom.xml`:

```
<parent>
  <groupId>org.springframework.boot</groupId>
  <artifactId>spring-boot-starter-parent</artifactId>
  <version>2.1.1.RELEASE</version>
  <relativePath/> <!-- lookup parent from repository -->
</parent>

<dependencyManagement>
  <dependencies>
    <dependency>
      <groupId>org.springframework.cloud</groupId>
      <artifactId>spring-cloud-dependencies</artifactId>
      <version>Greenwich.RC2</version>
      <type>pom</type>
      <scope>import</scope>
```

```
    </dependency>
  </dependencies>
</dependencyManagement>
```

Exploring centralized microservice configuration

Spring Cloud Config provides solutions for externalizing the configuration of a microservice. Let's understand the need to externalize the microservice configuration.

Problem statement

In microservice architectures, we typically have a number of small microservices interacting with each other instead of a set of big monolithic applications. Each microservice is typically deployed in multiple environments—development, testing, load test, staging, and production. In addition, there can be multiple instances of microservices in different environments.

For example, a specific microservice might be handling the heavy load. There might be multiple production instances for that microservice in production.

The configuration of an application typically contains the following:

- **Database configuration**: Details that are needed to connect to the database
- **Message broker configuration**: Any configuration that's needed to connect to AMQP or similar resources
- **External services configuration**: Other services that the microservice needs
- **Microservice configuration**: Typical configuration related to the business logic of the microservice

Each instance of a microservice can have its own configuration—different databases and different external services it consumes, among others. For example, if a microservice is deployed in five environments and there are four instances in each environment, the microservice can have a total of 20 different configurations.

The following diagram shows the typical configurations that are needed for Microservice A. We are looking at two instances in development, three instances in QA, one instance in stage, and four instances in production:

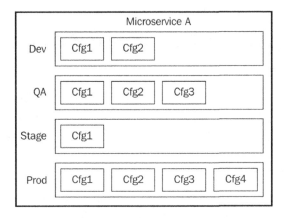

Solution

Maintaining the configurations for different microservices separately would make it difficult for the operations team. The solution, as shown in the following diagram, is to create a centralized **Configuration Server:**

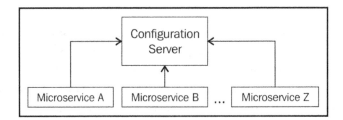

The centralized **Configuration Server** holds all of the configuration that belongs to all of the different microservices. This helps to keep the configuration separate from the application deployable.

The same deployable (EAR or WAR) can be used in different environments. However, all the configuration (things that vary between different environments) will be stored in the centralized configuration server.

An important decision that needs to be made would be to decide whether there are separate instances of centralized configuration servers for different environments. Typically, you would want access to your production configuration to be more restrictive compared to other environments. At a minimum, we recommend a separate centralized configuration server for production. Other environments can share one instance of the configuration server.

Options

The following screenshot shows the options that are provided in **SPRING INIITIALIZR** for Cloud Config Servers:

Cloud Config

☐ Config Client
 spring-cloud-config Client

☐ Config Server
 Central management for configuration via a git or svn backend

☐ Zookeeper Configuration
 Configuration management with Zookeeper and spring-cloud-zookeeper-config

☐ Consul Configuration
 Configuration management with Hashicorp Consul

In this chapter, we will configure a Cloud Config Server using Spring Cloud Config. Zookeeper and Consul are good alternatives, but Spring Cloud Config is the most popular option.

Spring Cloud Config

Spring Cloud Config provides support for centralized microservice configuration. It is a combination of two important components:

- **Spring Cloud Config Server**: Provides support for exposing centralized configuration backed up by a version control repository—**GIT** or subversion
- **Spring Cloud Config Client**: Provides support for applications to connect to Spring Cloud Config Server

The following diagram shows a typical microservice architecture using Spring Cloud Config. The configuration for multiple microservices is stored in a single **GIT** repository:

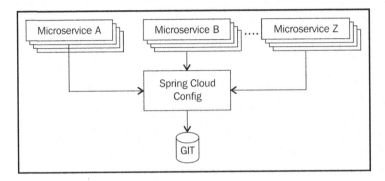

Implementing Spring Cloud Config Server

The following diagram shows the updated implementation of **Microservice A** and **Service Consumer** with Spring Cloud Config. In the following diagram, we will integrate **Microservice A** with **Spring Cloud Config** in order to retrieve its configuration from the local Git repository:

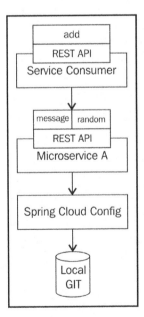

Implementing **Spring Cloud Config** entails the following steps:

1. Set up the **Spring Cloud Config** server.
2. Create a new service in **Microservice A** to return some information from the application configuration. We would use this service to test whether we are able to pick up configuration from the **Spring Cloud Config** server.
3. Set up a local Git repository and connect it to the **Spring Cloud Config** server.
4. Update **Microservice A** to use the configuration from Cloud Config Server by using Spring Cloud Config Client.

Setting up Spring Cloud Config Server

Let's set up Cloud Config Server using **SPRING INITIALIZR** (http://start.spring.io). The following screenshot shows the **GroupId** and **ArtifactId** to choose. Make sure that you select **Config Server** as a dependency:

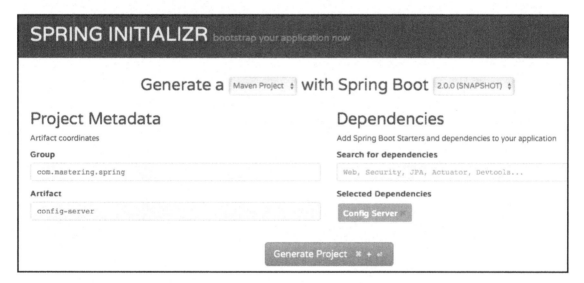

If you want to add Config Server to an existing application, use the dependency that's shown here:

```
<dependency>
  <groupId>org.springframework.cloud</groupId>
  <artifactId>spring-cloud-config-server</artifactId>
</dependency>
```

Once the project has been created, the first step is to add the `EnableConfigServer` annotation. The following snippet shows the annotation added to `ConfigServerApplication`:

```
@EnableConfigServer
@SpringBootApplication
public class ConfigServerApplication {
```

Before we start Config Server up, we will create a test service in Microservice A to return a message from the application configuration.

Creating a service in Microservice A to return a message from the application configuration

Let's create a service to return a simple message from the application configuration, that is, `application.properties`.

We learned about `@ConfigurationProperties` in Chapter 4, *Getting Started with Spring Boot*. Let's create a simple application configuration with one property—`message`:

```
@Component
@ConfigurationProperties("application")
public class ApplicationConfiguration {

    private String message;

    public String getMessage() {
      return message;
    }

    public void setMessage(String message) {
      this.message = message;
    }

}
```

A few important things to note are as follows:

- `@ConfigurationProperties("application")`: This defines a class defining `application.properties`.
- `private String message`: This defines one property—`message`. The value can be configured in `application.properties` with `application.message` as the key.

We can configure a value for the preceding component in `application.properties`, as shown in the following snippet:

```
application.message=Default Message
```

A couple of important things to note are as follows:

- `spring.application.name=microservice-a`: `spring.application.name` is used to give a name to the application.
- `application.message=Default Message`: This configures a default message for `application.message`.

Let's create a controller to read the message and return it, as shown in the following snippet:

```
@RestController
public class MessageController {

    @Autowired
    private ApplicationConfiguration configuration;

    @RequestMapping("/message")
    public Map<String, String> welcome() {

        Map<String, String> map = new HashMap<String, String>();
        map.put("message", configuration.getMessage());
        return map;

    }
}
```

Some important things to note are as follows:

- `@Autowired private ApplicationConfiguration configuration`: This autowires `ApplicationConfiguration` to allow you to read the configured message value.
- `@RequestMapping("/message") public Map<String, String> welcome()`: This exposes a simple service at the URI/`message`.
- `map.put("message", configuration.getMessage())`: The service returns a map with one entry. It has a key message, and the value is picked up from `ApplicationConfiguration`.

When the service is executed at `http://localhost:8080/message`, we get the following response:

```
{"message":"Default Message"}
```

Connecting Spring Cloud Config Server to a local Git repository

Let's get back to the Spring Cloud Config server we created earlier.

We want Cloud Config Server to pick up configuration from the Git repository. To start things off, we need to set up the Git repository.

 You can install Git for your specific operating system from `https://git-scm.com`.

The following commands will help you set up a simple local Git repository.

Switch to a directory of your choice after installing Git. Execute the following commands on a Terminal or Command Prompt:

```
mkdir git-localconfig-repo
cd git-localconfig-repo
git init
```

Now that the Git repository is ready, let's add configuration for Microservice A in the Git repository.

Create a file called `microservice-a.properties` in the `git-localconfig-repo` folder with the content shown here:

```
management.security.enabled=false
application.message=Message From Default Local Git Repository
```

Execute the following commands to add and commit `microservice-a.properties` to a local Git repository:

```
git add -A
git commit -m "default microservice a properties"
```

Now that we have the local Git repository ready with our configuration, we need to connect Config Server to it.

Let's configure `application.properties` in `config-server`, as shown here:

```
spring.application.name=config-server

server.port=8888

spring.cloud.config.server.git.uri-file:///in28Minutes/Books/MasteringSprin
g/git-localconfig-repo

#spring.cloud.config.server.git.uri=file://C:/dev/workspaces/workspace_mast
ring_spring/git-localconfig-repo
```

Some important things to note are as follows:

- `server.port=8888`: This configures the port for Config Server. `8888` is typically the most commonly used port for Config Server.
- `spring.cloud.config.server.git.uri=file:///in28Minutes/Books/Ma steringSpring/git-localconfig-repo`: This configures the URI to the local Git repository. If you want to connect to a remote Git repository, you can configure the URI of the Git repository here.
- `spring.cloud.config.server.git.uri=file://C:/dev/workspaces/wor kspace_mastring_spring/git-localconfig-repo`: This shows the corresponding configuration for Windows.

Start the server. When you hit the `http://localhost:8888/microservice-a/default` URL, you will see the following response:

```
{
  "name":"microservice-a",
  "profiles":[
    "default"
    ],
  "label":null,
  "version":null,
  "state":null,
  "propertySources":[
    {
      "name":"file:///in28Minutes/Books/MasteringSpring
      /git-localconfig-repo/microservice-a.properties",
      "source":{
        "application.message":"Message From Default
        Local Git Repository"
      }
    }]
}
```

Some important things to understand are as follows:

- `http://localhost:8888/microservice-a/default`: The URI format is `/{application-name}/{profile}[/{label}]`. Here, `application-name` is `microservice-a` and the profile is `default`.
- The service returns the configuration from `microservice-a.properties` since we are using the default profile. You can see it in the response in the `propertySources>name` field.
- `"source":{"application.message":"Message From Default Local Git Repository"}`: The content of the response is the content of the property file.

Creating a development environment-specific configuration for Microservice A

Let's create a specific configuration for `Microservice A` for the `dev` environment.

Create a new file in `git-localconfig-repo` with the name `microservice-a-dev.properties` with the content shown here:

```
application.message=Message From Dev Git Repository
```

Execute the following commands to `add` and `commit microservice-a-dev.properties` to the local Git repository:

```
git add -A
git commit -m "dev microservice a properties"
```

When you hit the `http://localhost:8888/microservice-a/dev` URL, you will see the following response:

```
{
    "name":"microservice-a","profiles":["dev"],
    "label":null,"version":null,"state":null,
    "propertySources":[
    {
      "name":"file:///in28Minutes/Books/MasteringSpring
       /git-localconfig-repo/microservice-a-dev.properties",
      "source":{  "application.message":"Message From Dev Git Repository"
    }
    },
    {
    "name":"file:///in28Minutes/Books/MasteringSpring
      /git-localconfig-repo/microservice-a.properties",
    "source":{
```

```
        "application.message":"Message From Default
        Local Git Repository"
    }}]
}
```

The response contains the `dev` configuration from `microservice-a-dev.properties`. The configuration from the default property file (`microservice-a.properties`) is also returned.

Properties configured in `microservice-a-dev.properties` (environment-specific properties) have higher priority than the defaults that are configured in `microservice-a.properties`.

Similar to `dev`, a separate configuration for `Microservice A` can be created for different environments. If there is a need for multiple instances in a single environment, a tag can be used to differentiate them. A URL of the `http://localhost:8888/microservice-a/dev/{tag}` format can be used to retrieve configuration based on the specific tag.

Application configuration for `Microservice A` on Cloud Config Server is ready. Let's connect `Microservice A` to Cloud Config Server.

Enhancing Microservice A to make it a Spring Cloud Config Client

Microservice A needs to talk to Spring Cloud Config Server to retrieve application configuration. How do we do this?

For starters, let's configure a dependency on Spring Cloud Config Client for `Microservice A`. The dependency is shown here. Add the following code to the `pom.xml` file of `Microservice A`:

```
<dependency>
  <groupId>org.springframework.cloud</groupId>
  <artifactId>spring-cloud-starter-config</artifactId>
</dependency>
```

Dependencies for Spring Cloud are managed differently from Spring Boot. We will use dependency management to manage dependencies. The following snippet will ensure that the correct versions of all Spring Cloud dependencies are used:

```
<dependencyManagement>
    <dependencies>
        <dependency>
            <groupId>org.springframework.cloud</groupId>
            <artifactId>spring-cloud-dependencies</artifactId>
```

```
            <version>Greenwich.RELEASE</version>
            <type>pom</type>
            <scope>import</scope>
        </dependency>
    </dependencies>
</dependencyManagement>
```

Rename `application.properties` in `Microservice A` to `bootstrap.properties`.

Configure it as follows:

```
spring.application.name=microservice-a
spring.cloud.config.uri=http://localhost:8888
```

Since we want `Microservice A` to connect to `Config Server`, we provide the URI of `Config Server` using `spring.cloud.config.uri`. Cloud Config Server is used to retrieve the configuration for Microservice A. Hence, the configuration is provided in `bootstrap.properties`.

 Spring Cloud Context: Spring Cloud introduces a few important concepts for the Spring application that's deployed in the Cloud. The Bootstrap Application Context is an important concept. It is the parent context for the microservice application. It is responsible for loading an external configuration (for example, from Spring Cloud Config Server) and decrypting configuration files (external and local). The Bootstrap context is configured using `bootstrap.yml` or `bootstrap.properties`. We had to change the name of `application.properties` to `bootstrap.properties` in `Microservice A` earlier because we want `Microservice A` to use the Config Server for bootstrapping.

An extract from the log when `Microservice A` is restarted is shown here:

```
Fetching config from server at: http://localhost:8888
Located environment: name=microservice-a, profiles=[default],
label=null, version=null, state=null
Located property source: CompositePropertySource
[name='configService', propertySources=[MapPropertySource
[name='file:///in28Minutes/Books/MasteringSpring/git-localconfig-
repo/microservice-a.properties']]]
```

The `Microservice A` service is using the configuration from `Spring Config Server` at `http://localhost:8888`.

The following is the response when `Message Service`
at `http://localhost:8080/message` is invoked:

```
{"message":"Message From Default Local Git Repository"}
```

The message is picked up from the `localconfig-repo/microservice-a.properties`
file.

You can set the active profile to `dev` to pick up the `dev` configuration:

```
spring.profiles.active=dev
```

The configuration for the service consumer microservice can also be stored in `local-config-repo` and exposed using Spring Config Server.

Getting an overview of event-driven approaches

In `Chapter 11`, *Getting Started with Microservices*, we talked about the shift to event-driven architectures with microservices. In general, asynchronous communication patterns are more scalable compared to synchronous communication.

There are two popular approaches for asynchronous communication:

- Spring JMS using the JMS API
- **Advanced Message Queuing Protocol (AMQP)**

Understanding Spring JMS using the JMS API

In the Java world, one of the most popular APIs for asynchronous communication is **JMS** (short for **Java Messaging Service**).

The JMS API defines the API for Java applications to communicate in a loosely coupled asynchronous approach by sending and receiving messages over message brokers. ActiveMQ is one of the most popular JMS-compliant message brokers.

Spring JMS simplifies JMS communication in Spring applications.

The following example shows a simple class sending a JMS message using Spring JMS:

```
public class SendJMSMessage {
    @Autowired
    private JmsTemplate jmsTemplate;

    @Autowired
    private Queue queue;
    public void simpleSend() {
        this.jmsTemplate.send(queue, new MessageCreator() {
            public Message createMessage(Session session) throws
JMSException {
                return session.createTextMessage("Send Message");
            }
        });
    }
}
```

JmsTemplate is a helper class that provides methods that can send and receive messages over message brokers. Queue is the representation for the message broker.

AMQP

AMQP (**Advanced Message Queueing Protocol**) is one of the most popular protocols for asynchronous communication. RabbitMQ, OpenAMQ, and StormMQ are some of the popular implementations.

AMQP is reliable and interoperable.

In the next section, we'll look at using RabbitMQ as the message broker and use the AMQP protocol to allow applications to be notified about configuration changes.

Getting started with Spring Cloud Bus

Spring Cloud Bus makes it seamless to connect microservices to lightweight message brokers such as Kafka and RabbitMQ.

The need for Spring Cloud Bus

Consider an example of making a configuration change in a microservice. Let's assume that there are five instances of `Microservice A` running in production. We need to make an emergency configuration change. For example, let's make a change in `localconfig-repo/microservice-a.properties`:

```
application.message=Message From Default Local Git Repository Changed
```

For `Microservice A` to pick up this configuration change, we need to invoke a `POST` request on `http://localhost:8080/actuator/refresh`. The following command can be executed at the Command Prompt to send a `POST` request:

```
curl -X POST http://localhost:8080/actuator/refresh
```

You will see the configuration change reflected at `http://localhost:8080/message`. The following is the response from the service:

```
{"message":"Message From Default Local Git Repository Changed"}
```

We have five instances of `Microservice A` running. The change in configuration is reflected only for the instance of Microservice A where the URL is executed. The other four instances will not receive the configuration change until the refresh request is executed on them.

If there are a number of instances of a microservice, then executing the refresh URL for each instance becomes cumbersome since you would need to do this for every configuration change.

Propagating configuration changes using Spring Cloud Bus

The solution is to use Spring Cloud Bus to propagate the configuration change to multiple instances over a message broker such as RabbitMQ.

The following diagram shows how different instances of a microservice (actually, they can be completely different microservices as well) are connected to a message broker using Spring Cloud Bus:

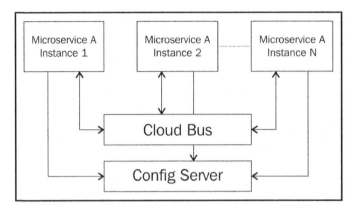

Each microservice instance will register with the Spring Cloud Bus at application startup.

When the refresh is called on one of the microservice instances, Spring Cloud Bus will propagate a change event to all of the microservice instances. The microservice instances will request the updated configuration from the configuration server upon receiving the change event.

Implementing Spring Cloud Bus

We will use RabbitMQ as the message broker. Ensure that you have installed and started up RabbitMQ before proceeding further.

 Installation instructions for RabbitMQ are provided at `https://www.rabbitmq.com/download.html`.

The next step is to add connectivity to Spring Cloud Bus for `Microservice A`. Let's add the following dependency in the `pom.xml` file of `Microservice A`:

```
<dependency>
<groupId>org.springframework.amqp</groupId>
<artifactId>spring-rabbit</artifactId>
</dependency>
```

We can run `Microservice A` on different ports by providing the port as one of the startup VM arguments. The following screenshot shows how you can configure the server port as the VM argument in Eclipse. The value that's being configured is `-Dserver.port=8081`:

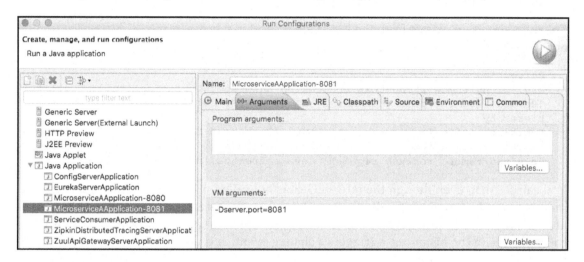

We will run `Microservice A` on ports `8080` (default) and `8081`. The following is an extract from the log when `Microservice A` is restarted:

```
o.s.integration.channel.DirectChannel : Channel 'microservice-
a.springCloudBusInput' has 1 subscriber(s).
Bean with name 'rabbitConnectionFactory' has been autodetected for JMX
exposure
Bean with name 'refreshBusEndpoint' has been autodetected for JMX exposure
Created new connection: SimpleConnection@6d12ea7c
[delegate=amqp://guest@127.0.0.1:5672/, localPort= 61741]
Channel 'microservice-a.springCloudBusOutput' has 1 subscriber(s).
 declaring queue for inbound: springCloudBus.anonymous.HK-
dFv8oRwGrhD4BvuhkFQ, bound to: springCloudBus
Adding {message-handler:inbound.springCloudBus.default} as a subscriber to
the 'bridge.springCloudBus' channel
```

All instances of `Microservice A` are registered with `Spring Cloud Bus` and listen to events on the Cloud Bus. The default configuration of RabbitMQ Connection is a result of the magic of autoconfiguration.

Let's update `microservice-a.properties` with a new message now:

```
    application.message=Message From Default Local Git Repository Changed
Again
```

Commit the file and fire a request to refresh the configuration on one of the instances, let's say, port `8080`, using the `http://localhost:8080/actuator/bus-refresh` URL:

```
curl -X POST http://localhost:8080/actuator/bus-refresh
```

The following is an extract from the log of the second instance of `Microservice A` running on port `8081`:

```
Refreshing
org.springframework.context.annotation.AnnotationConfigApplicationContext@5
10cb933: startup date [Mon Mar 27 21:39:37 IST 2017]; root of context
hierarchy
Fetching config from server at: http://localhost:8888
Started application in 1.333 seconds (JVM running for 762.806)
Received remote refresh request. Keys refreshed [application.message]
```

You can see that, even though the refresh URL is not called on port `8081`, the updated message is picked up from Config Server. This is because all instances of `Microservice A` are listening on the Spring Cloud Bus for change events. As soon as the refresh URL is called on one of the instances, it triggers a change event, and all the other instances pick up the changed configuration.

You will see the configuration change reflected in both instances of `Microservice A` at `http://localhost:8080/message` and `http://localhost:8081/message`. The following is the response from the service:

```
{"message":"Message From Default Local
   Git Repository Changed Again"}
```

Declarative REST client – Feign

Feign helps us to create REST clients for RESTful services with minimum configuration and code. All you need to define is a simple interface and use proper annotations.

`RestTemplate` is typically used to make REST service calls. Feign helps us write REST clients without the need for `RestTemplate` and the logic around it.

Feign integrates well with Ribbon (client-side load balancing) and Eureka (name server). We will look at this integration later in this chapter.

To use Feign, let's add the Feign starter to the `pom.xml` file of the Service Consumer microservice:

```
<dependency>
  <groupId>org.springframework.cloud</groupId>
  <artifactId>spring-cloud-starter-openfeign</artifactId>
</dependency>
```

We need to add `dependencyManagement` for Spring Cloud to the `pom.xml` file as this is the first Cloud dependency that the Service Consumer microservice will be using:

```
<dependencyManagement>
  <dependencies>
    <dependency>
      <groupId>org.springframework.cloud</groupId>
      <artifactId>spring-cloud-dependencies</artifactId>
      <version>Greenwich.RELEASE</version>
      <type>pom</type>
      <scope>import</scope>
    </dependency>
  </dependencies>
</dependencyManagement>
```

The next step is to add the annotation in order to enable scanning for Feign clients to `ServiceConsumerApplication`.

The following snippet shows the usage of the `@EnableFeignClients` annotation:

```
@EnableFeignClients("com.mastering.spring.consumer")
public class ServiceConsumerApplication {
```

We need to define a simple interface to create a Feign client for `random service`. The following snippet shows the details:

```
@FeignClient(name ="microservice-a", url="localhost:8080")
public interface RandomServiceProxy {
  @GetMapping(value = "/random")
  List<Integer> getRandomNumbers();
}
```

Some important things to note are as follows:

- `@FeignClient(name ="microservice-a", url="localhost:8080")`: The `FeignClient` annotation is used to declare that a REST client with the given interface needs to be created. We are hardcoding the URL of `Microservice A` for now. Later, we will look at how we can connect this to a name server and eliminate the need for hardcoding.

- `@RequestMapping(value = "/random", method = RequestMethod.GET)`: This specific GET service method is exposed at the URI, that is, `/random`.
- `public List<Integer> getRandomNumbers()`: This defines the interface of the service method.

Let's update `NumberAdderController` to use `RandomServiceProxy` in order to call the service. The following snippet shows the important details:

```
@RestController
public class NumberAdderController {

    @Autowired
    private RandomServiceProxy randomServiceProxy;

    @RequestMapping("/add")
    public Long add() {

        long sum = 0;
        List<Integer> numbers = randomServiceProxy.getRandomNumbers();

        for (int number : numbers) {
            sum += number;
        }

        return sum;
    }
}
```

A couple of important things to note are as follows:

- `@Autowired private RandomServiceProxy randomServiceProxy`: `RandomServiceProxy` is autowired in.
- `List<Integer> numbers = randomServiceProxy.getRandomNumbers()`: Look at how simple it is to use `FeignClient`. There's no need to play around with `RestTemplate` anymore.

When we invoke the add service in the Service Consumer microservice at `http://localhost:8100/add`, we will get the following response:

```
2103
```

GZIP compression can be enabled on Feign requests by configuring it, as shown in the following snippet:

```
feign.compression.request.enabled=true
feign.compression.response.enabled=true
```

Implementing load balancing for microservices

Microservices are the most important building blocks of Cloud-native architectures. Microservice instances are scaled up and down based on the load of a specific microservice. How do we ensure that the load is equally distributed among the different instances of microservices? That's where the magic of load balancing comes in. Load balancing is important in order to ensure that the load is equally distributed among the different instances of microservices.

Ribbon for client-side load balancing

As shown in the following diagram, Spring Cloud Netflix Ribbon provides client-side load balancing by using round-robin execution among the different instances of a microservice:

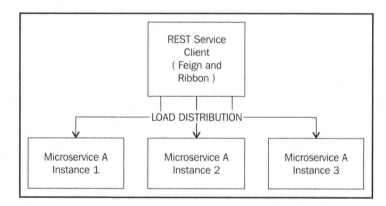

Implementing Ribbon in the Service Consumer microservice

We will add Ribbon to the Service Consumer microservice. This microservice will distribute the load among two instances of Microservice A.

Let's start by adding the Ribbon dependency to the `pom.xml` file of the Service Consumer microservice:

```
<dependency>
  <groupId>org.springframework.cloud</groupId>
  <artifactId>spring-cloud-starter-netflix-ribbon</artifactId>
</dependency>
```

Next, we can configure the URLs for the different instances of `Microservice A`. Add the following configuration to `application.properties` in the Service Consumer microservice:

```
microservice-a.ribbon.listOfServers=
http://localhost:8080,http://localhost:8081
```

We will then specify the `@RibbonClient` annotation on the service proxy—`microservice-a` in this example. The `@RibbonClient` annotation is used to specify a declarative configuration for a Ribbon client:

```
@FeignClient(name ="microservice-a")
@RibbonClient(name="microservice-a")
public interface RandomServiceProxy {
```

When you restart the Service Consumer microservice and hit the add service at `http://localhost:8100/add`, you will get the following response:

```
2705
```

This request is handled by an instance of `Microservice A` running on port 8080. An extract from the log is shown here:

```
c.m.s.c.c.RandomNumberController : Returning [487,
  441, 407, 563, 807]
```

When we hit the add service again at the same URL, `http://localhost:8100/add`, we get the following response:

```
3423
```

However, this time, the request is handled by an instance of `Microservice A` running on port 8081. An extract from the log is shown here:

```
c.m.s.c.c.RandomNumberController : Returning [661,
  520, 256, 988, 998]
```

We have now successfully distributed the load among the different instances of `Microservice A`. While this can be improved further, this is a good start.

While round robin (`RoundRobinRule`) is the default algorithm that's used by Ribbon, there are other options available:

- `AvailabilityFilteringRule` will skip servers that are down and that have a number of concurrent connections.
- `WeightedResponseTimeRule` will pick the server based on the response times. If a server takes a long time to respond, it will get fewer requests.

The algorithm to be used can be specified in the application configuration:

```
microservice-a.ribbon.NFLoadBalancerRuleClassName =
com.netflix.loadbalancer.WeightedResponseTimeRule
```

`microservice-a` is the name of the service we specified in the `@RibbonClient(name="microservice-a")` annotation.

The following diagram shows the architecture for the components we have set up already:

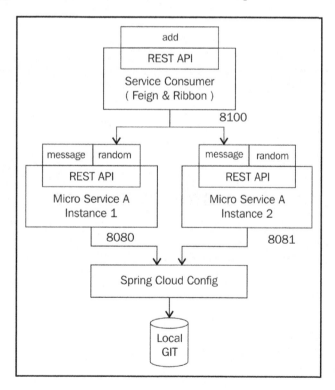

Understanding the need for a naming server

Microservice architectures involve a number of smaller microservices interacting with each other. Adding to this, there can be multiple instances of each microservice. Maintaining the external service connections and configurations manually would be difficult as new instances of microservices are dynamically created and destroyed. Name servers provide features of service registration and service discovery. Name servers allow microservices to register themselves and discover the URLs to other microservices they want to interact with.

Limitations of hardcoding microservice URLs

In the previous example, we added the following configuration to `application.properties` in the Service Consumer microservice:

```
random-proxy.ribbon.listOfServers=
    http://localhost:8080,http://localhost:8081
```

This configuration represents all the instances of Microservice A. Take a look at the following situations:

- A new instance of `Microservice A` is created.
- An existing instance of `Microservice A` is no longer available.
- `Microservice A` is moved to a different server.

In all of these instances, the configuration needs to be updated and the microservices need to be refreshed in order to pick up the changes.

The working of a naming server

The **Name Server** is an ideal solution for the preceding situation. The following diagram shows how name servers work:

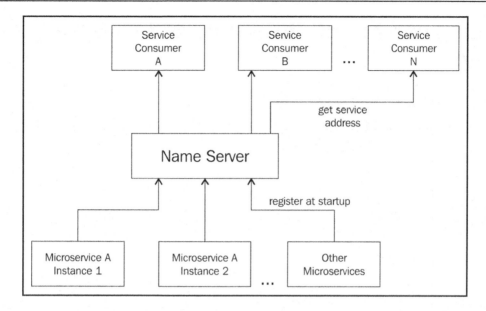

There are two important steps in interacting with naming servers:

1. **Registration**: All the microservices (different microservices and each of their instances) will register themselves with the name server as each microservice starts up.

2. **Find location(s) of other microservices**: When a service consumer wants to get the location of a specific microservice, it requests the name server. Whenever a service consumer looks up the name server with a microservice ID, it will get the list of the instances of that specific microservice.

 A unique microservice ID is assigned to each microservice. This is used as a key in the register request and the lookup request.

Naming server options supported by Spring Cloud

The following screenshot shows the different options that are available for service discovery in **SPRING INITIALIZR** (`http://start.spring.io`):

We are going to use Eureka as the name server for service discovery in our example. Zookeeper and Consul are also popular options for service discovery.

Implementing the Eureka naming service

The implementation of Eureka for our example involves the following steps:

1. Setting up Eureka Server.
2. Updating the `Microservice A` instances to register with Eureka Server.
3. Updating the Service Consumer microservice to use the `Microservice A` instances registered with Eureka Server.

Setting up Eureka Server

We will use **SPRING INITIALIZR** (`http://start.spring.io`) to set up a new project for Eureka Server. The following screenshot shows the **GroupId**, **ArtifactId**, and **Dependencies** to be selected:

The next step is to add the `EnableEurekaServer` annotation to the `SpringBootApplication` class. The following snippet shows the details:

```
@SpringBootApplication
@EnableEurekaServer
public class EurekaServerApplication {
```

The following snippet shows the configuration in `application.properties`:

```
server.port = 8761
eureka.client.registerWithEureka=false
eureka.client.fetchRegistry=false
```

We are using port 8761 for `Eureka Naming Server`. Launch `EurekaServerApplication`.

A screenshot of the Eureka dashboard at `http://localhost:8761` is shown here:

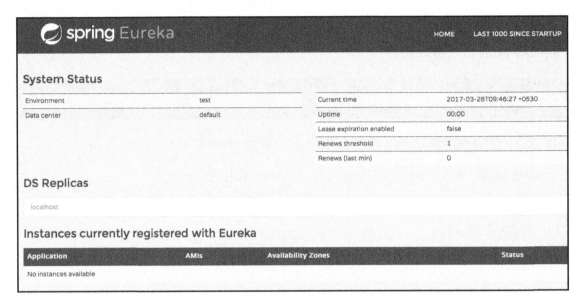

As of now, there are no applications registered with Eureka. In the next step, we'll register `Microservice A` and other services with Eureka.

Registering microservices with Eureka

To register any microservice with the Eureka name server, we need to add the dependency on a Eureka starter project. The following dependency needs to be added to the `pom.xml` file of `Microservice A`:

```
<dependency>
  <groupId>org.springframework.cloud</groupId>
  <artifactId>spring-cloud-starter-netflix-eureka-client</artifactId>
</dependency>
```

The next step is to add `EnableDiscoveryClient` to the `SpringBootApplication` classes. An example of `MicroserviceAApplication` is shown here:

```
@SpringBootApplication
@EnableDiscoveryClient
public class MicroserviceAApplication {
```

Spring Cloud Commons hosts the common classes that are used in different Spring Cloud implementations. A good example is an `@EnableDiscoveryClient` annotation. Different implementations are provided by Spring Cloud Netflix Eureka, Spring Cloud Consul Discovery, and Spring Cloud Zookeeper Discovery.

We will configure the URL of the naming server in the application configuration. For Microservice A, the application configuration is in the local Git repository file, `git-localconfig-repo/microservice-a.properties`:

```
eureka.client.serviceUrl.defaultZone=
  http://localhost:8761/eureka
```

When both instances of `Microservice A` are restarted, you will see these messages in the log of Eureka Server:

```
Registered instance MICROSERVICE-A/192.168.1.5:microservice-a
  with status UP (replication=false)
Registered instance MICROSERVICE-A/192.168.1.5:microservice-a:
  8081 with status UP (replication=false)
```

A screenshot of the Eureka dashboard at `http://localhost:8761` is as follows:

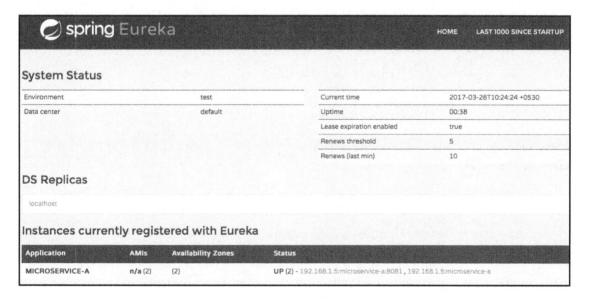

Two instances of `Microservice A` are now registered with Eureka Server. Similar updates can be done on Config Server in order to connect it to Eureka Server.

In the next step, we want to connect the Service Consumer microservice to pick up URLs of instances of `Microservice A` from Eureka Server.

Connecting the Service Consumer microservice with Eureka

The Eureka starter project needs to be added as a dependency in the `pom.xml` file of the Service Consumer microservice:

```
<dependency>
  <groupId>org.springframework.cloud</groupId>
  <artifactId>spring-cloud-starter-netflix-eureka-client</artifactId>
</dependency>
```

Currently, the URLs of the different instances of `Microservice A` are hardcoded in the Service Consumer microservice, as shown here, in `application.properties`:

```
microservice-a.ribbon.listOfServers=
  http://localhost:8080,http://localhost:8081
```

However, we don't want to hardcode `Microservice A` URLs. Instead, we want the Service Consumer microservice to get the URLs from Eureka Server. We do that by configuring the URL of Eureka Server in `application.properties` of the Service Consumer microservice. We will comment out the hardcoding of the `Microservice A` URLs:

```
#microservice-a.ribbon.listOfServers=
  http://localhost:8080,http://localhost:8081
eureka.client.serviceUrl.defaultZone=
  http://localhost:8761/eureka
```

Next, we will add `EnableDiscoveryClient` on the `ServiceConsumerApplication` class, as shown here:

```
@SpringBootApplication
@EnableFeignClients("com.mastering.spring.consumer")
@EnableDiscoveryClient
public class ServiceConsumerApplication {
```

Once the Service Consumer microservice is restarted, you will see that it will register itself with Eureka Server. The following is an extract from the log of Eureka Server:

```
Registered instance SERVICE-CONSUMER/192.168.1.5:
  service-consumer:8100 with status UP (replication=false)
```

In `RandomServiceProxy`, we have already configured a name for `microservice-a` on `FeignClient`, as shown here:

```
@FeignClient(name ="microservice-a")
@RibbonClient(name="microservice-a")
public interface RandomServiceProxy {
```

The Service Consumer microservice will use this ID (Microservice A) to query Eureka Server for instances. Once it gets the URLs from Eureka Service, it will invoke the service instance selected by Ribbon.

When the `add` service is invoked at `http://localhost:8100/add`, it returns an appropriate response.

Here's a quick review of the different steps that are involved:

1. As each instance of Microservice A starts up, it registers with the Eureka name server.
2. The Service Consumer microservice requests the Eureka name server for instances of Microservice A.
3. The Service Consumer microservice uses the Ribbon client-side load balancer to decide the specific instance of Microservice A to call.
4. The Service Consumer microservice calls a specific instance of Microservice A.

The biggest advantage of Eureka Service is that the Service Consumer microservice is now decoupled from Microservice A. Whenever new instances of Microservice A come up or an existing instance goes down, the Service Consumer microservice doesn't need to be reconfigured.

Understanding API gateways

Microservices architecture involves building a number of microservices. There are common features you will want to implement in each of these microservices. These common features are called cross-cutting concerns.

Let's look at some of the important cross-cutting concerns:

- **Authentication, authorization, and security**: How do we ensure that the microservice consumers are who they claim to be? How do we ensure that the consumers have the right access to microservices?

- **Rate limits:** There might be different kinds of API plans for consumers and different limits (the number of microservice invocations) for each plan. How do we enforce the limits on a specific consumer?
- **Dynamic routing**: Specific situations (for example, a microservice is down) might need dynamic routing.
- **Service aggregation**: The UI needs for mobile are different from the ones for desktop. Some microservice architectures have service aggregators tailored for a specific device.
- **Fault tolerance**: How do we ensure that failure in one microservice doesn't cause the entire system to crash?

When microservices talk directly with each other, these concerns have to be addressed by individual microservices. This kind of architecture may be difficult to maintain because each microservice might handle these concerns differently.

One of the most common solutions is to use an API gateway. All service calls to and between microservices should go through an API gateway. An API gateway typically provides the following features for microservices:

- Authentication and security
- Rate limiting
- Insights and monitoring
- Dynamic routing and static response handling
- Load shedding
- Aggregation of responses from multiple services

Implementing API gateway with Zuul

Zuul is part of the Spring Cloud Netflix project. It is an API gateway service that provides the capabilities of dynamic routing, monitoring, filtering, security, and more.

Implementing Zuul as an API gateway involves the following steps:

1. Setting up a new Zuul API gateway server.
2. Configuring Service Consumer to use Zuul API gateway.

Setting up a new Zuul API gateway server

We will use **SPRING INITIALIZR** (`http://start.spring.io`) to set up a new project for the Zuul API gateway. The following screenshot shows the **GroupId**, **ArtifactId**, and **Dependencies** to be selected:

The next step is to enable the Zuul proxy on the Spring Boot application. This is done by adding the `@EnableZuulProxy` annotation on the `ZuulApiGatewayServerApplication` class. The following snippet shows the details:

```
@EnableZuulProxy
@EnableDiscoveryClient
@SpringBootApplication
public class ZuulApiGatewayServerApplication {
```

We will run the Zuul proxy on port `8765`. The following snippet shows the configuration that's needed in `application.properties`:

```
spring.application.name=zuul-api-gateway
server.port=8765
eureka.client.serviceUrl.defaultZone=http://localhost:8761/eureka
```

We are configuring the port for the Zuul proxy and connecting it to the Eureka name server as well.

Configuring Zuul custom filters for logging every request

Zuul provides options to create custom filters so that you can implement typical API gateway functionality, such as authentication, security, and tracing. In this example, we will create a simple logging filter to log every request. The following snippet shows the details:

```
@Component
public class SimpleLoggingFilter extends ZuulFilter {

    @Override
    public String filterType() {
      return "pre";
    }

    @Override
    public int filterOrder() {
      return 1;
    }

    @Override
    public boolean shouldFilter() {
      return true;
    }
    // run method below

}
```

A few important things to note are as follows:

- `SimpleLoggingFilter extends ZuulFilter`: `ZuulFilter` is the base abstract class to create filters for Zuul. Any filter should implement the four methods listed here.
- `public String filterType()`: Possible return values are `"pre"` for prerouting filtering, `"route"` for routing to an origin, `"post"` for postrouting filters, and `"error"` for error handling. In this example, we want to filter before the request is executed. We return a value, that is, `"pre"`.
- `public int filterOrder()`: This defines the precedence for a filter.
- `public boolean shouldFilter()`: If the filter should only be executed in certain conditions, the logic can be implemented here. If you want the filter to always be executed, return `true`.

We can implement the logic for the filter in the `public Object run()` method. In our example, we are logging the request method and the URL of the request. The following snippet shows the implementation:

```
@Override
public Object run() {
   RequestContext context = RequestContext.getCurrentContext();
   HttpServletRequest httpRequest = context.getRequest();

   log.info(String.format("Request Method : %s n URL: %s",
                                   httpRequest.getMethod(),
httpRequest.getRequestURL().toString()));
   return null;
}
```

In the preceding method, we are logging some of the important request details.

When we start up the Zuul server by launching `ZuulApiGatewayServerApplication` as a Java application, you will see the following log in `Eureka Name Server`:

```
Registered instance ZUUL-API-GATEWAY/192.168.1.5:zuul-api-
   gateway:8765 with status UP (replication=false)
```

This shows that the Zuul API gateway is up and running. `Zuul API gateway` is also registered with `Eureka Server`. This allows microservice consumers to talk to the name server to get details about `Zuul API gateway`.

The following screenshot shows the Eureka dashboard at `http://localhost:8761`. You can see that instances of `Microservice A`, `service consumer`, and the `Zuul API Gateway` are now registered with `Eureka Server`:

Instances currently registered with Eureka

Application	AMIs	Availability Zones	Status
MICROSERVICE-A	n/a (1)	(1)	UP (1) - 192.168.1.5:microservice-a
SERVICE-CONSUMER	n/a (1)	(1)	UP (1) - 192.168.1.5:service-consumer:8100
ZUUL-API-GATEWAY	n/a (1)	(1)	UP (1) - 192.168.1.5:zuul-api-gateway:8765

The following is an extract from the `Zuul API gateway` log:

```
Mapped URL path [/microservice-a/**] onto handler of type [
class org.springframework.cloud.netflix.zuul.web.ZuulController]
Mapped URL path [/service-consumer/**] onto handler of type [
class org.springframework.cloud.netflix.zuul.web.ZuulController]
```

By default, all the services in `Microservice A` and the Service Consumer microservice are enabled for reverse proxying by Zuul.

Invoking microservices through Zuul

Let's invoke `random service` through the service proxy. The direct URL to a random microservice is `http://localhost:8080/random`. This is exposed by Microservice A, whose application name is `microservice-a`.

The URL structure to call a service through `Zuul API gateway` is `http://localhost:{port}/{microservice-application-name}/{service-uri}`. So, the `Zuul API gateway` URL for `random service` is `http://localhost:8765/microservice-a/random`. When you invoke `random service` through the API gateway, you get a response, as shown here. The response is similar to what you would typically get when directly calling the random service:

```
[73,671,339,354,211]
```

The following is an extract from the `Zuul Api gateway` log. You can see that the `SimpleLoggingFilter` that we created in `Zuul API gateway` is executed for the request:

```
c.m.s.z.filters.pre.SimpleLoggingFilter : Request Method : GET
URL: http://localhost:8765/microservice-a/random
```

The `add` service is exposed by Service Consumer, whose application name is `service-consumer` and the service URI is `/add`. So, the URL to execute the `add` service through the API gateway is `http://localhost:8765/service-consumer/add`. The response from the service is shown here. The response is similar to what you would typically get when directly calling the `add` service:

```
2488
```

The following is an extract from the `Zuul API gateway` log. You can see that the initial add service call is going through the API gateway:

```
2017-03-28 14:05:17.514 INFO 83147 --- [nio-8765-exec-1]
c.m.s.z.filters.pre.SimpleLoggingFilter : Request Method : GET
URL: http://localhost:8765/service-consumer/add
```

The `add` service calls `random service` on `Microservice A`. While the initial call to `add` service goes through the API gateway, the call from `add` service (the Service Consumer microservice) to `random service` (Microservice A) is not routed through the API gateway. In an ideal world, we would want all of the communication to take place through the API gateway.

In the next step, let's make the requests from the Service Consumer microservice go through the API gateway as well.

Configuring Service Consumer to use the Zuul API gateway

The following code shows the existing configuration of `RandomServiceProxy`, which is used to call `random service` on `Microservice A`. The name attribute in the `@FeignClient` annotation is configured to use the application name of Microservice A. The request mapping uses the `/random` URI:

```
@FeignClient(name ="microservice-a")
@RibbonClient(name="microservice-a")
public interface RandomServiceProxy {
@RequestMapping(value = "/random", method = RequestMethod.GET)
  public List<Integer> getRandomNumbers();
}
```

Now, we want the call to go through the API gateway. We need to use the application name of the API gateway and the new URI of `random service` in the request mapping. The following snippet shows the updated `RandomServiceProxy` class:

```
@FeignClient(name="zuul-api-gateway")
//@FeignClient(name ="microservice-a")
@RibbonClient(name="microservice-a")
public interface RandomServiceProxy {
  @GetMapping(value = "/microservice-a/random")
  //@RequestMapping(value = "/random", method = RequestMethod.GET)
  public List<Integer> getRandomNumbers();
}
```

When we invoke the add service at `http://localhost:8765/service-consumer/add`, we will see the typical response:

```
2254
```

However, now, we will see more things happen on the Zuul API gateway. The following is an extract from the `Zuul API gateway` log. You can see that the initial add service call on Service Consumer, as well as the `random service` call on `Microservice A`, are now being routed through the API gateway:

```
2017-03-28 14:10:16.093 INFO 83147 --- [nio-8765-exec-4]
c.m.s.z.filters.pre.SimpleLoggingFilter : Request Method : GET
URL: http://localhost:8765/service-consumer/add
2017-03-28 14:10:16.685 INFO 83147 --- [nio-8765-exec-5]
c.m.s.z.filters.pre.SimpleLoggingFilter : Request Method : GET
URL: http://192.168.1.5:8765/microservice-a/random
```

In this section, we saw a basic implementation of a simple logging filter on the Zuul API gateway. A similar approach can be used to implement filters for other cross-cutting concerns.

Understanding distributed tracing

In typical microservice architectures, there are a number of components involved. A typical call may involve more than four or five components. Think about these questions:

- How can we debug issues?
- How can we find out the root cause of a specific problem?

A typical solution is centralized logging with a dashboard.

We have all of the microservice logs consolidated in one place, and we are offering a dashboard on top of it.

Implementing Spring Cloud Sleuth and Zipkin

Spring Cloud Sleuth provides features to uniquely trace a service call across different microservice components. **Zipkin** is a distributed tracing system that's used to gather data that's needed to troubleshoot latency issues in microservices. We will be implementing a combination of Spring Cloud Sleuth and Zipkin to implement distributed tracing.

The following are the steps involved:

1. Integrate Microservice A, API gateway, and Service Consumer with Spring Cloud Sleuth.
2. Set up the Zipkin distributed tracing server.
3. Integrate Microservice A, API gateway, and Service Consumer with Zipkin.

Integrating microservice components with Spring Cloud Sleuth

When we call the add service on Service Consumer, it will invoke Microservice A through the API gateway. To be able to track the service call across different components, we would need something unique assigned to the request flow across components.

Spring Cloud Sleuth provides options to track a service call across different components using a concept called **span**. Each span has a unique 64-bit ID. The unique ID can be used to trace the call across components.

The following snippet shows the dependency for `spring-cloud-starter-sleuth`:

```
<dependency>
  <groupId>org.springframework.cloud</groupId>
  <artifactId>spring-cloud-starter-sleuth</artifactId>
</dependency>
```

We need to add the preceding dependency on Spring Cloud Sleuth to the following three projects:

- Microservice A
- Service Consumer
- Zuul API gateway server

We will start by tracing all of the service requests across microservices. To be able to trace all of the requests, we will need to configure a `Sampler` bean, as shown in the following snippet:

```
@Bean
public Sampler defaultSampler() {
  return Sampler.ALWAYS_SAMPLE;
}
```

The `Sampler` bean needs to be configured in the following microservice application classes:

- `MicroserviceAApplication`
- `ServiceConsumerApplication`
- `ZuulApiGatewayServerApplication`

When we invoke the `add` service at `http://localhost:8765/service-consumer/add`, we will see the typical response:

```
1748
```

However, you will start to see a few more details in the log entries. A simple entry from the Service Consumer microservice log is shown here:

```
2017-03-28 20:53:45.582 INFO [service-
consumer,d8866b38c3a4d69c,d8866b38c3a4d69c,true] 89416 --- [l-api-
gateway-5] c.netflix.loadbalancer.BaseLoadBalancer : Client:zuul-api-
gateway instantiated a
LoadBalancer:DynamicServerListLoadBalancer:{NFLoadBalancer:name=zuul-api-
gateway,current list of Servers=[],Load balancer stats=Zone stats:
{},Server stats: []}ServerList:null
```

For `[service-consumer,d8866b38c3a4d69c,d8866b38c3a4d69c,true]`—The first value, `service-consumer`, is the application name. The key part is the second value—`d8866b38c3a4d69c`. This is the value that can be used to trace this request across other microservice components.

The following are some other entries from the `service consumer` log:

```
2017-03-28 20:53:45.593 INFO [service-
consumer,d8866b38c3a4d69c,d8866b38c3a4d69c,true] 89416 --- [l-api-
gateway-5] c.n.l.DynamicServerListLoadBalancer : Using serverListUpdater
PollingServerListUpdater
 2017-03-28 20:53:45.597 INFO [service-
consumer,d8866b38c3a4d69c,d8866b38c3a4d69c,true] 89416 --- [l-api-
gateway-5] c.netflix.config.ChainedDynamicProperty : Flipping property:
zuul-api-gateway.ribbon.ActiveConnectionsLimit to use NEXT property:
niws.loadbalancer.availabilityFilteringRule.activeConnectionsLimit =
2147483647
2017-03-28 20:53:45.599 INFO [service-
consumer,d8866b38c3a4d69c,d8866b38c3a4d69c,true] 89416 --- [l-api-
gateway-5] c.n.l.DynamicServerListLoadBalancer :
DynamicServerListLoadBalancer for client zuul-api-gateway initialized:
DynamicServerListLoadBalancer:{NFLoadBalancer:name=zuul-api-gateway,current
list of Servers=[192.168.1.5:8765],Load balancer stats=Zone stats:
{defaultzone=[Zone:defaultzone; Instance count:1; Active connections count:
```

```
0; Circuit breaker tripped count: 0; Active connections per server: 0.0;]
  [service-consumer,d8866b38c3a4d69c,d8866b38c3a4d69c,true] 89416 ---
[nio-8100-exec-1] c.m.s.c.service.NumberAdderController : Returning 1748
```

The following is an extract from the `Microservice A` log:

```
[microservice-a,d8866b38c3a4d69c,89d03889ebb02bee,true] 89404
[nio-8080-exec-8] c.m.s.c.c.RandomNumberController : Returning [425, 55,
51, 751, 466]
```

The following is an extract from the Zuul API gateway log:

```
[zuul-api-gateway,d8866b38c3a4d69c,89d03889ebb02bee,true] 89397 ---
[nio-8765-exec-8] c.m.s.z.filters.pre.SimpleLoggingFilter : Request Method
: GET
URL: http://192.168.1.5:8765/microservice-a/random
```

As you can see in the preceding log extracts, we can use the second value in the log, called the span ID, to trace the service call across microservice components. In this example, the span ID is d8866b38c3a4d69c.

However, this requires searching through the logs of all of the microservice components. One option is to implement a centralized log using something like an **ELK** (short for **Elasticsearch**, **Logstash**, and **Kibana**) stack. We will take the simpler option of creating a Zipkin distributed tracing service in the next step.

Setting up a Zipkin distributed tracing server

The latest version of the Zipkin server JAR can be downloaded from https://search. maven.org/remote_content?g=io.zipkin.javaamp;a=zipkin-serveramp;v=LATESTamp;c= exec.

The following screenshot shows launching the Zipkin server as a JAR in a Mac Terminal:

```
rangaraokaranam$ ls
zipkin-server-2.11.12-exec.jar
rangaraokaranam$ RABBIT_URI=amqp://localhost java -jar zipkin-server-*-exec.jar
                                ********
                        **              **
                        *                *
                        **              **
                        **              **
                        **            **
                        **            **
                            ********
                            ****
                            ****
            ****            ****
          ******            ****                                    ***
        **********************************************************************
          *******            ****                                  ***
            ****            ****
                            **
                            **


            *****    **    *****    ** **    **    **  **
             **      **    **  *    ***      **    **** **
             **      **    *****    ****     **    **  ***
            ******   **    **       ** **    **    **  **

:: Powered by Spring Boot ::        (v2.1.1.RELEASE)
```

The command for Mac is as follows:

```
RABBIT_URI=amqp://localhost java -jar  zipkin-server-*-exec.jar
```

On Windows, you need two commands:

```
SET RABBIT_URI=amqp://localhost
java -jar  zipkin-server-*-exec.jar
```

Up until now, we used **SPRING INITIALIZR** to set up our projects. Since the Zipkin server is not available on **SPRING INITIALIZR** from Spring Boot 2.0.0.RELEASE, we use a different approach to set up the Zipkin server.

You can launch the Zipkin UI dashboard at `http://localhost:9411/`. The following is a screenshot of that. There is no data shown, as none of the microservices are connected to Zipkin yet:

Integrating microservice components with Zipkin

We will need to connect all of the microservice components that we want to trace with `Zipkin server`. Here is the list of components we will start with:

- Microservice A
- Service Consumer
- Zuul API gateway server

We want to connect to Rabbit MQ and Zipkin. All we need to do is add the following dependencies to the `pom.xml` file:

```
<dependency>
  <groupId>org.springframework.cloud</groupId>
  <artifactId>spring-cloud-starter-zipkin</artifactId>
</dependency>

<dependency>
  <groupId>org.springframework.amqp</groupId>
  <artifactId>spring-rabbit</artifactId>
</dependency>
```

Make sure that you rebuild all the applications and restart them.

Go ahead and execute the `add` service at `http://localhost:8100/add`. You can now see the details on the Zipkin dashboard. The following screenshot shows some of these details:

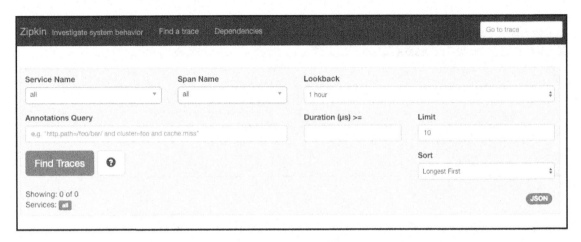

The first two rows show the failed requests. The third row shows the details of a successful request. We can further dig in by clicking on the successful row. The following screenshot shows the details that are displayed:

You can further dig in by clicking on the **Services** bar. The following screenshot shows the details that are displayed:

microservice-a.http:/microservice-a/random: 16.000ms

AKA: zuul-api-gateway,microservice-a

Date Time	Relative Time	Annotation	Address
3/28/2017, 10:08:08 PM	11.000ms	Client Send	192.168.1.5:8765 (zuul-api-gateway)
3/28/2017, 10:08:08 PM	14.000ms	Client Send	192.168.1.5:8765 (zuul-api-gateway)
3/28/2017, 10:08:08 PM	16.000ms	Server Receive	192.168.1.5:8080 (microservice-a)
3/28/2017, 10:08:08 PM	23.000ms	Server Send	192.168.1.5:8080 (microservice-a)
3/28/2017, 10:08:08 PM	27.000ms	Client Receive	192.168.1.5:8765 (zuul-api-gateway)

Key	Value
http.method	GET
http.path	/random
http.status_code	200
http.url	/random
Local Component	zuul
mvc.controller.class	RandomNumberController
mvc.controller.method	random
spring.instance_id	192.168.1.5:zuul-api-gateway:8765
spring.instance_id	192.168.1.5:microservice-a
Local Address	192.168.1.5:8765 (zuul-api-gateway)

In this section, we added distributed tracing for our microservices. We will now be able to visually track everything that is happening with our microservices. This will make it easy to track down and debug issues.

Implementing fault tolerance with Hystrix

Microservice architectures are built with a number of microservice components. What if one microservice goes down? Would all the dependent microservices fail and make the entire system collapse? Or would the error be gracefully handled and a degraded minimum functionality provided to the user? These questions decide the success of microservice architectures.

Microservice architectures should be resilient and be able to handle service errors gracefully. Hystrix provides fault-tolerant capabilities to microservices.

Integrating Hystrix into the Service Consumer microservice

We will add Hystrix to our Service Consumer microservice and enhance the add service in order to return a basic response even when Microservice A is down.

We will start by adding Hystrix Starter to the `pom.xml` file of the Service Consumer microservice. The following snippet shows the dependency details:

```
<dependency>
  <groupId>org.springframework.cloud</groupId>
  <artifactId>spring-cloud-starter-netflix-hystrix</artifactId>
</dependency>
```

Next, we will enable Hystrix auto-configuration by adding the `@EnableHystrix` annotation to the `ServiceConsumerApplication` class. The following snippet shows the details:

```
@SpringBootApplication
@EnableFeignClients("com.mastering.spring.consumer")
@EnableHystrix
@EnableDiscoveryClient
public class ServiceConsumerApplication {
```

`NumberAdderController` exposes a service with the `/add` request mapping. This uses `RandomServiceProxy` to fetch random numbers. What if this service fails? Hystrix provides a fallback. The following snippet shows how we can add a fallback method to a request mapping. All we need to do is add the `@HystrixCommand` annotation to the `fallbackMethod` attribute, thus defining the name of the fallback method—in this example, `getDefaultResponse`:

```
@HystrixCommand(fallbackMethod = "getDefaultResponse")
@RequestMapping("/add")
public Long add() {
  //Logic of add() method
}
```

Next, we define the `getDefaultResponse()` method with the same return type as the `add()` method. It returns a default hardcoded value:

```
public Long getDefaultResponse() {
  return 10000L;
 }
```

Let's bring down Microservice A and invoke `http://localhost:8100/add`. You will get the following response:

```
10000
```

When `Microservice A` fails, the Service Consumer microservice handles it gracefully and offers reduced functionality.

Summary

Spring Cloud makes it easy to add Cloud-native features to your microservices. In this chapter, we looked at some of the important patterns in developing Cloud-native applications and implemented them using various Spring Cloud projects.

We learned about managing microservices configuration with Spring Cloud Config, how to connect microservices and propagate configuration changes to all microservices using Spring Cloud Bus, and how to implement client-side load balancing with Ribbon. Then, we implemented location transparency with Eureka, an API gateway using Zuul, and used Spring Cloud Sleuth and Zipkin to implement distributed tracing. Finally, we implemented fault tolerance using Hystrix.

It is important to remember that the field of developing Cloud-native applications is still in its inception phase—in its first few years. It needs more time to mature. Expect some evolution in patterns and frameworks in the years to come.

In the next chapter, we'll shift our attention to one of the evolving programming techniques—Reactive programming.

Further reading

Spring Microservices, by Rajesh RV, is available at `https://www.packtpub.com/application-development/spring-microservices`.

13
Reactive Programming

Functional programming marks a shift from traditional imperatives to a more declarative style of programming. Reactive programming builds on top of functional programming to provide an alternative style.

In this chapter, we will discuss the basics of reactive programming.

The microservice architecture promotes message-based communication. One important tenet of reactive programming is building applications around events (or messages). Some of the important questions we will look at in this chapter include the following:

- What is reactive programming?
- What are the typical use cases?
- What kind of support does Java provide for it?
- How does Spring support reactive programming?
- What are the reactive features in Spring WebFlux?

Technical requirements

The following are the requirements for this chapter:

- Your favorite IDE, Eclipse
- Java 8+
- Maven 3.x
- An internet connection

The GitHub link for this chapter can be found at `https://github.com/PacktPublishing/Mastering-Spring-5.1/tree/master/Chapter13`

The reactive manifesto

Most applications from a few years ago had the luxury of the following:

- Multisecond response times
- Multiple hours of offline maintenance
- Smaller volumes of data

Times have changed. New devices (mobiles, tablets, and so on) and newer approaches (cloud-based) have emerged. In today's world, we are talking about the following:

- Sub second response times
- 100% availability
- An exponential increase in data volumes

Different approaches have emerged during the last few years to meet these emerging challenges. While reactive programming is not really a new phenomenon, it is one of the approaches that has been successful in dealing with these challenges.

The reactive manifesto (http://www.reactivemanifesto.org) aims to capture common themes.

> *"We believe that a coherent approach to systems architecture is needed, and we believe that all necessary aspects are already recognised individually: we want systems that are Responsive, Resilient, Elastic, and Message Driven. We call these Reactive Systems. Systems built as Reactive Systems are more flexible, loosely coupled, and scalable. This makes them easier to develop and amenable to change. They are significantly more tolerant of failure, and when failure does occur, they meet it with elegance rather than disaster. Reactive Systems are highly responsive, giving users effective interactive feedback."*

While the reactive manifesto clearly states the characteristics of responsive systems, it is not clear regarding how reactive systems are built.

Characteristics of reactive systems

The following diagram shows the important characteristics of reactive systems:

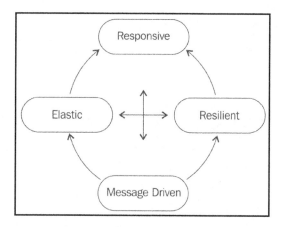

The important characteristics are as follows:

- **Responsive**: Systems respond in a timely manner to their users. Clear response time requirements are set, and the system meets them in all situations.
- **Resilient**: Distributed systems are built using multiple components. Failures can occur in any of these components. Reactive systems should be designed to contain failures within a localized space, for example, within each component. This prevents the entire system from going down if there is a local failure.
- **Elastic**: Reactive systems stay responsive under varying loads. When under a heavy load, these systems can add additional resources, releasing them when the load goes down. Elasticity is achieved using commodity hardware and software.
- **Message driven**: Reactive systems are driven by messages (or events). This ensures low coupling between components. This guarantees that the different components of the system can be scaled independently. Using non-blocking communication ensures that threads are alive for a shorter period of time.

Reactive systems are responsive to different kinds of stimulus. A few examples are as follows:

- **React to events**: Built based on message passing; reactive systems respond quickly to events.
- **React to load**: Reactive systems stay responsive under varying loads. They use more resources under high loads and release them under lower loads.
- **React to failures**: Reactive systems can handle failures gracefully. Components of reactive systems are built to localize failures. External components are used to monitor the availability of components and have the capability to replicate components when needed.

- **React to users**: Reactive systems are responsive to users. They do not waste time performing additional processing when consumers are not subscribed to specific events.

Reactive use case – a stock price page

While the reactive manifesto helps us to understand the characteristics of a reactive system, it does not really help with understanding how reactive systems are built. To understand this, we will consider the traditional approach to building a simple use case and compare it to the reactive approach.

The use case we want to build is a stock price page that displays the price of a specific stock. As long as the page remains open, we want to update the latest price of the stock on the page.

A quick look at the traditional approach

The traditional approach uses polling to check whether the stock price has changed. The following sequence diagram shows the traditional approach of building such a use case:

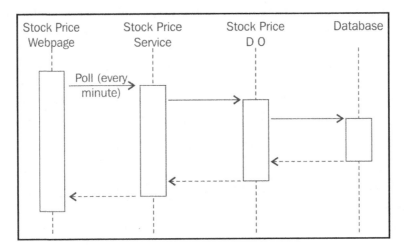

Once the page is rendered, it sends AJAX requests to the stock price service for the latest price, at regular intervals. These calls have to be done irrespective of whether the stock price has changed, since the web page does not have any knowledge of the stock price change.

How is the reactive approach different?

Reactive approaches involve connecting the different components involved to be able to react to events as they occur.

When the stock price web page is loaded, the web page registers for events from the stock price service. When the stock price change event occurs, an event is triggered. The latest stock price is updated on the web page. The following sequence diagram shows the reactive approach to building the stock price page:

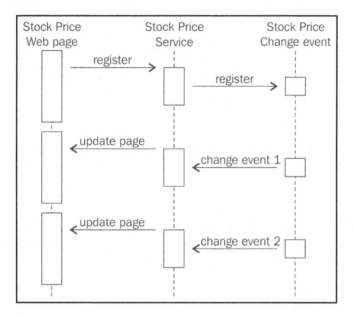

The reactive approach typically involves three steps:

1. Subscribing to events
2. The occurrence of events
3. Unregistering

When the stock price web page is initially loaded, it will subscribe to the stock price change event. The way you subscribe is different based on the reactive framework and/or the message broker (if any) that you use.

When the stock price change event for a specific stock occurs, a new event is triggered for all the subscribers of the event. The listener ensures that the web page is updated with the latest stock price.

Once the web page is closed (or refreshed), an unregister request is sent out by the subscriber.

Change events are no longer sent to the subscriber.

Comparing traditional and reactive approaches

The traditional approach is very simple. The reactive approach needs to implement a reactive subscribe and event chain. If the event chain involves a message broker, it becomes even more complex.

In the traditional approach, we poll for changes. This means that the entire sequence is triggered every minute (or at the specified interval), irrespective of whether there is a change in the stock price. In the reactive approach, once we register for the event, the sequence is triggered only when the stock price changes.

The lifetime of the threads in the traditional approach is longer. All resources used by the thread are locked for a longer duration. Considering the big picture of a server serving multiple requests at the same time, there will be more contention for threads and their resources. In the reactive approach, threads live for a short time, and, hence, there is less contention for resources.

Scaling in the traditional approach involves scaling up the database and creating more web servers. Because of the short lifetime of threads, the same infrastructure can handle more users in the reactive approach.

While the reactive approach has all the options of scaling of the traditional approach, it provides more distributed options. For example, the triggering of the stock price change event can be communicated to the application through a message broker, as shown in the following diagram:

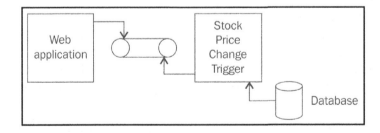

This means that the web application and the **Stock Price Change Trigger** application can be scaled independently of each other. This gives us more options in scaling up quickly when the need arises.

Implementing reactive programming in Java

Java 8 does not have any built-in support for reactive programming. A number of frameworks provide reactive features. We will implement reactive programming using reactive Streams, Reactor, and Spring WebFlux frameworks in subsequent sections.

Understanding Reactive Streams

> *"Reactive Streams is an initiative to provide a standard for asynchronous stream processing with non-blocking back pressure. This encompasses efforts aimed at runtime environments (JVM and JavaScript) as well as network protocols."*

> *- https://www.reactive-streams.org/*

A few important things to note are as follows:

- Reactive streams aim to define a minimal set of interfaces, methods, and protocols to enable reactive programming.
- Reactive streams aim to be a language-neutral approach with implementation in the Java (JVM-based) and JavaScript languages.
- Multiple transport streams (TCP, UDP, HTTP, and WebSockets) are supported.

Let's add the Maven dependencies for reactive streams to `pom.xml`:

```
<dependency>
  <groupId>org.reactivestreams</groupId>
  <artifactId>reactive-streams</artifactId>
  <version>1.0.0</version>
</dependency>

<dependency>
  <groupId>org.reactivestreams</groupId>
  <artifactId>reactive-streams-tck</artifactId>
  <version>1.0.0</version>
  <scope>test</scope>
</dependency>
```

A few of the important interfaces defined in `reactive-streams` are as follows:

```java
public interface Subscriber<T> {
  public void onSubscribe(Subscription s);
  public void onNext(T t);
  public void onError(Throwable t);
  public void onComplete();
}

public interface Publisher<T> {
  public void subscribe(Subscriber<? super T> s);
}

public interface Subscription {
  public void request(long n);
  public void cancel();
}
```

A few important things to note are as follows:

- **Interface Publisher**: `Publisher` provides a stream of elements in response to the demand received from its subscribers. A publisher can serve any number of subscribers. The subscriber count might vary with time.
- **Interface Subscriber:** `Subscriber` registers to listen to the stream of events. Subscribing is a two-step process. The first step is calling `Publisher.subscribe(Subscriber)`. The second step involves making a call to `Subscription.request(long)`. Once these steps are completed, the subscriber can start processing notifications using the `onNext(T t)` method. The `onComplete()` method signals the end of the notifications. The demand can be signaled via `Subscription.request(long)` whenever the `Subscriber` instance is capable of handling more.
- **Interface Subscription:** `Subscription` represents the link between one `Subscriber` and its `Publisher`. A subscriber can request more data using `request(long n)`. It can cancel the subscription to notifications using the `cancel()` method.

Exploring the Reactor framework

Reactor is a reactive framework from the Spring Pivotal team. It builds on top of reactive streams. As we will discuss later in this chapter, Spring Framework 5.0 uses the Reactor framework to enable Reactive web features.

The dependencies for Reactor are as follows:

```
<dependency>
  <groupId>io.projectreactor</groupId>
  <artifactId>reactor-core</artifactId>
  <version>3.0.6.RELEASE</version>
</dependency>

<dependency>
  <groupId>io.projectreactor.addons</groupId>
  <artifactId>reactor-test</artifactId>
  <version>3.0.6.RELEASE</version>
</dependency>
```

Reactor adds a couple of important things on top of the `Subscriber`, `Consumer`, and `Subscriptions` terminologies introduced by Reactive Streams:

- **Flux**: Flux represents a Reactive stream that emits 0 to n elements.
- **Mono**: Mono represents a Reactive stream that emits either no elements or one element.

In subsequent examples, we will create stub `Mono` and `Flux` objects, which will be pre-configured to emit elements at specific intervals. We will create consumers (or observers) to listen to these events and react to them.

Using Mono to emit one element

Creating `Mono` is very simple. The following `Mono` emits one element after a delay of 5 seconds:

```
Mono<String> stubMonoWithADelay = Mono.just("Ranga")
.delayElement(Duration.ofSeconds(5));
```

We want to listen to the events from `Mono` and log them to the console. We can do that using the statement specified here:

```
stubMonoWithADelay.subscribe(System.out::println);
```

However, if you run the program with the two preceding statements in a `Test` annotation, as shown in the following code, you will see that nothing is printed to the console:

```
@Test
public void monoExample() throws InterruptedException {

    Mono<String> stubMonoWithADelay = Mono.just("Ranga")
```

```
.delayElement(Duration.ofSeconds(5));

    stubMonoWithADelay.subscribe(System.out::println);

}
```

Nothing is printed to the console because the `Test` execution ends before `Mono` emits the element after 5 seconds. To prevent this, let's delay the execution of `Test` using `Thread.sleep`:

```
@Test
public void monoExample() throws InterruptedException {

    Mono<String> stubMonoWithADelay = Mono.just("Ranga")
.delayElement(Duration.ofSeconds(5));

    stubMonoWithADelay.subscribe(System.out::println);

    Thread.sleep(10000);

}
```

When we create a subscriber using `stubMonoWithADelay.subscribe(System.out::println)`, we are using the functional programming feature introduced in Java 8; `System.out::println` is a method definition. We are passing the method definition as a parameter to a method.

This is possible because of a specific functional interface called `Consumer`. A functional interface is an interface with only one method. The `Consumer` functional interface is used to define an operation that accepts a single input argument and returns no result. An outline of the `Consumer` interface is shown in the following snippet:

```
@FunctionalInterface
public interface Consumer<T> {

  void accept(T t);

}
```

Instead of using a lambda expression, we can explicitly define `Consumer` as well. The following code snippet shows the important details:

```
class SystemOutConsumer implements Consumer<String> {

  @Override
  public void accept(String t) {
```

```
        System.out.println("Received " + t + " at " + new Date());
    }

}

@Test
public void monoExample() throws InterruptedException {

    Mono<String> stubMonoWithADelay =  Mono.just("Ranga")
.delayElement(Duration.ofSeconds(5));

    stubMonoWithADelay.subscribe(new SystemOutConsumer());

    Thread.sleep(10000);

}
```

Bear in mind the following:

- `class SystemOutConsumer implements Consumer<String>`: We create a `SystemOutConsumer` class that implements the `Consumer` functional interface. The type of input is `String`.
- `public void accept(String t)`: We define the `accept` method to print the content of the string to the console.
- `stubMonoWithADelay.subscribe(new SystemOutConsumer())`: We create an instance of `SystemOutConsumer` to subscribe to the events.

The output is shown in the following screenshot:

We can have multiple subscribers listening to events from a `Mono` or `Flux`. The following snippet shows how we can create an additional subscriber:

```
class WelcomeConsumer implements Consumer<String> {

  @Override
  public void accept(String t) {
    System.out.println("Welcome " + t);
  }

}
```

```
@Test
public void monoExample() throws InterruptedException {

    Mono<String> stubMonoWithADelay = Mono.just("Ranga")
.delayElement(Duration.ofSeconds(5));

    stubMonoWithADelay.subscribe(new SystemOutConsumer());

    stubMonoWithADelay.subscribe(new WelcomeConsumer());

    Thread.sleep(10000);

}
```

A couple of important things to note are as follows:

- `class WelcomeConsumer implements Consumer<String>`: We are creating another `Consumer` class, `WelcomeConsumer`.
- `stubMonoWithADelay.subscribe(new WelcomeConsumer())`: We are adding an instance of `WelcomeConsumer` as a subscriber to the events from `Mono`.

The output is shown in the following screenshot:

```
19:29:36.538 [main] DEBUG reactor.util.Loggers$LoggerFactory - Using Slf4j logging framework
Welcome Ranga
Received Ranga at Thu Apr 27 19:29:41 IST 2017
```

Using Flux to emit multiple elements

`Flux` represents a reactive stream emitting 0 to n elements. The following snippet shows a simple `Flux` example:

```
@Test
public void simpleFluxStream() {
    Flux<String> stubFluxStream = Flux.just("Jane", "Joe");
    stubFluxStream.subscribe(new SystemOutConsumer());
}
```

A couple of important things to note are as follows:

- `Flux<String> stubFluxStream = Flux.just("Jane", "Joe")`: We are creating a `Flux` using the `Flux.just` method. It can create simple streams with hard-coded elements.
- `stubFluxStream.subscribe(new SystemOutConsumer())`: We are registering an instance of `SystemOutConsumer` as a subscriber on `Flux`.

The output is shown in the following screenshot:

```
<terminated> SpringReactiveTest.simpleFluxStream [JUnit] /Library/Java/JavaVirtualMachines/jdk1.8.0_31.jdk/Contents/
19:19:47.896 [main] DEBUG reactor.util.Loggers$LoggerFactory - Using Slf4j logging framework
Received Jane at Thu Apr 27 19:19:47 IST 2017
Received Joe at Thu Apr 27 19:19:47 IST 2017
```

The following snippet shows a more complex example of a `Flux` with two subscribers:

```
private static List<String> streamOfNames =
Arrays.asList("Ranga", "Adam", "Joe", "Doe", "Jane");
@Test
public void fluxStreamWithDelay() throws InterruptedException {
  Flux<String> stubFluxWithNames =
  Flux.fromIterable(streamOfNames)
  .delayElements(Duration.ofMillis(1000));
  stubFluxWithNames.subscribe(new SystemOutConsumer());
  stubFluxWithNames.subscribe(new WelcomeConsumer());
  Thread.sleep(10000);
}
```

A few important things to note are as follows:

- `Flux.fromIterable(streamOfNames).delayElements(Duration.ofMillis(1000))`: Creates a `Flux` from the specified list of strings. Elements are emitted at the specified delay of 1,000 milliseconds.
- `stubFluxWithNames.subscribe(new SystemOutConsumer())` and `stubFluxWithNames.subscribe(new WelcomeConsumer())`: We are registering two subscribers on `Flux`.
- `Thread.sleep(10000)`: Similar to the first `Mono` example; we introduce `sleep` to make the program wait until all the elements from the `Flux` are emitted.

The output is shown in the following screenshot:

```
<terminated> SpringReactiveTest.fromAList [JUnit] /Library/Java/JavaVirtualMachines/jdk1.8.0_31.jdk/Contents/Home/bin/
19:32:49.795 [main] DEBUG reactor.util.Loggers$LoggerFactory - Using Slf4j logging framework
Welcome Ranga
Received Ranga at Thu Apr 27 19:32:50 IST 2017
Welcome Adam
Received Adam at Thu Apr 27 19:32:51 IST 2017
Welcome Joe
Received Joe at Thu Apr 27 19:32:52 IST 2017
Welcome Doe
Received Doe at Thu Apr 27 19:32:53 IST 2017
Welcome Jane
Received Jane at Thu Apr 27 19:32:54 IST 2017
```

In this section, we understood how to use `Flux`—a stream with multiple elements.

Creating Reactive web applications with Spring Web Reactive

Spring Web Reactive is one of the most important new features in Spring Framework 5. It brings in reactive capabilities for web applications.

Spring Web Reactive is based on the same fundamental programming model as Spring MVC. The following table provides a quick comparison of the two frameworks:

Parameters	Spring MVC	Spring Web Reactive
Use	Traditional web application	Reactive web application
Programming Model	`@Controller` with `@RequestMapping`	The same as Spring MVC
Base API	The servlet API	Reactive HTTP
Runs on	Servlet containers	Servlet containers(less than 3.1), Netty, and Undertow

In the subsequent steps, we implement a simple use case for Spring Web Reactive.

The following are the important steps involved:

- Creating a project using Spring Initializr
- Creating a Reactive controller returning an event stream (Flux)
- Creating an HTML view

Creating a project using Spring Initializr

Let's start by creating a new project using **SPRING INITIALIZR** (`http://start.spring.io/`). The following screenshot shows the details:

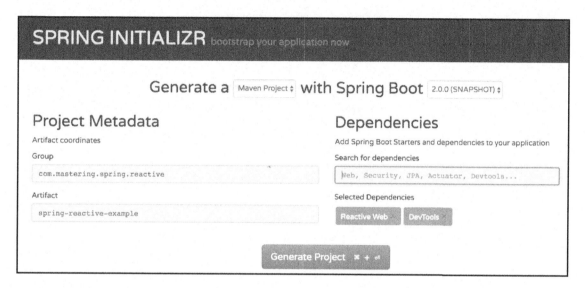

A few things to note are as follows:

- **Group**: `com.mastering.spring.reactive`
- **Artifact**: `spring-reactive-example`
- **Dependencies**: `ReactiveWeb` (to build a reactive web application) and `DevTools` (for auto-reload when the application code is changed)

Click **Generate**, and import the project into your IDE as a Maven project.

Important dependencies in the `pom.xml` file are as follows:

```xml
<dependency>
  <groupId>org.springframework.boot</groupId>
  <artifactId>spring-boot-starter</artifactId>
</dependency>

<dependency>
  <groupId>org.springframework.boot</groupId>
  <artifactId>spring-boot-devtools</artifactId>
</dependency>

<dependency>
```

```
        <groupId>org.springframework.boot</groupId>
        <artifactId>spring-boot-starter-webflux</artifactId>
    </dependency>

    <dependency>
        <groupId>org.springframework.boot</groupId>
        <artifactId>spring-boot-starter-test</artifactId>
        <scope>test</scope>
    </dependency>
```

The `spring-boot-starter-webflux` dependency is the most important dependency for Spring Web Reactive. The following snippet shows the dependencies defined in `spring-boot-starter-webflux`:

```
    <dependency>
        <groupId>org.springframework.boot</groupId>
        <artifactId>spring-boot-starter</artifactId>
    </dependency>

    <dependency>
        <groupId>org.springframework.boot</groupId>
        <artifactId>spring-boot-starter-reactor-netty</artifactId>
    </dependency>

    <dependency>
        <groupId>com.fasterxml.jackson.core</groupId>
        <artifactId>jackson-databind</artifactId>
    </dependency>

    <dependency>
        <groupId>org.hibernate</groupId>
        <artifactId>hibernate-validator</artifactId>
    </dependency>

    <dependency>
        <groupId>org.springframework</groupId>
        <artifactId>spring-web</artifactId>
    </dependency>

    <dependency>
        <groupId>org.springframework</groupId>
        <artifactId>spring-webflux</artifactId>
    </dependency>
```

The preceding snippet shows the important building blocks of Spring Reactive—`spring-webflux`, `spring-web`, and `spring-boot-starter-reactor-netty`. **Netty** is the default embedded Reactive server.

Creating a reactive controller – StockPriceEventController

Creating a Spring Reactive controller is very similar to creating a Spring MVC controller. The basic constructs are the same: `@RestController` and the different `@RequestMapping` annotations. The following snippet shows a simple reactive controller named `StockPriceEventController`:

```java
@RestController
public class StockPriceEventController {

    @GetMapping("/stocks/price/{stockCode}")
    Flux < String > retrieveStockPriceHardcoded
                            (@PathVariable("stockCode") String
stockCode) {
        return Flux.interval(Duration.ofSeconds(5))
                    .map(l -> getCurrentDate() + " : "
                        + getRandomNumber(100, 125))
                    .log();
    }

    private String getCurrentDate() {
        return (new Date()).toString();
    }

    private int getRandomNumber(int min, int max) {
        return ThreadLocalRandom.current().nextInt(min, max + 1);
    }

}
```

A few important things to note are as follows:

- `@RestController` and `@GetMapping("/stocks/price/{stockCode}")`: Basic constructs are the same as Spring MVC. We are creating a mapping to the specified URI.
- `Flux<String> retrieveStockPriceHardcoded(@PathVariable("stockCode") String stockCode)`: Flux represents a stream of 0 to *n* elements. The return type, `Flux<String>`, indicates that this method returns a stream of values representing the current price of a stock.
- `Flux.interval().map(l -> getCurrentDate() + " : " + getRandomNumber(100, 125))`: We are creating a hard-coded Flux returning a stream of random numbers.

- `Duration.ofSeconds(5)`: Stream elements are returned every 5 seconds.
- `Flux.<<*****>>.log()`: Invoking the `log()` method on `Flux` helps observe all Reactive streams signals and trace them using logger support.
- `private String getCurrentDate()`: Returns the current time as a string.
- `private int getRandomNumber(int min, int max)`: Returns a random number between `min` and `max`.

Creating an HTML view – stock-price.html

In the previous step, *Creating a reactive controller*—`StockPriceEventController`, we mapped a `Flux` stream to the `"/stocks/price/{stockCode}"` URL. In this step, let's create a view to show the current value of the stock on the screen.

We will create a simple static HTML page (`resources/static/stock-price.html`) with a button to start retrieving from the stream. The following snippet shows the HTML:

```
<p>
  <button id="subscribe-button">Get Latest IBM Price</button>
  <ul id="display"></ul>
</p>
```

We want to create a JavaScript method to register with the stream and append new elements to a specific `div`. The following snippet shows the JavaScript method:

```
function registerEventSourceAndAddResponseTo(uri, elementId) {
  var stringEvents = document.getElementById(elementId);
  var stringEventSource = new EventSource(uri);
  stringEventSource.onmessage = function(e) {
    var newElement = document.createElement("li");
    newElement.innerHTML = e.data;
    stringEvents.appendChild(newElement);
  }
}
```

The `EventSource` interface is used to receive server-sent events. It connects to a server over HTTP and receives events in a `text/event-stream` format. When it receives an element, the `onmessage` method is called. The connection remains open until the `close` method is called.

The following snippet shows the code to register the `onclick` event for the get latest IBM price button:

```
addEvent("click", document.getElementById('subscribe-button'),
function() {
        registerEventSourceAndAddResponseTo("/stocks/price/IBM",
        "display");
    }
);
function addEvent(evnt, elem, func) {
  if (typeof(EventSource) !== "undefined") {
    elem.addEventListener(evnt,func,false);
  }
  else { // No much to do
    elem[evnt] = func;
  }
}
```

Launching SpringReactiveExampleApplication

Launch the `SpringReactiveExampleApplication` application class as a Java application. One of the last messages you would see in the start up log is `Netty started on port(s): 8080`. **Netty** is the default embedded server for Spring Reactive.

The following screenshot shows the browser when you navigate to the `localhost:8080/stock-price.html` URL:

When the **Get Latest IBM Price** button is clicked, `EventSource` kicks in and registers for events from "`/stocks/price/IBM`". As soon as an element is received, it is shown on the screen.

The following screenshot shows the screen after a few events are received. You can observe that an event is received every 5 seconds:

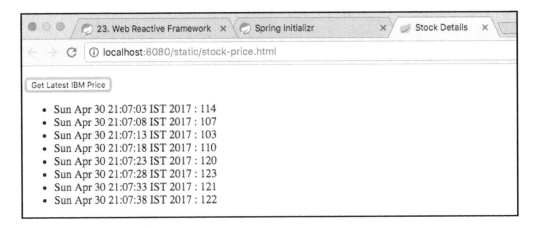

The next screenshot shows an extract from the log after the browser window is closed:

```
[ctor-http-nio-2] reactor.Flux.OnAssembly.1          : | onSubscribe([Fuseable] FluxOnAssembly.OnAssemblySubscriber)
[ctor-http-nio-2] reactor.Flux.OnAssembly.1          : | request(1)
[    parallel-1] reactor.Flux.OnAssembly.1           : | onNext(Sun Apr 30 21:07:03 IST 2017 : 114)
[ctor-http-nio-2] reactor.Flux.OnAssembly.1          : | request(31)
[    parallel-1] reactor.Flux.OnAssembly.1           : | onNext(Sun Apr 30 21:07:08 IST 2017 : 107)
[    parallel-1] reactor.Flux.OnAssembly.1           : | onNext(Sun Apr 30 21:07:13 IST 2017 : 103)
[    parallel-1] reactor.Flux.OnAssembly.1           : | onNext(Sun Apr 30 21:07:18 IST 2017 : 110)
[    parallel-1] reactor.Flux.OnAssembly.1           : | onNext(Sun Apr 30 21:07:23 IST 2017 : 120)
[    parallel-1] reactor.Flux.OnAssembly.1           : | onNext(Sun Apr 30 21:07:28 IST 2017 : 123)
[    parallel-1] reactor.Flux.OnAssembly.1           : | onNext(Sun Apr 30 21:07:33 IST 2017 : 121)
[    parallel-1] reactor.Flux.OnAssembly.1           : | onNext(Sun Apr 30 21:07:38 IST 2017 : 122)
[    parallel-1] reactor.Flux.OnAssembly.1           : | onNext(Sun Apr 30 21:07:43 IST 2017 : 119)
[    parallel-1] reactor.Flux.OnAssembly.1           : | onNext(Sun Apr 30 21:07:48 IST 2017 : 100)
[    parallel-1] reactor.Flux.OnAssembly.1           : | onNext(Sun Apr 30 21:07:53 IST 2017 : 109)
[    parallel-1] reactor.Flux.OnAssembly.1           : | onNext(Sun Apr 30 21:07:58 IST 2017 : 123)
[    parallel-1] reactor.Flux.OnAssembly.1           : | onNext(Sun Apr 30 21:08:03 IST 2017 : 123)
[    parallel-1] reactor.Flux.OnAssembly.1           : | onNext(Sun Apr 30 21:08:08 IST 2017 : 124)
[    parallel-1] reactor.Flux.OnAssembly.1           : | onNext(Sun Apr 30 21:08:13 IST 2017 : 120)
[    parallel-1] reactor.Flux.OnAssembly.1           : | onNext(Sun Apr 30 21:08:18 IST 2017 : 108)
[    parallel-1] reactor.Flux.OnAssembly.1           : | onNext(Sun Apr 30 21:08:23 IST 2017 : 107)
[    parallel-1] reactor.Flux.OnAssembly.1           : | onNext(Sun Apr 30 21:08:28 IST 2017 : 122)
[    parallel-1] reactor.Flux.OnAssembly.1           : | onNext(Sun Apr 30 21:08:33 IST 2017 : 104)
[    parallel-1] reactor.Flux.OnAssembly.1           : | onNext(Sun Apr 30 21:08:38 IST 2017 : 118)
[    parallel-1] reactor.Flux.OnAssembly.1           : | onNext(Sun Apr 30 21:08:43 IST 2017 : 102)
[    parallel-1] reactor.Flux.OnAssembly.1           : | onNext(Sun Apr 30 21:08:48 IST 2017 : 102)
[    parallel-1] reactor.Flux.OnAssembly.1           : | onNext(Sun Apr 30 21:08:53 IST 2017 : 103)
[    parallel-1] reactor.Flux.OnAssembly.1           : | onNext(Sun Apr 30 21:08:58 IST 2017 : 117)
[    parallel-1] reactor.Flux.OnAssembly.1           : | request(24)
[    parallel-1] reactor.Flux.OnAssembly.1           : | onNext(Sun Apr 30 21:09:03 IST 2017 : 104)
[ctor-http-nio-2] reactor.Flux.OnAssembly.1          : | cancel()
```

You can observe a sequence of `onNext` method calls, which are triggered as soon as the element is available. When the browser window is closed, the `cancel()` method is called to terminate the stream.

In this example, we created a controller returning an event stream (as `Flux`) and a web page registering to the event stream using `EventSource`. In the next example, let's take a look at extending the reach of an event stream to the database.

Integrating with reactive databases

All normal database operations are blocking; that is, the thread waits until a response is received from the database.

To fully benefit from reactive programming, end-to-end communication has to be reactive, that is, based on event streams.

`ReactiveMongo` is designed to be reactive and to avoid blocking operations. All operations, including select, update, or delete, return immediately. Data can be streamed into and out of the database using event streams.

In this section, we will use the Spring Boot Reactive MongoDB starter to create a simple example connecting to `ReactiveMongo`.

The following steps are involved:

1. Integrating the Spring Boot Reactive MongoDB starter
2. Creating a model object to the `Stock` document
3. Creating `reactiveCrudRepository`
4. Initializing stock data using the command-line runner
5. Creating reactive methods in the REST controller
6. Updating the view to subscribe to the event stream

Integrating the Spring Boot Reactive MongoDB starter

To connect to the `ReactiveMongo` database, Spring Boot provides a starter project—the Spring Boot Reactive MongoDB starter. Let's add this to our `pom.xml` file:

```
<dependency>
  <groupId>org.springframework.boot</groupId>
  <artifactId>spring-boot-starter-data-mongodb-
    reactive</artifactId>
</dependency>
```

The `spring-boot-starter-data-mongodb-reactive` starter brings in the `spring-data-mongodb`, `mongodb-driver-async`, and `mongodb-driver-reactivestreams` dependencies. The following snippet shows the important dependencies in the `spring-boot-starter-data-mongodb-reactive` starter:

```
<dependency>
  <groupId>org.springframework.data</groupId>
  <artifactId>spring-data-mongodb</artifactId>
  <exclusions>
   <exclusion>
     <groupId>org.mongodb</groupId>
     <artifactId>mongo-java-driver</artifactId>
   </exclusion>
   <exclusion>
     <groupId>org.slf4j</groupId>
     <artifactId>jcl-over-slf4j</artifactId>
   </exclusion>
  </exclusions>
</dependency>

<dependency>
 <groupId>org.mongodb</groupId>
 <artifactId>mongodb-driver</artifactId>
</dependency>

<dependency>
 <groupId>org.mongodb</groupId>
 <artifactId>mongodb-driver-async</artifactId>
</dependency>

<dependency>
 <groupId>org.mongodb</groupId>
 <artifactId>mongodb-driver-reactivestreams</artifactId>
</dependency>

<dependency>
 <groupId>io.projectreactor</groupId>
 <artifactId>reactor-core</artifactId>
</dependency>
```

The `EnableReactiveMongoRepositories` annotation enables the `ReactiveMongo` features. The following snippet shows it being added to the `SpringReactiveExampleApplication` class:

```
@SpringBootApplication
@EnableReactiveMongoRepositories
public class SpringReactiveExampleApplication {
```

Creating a model object – a stock document

We will create the `Stock` document class, as shown in the following code. It contains three member variables—code, name, and `description`:

```
@Document
public class Stock {
  private String code;
  private String name;
  private String description;
    //Getters, Setters and Constructor
}
```

Creating ReactiveCrudRepository

Traditional Spring data repositories are blocking. Spring data introduces a new repository for interaction with reactive databases. The following code shows some of the important methods declared in the `ReactiveCrudRepository` interface:

```
@NoRepositoryBean
public interface ReactiveCrudRepository<T, ID extends Serializable>
extends Repository<T, ID> {
  <S extends T> Mono<S> save(S entity);
  Mono<T> findById(ID id);
  Mono<T> findById(Mono<ID> id);
  Mono<Boolean> existsById(ID id);
  Flux<T> findAll();
  Mono<Long> count();
  Mono<Void> deleteById(ID id);
  Mono<Void> deleteAll();
  }
```

All the methods in the preceding interface are non-blocking. They return either `Mono` or `Flux`, which can be used to retrieve elements when events are triggered.

We want to create a repository for the `Stock` document object. The following snippet shows the definition of `StockMongoReactiveCrudRepository`. We extend `ReactiveCrudRepository` with `Stock` as the document being managed and a key of the `String` type:

```
public interface StockMongoReactiveCrudRepository
extends ReactiveCrudRepository<Stock, String> {
}
```

Initializing stock data using CommandLineRunner

Let's use `CommandLineRunner` to insert some data into `ReactiveMongo`. The following snippet shows the details added to `SpringReactiveExampleApplication`:

```
@Bean
CommandLineRunner initData(
StockMongoReactiveCrudRepository mongoRepository) {
  return (p) -> {
  mongoRepository.deleteAll().block();
  mongoRepository.save(
  new Stock("IBM", "IBM Corporation", "Desc")).block();
  mongoRepository.save(
  new Stock("GGL", "Google", "Desc")).block();
  mongoRepository.save(
  new Stock("MST", "Microsoft", "Desc")).block();
  };
}
```

The `mongoRepository.save()` method is used to save the `Stock` document to `ReactiveMongo`. The `block()` method ensures that the `save` operation is completed before the next statement is executed.

Creating reactive methods in the REST controller

We can now add in the controller methods to retrieve details using `StockMongoReactiveCrudRepository`:

```
@RestController
public class StockPriceEventController {
  private final StockMongoReactiveCrudRepository repository;
  public StockPriceEventController(
  StockMongoReactiveCrudRepository repository) {
    this.repository = repository;
  }

@GetMapping("/stocks")
Flux<Stock> list() {
  return this.repository.findAll().log();
}

@GetMapping("/stocks/{code}")
Mono<Stock> findById(@PathVariable("code") String code) {
  return this.repository.findById(code).log();
}
}
```

A few important things to note are as follows:

- `private final StockMongoReactiveCrudRepository repository`: `StockMongoReactiveCrudRepository` **is injected using the constructor injection.**
- `@GetMapping("/stocks") Flux<Stock> list()`: **Exposes a** `GET` **method to retrieve a list of stocks. It returns a** `Flux` **indicating that this will be a stream of stocks.**
- `@GetMapping("/stocks/{code}") Mono<Stock> findById(@PathVariable("code") String code)`: `findById` **returns a** `Mono`, **indicating that it will return** `0` **or** `1` **stock element(s).**

Updating the view to subscribe to the event stream

We want to update the view with new buttons to trigger events to list all stocks and show the details of a specific stock. The following snippet shows the code to be added to `resources\static\stock-price.html`:

```
<button id="list-stocks-button">List All Stocks</button>
<button id="ibm-stock-details-button">Show IBM Details</button>
```

The following snippet enables click events on the new buttons and triggers a connection with their respective events:

```
<script type="application/javascript">
addEvent("click",
document.getElementById('list-stocks-button'),
function() {
  registerEventSourceAndAddResponseTo("/stocks","display");
 }
);
addEvent("click",
document.getElementById('ibm-stock-details-button'),
function() {
  registerEventSourceAndAddResponseTo("/stocks/IBM","display");
}
);
</script>
```

Launching SpringReactiveExampleApplication

You will need to first install and launch MongoDB on your machine.

Instructions to install and launch MongoDB can be found on the MongoDB website at https://docs.mongodb.com/manual/installation/.

Launch the `SpringReactiveExampleApplication` class. The following screenshot shows the screen loading the page at `http://localhost:8080/stock-price.html`:

The following screenshot shows the screen when the stock list is clicked on:

The following screenshot shows the screen when the **Show IBM Details** button is clicked on:

In this section, we quickly implemented a reactive solution for MongoDB. We saw that `ReactiveMongo` is designed to be reactive and avoids blocking operations.

Summary

In this chapter, we took a quick peek into the world of reactive programming. We discussed the important frameworks in the Java Reactive world—reactive streams, Reactor, and Spring Web Flux. We implemented a simple web page using event streams.

Reactive programming is not a silver bullet. While it might not be the correct option for all use cases, it is a possible option you should evaluate. Its language, framework support, and the use of reactive programming are in the initial stages of evolution.

In the next chapter, we will move on to discuss the best practices in developing applications using Spring Framework.

Spring Best Practices

In previous chapters, we've discussed a number of Spring projects—Spring MVC, Spring Boot, Spring Cloud, Spring Cloud Data Flow, and Spring Reactive.

The challenges with enterprise application development do not end with choosing the right framework. One of the biggest challenges is the appropriate use of frameworks. In this chapter, we will discuss the best practices of enterprise application development with the Spring Framework.

We will talk about best practices related to the following topics:

- The structure of enterprise applications
- Spring configuration
- Managing dependency versions
- Exception handling
- Unit testing
- Integration testing
- Session management
- Caching
- Logging

Adhering to Maven's standard directory layout

Maven defines a standard directory layout for all projects. Once all projects adopt this layout, it allows developers to switch between projects with ease.

The great thing is that once you create a project with **SPRING INITIALIZR**, you can follow all of the Maven conventions.

The following screenshot shows an example directory layout for a web project:

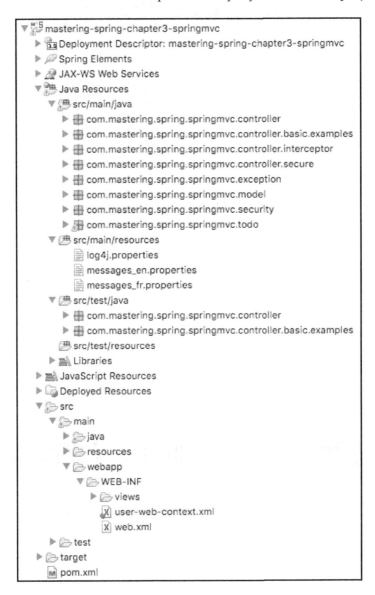

The following sets out some of the important standard directories:

- `src/main/java`: All application-related source code
- `src/main/resources`: All application-related resources—Spring context files, property files, logging configuration, and so on
- `src/main/webapp`: All resources related to the web application—view files (JSP, view templates, static content, and so on)
- `src/test/java`: All unit testing code
- `src/test/resources`: All resources related to unit testing

Building applications using a layered architecture

One of the core design aims is the **separation of concerns (SoC)**. A good practice, irrespective of the size of an application or microservice, is to create a layered architecture.

Each layer in a layered architecture should have one concern and it should implement it well. Layering the applications also helps in simplifying unit tests. The code in each layer can be completely unit tested by mocking out the layer that follows. The following diagram shows some of the important layers in a typical microservice/web application:

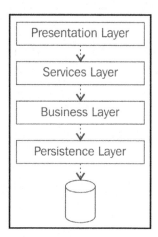

The layers shown in the preceding diagram are as follows:

- **Presentation layer**: In a microservice, the presentation layer is where the REST controllers reside. In a typical web application, this layer would also contain the view-related content—JSPs, templates, and static content. The presentation layer talks to the services layer.
- **Services layer**: This acts a facade to the business layer. Different views—mobile, web, and tablets—might need different kinds of data. The services layer understands their needs and provides the correct data based on the presentation layer.
- **Business layer**: This is where all the business logic is. Another best practice is to put most of the business logic into the domain model. The business layer talks to the data layer to get the data and add business logic on top of it.
- **Persistence layer**: This takes care of retrieving and storing data to the database. This layer typically contains the JPA mappings or the JDBC code.

Having separate context files for different layers

It is recommended that you have different Spring contexts for each of the layers. This helps in separating the concerns of each layer and helps with the unit testing code for the specific layer.

An application `context.xml` can be used to import contexts from all the layers. This can be a context that is loaded when an application is run. Some of the possible Spring context names are listed here:

- `application-context.xml`
- `presentation-context.xml`
- `services-context.xml`
- `business-context.xml`
- `persistence-context.xml`

As we move away from XML configuration toward Java configuration, we can have separated configuration classes by layer, as an alternative:

- `PresentationConfig.java`
- `ServicesConfig.java`
- `BusinessConfig`
- `PersistenceConfig`

Separating api and impl for important layers

Another best practice to ensure loosely coupled application layers is to have separate `api` and implementation modules in each layer. This helps in creating a clear separation between the two layers. The implementation of the layer can be changed without affecting the layers above it.

The following screenshot shows the data layer with two submodules (`api` and `impl`):

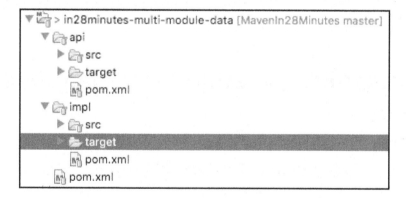

The data `pom.xml` defines these two child modules:

```
<modules>
  <module>api</module>
  <module>impl</module>
</modules>
```

The `api` module is used to define the interface that the data layer offers. The `impl` module is used to create the implementation.

The business layer should be built using the API from the data layer. The business layer should not depend on the implementation (the `impl` module) of the data layer.

The following snippet shows an extract from the `pom.xml` file of the business layer:

```xml
<dependency>
  <groupId>com.in28minutes.example.layering</groupId>
  <artifactId>data-api</artifactId>
</dependency>

<dependency>
  <groupId>com.in28minutes.example.layering</groupId>
  <artifactId>data-impl</artifactId>
  <scope>runtime</scope>
</dependency>
```

While `data-api` dependency has the default scope-compile, the `data-impl` dependency has a scope runtime. This ensures that the `data-impl` module is not available during the compilation of the business layer.

While separate, `api` and `impl` can be implemented for all layers; it is recommended that you use it at least for the business layer.

Understanding exception handling best practices

Having good exception handling is important to ensure the following:

- Your users know who to contact to seek help or support.
- Your developers/support team have the information to solve the problem.

In the Java world, we have two types of exceptions:

- **Checked exceptions**: When a service method throws this exception, all the consumer methods should either handle or throw the exception.
- **Unchecked exceptions**: The consumer method is not required to handle or throw the exception thrown by the service method.

`RuntimeException` and all its subclasses are unchecked exceptions. All other exceptions are checked exceptions.

Checked exceptions can make your code hard to read. This can be seen in the following example:

```
PreparedStatement st = null;
try {
    st = conn.prepareStatement(INSERT_TODO_QUERY);
    st.setString(1, bean.getDescription());
    st.setBoolean(2, bean.isDone());
    st.execute();
    } catch (SQLException e) {
      logger.error("Failed : " + INSERT_TODO_QUERY, e);
      } finally {
        if (st != null) {
          try {
            st.close();
            } catch (SQLException e) {
            // Ignore - nothing to do..
            }
        }
      }
    }
```

The declaration of the `execute` method in the `PreparedStatement` class is as follows:

```
boolean execute() throws SQLException
```

`SQLException` is a checked exception. So, any method that calls the `execute()` method should either handle the exception or throw it. In the preceding example, we handle the exception using a `try-catch` block.

Spring's approach to exception handling

Spring takes a different approach to this problem. It makes most of the exceptions unchecked. The code becomes simple as shown in the following example:

```
jdbcTemplate.update(INSERT_TODO_QUERY,
bean.getDescription(),bean.isDone());
```

The `update` method in `JDBCTemplate` does not declare throwing any exceptions.

The recommended approach

We recommend an approach very similar to the one used by the Spring Framework. When deciding what exceptions to throw from a method, always think about the method's consumer.

Can the consumer of the method do something about the exception?

In the preceding example of approach handling, if the execution of the query failed, the `consumer` method would not be able to do anything except show an error page to the user. In that kind of a scenario, we should not complicate things and force the consumer to handle the exception.

We recommend the following approach to exception handling in applications:

- Think about the consumer. If the consumer of the method cannot do anything useful (except logging or showing an error page) about the exception, make it unchecked.
- In the topmost layer, typically the presentation layer, you have to `catch all` exception handling to display an error page or to send an error response to the consumer.

Keeping your Spring configuration light

One of the problems with Spring before annotations was the size of the application context XML files. Application context XML files ran into hundreds (sometimes thousands) of lines. However, with annotations, there is no longer a need for such long application context XML files.

We recommend that you use component scans to locate and autowire the beans instead of manually wiring the beans in XML files. Keep your application context XML files very small. We recommend that you use Java `@Configuration` whenever framework-related configuration is needed.

Using the basePackageClasses attribute in ComponentScan

When using a component scan, we recommend that you use the `basePackageClasses` attribute. The following snippet shows an example of this:

```
@ComponentScan(basePackageClasses = ApplicationController.class)
public class SomeApplication {
```

The `basePackageClasses` attribute is the type-safe alternative to `basePackages()` and can be used to specify which packages to scan for the annotated components. The package of each specified class will be scanned.

This will ensure that, even when the package is renamed or moved, the component scan would work as expected.

Not using version numbers in schema references

Spring can recognize the correct version of the schemas from the dependencies. Hence, it is no longer necessary to use version numbers in the schema references. The following class snippet shows an example of this:

```
<?xml version="1.0" encoding="UTF-8"?>
<beans xmlns="http://www.springframework.org/schema/beans"
  xmlns:xsi="http://www.w3.org/2001/XMLSchema-instance"
  xmlns:context="http://www.springframework.org/schema/context"
  xsi:schemaLocation="http://www.springframework.org/schema/beans
http://www.springframework.org/schema/beans/spring-beans.xsd
  http://www.springframework.org/schema/context/
  http://www.springframework.org/schema/context/spring-
  context.xsd">
  <!-- Other bean definitions-->
</beans>
```

The preceding snippet does not specify a Spring version. It is generic. This will not need to change even when you upgrade your Spring version.

Preferring constructor injection for mandatory dependencies

In Chapter 2, *Dependency Injection and Unit Testing*, we looked at the different kinds of dependency injection options used with Spring. Typically, there are two kinds of dependencies for beans:

- **Mandatory dependencies**: These are the dependencies that you want to be available for the bean. If the dependency is not available, you would want the context to fail to load up.
- **Optional dependencies**: These are dependencies that are optional. They are not always available. It's fine to load the context even if these are not available.

We recommend that you wire mandatory dependencies using constructor injection instead of setter injection. This would ensure that the context would fail to load if the mandatory dependency is missing. The following snippet shows an example of this:

```
public class SomeClass {
  private MandatoryDependency mandatoryDependency
  private OptionalDependency optionalDependency;
  public SomeClass(MandatoryDependency mandatoryDependency) {
    this.mandatoryDependency = mandatoryDependency;
  }
public void setOptionalDependency(
OptionalDependency optionalDependency) {
    this.optionalDependency = optionalDependency;
  }
  //All other logic
}
```

Managing dependency versions for Spring projects

Projects depend on other frameworks, also called dependencies. It is important to manage the versions of the framework dependencies used. If you are using Spring Boot, the simplest option to manage dependency versions is to use `spring-boot-starter-parent` as the parent POM. This is the option we used in all our project examples in this book:

```
<parent>
  <groupId>org.springframework.boot</groupId>
  <artifactId>spring-boot-starter-parent</artifactId>
```

```
        <version>${spring-boot.version}</version>
        <relativePath /> <!-- lookup parent from repository -->
    </parent>
```

Versions of more than 200 dependencies are managed by `spring-boot-starter-parent`. Before a Spring Boot release, it is ensured that all the versions of these dependencies play well together. The following code shows some of the dependency versions that are managed:

```
<activemq.version>5.14.3</activemq.version>
<ehcache.version>2.10.3</ehcache.version>
<elasticsearch.version>2.4.4</elasticsearch.version>
<h2.version>1.4.193</h2.version>
<jackson.version>2.8.7</jackson.version>
<jersey.version>2.25.1</jersey.version>
<junit.version>4.12</junit.version>
<mockito.version>1.10.19</mockito.version>
<mongodb.version>3.4.2</mongodb.version>
<mysql.version>5.1.41</mysql.version>
<reactor.version>2.0.8.RELEASE</reactor.version>
<reactor-spring.version>2.0.7.RELEASE</reactor-spring.version>
<selenium.version>2.53.1</selenium.version>
<spring.version>4.3.7.RELEASE</spring.version>
<spring-amqp.version>1.7.1.RELEASE</spring-amqp.version>
<spring-cloud-connectors.version>1.2.3.RELEASE</spring-cloud-connectors.version>
<spring-batch.version>3.0.7.RELEASE</spring-batch.version>
<spring-hateoas.version>0.23.0.RELEASE</spring-hateoas.version>
<spring-kafka.version>1.1.3.RELEASE</spring-kafka.version>
<spring-restdocs.version>1.1.2.RELEASE</spring-restdocs.version>
<spring-security.version>4.2.2.RELEASE</spring-security.version>
<thymeleaf.version>2.1.5.RELEASE</thymeleaf.version>
```

It is recommended that you do not override any of the versions of the managed dependencies in the project POM file. This ensures that when we upgrade our Spring Boot version, we would get the latest version upgrades for all of the dependencies.

Sometimes, you have to use a custom corporate POM as a parent POM. The following snippet shows how to manage dependency versions in this scenario:

```
<dependencyManagement>
  <dependencies>
    <dependency>
      <groupId>org.springframework.boot</groupId>
      <artifactId>spring-boot-dependencies</artifactId>
      <version>${spring-boot.version}</version>
      <type>pom</type>
```

```
        <scope>import</scope>
      </dependency>
    </dependencies>
</dependencyManagement>
```

If you are not using Spring Boot, then you can manage all basic Spring dependencies using Spring BOM as shown in the following example:

```
<dependencyManagement>
  <dependencies>
    <dependency>
      <groupId>org.springframework</groupId>
      <artifactId>spring-framework-bom</artifactId>
      <version>${org.springframework-version}</version>
      <type>pom</type>
      <scope>import</scope>
    </dependency>
  </dependencies>
</dependencyManagement>
```

In summary, we recommend either using a Spring Boot starter parent or Spring BOM to manage versions of the Spring Framework used in your projects.

Exploring unit testing best practices

While the basic aim of unit testing is to find defects, approaches for writing unit tests for each of the layers are different. In this section, we will take a quick look at unit testing examples and best practices for different layers.

Writing tests for the business layer

When writing tests for the business layer, we recommend that you avoid using the Spring Framework in the unit tests. This will ensure that your tests are framework independent and will run faster.

The following code is an example of a unit test written without using the Spring Framework:

```
@RunWith(MockitoJUnitRunner.class)
public class BusinessServiceMockitoTest {

    private static final User DUMMY_USER = new User("dummy");
```

```
@Mock
private DataService dataService;

@InjectMocks
private BusinessService service = new BusinessServiceImpl();

@Test
public void testCalculateSum() {

BDDMockito.given(dataService.retrieveData(Matchers.any(User.class)))
                .willReturn(Arrays.asList(new Data(10), new Data(15), new
Data(25)));

    long sum = service.calculateSum(DUMMY_USER);

    assertEquals(10 + 15 + 25, sum);

    }
}
```

The Spring Framework is used to wire dependencies in the running application. However, in your unit tests, using the @InjectMocks Mockito annotation in combination with @Mock is the best option.

Writing tests for the web layer

Unit tests for web layers involve testing the controllers—REST and otherwise—so we recommend the following:

- Using Mock MVC for web layers built on Spring MVC.
- Jersey Test Framework is a good choice for REST services built using Jersey and JAX-RS.

A quick example of setting up the Mock MVC framework is shown in the following example:

```
@RunWith(SpringRunner.class)
@WebMvcTest(TodoController.class)
public class TodoControllerTest {

    @Autowired
    private MockMvc mvc;

    @MockBean
    private TodoService service;
```

```
        //Tests

    }
```

Using `@WebMvcTest` will allow us to use autowire `MockMvc` and execute web requests. A great feature of `@WebMVCTest` is that it only instantiates the controller components. All other Spring components are expected to be mocked and can be autowired using `@MockBean`.

Writing tests for the data layer

Spring Boot offers a simple annotation, `@DataJpaTest`, for data layer unit tests. A simple example is listed here:

```
@DataJpaTest
@RunWith(SpringRunner.class)
public class UserRepositoryTest {

    @Autowired
    UserRepository userRepository;

    @Autowired
    TestEntityManager entityManager;

  //Test Methods

    }
```

`@DataJpaTest` may also inject a `TestEntityManager` bean, which provides an alternative to the standard JPA `entityManager` specifically designed for tests.

If you want to use `TestEntityManager` outside of `@DataJpaTest`, you can also use the `@AutoConfigureTestEntityManager` annotation.

Data JPA tests are run against an embedded database by default. This ensures that tests can be run as many times as you want without affecting the database.

Other application development best practices

We recommend that you follow the **test-driven development (TDD)** approach to develop code. Writing tests before code results in a clear understanding of the complexity and dependencies of the code unit being written. In my experience, this leads to better design and better code.

The best projects that I worked on recognize that unit tests are more important than the source code. Applications evolve. Previous architectures from a few years back are legacy today. By having great unit tests, we can continuously refactor and improve our projects.

A few guidelines about unit tests are listed here:

- Unit tests should be readable. Other developers should be able to understand the test in less than 15 seconds. Aim for tests that serve as documentation for the code.
- Unit tests should fail only when there is a defect in the production code. This seems simple. However, if unit tests use external data, they can fail when external data changes. Over a period of time, developers lose confidence in unit tests.
- Unit tests should run quickly. Slow tests are run infrequently, losing all benefits associated with unit testing.
- Unit tests should be run as part of **continuous integration** (CI). As soon as there is a commit in the version control, the build (with unit tests) should run and notify developers in case of failure.

Exploring integration testing best practices

While unit tests test a specific layer, integration tests are used to test the code in multiple layers. To keep the tests repeatable, we recommend that you use an embedded database instead of a real database for integration tests and create a separate profile for integration tests using an embedded database. This ensures that each developer has their own database to run the tests against. Let's look at a few simple examples.

This is an example of an `application.properties` file:

```
app.profiles.active: production
```

This is an example of an `application-production.properties` file:

```
app.jpa.database: MYSQL
app.datasource.url: <<VALUE>>
app.datasource.username: <<VALUE>>
app.datasource.password: <<VALUE>>
```

And here is an example of an `application-integration-test.properties` file:

```
app.jpa.database: H2
app.datasource.url=jdbc:h2:mem:mydb
app.datasource.username=sa
app.datasource.pool-size=30
```

We would need to include the H2 driver dependency in the test scope, as shown in the following snippet:

```
<dependency>
  <groupId>mysql</groupId>
  <artifactId>mysql-connector-java</artifactId>
  <scope>runtime</scope>
</dependency>

<dependency>
  <groupId>com.h2database</groupId>
  <artifactId>h2</artifactId>
  <scope>test</scope>
</dependency>
```

An example integration test using `@ActiveProfiles("integration-test")` is as follows. The integration tests will now run using an embedded database:

```
@ActiveProfiles("integration-test")
@RunWith(SpringRunner.class)
@SpringBootTest(classes = Application.class,
                webEnvironment =
SpringBootTest.WebEnvironment.RANDOM_PORT)
    public class TodoControllerIT {

    @LocalServerPort
    private int port;

    private TestRestTemplate template = new TestRestTemplate();

    //Tests

}
```

Integration tests are critical for the continuous delivery of working software. The features that Spring Boot provides make it easy to implement integration tests.

For more details about implementing unit and integration tests with Spring Boot, we recommend reading `Chapter 7`, *Unit Testing REST API with Spring Boot.*

Using Spring Session to manage session

Managing the session state is one of the important challenges in distributing and scaling web applications. HTTP is a stateless protocol. The state of user interactions with web applications is typically managed in `HttpSession`.

> We recommend making all your REST APIs stateless.

It is important to have as little data as possible in a session. Focus on identifying and removing data that is not needed in the session.

Consider a distributed application with three instances, as shown in the following diagram. Each of these instances has its own local session copy:

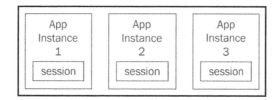

Imagine a user is being currently served from **App Instance 1**. Imagine that **App Instance 1** goes down and the load balancer sends the user to **App Instance 2**. **App Instance 2** is not aware of the session state that was available with **App Instance 1**. The user has to log in and start again. That's not good user experience.

Spring Session provides features to externalize your session store. Instead of using local `HttpSession`, Spring Session provides alternatives to store the session state to different data stores as shown in the following diagram:

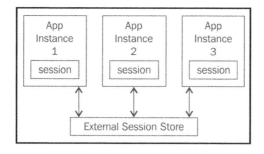

Spring Session also provides a clear SoC. The application code remains the same irrespective of the session data store being used. We can switch between session data stores through configuration.

Implementing Spring Session with Redis

In this example, we will connect Spring Session to use a Redis session store. While the code to put data into session remains the same, the data would be stored to Redis instead of an HTTP session.

 Redis is an in-memory data store. It has many use cases, typically as a quick database for caching and sometimes even as a message broker.

The following list shows the three simple steps involved:

1. Add dependencies for Spring Session.
2. Configure the filter to replace `HttpSession` with Spring session.
3. Enable filtering for Tomcat by extending `AbstractHttpSessionApplicationInitializer`.

Adding dependencies for Spring Session

The dependencies needed for Spring Session connecting to a Redis store are `spring-session-data-redis` and `lettuce-core` as shown in the following example:

```
<dependency>
  <groupId>org.springframework.session</groupId>
  <artifactId>spring-session-data-redis</artifactId>
  <type>pom</type>
</dependency>

<dependency>
  <groupId>io.lettuce</groupId>
  <artifactId>lettuce-core</artifactId>
</dependency>
```

Configuring the filter to replace a HttpSession with Spring Session

The following configuration creates a servlet filter to replace HTTPSession with a session implementation from Spring Session—Redis data store:

```
@EnableRedisHttpSession
public class ApplicationConfiguration {

  @Bean
  public LettuceConnectionFactory connectionFactory() {
    return new LettuceConnectionFactory();
  }

}
```

Enabling filtering for Tomcat by extending AbstractHttpSessionApplicationInitializer

In the previous step, the servlet filter needs to be enabled on every request to the servlet container (Tomcat). The following snippet shows the code involved:

```
public class Initializer extends
AbstractHttpSessionApplicationInitializer {

    public Initializer() {
       super(ApplicationConfiguration.class);
    }

}
```

That's all the configuration you would need. The great thing with Spring Session is that when talking to HTTPSession, your application code does not change! You can continue using the HttpSession interface, but in the background, Spring Session ensures that the session data is stored to an external data store (Redis in this example):

```
req.getSession().setAttribute(name, value);
```

Spring Session provides simple options to connect to an external session store. Backing up your session on an external session store ensures that your user can fail even when one of your application instances goes down.

Exploring caching best practices

Caching is essential when building a performant application. You would not want to hit the external service or the database all the time. Data that does not change frequently can be cached.

Spring provides transparent mechanisms to connect and use a cache. The following steps are involved in enabling a cache on an application:

1. Add the `spring-boot-starter-cache` dependency.
2. Add caching annotations.

Let's discuss these in detail.

Adding the spring-boot-starter-cache dependency

The following snippet shows the `spring-boot-starter-cache` dependency. It brings in all the dependencies and auto-configuration needed to configure a cache:

```
<dependency>
  <groupId>org.springframework.boot</groupId>
  <artifactId>spring-boot-starter-cache</artifactId>
</dependency>
```

Adding caching annotations

The next step is to add the caching annotations, indicating when something needs to be added or removed from the cache. The following snippet shows an example:

```
@Component
public class ExampleRepository implements Repository {
  @Override
  @Cacheable("something-cache-key")
  public Something getSomething(String id) {
      //Other code
  }
}
```

Some of the annotations that are supported are as follows:

- `Cacheable`: This is used to cache the result of a method invocation. The default implementation constructs the key based on the parameters passed to the method. The method will not be invoked if the value is found in the cache.
- `CachePut`: This is similar to `@Cacheable`. A significant difference is that the method is always invoked and the result is put in a cache.
- `CacheEvict`: This triggers an evict for a specific element from the cache. Typically done when an element is deleted or updated.

A few other important things to note about Spring caching are as follows:

- The default cache used is `ConcurrentHashMap`.
- The Spring caching abstraction is JSR-107 compliant.
- Other caches that can be auto configured include Ehcache, Redis, and Hazelcast.

Spring Boot Cache starter makes it easy to integrate caching into your application with simple easy-to-use annotations.

Understanding best practices for logging

Spring and Spring Boot depend on commons-logging APIs. They are not dependent on any other logging frameworks. Spring Boot provides starters to simplify the configuration of specific logging frameworks.

Using the Logback framework

The `spring-boot-starter-logging` starter is all that you need to use the `Logback` framework. This dependency is the default logging included in most of the starters, including `spring-boot-starter-web`. The dependency is shown in the following example:

```
<dependency>
  <groupId>org.springframework.boot</groupId>
  <artifactId>spring-boot-starter-logging</artifactId>
</dependency>
```

The following snippet shows `logback` and the related dependencies included in `spring-boot-starter-logging`:

```xml
<dependency>
  <groupId>ch.qos.logback</groupId>
  <artifactId>logback-classic</artifactId>
</dependency>

<dependency>
  <groupId>org.slf4j</groupId>
  <artifactId>jcl-over-slf4j</artifactId>
</dependency>

<dependency>
  <groupId>org.slf4j</groupId>
  <artifactId>jul-to-slf4j</artifactId>
</dependency>

<dependency>
  <groupId>org.slf4j</groupId>
  <artifactId>log4j-over-slf4j</artifactId>
</dependency>
```

log4j2

To use `log4j2`, we need to use `spring-boot-starter-log4j2`. When we use starters such as `spring-boot-starter-web`, we need to ensure that we exclude the dependency in `spring-boot-starter-logging`. The following snippet shows details of this:

```xml
<dependency>
  <groupId>org.springframework.boot</groupId>
  <artifactId>spring-boot-starter</artifactId>
  <exclusions>
    <exclusion>
      <groupId>org.springframework.boot</groupId>
      <artifactId>spring-boot-starter-logging</artifactId>
    </exclusion>
  </exclusions>
</dependency>

<dependency>
  <groupId>org.springframework.boot</groupId>
  <artifactId>spring-boot-starter-log4j2</artifactId>
</dependency>
```

The following snippet shows the dependencies used in the `spring-boot-starter-log4j2` starter:

```
<dependency>
  <groupId>org.apache.logging.log4j</groupId>
  <artifactId>log4j-slf4j-impl</artifactId>
 </dependency>

<dependency>
   <groupId>org.apache.logging.log4j</groupId>
   <artifactId>log4j-api</artifactId>
</dependency>

<dependency>
  <groupId>org.apache.logging.log4j</groupId>
  <artifactId>log4j-core</artifactId>
</dependency>

  <dependency>
    <groupId>org.slf4j</groupId>
    <artifactId>jul-to-slf4j</artifactId>
  </dependency>
```

Providing framework independent configuration

Irrespective of the `logging` framework used, Spring Boot allows a few basic configuration options in application properties. A few examples are shown in the following snippet:

```
logging.level.org.springframework.web=DEBUG
logging.level.org.hibernate=ERROR
logging.file=<<PATH_TO_LOG_FILE>>
```

In the age of microservices, irrespective of the framework you use for `logging`, we recommend that you log to the console (instead of a file) and use a centralized logging store tool to capture logs from all microservice instances.

By default, Spring and Spring Boot use the commons-logging APIs. We use Spring Boot starters to simplify the configuration of specific logging frameworks.

Summary

In this chapter, we looked at some of the best practices in developing Spring-based applications. We covered best practices in structuring our projects—layering, following the Maven standard directory layout, and using `api` and implementation modules. We also discussed how to keep our Spring configuration to a minimum. We looked at best practices related to logging, caching, session management, and exception handling.

Understanding all this helps you to provide the best possible implementations for your Spring projects.

In the next chapter, we'll learn a new language—Kotlin. We will learn the basics of implementing a Spring project with Kotlin.

Working with Kotlin in Spring

15

Kotlin is a statically typed **Java Virtual Machine (JVM)** language, enabling code that is expressive, short, and readable. Kotlin is created by JetBrains, the team behind the IntelliJ IDE. In the last few years, Kotlin has picked up steam and is now the preferred language for developing Android applications.

Kotlin has a concise syntax and can make developing web applications easier. Recognizing this potential, the Spring Frameworks provided support for Kotlin, starting from version 5.0.

In this chapter, we will explore some of the important features of Kotlin and learn how to create a basic REST service with Kotlin and Spring Boot.

By the end of this chapter, you will understand the following:

- What is Kotlin?
- How does Kotlin compare with Java?
- How to create a Kotlin project in Eclipse
- How to create a Spring Boot project with Kotlin
- How to implement and unit test a simple Spring Boot REST service using Kotlin

Technical requirements

The following are the requirements for this chapter:

- Your favorite IDE, Eclipse
- Kotlin 1.3+
- Java 8+
- Maven 3.x
- Internet Connectivity

The GitHub link for this chapter can be found at `https://github.com/PacktPublishing/Mastering-Spring-5.1/tree/master/Chapter15`

Getting started with Kotlin

Kotlin is an open source, statically typed language that can be used to build applications that run on the JVM, Android, and JavaScript platforms. Kotlin is developed by JetBrains under the Apache 2.0 license and the source code is available on GitHub (`https://github.com/jetbrains/kotlin`).

A couple of quotes from Andrey Breslav, the lead language designer for Kotlin, are listed as follows. These help us to understand the thought process behind Kotlin:

> *The primary purpose of Project Kotlin is to create for developers a general-purpose language that can serve as a useful tool that is safe, concise, flexible, and 100 percent Java-compatible.*

> *- Andrey Breslav*

> *Kotlin is designed to be an industrial-strength object-oriented language, and a "better language" than Java, but still be fully interoperable with Java code, allowing companies to make a gradual migration from Java to Kotlin.*

> *- Andrey Breslav*

Kotlin is one of the official languages supported by Android. The official Android developer page for Kotlin (`https://developer.android.com/kotlin/index.html`) highlights the important reasons why Kotlin is quickly becoming popular with developers:

> *Kotlin is expressive, concise, extensible, powerful, and a joy to read and write. It has wonderful safety features in terms of nullability and immutability, which aligns with our investments to make Android apps healthy and performant by default. Best of all, it's interoperable with our existing Android languages and runtime.*

Some of the important things about Kotlin include the following:

- Complete compatibility with Java. You can call Java code from Kotlin and vice versa.
- Concise and readable language. The Kotlin FAQ (`http://kotlinlang.org/docs/reference/faq.html`) estimates a 40 percent reduction in the number of lines of code.

- Support for both functional and object-oriented programming.
- IntelliJ IDEA, Android Studio, Eclipse, and NetBeans are the IDEs that have support for Kotlin. While the support is not as good as that for Java, it is improving by the day.
- All major build tools – Gradle, Maven, and Ant – have support for building Kotlin projects.

Comparing Kotlin and Java

One of the important reasons for the popularity of Java is the Java platform including the JVM. The Java platform provides security and portability for the Java language. A number of languages emerged in the last few years that aimed to leverage the advantages of the Java platform. They compile to the bytecode and can run on the JVM. These languages include the following frameworks:

- Clojure
- Groovy
- Scala
- JRuby
- Jython

Kotlin aims to address some of the important issues in the Java language and provide a concise alternative. Some of the important differences with the Java language are as follows.

Creating variables and understanding type inference

Kotlin infers the type of a variable from the value assigned to it. In the following example, intVariable is assigned a type of Int:

```
//Type Inference
var intVariable = 10
```

Since Kotlin is type-safe, the following snippet will result in a compilation error if uncommented:

```
//intVariable = "String"
//If uncommented -> Type mismatch:
//inferred type is String but Int was expected
```

Understanding the immutability of variables

Typically, like all other programming languages, the values of variables can be changed. The following snippet shows an example:

```
var variable = 5

variable = 6 //You can change value
```

However, if `val` (instead of `var`) is used to define a variable, then the variable is immutable. The value of the variable cannot be changed. This is similar to `final` variables in Java. Consider the following code:

```
val immutable = 6

//immutable = 7 //Val cannot be reassigned
```

A quick look at the type system

In Kotlin, everything is an object. There are no primitive variables.

The following are the important numeric types:

- `Double`: 64 bit
- `Float`: 32 bit
- `Long`: 64 bit
- `Int`: 32 bit
- `Short`: 16 bit
- `Byte`: 8 bit

Unlike Java, Kotlin does not treat characters as a numeric type. Any numeric operation on a character will result in a compilation error. Consider the following code:

```
var char = 'c'

//Operator '==' cannot be applied to 'Char' and 'Int'
//if(char==1) print (char);
```

Understanding null safety

Java programmers are very familiar with `java.lang.NullPointerException`. Any operations performed on an `object` variable referencing null will throw `NullPointerException`.

Kotlin's type system aims to eliminate `NullPointerException`. Normal variables cannot hold null. The following code snippet will not compile if uncommented:

```
var string: String = "abc"
//string = null //Compilation Error
```

To be able to store null in a variable, a special declaration needs to be used. That is, the type followed by ?. For example, consider the following `String?` object:

```
var nullableString: String? = "abc"

nullableString = null
```

Once a variable is declared to be nullable, only safe (?) or non-null asserted (!!.) calls are allowed. Direct references will result in a compilation error, which is shown as follows:

```
//Compilation Error
//print(nullableString.length)

if (nullableString != null) {
 print(nullableString.length)
}

 print(nullableString?.length)
```

We looked at important differences between variables – types and null safety – in Java and Kotlin. Let's shift our attention to methods.

Defining functions in Kotlin

In Kotlin, functions are declared using the `fun` keyword. The following code snippet shows an example:

```
fun helloBasic(name: String): String {
  return "Hello, $name!"
}
```

Function arguments are specified in brackets after the function name. `name` is an argument of the `String` type. The function return type is specified after the arguments. The return type of the function is `String`.

The following line of code shows the invocation of the `helloBasic` function:

```
println(helloBasic("foo")) // => Hello, foo!
```

Kotlin also allows names to be added. The following line of code shows an example:

```
println(helloBasic(name = "bar"))
```

Function arguments can optionally have a default argument value:

```
fun helloWithDefaultValue(name: String = "World"): String {
 return "Hello, $name!"
}
```

The following line of code shows the invocation of the `helloWithDefaultValue` function without specifying any parameters. The default value of the name argument is used:

```
println(helloWithDefaultValue()) //Hello, World
```

If a function has just one expression, then it can be defined on a single line. The `helloWithOneExpression` function is a simplified version of the `helloWithDefaultValue` function. The return type is inferred from the value:

```
fun helloWithOneExpression(name: String = "world") = "Hello, $name!"
```

Functions returning void and having only one expression can also be defined on a single line. The following code snippet shows an example:

```
fun printHello(name: String = "world") = println("Hello, $name!")
```

Playing with arrays

Arrays are represented by an `Array` class in Kotlin. The following code snippet shows some of the important properties and methods in the `Array` class:

```
class Array<T> private constructor() {

  val size: Int

  operator fun get(index: Int): T

  operator fun set(index: Int, value: T): Unit

  operator fun iterator(): Iterator<T>

  // ...
}
```

An array can be created using the `intArrayOf` function:

```
val intArray = intArrayOf(1, 2, 10)
```

The following code snippet shows some of the important operations that can be performed on an array:

```
println(intArray[0])//1
println(intArray.get(0))//1

println(intArray.all { it > 5 }) //false
println(intArray.any { it > 5 }) //true

println(intArray.asList())//[1, 2, 10]

println(intArray.max())//10
println(intArray.min())//1
```

Exploring Kotlin collections

Kotlin has simple functions to initialize collections. The following line of code shows an example of initializing a list:

```
val countries = listOf("India", "China", "USA")
```

The following code snippet shows some of the important operations that can be performed on a list:

```
println(countries.size)//3

println(countries.first())//India

println(countries.last())//USA

println(countries[2])//USA
```

Lists, created with `listOf`, are immutable in Kotlin. To be able to change the content of a list, the `mutableListOf` function needs to be like this:

```
//countries.add("China") //Not allowed
val mutableContries = mutableListOf("India", "China", "USA")

mutableContries.add("China")
```

The `mapOf` function is used to initialize a map, as shown in the following code snippet:

```
val characterOccurances = mapOf("a" to 1, "h" to 1, "p" to 2, "y" to
1)//happy

println(characterOccurances)//{a=1, h=1, p=2, y=1}
```

The following line of code shows the retrieval of a value for a specific key:

```
println(characterOccurances["p"])//2
```

A map can be destructured into its key value constituents in a loop. The following lines of code show the details:

```
for ((key, value) in characterOccurances) {
  println("$key -> $value")
}
```

No checked exceptions

Checked exceptions in Java have to be handled or rethrown. This results in a lot of unnecessary code. The following example shows the `try` `catch` block how to handle the checked exceptions thrown by `new FileReader("pathToFile")` - `throws FileNotFoundException` and `reader.read()` - `throws IOException`:

```
public void openSomeFileInJava(){
  try {
```

```
        FileReader reader = new FileReader("pathToFile");
        int i=0;
        while(i != -1){
          i = reader.read();
          //Do something with what was read
        }
    reader.close();
  } catch (FileNotFoundException e) {
      //Exception handling code
    } catch (IOException e) {
    //Exception handling code
  }
}
```

Kotlin does not have any checked exceptions. It's up to the client code to decide whether they want to handle the exception. Exception handling is not forced on the client.

Using a data class for beans

Typically, we will create a number of bean classes to hold data. Kotlin introduces the concept of a data class. The following block of code shows the declaration of a data class:

```
data class Address(val line1: String,
                   val line2: String,
                   val zipCode: Int,
                   val state: String,
                   val country: String)
```

Kotlin provides a primary constructor, equals(), hashcode(), and a few other utility methods for data classes. The following lines of code shows the creation of an object using the constructors:

```
val myAddress = Address("234, Some Apartments",
                                "River Valley Street", 54123, "NJ",
  "USA")
```

Kotlin also provides a toString object:

```
println(myAddress)

//Address(line1=234, Some Apartments, line2=River Valley
//Street, zipCode=54123, state=NJ, country=USA)
```

The `copy` function can be used to make a copy (clone) of an existing `data` class object. The following code snippet shows the details:

```
val myFriendsAddress = myAddress.copy(line1 = "245, Some Apartments")

println(myFriendsAddress)

//Address(line1=245, Some Apartments, line2=River Valley
//Street, zipCode=54123, state=NJ, country=USA)
```

An object of a `data` class can easily be destructured. The following line of code shows the details. `println` makes use of string templates to print the value:

```
val (line1, line2, zipCode, state, country) = myAddress;

println("$line1 $line2 $zipCode $state $country");
//234, Some Apartments River Valley Street 54123 NJ USA
```

In this section, we looked at the important differences between Java and Kotlin. Java developers should be able to quickly pick up Kotlin skills as the fundamental concepts are similar.

Creating a Kotlin project in Eclipse

Before we are able to use Kotlin in Eclipse, we will need to install the Kotlin plugin in Eclipse.

Kotlin plugin

The Kotlin plugin can be installed from `https://marketplace.eclipse.org/content/kotlin-plugin-eclipse`:

1. Click on the **Install** button, as shown in the following screenshot:

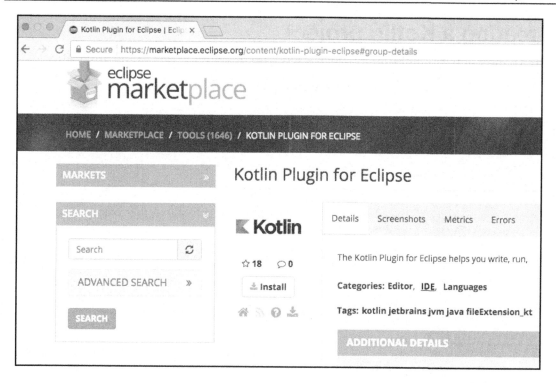

2. Choose **Kotlin Plugin for Eclipse 0.8.2** and click on the **Confirm** button, as shown in the following screenshot:

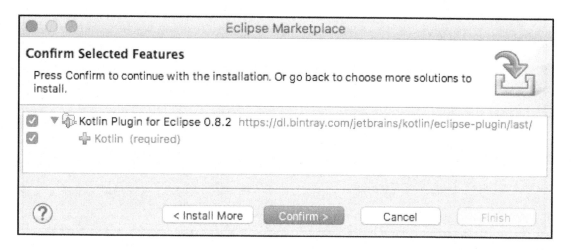

Accept defaults in the subsequent steps to install the plugin. The installation will take a little while. Restart Eclipse once the installation of the plugin is complete.

Creating a Kotlin project

Let's create a new Kotlin Project to get started with developing our Kotlin application:

1. In Eclipse, click on **File** | **New** | **Project**..., as shown in the following screenshot:

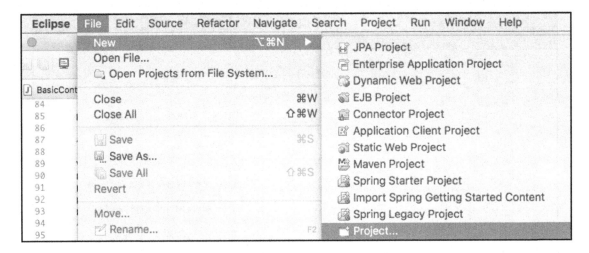

2. Choose **Kotlin Project** from the list:

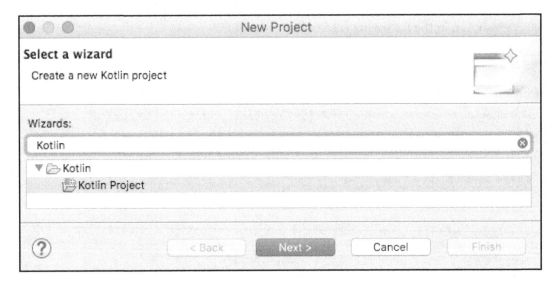

3. Provide `Kotlin-Hello-World` as the name of the project, accept all defaults, and click on **Finish**. Eclipse will create a new Kotlin project.

4. The following screenshot shows the structure of a typical Kotlin project. Both `Kotlin Runtime Library` and `JRE System Library` are available in the project:

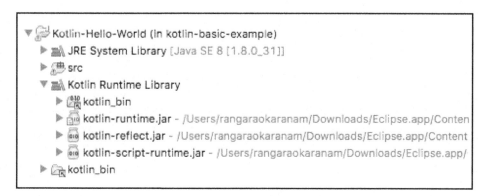

Creating a Kotlin class

To create a new Kotlin class, perform the following steps:

1. Right-click on the folder and choose **New** | **Other**, as shown in the following screenshot:

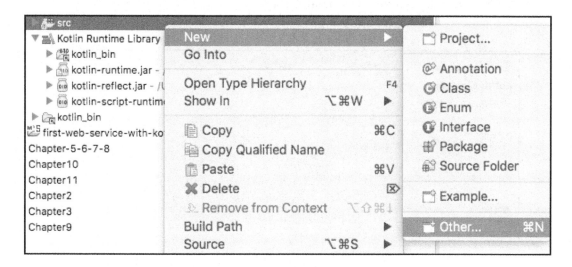

2. Choose the class, as shown in the following screenshot:

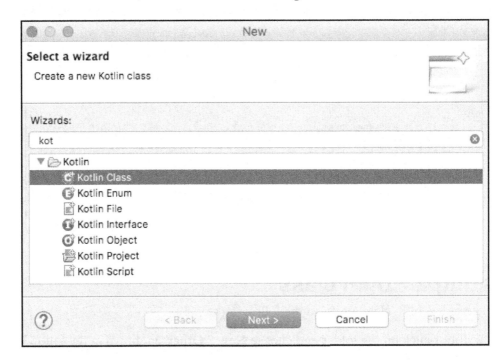

3. Give your new Kotlin class a name (HelloWorld) and a package (com.mastering.spring.kotlin.first). Click on **Finish**:

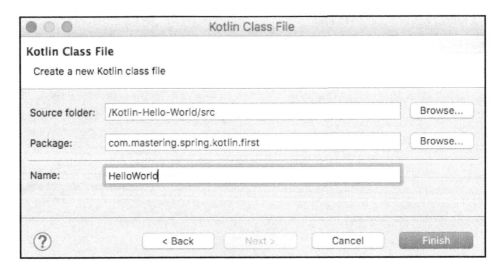

4. Create a `main` function, as shown in the following lines of code:

```
fun main(args: Array<String>) {
 println("Hello, world!")
}
```

We will look at the result of running this program in the next section.

Running a Kotlin class

To run a Kotlin class, right-click on the `HelloWorld.kt` file and click on **Run As** | **Kotlin Application**, as shown in the following screenshot:

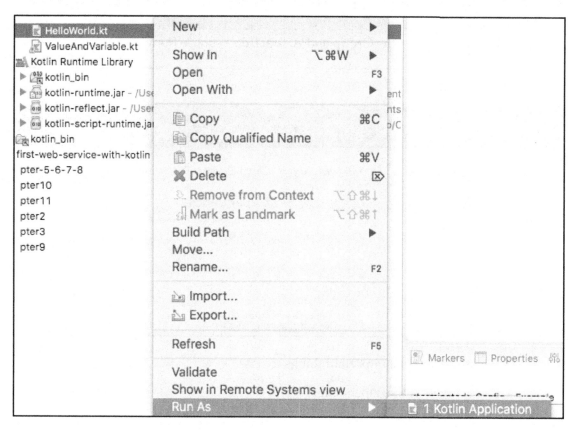

`Hello, World` is printed on the console, as shown here:

In this section, we quickly created a Kotlin project in Eclipse and ran a simple Kotlin application. In the next section, let's create a Spring Boot project using Kotlin.

Creating a Spring Boot project using Kotlin

We will use **Spring Initializr** (`http://start.spring.io`) to initialize a Kotlin project. The following screenshot shows the **Group** and **ArtifactId** to choose from:

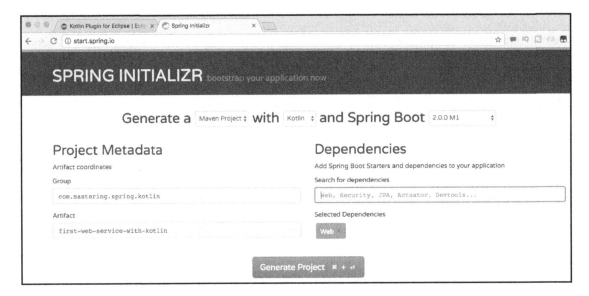

The following are a couple of important things to note:

- Choose **Web** as the dependency.
- Choose **Kotlin** as the language (the second drop-down option in the top of the screenshot).
- Click on **Generate Project** and import the downloaded project into Eclipse as a Maven project.

The following screenshot shows the structure of the generated project:

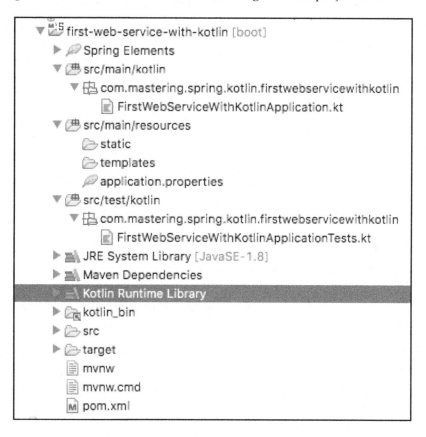

The following are some of the important things to note:

- `src/main/kotlin`: This is the folder where all the Kotlin source code is present. This is similar to `src/main/java` in a Java project.
- `src/test/kotlin`: This is the folder where all the Kotlin test code is present. This is similar to `src/test/java` in a Java project.
- Resource folders are the same as a typical Java project: `src/main/resources` and `src/test/resources`.
- Instead of **JRE System Library**, **Kotlin Runtime Library** is used as the execution environment.

Adding dependencies and plugins to pom.xml

In addition to the normal dependencies in a Java Spring Boot project, there are two additional dependencies in `pom.xml`:

```xml
<dependency>
  <groupId>org.jetbrains.kotlin</groupId>
  <artifactId>kotlin-stdlib-jre8</artifactId>
  <version>${kotlin.version}</version>
</dependency>

<dependency>
  <groupId>org.jetbrains.kotlin</groupId>
  <artifactId>kotlin-reflect</artifactId>
  <version>${kotlin.version}</version>
</dependency>
```

The following are a couple of important things to note:

- `kotlin-stdlib-jre8`: The standard library supporting the new JDK APIs added in Java 8
- `kotlin-reflect`: The runtime component for using reflection features on a Java platform

In addition to `spring-boot-maven-plugin`, `kotlin-maven-plugin` is added in as a plugin in `pom.xml`. `kotlin-maven-plugin` compiles Kotlin sources and modules. This plugin is configured to be used during the `compile` and `test-compile` phases. The following piece of code shows the details:

```xml
<plugin>
 <artifactId>kotlin-maven-plugin</artifactId>
 <groupId>org.jetbrains.kotlin</groupId>
 <version>${kotlin.version}</version>
 <configuration>
   <compilerPlugins>
     <plugin>spring</plugin>
   </compilerPlugins>
   <jvmTarget>1.8</jvmTarget>
 </configuration>
<executions>
<execution>
  <id>compile</id>
  <phase>compile</phase>
  <goals>
    <goal>compile</goal>
  </goals>
```

```
        </execution>
        <execution>
          <id>test-compile</id>
          <phase>test-compile</phase>
          <goals>
            <goal>test-compile</goal>
          </goals>
        </execution>
      </executions>
      <dependencies>
        <dependency>
          <groupId>org.jetbrains.kotlin</groupId>
          <artifactId>kotlin-maven-allopen</artifactId>
          <version>${kotlin.version}</version>
        </dependency>
      </dependencies>
    </plugin>
```

Spring Boot application class

The following code block shows the generated `SpringBootApplication` class,
`FirstWebServiceWithKotlinApplication`. We made the class open to enable Spring
Boot to override it:

```
@SpringBootApplication
open class FirstWebServiceWithKotlinApplication
fun main(args: Array<String>) {
  SpringApplication.run(
        FirstWebServiceWithKotlinApplication::class.java,
      *args)
}
```

The following are a few important things to note:

- The package, import, and annotations are the same as that of a Java class.
- The declaration of the main function in Java was `public static void
  main(String[] args)`. In the preceding example, we are using the Kotlin
  function syntax. Kotlin does not have static methods. Any function declared
  outside of a class can be called without needing a class reference.
- Launching `SpringApplication` in Java is done using
  `SpringApplication.run(FirstWebServiceWithKotlinApplication.clas
  s, args)`. In the latest versions of Spring Boot, this can also be done
  using `runApplication<FirstWebServiceWithKotlinApplication>(*args
)`.

- :: is used to obtain a Kotlin class runtime reference. So, `FirstWebServiceWithKotlinApplication::class` gives us a runtime reference to the Kotlin class. To obtain a Java class reference, we need to use the `.java` property on the reference. So, in Kotlin, the syntax is `FirstWebServiceWithKotlinApplication::class.java`.
- In Kotlin, `*` is called a spread operator. It is used when passing an array to a function accepting variable arguments. So, we will use `*args` to pass the array to the `run` method.

The application can be launched by running `FirstWebServiceWithKotlinApplication` as a Kotlin application.

Spring Boot application test class

Now that we have the application running, let's shift our attention towards unit tests.

The following code snippet shows the generated `SpringBootApplicationTest` class, `FirstWebServiceWithKotlinApplicationTests`:

```
@RunWith(SpringRunner::class)
@SpringBootTest
class FirstWebServiceWithKotlinApplicationTests {
  @Test
  fun contextLoads() {
  }
}
```

The following are a few important things to note:

- The package, import, and annotations are the same as that of a Java class.
- :: is used to obtain a Kotlin class runtime reference. Compared to `@RunWith(SpringRunner.class)` in Java, the Kotlin code uses `@RunWith(SpringRunner::class)`.
- The declaration of the test class uses the Kotlin function syntax.

Implementing the REST service using Kotlin

We will start with creating a service returning a hardcoded string. After that, we will discuss an example of returning a proper JSON response. We will also look at an example of passing a path parameter.

A simple method returning a string

Let's start with creating a simple REST service returning a `welcome` message:

```kotlin
@RestController
class BasicController {
  @GetMapping("/welcome")
  fun welcome() = "Hello World"
}
```

A comparable Java method is shown as follows. A major difference is how we are able to define a function in one line in Kotlin, with `fun welcome() = "Hello World"`:

```java
@GetMapping("/welcome")
public String welcome() {
   return "Hello World";
}
```

If we run `FirstWebServiceWithKotlinApplication.kt` as a Kotlin application, it will start up the embedded Tomcat container. We can launch the URL (`http://localhost:8080/welcome`) in the browser, as shown in the following screenshot:

Writing a unit test

Let's quickly write a unit test to test the preceding controller method:

```kotlin
@RunWith(SpringRunner::class)
@WebMvcTest(BasicController::class)
class BasicControllerTest {

  @Autowired
  lateinit var mvc: MockMvc;

  @Test
  fun `GET welcome returns "Hello World"`() {
    mvc.perform(
```

```
        MockMvcRequestBuilders.get("/welcome").accept(
        MediaType.APPLICATION_JSON))
        .andExpect(status().isOk())
        .andExpect(content().string(equalTo("Hello World")));
    }

    }
```

In the preceding unit test, we will launch a Mock MVC instance with `BasicController`. A few quick things to note are as follows:

- The `@RunWith(SpringRunner.class)` and `@WebMvcTest(BasicController::class)` annotations: They are similar to Java, except for the class references.
- `@Autowired lateinit var mvc: MockMvc`: This autowires the `MockMvc` bean that can be used to make requests. Properties declared as non-null must be initialized in the constructor. For properties that are autowired through the dependency injection, we can avoid null checks by adding `lateinit` to the variable declaration.
- `fun` \`GET welcome returns "Hello World"\` `()`: This is a unique feature of Kotlin. Instead of giving the test method a name, we are giving a description for the test. This is awesome because, ideally, the test method will not be called from another method.
- `mvc.perform(MockMvcRequestBuilders.get("/welcome").accept(Media Type.APPLICATION_JSON))`: This performs a request to `/welcome` with the `Accept` header value, `application/json`, which is similar to the Java code.
- `andExpect(status().isOk())`: This expects that the status of the response is `200` (success).
- `andExpect(content().string(equalTo("Hello World")))`: This expects that the content of the response is equal to `"Hello World"`.

Writing an integration test

When we do integration testing, we will want to launch the embedded server with all the controllers and beans that are configured. The following block of code shows how we can create a simple integration test:

```
    @RunWith(SpringRunner::class)
    @SpringBootTest(webEnvironment =
SpringBootTest.WebEnvironment.RANDOM_PORT)

    class BasicControllerIT {
```

```
@Autowired
lateinit var restTemplate: TestRestTemplate

@Test
fun `GET welcome returns "Hello World"`() {
  // When
  val body = restTemplate.getForObject("/welcome",
  String::class.java)
  // Then
  assertThat(body).isEqualTo("Hello World")
}

}
```

A few important things to note are as follows:

- @RunWith(SpringRunner::class), @SpringBootTest(webEnvironment = SpringBootTest.WebEnvironment.RANDOM_PORT): SpringBootTest provides additional functionality on top of the Spring TestContext. It provides support to configure the port for a fully running container and TestRestTemplate (to execute requests). This is similar to the Java code, except for the class reference.
- @Autowired lateinit var restTemplate: TestRestTemplate: TestRestTemplate is typically used in integration tests. It provides additional functionality on top of the RestTemplate, which is especially useful in the integration of the test context. It does not follow redirects so that we can assert the response location. lateinit allows us to avoid null checks for the autowired variables.

Simple REST method returning an object

We will create a simple WelcomeBean **POJO** (short for **Plain Old Java Object**) with a member field called message and one argument constructor, as shown in the following line of code:

```
data class WelcomeBean(val message: String = "")
```

The corresponding Java class is listed as follows:

```
public class WelcomeBean {

  private String message;

  public WelcomeBean(String message) {
```

```
        super();
        this.message = message;
    }

    public String getMessage() {
      return message;
    }
  }
}
```

Kotlin automatically adds constructors and other utility methods to the data classes.

In the previous method, we returned a string. Let's create a method that returns a proper JSON response. Take a look at the following method:

```
@GetMapping("/welcome-with-object")
fun welcomeWithObject() = WelcomeBean("Hello World")
```

The method returns a simple WelcomeBean initialized with a "Hello World" message.

Executing a request

Let's send a test request and see what response we get. The following screenshot shows the output:

```
localhost:8080/welcome-with-object
```

```
{"message":"Hello World"}
```

The response for the http://localhost:8080/welcome-with-object URL is shown as follows:

```
{"message":"Hello World"}
```

Writing a unit test

Let's quickly write a unit test checking for the JSON response and then add the test to BasicControllerTest:

```
@Test
fun `GET welcome-with-object returns "Hello World"`() {
    mvc.perform(MockMvcRequestBuilders.get("/welcome-with-object")
```

```
.accept(MediaType.APPLICATION_JSON))
        .andExpect(status().isOk())
        .andExpect(content().string(containsString("Hello World")));
}
```

This test is very similar to the earlier unit test, except that we are using `containsString` to check whether the content contains a `"Hello World"` substring.

Writing an integration test

Let's shift our focus to writing an integration test and then add a method to `BasicControllerIT`, as shown in the following code snippet:

```
@Test
fun `GET welcome-with-object returns "Hello World"`() {

    // When
    val body = restTemplate.getForObject("/welcome-with-object",
    WelcomeBean::class.java)

    // Then
    assertThat(body.message, containsString("Hello World"));
}
```

This method is similar to the earlier integration test, except that we are asserting for a substring in the `assertThat` method.

GET method with path variables

Let's shift our attention to path variables. Path variables are used to bind values from the URI to a variable in the controller method. In the following example, we want to parameterize the name so that we can customize the welcome message with a name:

```
@GetMapping("/welcome-with-parameter/name/{name}")
fun welcomeWithParameter(@PathVariable name: String) =
                                    WelcomeBean("Hello World,
$name")
```

The following are a few important things to note:

- `@GetMapping("/welcome-with-parameter/name/{name}")`: `{name}` indicates that this value will be the variable. We can have multiple variable templates in a URI.

- `welcomeWithParameter(@PathVariable String name)`: `@PathVariable` ensures that the variable value from the URI is bound to the variable name.
- `fun welcomeWithParameter(@PathVariable name: String) = WelcomeBean("Hello World, $name")`: We are using the Kotlin single expression function declaration to directly return the created `WelcomeBean`. `"Hello World, $name"` makes use of Kotlin string templates. `$name` will be replaced by the value of the path variable name.

Executing a request

Let's send a test request and see what response we get. The following screenshot shows the response:

The response for the `http://localhost:8080/welcome-with-parameter/name/Buddy` URL is as follows:

```
{"message":"Hello World, Buddy!"}
```

As expected, the name in the URI is used to form the message in the response.

Writing a unit test

Let's quickly write a unit test for the preceding method. We will want to pass a name as a part of the URI and check whether the response contains the name. The following code shows how we can do that:

```
@Test
fun `GET welcome-with-parameter returns "Hello World, Buddy"`() {
   mvc.perform(MockMvcRequestBuilders.get("/welcome-with-
parameter/name/Buddy")
.accept(MediaType.APPLICATION_JSON))
        .andExpect(status().isOk())
        .andExpect(content().string(containsString("Hello World,
Buddy")));
   }
```

A few important things to note are as follows:

- `MockMvcRequestBuilders.get("/welcome-with-parameter/name/Buddy")`: This matches with the variable template in the URI. We will pass in the name.
- `.andExpect(content().string(containsString("Hello World, Buddy")))`: We expect the response to contain the message with the name.

Writing an integration test

The integration test for the preceding method is very simple. Take a look at the following `test` method:

```
@Test
fun `GET welcome-with-parameter returns "Hello World"`() {

    // When
    val body = restTemplate.getForObject("/welcome-with-parameter/name/Buddy",

                                        WelcomeBean::class.java)

    // Then
    assertThat(body.message, containsString("Hello World, Buddy"));
}
```

A few important things to note are as follows:

- `restTemplate.getForObject("/welcome-with-parameter/name/Buddy", WelcomeBean::class.java)`: This matches against the variable template in the URI. We are passing in the name `Buddy`.
- `assertThat(response.getBody(), containsString("Hello World, Buddy"))`: We expect the response to contain the message with the name.

In this section, we looked at the basics of creating a simple REST service with Spring Boot. We also ensured that we have good unit tests and integration tests.

Summary

Kotlin helps a developer write concise, readable code. It fits hand in glove with the philosophy of Spring Boot to make application development easier and faster.

In this chapter, we started with understanding Kotlin and how it compares with Java. We built a couple of simple REST services with Spring Boot and Kotlin. We saw examples of how coding with Kotlin for services and unit tests is concise.

Kotlin has made great strides in the last couple of years—becoming an officially supported language for Android was a great first step. Support for Kotlin in Spring Framework 5.0 is the icing on the cake. The future of Kotlin depends on how successful it is with the larger Java development community. It has the potential to be an important tool in your arsenal.

Other Books You May Enjoy

If you enjoyed this book, you may be interested in these other books by Packt:

Hands-On Full Stack Development with Spring Boot 2 and React - Second Edition

Juha Hinkula

ISBN: 978-1-83882-236-1

- Create a RESTful web service with Spring Boot
- Grasp the fundamentals of dependency injection and how to use it for backend development
- Discover techniques for securing the backend using Spring Security
- Understand how to use React for frontend programming
- Benefit from the Heroku cloud server by deploying your application to it
- Delve into the techniques for creating unit tests using JUnit
- Explore the Material UI component library to make more user-friendly user interfaces

Spring 5.0 Projects
Nilang Patel

ISBN: 978-1-78839-041-5

- Build Spring based application using Bootstrap template and JQuery
- Understand the Spring WebFlux framework and how it uses Reactor library
- Interact with Elasticsearch for indexing, querying, and aggregating data
- Create a simple monolithic application using JHipster
- Use Spring Security and Spring Security LDAP and OAuth libraries for Authentication
- Develop a microservice-based application with Spring Cloud and Netflix
- Work on Spring Framework with Kotlin

Leave a review - let other readers know what you think

Please share your thoughts on this book with others by leaving a review on the site that you bought it from. If you purchased the book from Amazon, please leave us an honest review on this book's Amazon page. This is vital so that other potential readers can see and use your unbiased opinion to make purchasing decisions, we can understand what our customers think about our products, and our authors can see your feedback on the title that they have worked with Packt to create. It will only take a few minutes of your time, but is valuable to other potential customers, our authors, and Packt. Thank you!

Index

C

View
  controller redirecting, with form 76
  controller redirecting, with model 74
  controller redirecting, with ModelAndView 75
  creating 72, 75, 76
  creating, with form 78, 79
  used, for creating simple controller flow 72
Visual Studio Code IDE
  React application, importing into 337
  reference 337

W

weaving, types
  about 187
  Binary Weaving 187
  Compile-Time Weaving 187
  Runtime Weaving 187
Web Application Archive (WAR) 163
web layer
  tests, writing 515
welcome message, creating with name path
    variable
  about 218
  request, executing 218
wiring 39

X

XML configuration
  application context, launching with 50
  using, for application context 49
  versus Java configuration 49
XML Spring configuration
  defining 49

Y

YAML configuration
  exploring 161, 162

Z

Zipkin distributed tracing server
  setting up 467
Zipkin
  about 464
  implementing 464
  microservice components, integrating with 469, 471
Zuul API gateway server
  setting up 459
Zuul custom filters
  configuring, for logging every request 460, 462
Zuul
  about 416
  microservices, invoking through 462
  used, for implementing API gateway 458

Made in the USA
Coppell, TX
26 January 2020